Disgust
AND ITS DISORDERS

Disgust
AND ITS DISORDERS

THEORY, ASSESSMENT,
and TREATMENT IMPLICATIONS

EDITED BY

Bunmi O. Olatunji and Dean McKay

AMERICAN PSYCHOLOGICAL ASSOCIATION
WASHINGTON, DC

Published by
American Psychological Association
750 First Street, NE
Washington, DC 20002
www.apa.org

To order
APA Order Department
P.O. Box 92984
Washington, DC 20090-2984
Tel: (800) 374-2721; Direct: (202) 336-5510
Fax: (202) 336-5502; TDD/TTY: (202) 336-6123
Online: www.apa.org/books/
E-mail: order@apa.org

In the U.K., Europe, Africa, and the Middle East, copies may be ordered from
American Psychological Association
3 Henrietta Street
Covent Garden, London
WC2E 8LU England

Typeset in Goudy by Circle Graphics, Inc., Columbia, MD

Printer: Maple-Vail Book Manufacturing, Binghamton, NY
Cover Designer: Berg Design, Albany, NY
Technical/Production Editor: Tiffany L. Klaff

The opinions and statements published are the responsibility of the authors, and such opinions and statements do not necessarily represent the policies of the American Psychological Association.

Library of Congress Cataloging-in-Publication Data

Disgust and its disorders : theory, assessment, and treatment implications / edited by Bunmi O. Olatunji and Dean McKay.—1st ed.
    p. ; cm.
  Includes bibliographical references and index.
  ISBN-13: 978-1-4338-0397-0
  ISBN-10: 1-4338-0397-6
  1. Aversion. I. Olatunji, Bunmi O. II. McKay, Dean, 1966– III. American Psychological Association.
  [DNLM: 1. Phobic Disorders—psychology. 2. Phobic Disorders—therapy. 3. Affective Symptoms—complications. 4. Cross-Cultural Comparison. 5. Emotions. 6. Psychotherapy—methods. WM 178 D611 2009]

    RC455.4.A94D57 2009
    616.85'225—dc22
                        2008016943

British Library Cataloguing-in-Publication Data

A CIP record is available from the British Library.

Printed in the United States of America
First Edition

To my parents, who never gave me a reason to be disgusted
—*Bunmi O. Olatunji*

For Dawn and Rebecca, who never grew disgusted with my long work hours
—*Dean McKay*

CONTENTS

Contributors .... *xi*

Foreword .... *xv*
Sheila R. Woody

Introduction: The Emerging Importance of Disgust in Psychopathology ... 3
Bunmi O. Olatunji and Dean McKay

I. Theory and Assessment 7

Chapter 1.   Disgust: The Body and Soul Emotion
               in the 21st Century 9
               Paul Rozin, Jonathan Haidt, and Clark McCauley

Chapter 2.   Disgust Sensitivity: Psychometric Overview
               and Operational Definition 31
               Bunmi O. Olatunji and Josh M. Cisler

Chapter 3.   Disgust: A Cognitive Approach 57
               Nathan L. Williams, Kevin M. Connolly,
               Josh M. Cisler, Lisa S. Elwood, Jeffrey L. Willems,
               and Jeffrey M. Lohr

II. Response Patterns **75**

Chapter 4.   The Acquisition and Maintenance of Disgust:
               Developmental and Learning Perspectives 77
               Craig N. Sawchuk

Chapter 5.   A Cross-Cultural Perspective on Disgust 99
               Lisa S. Elwood and Bunmi O. Olatunji

Chapter 6.   The Psychophysiology of Disgust: Motivation,
               Action, and Autonomic Support 123
               Scott R. Vrana

Chapter 7.   The Functional Neuroanatomy of Disgust 145
               Anne Schienle

III. Disorders of Disgust **167**

Chapter 8.   Disgust and Animal Phobias 169
               Graham C. L. Davey and Sarah Marzillier

Chapter 9.   Disgust and Blood-Injury-Injection Phobia 191
               Andrew C. Page and Benjamin J. Tan

Chapter 10.   The Intersection of Disgust and
               Contamination Fear 211
               Dean McKay and Melanie W. Moretz

Chapter 11.   Food, Body, and Soul: The Role of Disgust
               in Eating Disorders 229
               Nicholas Troop and Anna Baker

Chapter 12.   Sex and the Sexual Dysfunctions: The Role
               of Disgust and Contamination Sensitivity 253
               Peter J. de Jong and Madelon L. Peters

Chapter 13.   The Treatment of Disgust 271
               Suzanne A. Meunier and David F. Tolin

Chapter 14.   Disgust and Psychopathology: Next Steps in
              an Emergent Area of Treatment and Research............ 285
              Dean McKay and Bunmi O. Olatunji

Author Index 293

Subject Index 309

About the Editors... 323

CONTRIBUTORS

Anna Baker, PhD, Department of Psychology, London Metropolitan University, London, England

Josh M. Cisler, Department of Psychology, University of Arkansas, Fayetteville

Kevin M. Connolly, Department of Psychology, University of Arkansas, Fayetteville

Graham C. L. Davey, PhD, Department of Psychology, University of Sussex, Brighton, England

Peter J. de Jong, PhD, Department of Clinical and Developmental Psychology, University of Groningen, Groningen, The Netherlands

Lisa S. Elwood, Department of Psychology, University of Arkansas, Fayetteville

Jonathan Haidt, PhD, Department of Psychology, University of Virginia, Charlottesville

Jeffrey M. Lohr, PhD, Department of Psychology, University of Arkansas, Fayetteville

Sarah Marzillier, PhD, Sussex Partnership National Health Service Trust, Worthing, West Sussex, England

Clark McCauley, PhD, Department of Psychology, Bryn Mawr University, Bryn Mawr, PA

Dean McKay, PhD, ABPP, Department of Psychology, Fordham University, Bronx, NY

Suzanne A. Meunier, PhD, The Institute of Living, Hartford Hospital, Hartford, CT

Melanie W. Moretz, Department of Psychology, Fordham University, Bronx, NY

Bunmi O. Olatunji, PhD, Department of Psychology, Vanderbilt University, Nashville, TN

Andrew C. Page, PhD, School of Psychology, University of Western Australia, Perth

Madelon L. Peters, PhD, Department of Health Sciences, University of Maastricht, Maastricht, The Netherlands

Paul Rozin, PhD, Department of Psychology, University of Pennsylvania, Philadelphia

Craig N. Sawchuk, PhD, Department of Psychiatry and Behavioral Sciences, University of Washington School of Medicine, Seattle

Anne Schienle, PhD, Department of Psychology, University of Trier, Trier, Germany

Benjamin J. Tan, PhD, School of Psychology, University of Western Australia, Perth

David F. Tolin, PhD, ABPP, The Institute of Living, Hartford Hospital, Hartford, CT; Yale University School of Medicine, New Haven, CT

Nicholas Troop, PhD, School of Psychology, University of Hertfordshire, Hatfield, England

Scott R. Vrana, PhD, Department of Psychology, Virginia Commonwealth University, Richmond

Jeffrey L. Willems, Department of Psychology, University of Arkansas, Fayetteville

Nathan L. Williams, PhD, Department of Psychology, University of Arkansas, Fayetteville

Sheila R. Woody, PhD, Department of Psychology, University of British Columbia, Vancouver, Canada

FOREWORD

SHEILA R. WOODY

Compared with other emotions like fear or sadness, there has not been a lot of research on disgust. I'm not sure why this is, although I suspect many people are put off that disgust is a favorite emotion among children and adolescent boys but not among "ladies" and "gentlemen."

But what is disgust? It is clearly a defensive or aversive emotion (as compared with appetitive emotions), but how does it relate to other emotions in this category? What delineates it from related phenomena such as distaste, feeling contaminated, contempt, shame? Is an infant's facial expression of distaste, for example, sufficient evidence of the experience of disgust? Are conditioned food aversions examples of acquired disgust? Also of importance, do other animals experience disgust? Is disgust just one construct, one emotion— or are there subtypes or domains of disgust? If there are distinct types of disgust, what distinguishes them? How are the different types evoked? How do they fit (or fail to fit) with particular types of psychopathology? Do they share a common neural pathway? Does odor have a special neuroanatomical association with disgust? How about nausea?

Other important questions include why disgust exists, in the sense of what function it serves, and the chapters in this book provide diverse theories on this question. How does disgust develop, and how is it acquired? What does it mean that phobias of creepy animals are associated with elevated disgust sensitivity? What comprises a pathological or maladaptive disgust response? How can we reduce or eliminate those learned responses? This volume answers these questions with the best information currently available.

In the past 20 years, research on disgust has proliferated, thanks mainly to the contributors to this book. Fittingly, chapter 1 is written by Paul Rozin, along with Johathan Haidt and Clark McCauley, some of the collaborators with whom he has uniquely sparked interest in the topic of disgust. Paul's lab has produced a long series of elegant and creative studies that serve as prototypes for connecting humor and curiosity with good research design. He and his collaborators have also produced the most widely used measures of disgust sensitivity, tools that have certainly pushed the field forward. Graham Davey, who contributed to chapter 8, has also had enormous impact on the study of disgust through his disease avoidance model, which provided testable hypotheses about the functioning of disgust. Andrew Page did the field a similar service with his theory about the role of disgust in blood-injury-injection phobia.

Better known to me personally are the cast of characters who are affiliated in one way or another with the University of Arkansas program, who have worked together in a collaborative effort to better understand the relationship between disgust and anxiety disorders. This group of researchers, now located in universities across the United States, includes one of the editors, Bunmi Olatunji, as well as Craig Sawchuk and David Tolin. Peter de Jong and Dean McKay are honorary members of this group (in my mind, anyway) because they worked as collaborators and mentors to Bunmi on his predoctoral National Institute of Mental Health Ruth L. Kirschstein National Research Service Award project. These researchers (and Jeff Lohr, who is responsible for bringing them all together) are collectively responsible for a body of research that has helped to define the boundaries of disgust and anxiety and shed light on the role of disgust in contamination fears and washing compulsions. It is important to note that they have used diverse methods to test the role of conditioning, evaluative learning, and emotional and information processing in maladaptive disgust reactions.

As one quickly sees when reading and discussing empirical research on disgust, the scholarly business of designing and conducting experiments about disgust also has a lighthearted side and can be a lot of fun. Lab meetings about disgust research involve quite a bit more giggling than lab meetings on most other topics in psychology. Once when I was meeting with graduate students to plan some studies on disgust, we were brainstorming about useful elicitors of disgust we could apply in the lab. As usual, the conversation was punctuated by twitters of amusement. When I suggested having a spider walk across a cracker that research participants would then be invited to eat, one student cried out in horror. In all seriousness, he felt I had crossed the line from disgusting (giggle, giggle) to dangerous (not funny, unethical) because, in his view, the spider may carry harmful germs on its feet.

Although disgust has its amusing side, research questions about disgust are very serious. The contributions to this volume include consideration of some of these almost philosophical topics (as well as practical topics like psychometric properties of measures of disgust sensitivity). The authors present thorough reviews of the current state of the literature on various aspects of disgust, but they also openly grapple with aspects of basic questions about disgust that remain mysteries. The overall effect is to stoke curiosity about this understudied emotion.

For those who are interested in disgust, these chapters give thoughtful treatment to such serious questions and provide a useful compendium of relevant research results. Although this scholarly book refrains from making the easy jokes about this topic, feel free to let yourself smile on occasion when you read about some of the studies the contributors have conducted—or when you design your own. No one said research in psychology couldn't be fun!

Disgust

AND ITS DISORDERS

INTRODUCTION: THE EMERGING IMPORTANCE OF DISGUST IN PSYCHOPATHOLOGY

BUNMI O. OLATUNJI AND DEAN McKAY

Clinical science advances primarily through two traditions—observations from case data and through efforts to explain experimental data that does not conform to the expected outcomes. Most of the accumulated data in clinical psychology addresses problems associated with anxiety, depression, and thought disturbance (i.e., psychosis). In some ways, it can be reasonably claimed that these problems have been the focus of most research because of client report of primary disturbance (case data tradition) or through variance explained in experimental research (experimental tradition).

In the case data tradition, the reliance on the primary presenting problem as described by the client is useful. However, clients often struggle to correctly identify the variables that are most salient in producing discomfort. This concept is not a new one in clinical psychology, and practitioners have a wealth of theoretical and assessment approaches to identify the salient causes and consequences of the presenting problem. This is true if one is a practitioner in the Freudian tradition (i.e., Fenichel, 1945) on the one hand or in the applied behavior analysis tradition (i.e., Skinner, 1938) on the other. What happens if a salient variable is not identified by the client and the existing clinical theory fails to account for it as well?

In the experimental data tradition, research protocols are developed on the basis of existing theory, and phenomena that are difficult to explain may be evaluated with data collected in the scientific enterprise, or it may require the examination of, potentially, variables noted from the laboratory sessions that form the basis of later experiments. However the additional analyses and future investigations are constrained by the theory guiding the researcher. What happens if the theory and investigations are not sensitive to the potential third variable causes that can be important, yet still do not rise to the awareness of the experimenter?

The role of disgust in psychopathology illustrates the problems raised above in both the case data and experimental lab traditions. Disgust is an emotional state that often escapes the attention of clients presenting for treatment of conditions where avoidance is a primary component of the disorder. The reasons for this are not yet well understood, but it is more often the case that clients will report feeling anxious or describe the physical events related to disgust as anxiety (i.e., potential epiphenomena). Disgust is an emotional state that, until recently, was ignored by experimenters. The reasons are also hard to clearly see, but among the potential hypotheses are (a) it was assumed that disgust did not account for significant amounts of variance, (b) that it was theoretically unrelated or implausibly related to psychopathology, or (c) that researchers were reluctant to study the area because of their own aversive responses. Despite the shortcomings in these two traditions, it appears that disgust has arrived as an important emotion in understanding psychopathology (McNally, 2002).

The past 2 decades have been an exciting time for researchers to examine disgust in psychopathology. What began as a relatively narrow line of inquiry in regard to the role of disgust in phobias (Matchett & Davey, 1991) has grown to include an impressive array of different psychological disorders (Olatunji & McKay, 2007). Until 1991, when Matchett and Davey described the disease-avoidance model, and for a few years after, disgust was largely ignored in the scientific literature. Although the scientific community had an aversion to studying disgust in at least the same degree that individuals with disgust-based conditions avoided certain objects and situations, it now appears obvious to study this emotion in relation to a wide range of problems.

The starting point for this line of inquiry, the disease-avoidance model of phobias, was based on some fundamental aspects of disgust that are not shared by other emotions. Essentially, disgust is a communicable emotion, transmitted by objects, and easily transferred to otherwise neutral stimuli. The natural starting point, phobias, was quite narrow, restricted to insects and animals. The chapters in this book illustrate how far this literature has gone since then and where contributors have conducted research on other anxiety disorders, sexual dysfunction, and eating disorders.

It is interesting to note that disgust was ignored for so long. Disgust is a primary emotion, readily identified in facial expressions across cultures and through specific psychophysiological responses and neural structures. It is not the only underexamined emotional state, but other primary emotions, even those considered emergent, have enjoyed greater research scrutiny. If we were to examine the research into two other understudied emotional states in psychopathology research—anger and happiness—then disgust is considerably less represented in the literature. Figure 1 displays the number of citations in PsycLIT when the terms *anger, happiness,* or *disgust* were paired with the word *disorder*. Throughout the time frame considered, disgust is always lower than even happiness, an emotional state not typically associated with psychopathology because other emotional states readily describe the absence of happiness (i.e., sadness).

Fortunately, when clinical researchers finally turned their attention to disgust, there was already a comprehensive model of the emotional state available (Rozin & Fallon, 1987). As the chapters in this book illustrate, the experimentally verified components of disgust have proven valuable in describing and predicting many psychopathological states. An important next step will involve the development of treatments aimed at addressing disgust. Several authors in this volume attempt to grapple with this problem, with some encouraging signs.

The complexity of disgust is highlighted in this volume by the chapters involving response patterns. Compared with other emotional states, disgust

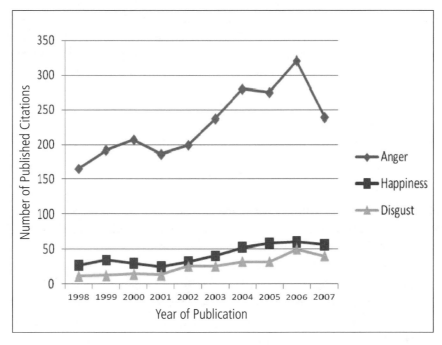

Figure 1. Citations for disgust, anger, and happiness with *disorder* as the search term, 1998–2007.

is unique in its responses and correlates. For example, Anne Schienle (chap. 7, this volume) illustrates the unique neuroanatomy of disgust. These findings and others involving patterns of acquisition (Craig N. Sawchuk, chap. 4, this volume) and psychophysiological response (Scott R. Vrana, chap. 6, this volume) illustrate well the need for additional treatment approaches, because these findings are separate from those approaches clinicians are accustomed to treating.

The final part of the book deals with the research on specific conditions that have been linked to disgust. Given the long-ignored status of disgust, most of the emerging research has been focused not only on identifying the role of disgust in psychopathology but also the degree that it is unique and separate from other emotional states that had been previously viewed as central (or exclusive) to the various conditions under study. For example, in phobias and other avoidance conditions, it had been previously assumed that anxiety was the sole emotional determinant of avoidance. It now appears that this is not the case (see chaps. 8, 9, and 10, this volume).

Now that disgust has arrived, there is much more work to be done. This book examines and compiles the existing research on the topic, but it is clear that much more has to be done to fully understand how disgust plays a role in psychopathology, and how it does not. We started by discussing clinical and experimental traditions. It is possible that disgust was ignored in many cases because it did not, in fact, play a role in explaining the clinical phenomena at hand. As areas of investigation become more sophisticated, these distinctions become clearer. Therefore, whereas disgust appears to clearly play a role in many of the conditions discussed in this text, and likely plays a role in several others not yet in a text of this sort because the research is still in its infancy, we hope that the material in this book will allow investigators to identify the limits of explanatory domains for disgust and give it the rightful place in our therapeutic endeavors.

REFERENCES

Fenichel, O. (1945). *The psychoanalytic theory of neurosis*. New York: Norton.

Matchett, G., & Davey, G. C. L. (1991). A test of a disease-avoidance model of animal phobias. *Behaviour Research and Therapy, 29*, 91–94.

McNally, R. J. (2002). Disgust has arrived. *Journal of Anxiety Disorders, 16*, 561–566.

Olatunji, B. O., & McKay, D. (2007). Disgust and psychiatric illness: Have we remembered? *British Journal of Psychiatry, 190*, 457–459.

Rozin, P., & Fallon, A. E. (1987). A perspective on disgust. *Psychological Review, 94*, 23–41.

Skinner, B. F. (1938). *The behavior of organisms*. New York: Century-Appleton-Crofts.

I

THEORY AND ASSESSMENT

1

DISGUST: THE BODY AND SOUL EMOTION IN THE 21ST CENTURY

PAUL ROZIN, JONATHAN HAIDT, AND CLARK McCAULEY

The present volume is, we believe, the first-ever edited volume devoted to the emotion of disgust. In this chapter, we (a) address why disgust was almost completely ignored until about 1990 and why there has been a great increase in attention to disgust since then; (b) outline an integrative, body-to-soul preadaptation theory of disgust; and (c) identify some specific features of disgust that make it particularly susceptible to laboratory research and particularly appropriate to address some fundamental issues in psychology. In the final section, we outline some new questions raised by research targeting brain mechanisms, psychopathology, the psychometric structure of disgust, and disgust and morality. We conclude by indicating some important aspects of disgust that have yet to receive systematic investigation.

WHY THE DELAY? A CENTURY OF IGNORING DISGUST

Disgust got off to a good start in Charles Darwin's (1872/1998) classic, *The Expression of the Emotions in Man and Animals*. Darwin listed disgust as 1 of 32 emotions and made it an important component of chapter 11, "Disdain–Contempt–Disgust–Guilt–Pride, etc." He even included a page with drawings of expressions indicating disgust. As emotion research developed within psychology, however, disgust (and most of the other emotions mentioned by Darwin) dropped out of the picture. Attention converged on sadness, anger, and fear (and only recently on happiness as well).

Thus, in William James's (1890/1950) classic chapter on emotion, the word *disgust/disgusted/disgusting* is mentioned 3 times in comparison with *anger/angry* (20 times, plus 11 for *rage*) and *fear/afraid/fright* (42 mentions). The indexes of 15 major introductory psychology textbooks from 1890 to 1958 contain a total of 5 page references to disgust, as opposed to 46 for anger and 85 for fear. (The titles of these texts, a convenience sample of the texts available in the University of Pennsylvania library, are listed on p. 368 of Rozin, 2006.)

This lack of interest in disgust is surprising because disgust meets Ekman's (1992) standard criteria for being a basic emotion as well as any other candidate, and it is usually included in lists of basic emotions, which typically also include anger, fear, happiness, sadness, and surprise. The landmark books on emotion (Izard, 1977; Lazarus, 1991; Plutchik, 1980; Tomkins, 1963) give considerable attention to disgust, and there is one classic article by Angyal (1941). However, as a topic for either research or attention in the teaching of psychology, disgust was almost absent until the last decade of the 20th century.

This absence in the more recent literature was documented by Olatunji and Sawchuk (2005), who carried out a search for anger, fear, and disgust on the PsycINFO reference database from 1960 to 2003. There were virtually no articles on disgust until the 1990s.

There is no simple explanation for this neglect, but four factors may have contributed. First, all human endeavors, starting with perception and attention, involve information overload and filtering out most of the input. Limited cognitive resources for humans and limited human resources for research in academic psychology virtually require a selection of a small subset of possible topics for study and attention (Rozin, 2007). Therefore, of Darwin's 32 candidate emotions, it is not surprising that only a few became the targets for major research programs.

Second, fear is easy to see and study in many animals and is obviously fundamental in many forms of human psychopathology. Anger as a source of violence has clear relevance to social problems. Therefore, it is not surprising that fear and anger receive much more attention than disgust.

As was already noted, from William James onward psychologists have focused on fear and anger in trying to understand both everyday problems and pathologies. A search of two linguistic databases from the Linguistic Data Consortium (http://www.ldc.upenn.edu)—a large compendium of English language news sources, and a more modest base of spoken English sampled from transcriptions of telephone conversations—revealed the following. In the news database, there were 17,663 citations to disgust (*disgust, disgusted, disgusting*) compared with 177,018 for *anger/angry*, and 285,194 for *fear/afraid*. That is, relative to *disgust*, citations to *anger* were 10 times more common and citations to *fear* were 16 times more common. In the conversation database, however, the ratios were 1.4:1 for *anger* and 7:1 for *fear*. These lower ratios suggest that the term *disgust* is relatively more frequent in common speech than it is in writing.

A third reason may be that disgust, as its name suggests, is particularly associated with food and eating. Psychologists have sought general mechanisms of behavior rather than focusing on specific domains of life (Rozin, 2006), and the food domain, in particular, has received little attention (Rozin, 2006, 2007).

A fourth reason for disgust avoidance may simply be that disgust is disgusting. Pelham, Mirenberg, and Jones (2002) demonstrated that tiny flashes of affective positivity influence people to choose marriage partners and careers whose names resemble their own (e.g., men named Lawrence are more likely than average to become lawyers and marry women named Laurie). It seems likely, therefore, that when graduate students choose research topics, many are steered away from the revolting subject matter of disgust.

Thus, psychologists' weak attention to disgust may be a result of some combination of the following factors: (a) Disgust was lost in Darwin's long list of emotions, (b) disgust lost out to fear and anger in the race to be relevant to human problems, (c) disgust was seen as relevant to only that narrow part of human behavior related to food and eating, and (d) disgust research is avoided as disgust is avoided.

WHY NOW? DOCUMENTING THE RISE OF INTEREST IN DISGUST

The analysis by Olatunji and Sawchuk (2005) indicated a notable rise in disgust citations in the 1990s, stabilizing at about 50 per year in the first decade of the 21st century. Compared with about 500 citations for anger and 1,200 for fear, disgust citations are still modest, but the increase is impressive. Disgust seems now to have assumed the place that would be accorded to it in terms of its relative frequency in English-language news sources, although still well below its status in English-language conversations (see the Linguistic Data Consortium, http://www.ldc.upenn.edu/).

We are not aware of any academically oriented books on disgust before 1997; however, since the publication of William Ian Miller's (1997) *The Anatomy of Disgust*, at least one other book has focused on disgust (S. B. Miller, 2004), and two well-regarded psychology trade books have given prominent attention to disgust (Bloom, 2004; Pinker, 1997). Interest in the involvement of disgust in anxiety disorders (particularly phobias and obsessive–compulsive disorders [OCD]) was signaled by special issues devoted to disgust in the *Journal of Anxiety Disorders* (McKay, 2002) and the *Journal of Behavior Therapy and Experimental Psychiatry* (Olatunji & McKay, 2006).

We recently coded all 139 abstracts in the PsycINFO database that mentioned disgust in the title, abstract, or key phrase from 2001 through 2006. Our analysis showed that the largest focus of recent work is the link between disgust and psychopathology (primarily but not entirely phobias and OCD; 37% of references), followed by neurological, neuroanatomical, and neurochemical aspects of disgust (18% of references). None of the remaining topics had 7% or more of the references. Some of the more common of these smaller categories were the psychometrics and structure of disgust, contamination and odor, dynamics of disgust (especially moment-to-moment changes and interactions with other emotions), moral disgust, psychophysiology, development, and expression.

THE BODY-TO-SOUL PREADAPTATION THEORY OF DISGUST

One reason for the recent explosion of interest in disgust may be the growing recognition that disgust is related to many social, cultural, and even spiritual issues. In 1993, we developed a theory of disgust to explain how this originally food-related emotion expanded, both in biological and in cultural evolution, to become a guardian of the body, the social order, and the soul (the body-to-soul preadaptation theory). We began with the recognition that disgust was at its core a food-rejection emotion (Rozin & Fallon, 1987), but that, cross-culturally, disgust elicitors come from a wide variety of domains. We suggested that foods and body products are the core disgust elicitors, the elicitors for which the brain was most directly shaped by natural selection, probably to avoid biological pathogens (Rozin & Fallon, 1987; Rozin, Haidt, & McCauley, 1993, 2000; Rozin, Haidt, McCauley, & Imada, 1997). In our view, this powerful core disgust system, which stimulates a sense of repulsion and a withdrawal from the elicitor, was preadapted for easy extension to other threatening entities, including social and moral threats. The act of making something disgusting means producing internalized motivation to avoid it.

What is done with feces in toilet training can be done with other things, including inappropriate sex, poor hygiene, violations of the body envelope (e.g., the stump from an amputated hand, or viscera exposed by a wound), and death. Although many of these avoidances may have some health benefits, conscious justifications often have little to do with health. Large families of disgust elicitors are features that humans share with animals: eating/food, excreting, sex, soft body interiors, and death. Rozin et al. (1993, 2000) formulated this entire set of elicitors as reminders of our animal nature. In this view, humans display in most cultures a strong desire to be seen as qualitatively distinct from other animals, that is, to be "more than animals." Disgust is in the service of this desire by causing us to recoil from reminders of our animal nature.

Perhaps the most threatening characteristic that humans share with other animals is mortality, and avoidance of contact with death, either physically or mentally, seems to be central to disgust. The quintessential odor of disgust, the putrid odor, is the odor of decaying animal flesh. Our linking of disgust and death, inspired in part by Ernest Becker's (1973) *The Denial of Death*, paralleled the development of terror management theory in social psychology (Greenberg, Pyszczynski, & Solomon, 1986; Solomon, Greenberg, & Pyszczynski, 1991). Terror management theory, also rooted in Becker's ideas, highlights the importance of commitment to cultural norms as a defense against individual mortality. Direct linkages between mortality salience and disgust have been established (Cox, Goldenberg, Pyszczynski, & Weise, 2006; Goldenberg et al., 2001).

Our further analysis suggested two other domains of disgust elicitors not related to our animal nature. One is *interpersonal disgust*, which is disgust at other persons, particularly strangers and outgroups. A second is *moral disgust*, in which disgust is harnessed to produce offense at certain culturally determined moral violations. In terms of Shweder's cross-cultural taxonomy of moral systems (community, autonomy, divinity [CAD]; Shweder, Much, Mahapatra, & Park, 1997), disgust seems to be the emotion linked to violations of divinity (the CAD triad hypothesis; Rozin, Lowery, Imada, & Haidt, 1999). Haidt and his colleagues (Haidt, 2001; Haidt, Koller, & Dias, 1993; Wheatley & Haidt, 2005) have demonstrated that disgust plays a direct role in many moral judgments. Disgust is now a part of moral psychology.

WHAT (ELSE) MAKES DISGUST (SUDDENLY) SO INTERESTING?

Disgust has a number of special properties that might account for its recent and rapid rise as an object of interdisciplinary study. We have identified six properties that ought to continue to motivate more research in the future.

Convenience

Psychologists have understandably tried to bring their research into the laboratory, to establish more control and allow for experimentation. One of the challenges of emotion research is that, ethically, it is difficult to elicit strong emotions in the laboratory. In particular, it is ethically problematic to elicit fear or anger in a realistic way in the laboratory. It is relatively easy, however, to stimulate disgust in the laboratory—even in an fMRI scanner—and this can be done in ethically acceptable and ecologically valid ways. One can present real disgust elicitors, in photograph or in reality (e.g., a cockroach) and produce strong disgust in participants. We have done this by using over 20 different real elicitors (Rozin, Haidt, McCauley, Dunlop, & Ashmore, 1999).

Contamination

Contamination is a special property of disgust elicitors; it has the power to render a good food inedible by mere brief contact (Rozin, Millman, & Nemeroff, 1986). Examples of contamination seem to follow the sympathetic magical law of contagion: "Once in contact, always in contact." Sensitivity to contagion appears to be present in all adult humans but absent in children (see Fallon, Rozin, & Pliner, 1984; reviewed in Rozin & Nemeroff, 1990). Contamination effects, for which disgusting entities are particularly good elicitors, are of interest to researchers in judgment and decision making, because the effects are powerful and often "irrational."

It is important to recognize that contagion effects can be obtained with disgust elicitors that are not directly mediated (in contemporary humans) by a fear of infection. Although individuals typically justify their rejection of a juice contacted by a cockroach in terms of health risks, their aversion is not reduced significantly if the cockroach is sterilized (Rozin et al., 1986). Contamination effects connect disgust research with work on essentialism in developmental psychology and likewise with the study of obsessive–compulsive disorder.

The Disgust Scale

The availability of a tool often stimulates research and makes what the tool measures more salient; this seems to have happened for disgust. The Disgust Scale (Haidt, McCauley, & Rozin, 1994) has become a widely used instrument, and because it was designed to investigate many subtypes of disgust, rather than providing an overall score, it has stimulated discussion of the structure of disgust and of the relationships between subtypes of disgust and specific mental disorders (Olatunji et al., 2007; information about the Disgust Scale is available at http://www.people.virginia.edu/~jdh6n/disgustscale.html).

Affective Neuroscience

Two important neuroscience findings launched an extensive exploration of disgust and the brain, motivated in part by the rapid development of brain scanning methodologies. Sprengelmeyer et al. (1996) made the remarkable finding that individuals with Huntington's disease, a hereditary but late-onset disorder principally of the motor system, showed a surprisingly specific deficit in recognizing disgust faces. Along with work on fear and the amygdala, this was one of the first findings to suggest that different emotions might have different mediating brain loci in humans. The presence of this deficit in carriers of Huntington's disease, who do not yet show the late onset motor symptoms, is particularly striking (Gray, Young, Barker, Curtis, & Gibson, 1997).

An extensive series of brain scanning studies arose at about the same time, starting with the work of Phillips et al. (1997). These studies showed that some brain areas—particularly the anterior insula, some basal ganglia structures, and some parts of the frontal cortex—are specifically involved in the experience of disgust. This work connects disgust research with neuroscience, one of the most rapidly growing areas in psychology in which the ease of eliciting disgust in a realistic way has great appeal. Neuroscience research promises both to enlighten us about the brain mechanisms of disgust and to provide tests of some psychological ideas about disgust—for example, whether all types of disgust are linked in the brain to a food–taste–smell system and whether moral disgust shares circuitry with core disgust.

Anxiety Disorders

The central role of disgust in some anxiety disorders was suggested by Davey and his collaborators (Davey, 1993; Matchett & Davey, 1991), when they pointed out that disgust is an important and previously ignored aspect of phobias. In addition, their disease-avoidance interpretation of disgust elicitors provided a conceptual link between research on disgust and research on phobias. The disgust–phobia link is now a major line of research, followed up by Davey and his group, and Woody and Teachman (2000), among others. Power and Dalgleish (1997) emphasized this and other links between disgust and psychopathology.

Disgust is also known to be central to OCD. The link is substantively clear, at least for the case of the contamination variety of OCD, which seems to relate to both enhanced disgust and enhanced contamination sensitivity. The disgust–OCD link appeared in print from a number of different sources in the period of 1999–2001, and a whole set of studies relating disgust sensitivity to clinical OCD, or to OCD tendencies, are now in the literature (reviewed by Berle & Phillips, 2006; Husted, Shapira, & Goodman, 2006; Olatunji & Sawchuk, 2005).

Public Interest

Although psychology has not been driven, to a major degree, by what the public finds interesting (Rozin, 2006), public interest may have some effect, and disgust is of interest to many people. Media interest in research on disgust has been high, and popular television programs such as *Fear Factor* speak to its appeal.

THE FUTURE OF DISGUST RESEARCH

Disgust has, until recently, been a hole in emotion research. As a hole fills, subholes are often created (Rozin, 2007). Currently, brain research and psychopathology are the two enthusiasms that are filling in parts of the disgust hole and leaving subholes. We review here some research directions we think are promising that have yet to receive significant attention. The first two areas (brain mechanisms and psychopathology) are well developed, but we indicate some possible lines of work within these areas that have yet to be explored. The remaining areas have received little or no attention.

Brain Mechanisms

We expect to see many more brain scan studies that indicate activation of brain areas during the elicitation or expression of disgust, and of contamination as well. These, plus analyses of disgust deficits resulting from brain damage, can be expected to provide more details of the brain circuits that may be dedicated to disgust and also to test some psychological claims. For example, it should be possible, as studies have already suggested (Moll et al., 2005), to indicate the degree of shared and distinct circuitry for core versus moral or other varieties of disgust. Brain scan studies are also likely to shed light on the relations among disgust and related emotions, such as contempt, anger, shame, and fear.

Evidence that Huntington carriers have a severe deficit in disgust recognition (Gray et al., 1997; Sprengelmeyer et al., 1996) points to potentially exciting psychological studies. These unfortunate individuals may allow us to study what it is like to grow up in an environment in which the most prominent signal of disgust (the face of others) is not processed. If disgust is the emotion of civilization, then what are the consequences for a Huntington carrier?

Disgust and Psychopathology

Similarly, we expect to see many more studies of the relation between OCD and phobias, on one hand, and disgust and contamination sensitivity on the other hand. The mixture of fear and disgust in many phobias needs attention (Davey, 1993) and is getting further elaboration (Davey, 1993). Contamination sensitivity is part of the Disgust Scale (Haidt et al., 1994) and correlates with sensitivity to the domain-specific areas of disgust, and all eight of the original components of the Disgust Scale correlate with measures of OCD tendencies (Olatunji, Lohr, Sawchuk, & Tolin, 2007; Olatunji, Williams, Lohr, & Sawchuk, 2005). Conceptually, however, we can separate three factors: (a) how disgusting something is, (b) the extent to which it is transmitted by contact (contagion potential), and (c) the indelibility of this transfer (related to spiritual vs. material essence; Nemeroff & Rozin, 1994). It is possible, but not necessary, that OCD involves high levels of all three of these factors.

In addition, there have been suggestions of the involvement of disgust in a wide range of disorders beyond OCD and phobias, so there is likely more in store about disgust and psychopathology (Davey, Buckland, Tantow, & Dallos, 1998; Power & Dalgleish, 1997; Schienle et al., 2003).

Disgust, Animal Reminders, and Death

Our designation of animal nature reminders as a domain of disgust, one that falls between core disgust and social and moral disgust, is a theoretical claim. It has received some empirical support from studies on the psychometric structure of disgust (Olatunji, Williams, et al., 2007), but it needs refinement and more evidence. Of particular interest is the link between death and disgust. In Becker's (1973) analysis, in which mortality is the basic human dilemma (as opposed to Freud's emphasis on sex and aggression), disgust becomes a mechanism of denial or repression because disgust causes withdrawal from thoughts about, or contact with, death. Terror management theory, currently a productive line of empirical research, will no doubt make many more connections with the study of disgust.

Development of Disgust and Contamination

We presume that toilet training is an early and important disgust experience, in cultures that have toilet training. It seems that with the rejection of psychoanalysis, a baby or two may have been thrown out with the bathwater. There is minimal work in psychology now on either toilet training or weaning, two of Freud's favorite developmental issues (Rozin, 2006). Because feces are probably the universal primal disgust, toilet training is a valuable arena in which to study the acquisition of disgust. The conversion of feces from a desired to a detested and disgusting substance is a major transformation that could be a model system for the study of the acquisition of strong affect of many kinds, including social emotions of shame, guilt, and embarrassment.

The spread of disgust from feces to other body products, foods of animal origin, and eventually other entities presents a fascinating developmental problem. Does the acquisition of disgust follow in any way the sequence we have proposed for the cultural evolution of disgust? To what extent are disgusts acquired secondarily (Rozin & Fallon, 1987) by generalization from already disgusting entities (see Ferenczi, 1914/1952)? To what extent are disgusts generated by pairing with disgust faces or other indicators of offense? Can the acquisition of disgust sensitivities be understood as a form of evaluative conditioning?

We presume that basic disgust socialization begins in parent–child or sibling–child interactions, but this has not been studied. Today we have only a few studies showing a modest level of family (parent–child) resemblance in disgust sensitivity (Davey, Forster, & Mayhew, 1991; Rozin, Fallon, & Mandell, 1984).

Contamination sensitivity is not present in children below the age of about 4 years (Fallon et al., 1984; Siegal, 1988). If, as we have suggested, contamination sensitivity is central to disgust, then disgust does not appear in full until about this age. All indications are that the contamination response (to feces and many other objects of disgust, depending on the culture) is universal among adults and universally absent in young children and all animals. How is the idea of "once contact, always in contact" acquired? Does it depend, for example, on cognition about the action of invisible entities, such as germs (Rosen & Rozin, 1993)?

To what extent is the development of disgust and contamination different in different cultures? Does it relate, for example, to the manner and severity of toilet training? We have a little cross-cultural evidence suggesting similarity in contagion sensitivity in American and Hindu Indian children in the preschool to early school years, but with contagion sensitivity appearing somewhat earlier in Indian children and with a greater focus on interpersonal contagion in the Indian children (Hejmadi, Rozin, & Siegal, 2004). These questions have so far attracted relatively little research attention.

Disgust in Human History

Disgust, as we have defined it, including contamination and ideational (as opposed to sensory) food rejection, is uniquely human. The cognitive sophistication required to react to the nature or history of an object appears only in humans older than 3 or 4 years. Of course, a disgust progenitor, a rejection system with appropriate expressions for bad-tasting foods (e.g., mouth gape in response to bitter taste), exists in many mammals and in human infants. Nevertheless, and despite its obvious biological significance, disgust may be the last of the "basic" emotions to have emerged in human evolution.

We have no idea when in history ideational rejections of foods (on the basis of their nature or origin rather than sensory properties) arose. Disgust is clearly part (although not all) of the particular food taboos found in ancient Hinduism and Judaism. In Western European history, especially around eating and the table, disgust played a role in many of the changes in manners and mores during the 1,000 plus years that have been well chronicled (Elias, 1939/1978; Kass, 1994; W. I. Miller, 1997).

Two events in Western European history have special relevance for the cultural evolution of disgust. One is the acceptance of Darwin's theory of evolution by natural selection. The pre-Darwinian mentality (Thomas, 1983) with respect, for example, to human relations to animals, was quite different from the view that emerged in the 50 to 100 years after the publication of Darwin's *On the Origin of Species* in 1859. Animal-nature disgust might well have changed considerably as thinking about animals changed.

The second major event, less than half a century after Darwin's *Origin*, is the rise of germ theory. Germ theory provides a scientific basis for the contagion ideas that preceded it by thousands of years. Scientific demonstration of potent invisible entities is likely to have had a significant impact on lay thinking about contamination and disgust. A particularly illuminating examination of this possibility was carried out by Barnes (2006), who studied the public and medical professional reactions to sewage backups in Paris ("the great stinks of Paris") in the middle and late 19th century. The major great stink of Paris occurred just as germ theory was taking root in France. The "sanitary-bacteriological-synthesis" or the "marriage of filth and germs" is described by Barnes as a fascinating convergence of intuition-based attitudes to illness and death with the scientific advances associated with germ theory.

So far as we are aware, the history of disgust and contamination in East Asian, South Asian, African, and American Indian cultures is unexplored territory.

Disgust in Relation to Other Emotions

Among emotions, disgust is perhaps closest to contempt. Tomkins (1963) and W. I. Miller (1997) have had much of interest to say about these two emotions. Tomkins linked contempt more to smell and disgust more to taste, and Miller conceived of contempt as more linked to pride, superiority, and indifference than disgust. These suggestions fit with the CAD hypothesis that disgust is the moral emotion associated with violation of the ethic of divinity, whereas contempt is the emotion associated with violation of the ethic of community (including hierarchy and respect; Rozin, Lowery, et al., 1999).

Disgust and shame is another pair of related emotions. In one perspective, disgust is an other-directed moral emotion, and shame is a similar but more self-directed emotion. Finally, there seem to be relationships between disgust and hatred that must be worked out (see discussions in Tomkins, 1963, and W. I. Miller, 1997). In general, the relation between disgust and other social emotions is yet to be explored.

Intergroup Disgust

Disgust may play an important role in intergroup relations. Dehumanization seems to be involved in negative attitudes to, harsh treatment of, and even genocide directed at particular groups (Chirot & McCauley, 2006). Haslam (2006) distinguished between *animalistic dehumanization* that makes the enemy more like animals and *mechanistic dehumanization* that makes the enemy less human by denying them uniquely human characteristics that makes them more like a machine. Haslam suggested that disgust is the emotional reaction associated with animalistic dehumanization.

Similarly, Des Pres (1976) suggested that an important support for Nazis killing Jews and other inmates in concentration camps was the animal dehumanization imposed on them by the living conditions they were subjected to. Nazis found it easier to kill animals than humans. According to Des Pres, those prisoners who resisted animalization (e.g., by washing themselves even with muddy water) were more likely to survive.

Fiske, Cuddy, Glick, and Xu (2002) suggested that groups perceived as lower in status and dissimilar to the reference group tend to be viewed by the reference group with disgust and contempt. Related results suggest that disgust sensitivity is positively correlated with negative attitudes to foreigners, immigrants, outgroups, and deviant individuals (Faulkner, Schaller, Park, & Duncan, 2004; Hodson & Costello, 2007; Navarette & Fessler, 2006). This relation may be mediated by fear of infection or contamination (Faulkner et al., 2004; Navarette & Fessler, 2006). Thus, in the context of intergroup relations, disgust may serve as both a response to a threat of contamination and a justification for hostility that can extend to mass murder.

Disgust, Morality, and the Way Culture Shapes Disgust

Disgust has stimulated research and thinking about morality in two ways. It has provided another dimension in our understanding of emotion and morality, moving beyond the usual focus on anger. Thus, by a process of moralization, certain activities that were once morally neutral or even status positive (e.g., cigarette smoking) become morally negative (Rozin, 1997). When this occurs in body-related domains, there is reason to believe that disgust is recruited as an emotional response, as for example in reaction to cigarettes, cigarette ashes, and even smokers (Rozin & Singh, 1999).

Second, studies related to disgust have contributed to debate about the relative role of rationality and affect or emotion in moral judgment. It is no accident that the major presentation of the intuitionist position in moral psychology (Haidt, 2001) came from a psychologist whose interest in moral judgment originated in research on disgust (Haidt et al., 1993). Haidt and Bjorklund (2008) suggested that affectively laden intuitions—some related to disgust—drive moral judgment as well as political ideology; Inbar, Pizarro, and Bloom (in press) found that political conservatives score higher in disgust sensitivity. Future research might examine individual differences in disgust sensitivity within cultures as a partial account of differences in political ideology.

Structure of the Domains of Disgust

There is much yet to learn about the linkage between the various domains of disgust. Our preadaptive account provides one among a possible set of taxonomies. Psychometric research, such as the work of Olatunji, Williams, et al. (2007), promises to help us to carve the categories of disgust at their joints. Work on psychophysiology and brain activation or lesions will help us to see what disgust elicitors share common mechanisms.

Contamination

Nemeroff and Rozin (1994) identified two models of contagion, at least for Americans. In one model, material essence, the source of contagion behaves like a microscopic particle. It can be eliminated by washing, sterilization, or some other physical procedure. In the other model, spiritual essence, the essence seems to be permanent and indestructible. For most people, aversion to Adolf Hitler's sweater seems to be based on a spiritual essence that cannot be washed away. Yet many of those same people say that their aversion to a sweater worn by someone with hepatitis can be eliminated with sufficient washing and sterilizing.

The cognitions and feelings behind these two types of contagions, usually linked with disgust, need to be understood, as well as the causes of between- and within-culture differences in the properties of essence and the type of essence that is assumed to be transmitted by contact with disgusting or other negative entities. A particularly important feature of contagion, paralleled by disgust, is the journey from the physical to the moral. Although moral contagion is often indelible, it is sometimes treated as if it is physical. A promising line of research recently demonstrated the effectiveness, for Americans, of *washing,* a physical cleansing operation, as a way of ridding the self of moral contamination (Zhong & Liljenquist, 2006).

Unmaking Disgust

We live in a disgusting, contaminated world. Almost everything we interact with—chairs, doorknobs, air, food—has been in contact with other human beings. This could be crippling, but most people come to terms with it by a combination of habituation, reframing, and retreating to ritual and sacred law. We do not know the dynamics of how this occurs, but it is obvious that we ignore many potential disgust elicitors in daily life, unless called to our attention. Doorknobs, for instance, tend to escape our attention except when, for example, an unsavory looking person handles a doorknob while exiting a public bathroom as we are about to reach for the same doorknob.

Habituation must surely play a major role, and one critical issue is how specific the habituation might be. This issue is especially notable for professions in which disgust elicitors are salient: surgeons, morticians, and individuals who work with garbage. We recently showed what looks like habituation to the disgust-eliciting properties of cadavers in medical students who spend months dissecting a cadaver, but this appears quite specific to death-related disgust elicitors and perhaps does not even extend to still-warm dead bodies (Rozin, 2008). Contamination-sensitive religions, particularly Hinduism and Judaism, have ritual ways of dealing with contamination, including washing and establishing acceptable thresholds for contamination (e.g., the 1/60th rule for contamination in the rules of Kashrut; Grunfeld, 1982; Nemeroff & Rozin, 1992).

It is easy to imagine experimental investigations of habituation to disgust. How often would an undergraduate need to experience putting a pin in the eye of a refrigerated sheep's head, for instance, to find this experience more boring than disgusting? How long would habituation endure after the last trial? What cultural differences might appear in habituation experiments? Happily, experiments of this kind are unlikely to attract the concern of Institutional Review Boards. Much needs to be done to understand how human beings in different cultures deal with the fact that they live in a contaminated world.

Disgust and the Holes in the Body

Disgust centers on the holes in the body. Most of the most disgusting body products (e.g., feces, vomit) emanate from holes, and the holes are also foci for disgust sensitivity. There has been minimal work on the holes in the body, perhaps part of the general reaction formation to Freudian conceptions (Rozin, 2006, 2007). But holes, especially Freud's "big three" (mouth, anus, genitals) have too much to do with disgust to be ignored. They can be viewed as the most vulnerable gateways between the self and the body, between inside and outside; conversely, they can be seen as guardians of the body, protectors from the possibility of physical contamination (Fessler & Haley, 2006; S. B. Miller, 2004; W. I. Miller, 1997; Rozin, Nemeroff, Horowitz, Gordon, & Voet, 1995).

Dynamics of Disgust

Disgust, similar to other emotions, unfolds in a matter of seconds. Appraisals, expressions, behaviors, and physiological events, all occur in this period and influence one another. Scherer and Wallbott (1994) provided a general framework for understanding the pattern of events across a number of emotions, including disgust. Also, some psychophysiological studies begin to give a sense of the sequence of physiological components of disgust (Levenson, 1992; Stark, Walter, Schienle, & Vaitl, 2005). Still, psychologists know relatively little about the time course of the multiple aspects of the experience of disgust.

Finally, there is the issue of how disgust may interact with other emotions, either in alternation or blending. The close interplay and sequencing of different emotional states is a general problem for researchers interested in emotions (e.g., Marzillier & Davey, 2005).

Biological and Cultural Evolution of Disgust

One of the fundamental aspects of understanding anything in psychology is to understand the degree to which it has evolutionary origins, and if so, what they are. Disgust came on the stage of psychology, in part, through the writings of Darwin (1872/1998). In its original form, disgust is clearly an adaptive mechanism to protect the body or rid it of potentially harmful or contaminated foods, and perhaps to communicate information about these threats to conspecifics. Several other investigators have also proposed that disgust and contamination sensitivity originated as adaptive responses to the prospect of microbial infection (Curtis, Aunger, & Rabie, 2004; Curtis & Biran, 2001; Davey, 1993; Faulkner et al., 2004; Fessler & Haley, 2006). It seems likely that humans evolved a predisposition to find certain objects and smells disgusting, particularly for such things as feces and corpses that have long been major disease vectors within human communities. Fessler (e.g., Fessler & Haley, 2006) and Schaller (e.g., Schaller & Neuberg, 2007) have been particularly active in promoting evolutionary insights into disgust and contagion. One of the most interesting problems that remains is how genetic and cultural evolution may have intertwined so that this originally food-related emotion now serves many culturally variable social functions (e.g., maintaining group boundaries and guarding against spiritual pollution).

Humor

We close with an unusual and appropriately amusing aspect of disgust. As noted in the foreword to this volume, disgust is often funny. It is a major part of the humor of young boys, and it has its own genre of jokes (Fine, 1988; W. I. Miller, 1997). It seems that, like chili pepper, roller coaster rides, and horror movies, disgust can be enjoyable when it elicits a negative emotion or feeling in an environment in which cognitions indicate there is no real threat (McCauley, 1998; Rozin, 1990; Rozin & Schiller, 1980). Participants in studies on disgust often laugh and show signs of amusement (Hemenover & Schimmack, 2007; Rozin, Haidt, et al., 1999). We have called this *benign masochism* (Rozin, 1990). It plays a substantial role in human life, including in the experience of disgust. Benign masochism seems to depend on a competition between an emotion of the body and an emotion of civilization; the civilized mind seems to take pleasure in the fact that it can rise above its animal instincts.

CONCLUSION

Many have observed that a good piece of research raises more questions than it answers. The first decade or 2 of intensive research on disgust has raised more questions than it has answered. In our view, the most significant question is how a mouth- and food-oriented rejection mechanism, a "get-this-out-of-my-body" emotion, has been elaborated (culturally and biologically) into a broad and meaning-rich emotion that protects not just the body but also the soul. This book will set an agenda for the next decade; there is much to do.

REFERENCES

Angyal, A. (1941). Disgust and related aversions. *Journal of Abnormal and Social Psychology, 36*, 393–412.

Barnes, D. S. (2006). *The great stink of Paris and the nineteenth-century struggle against filth and germs*. Baltimore: Johns Hopkins University Press.

Becker, E. (1973). *The denial of death*. New York: Free Press.

Berle, D., & Phillips, E. S. (2006). Disgust and obsessive–compulsive disorder: An update. *Psychiatry, 69*, 228–238.

Bloom, P. (2004). *Descartes' baby: How the science of child development explains what makes us human*. New York: Basic Books.

Chirot, D., & McCauley, C. (2006). *Why not kill all of them? The logic and prevention of mass political murder*. Princeton, NJ: Princeton University Press.

Cox, C. R., Goldenberg, J. L., Pyszczynski, T., & Weise, D. (2006). Disgust, creatureliness and the accessibility of death-related thoughts. *European Journal of Social Psychology, 37*, 494–507.

Curtis, V., Aunger, R., & Rabie, T. (2004). Evidence that disgust evolved to protect from risk of disease. *Proceedings of the Royal Society B, 271*(Suppl.), S131–S133.

Curtis, V., & Biran, A. (2001). Dirt, disgust, and disease. Is hygiene in our genes? *Perspectives in Biology and Medicine, 44*, 17–31.

Darwin, C. (1859). *On the origin of species by means of natural selection, or the preservation of favoured races in the struggle for life*. London: Murray.

Darwin, C. (1998). *The expression of the emotions in man and animals: Definitive edition* (3rd ed.). New York: Oxford University Press. (Original work published 1872)

Davey, G. C. L. (1993). Factors influencing self-rated fear to a novel animal. *Cognition & Emotion, 7,* 461–471.

Davey, G. C. L., Buckland, G., Tantow, B., & Dallos, R. (1998). Disgust and eating disorders. *European Eating Disorders Review, 6,* 201–211.

Davey, G. C. L., Forster, L., & Mayhew, G. (1991). Familial resemblance in disgust sensitivity and animal phobias. *Behaviour Research and Therapy, 31,* 41–50.

Des Pres, T. (1976). *The survivor: An anatomy of life in the death camps.* Oxford, England: Oxford University Press.

Ekman, P. (1992). An argument for basic emotions. *Cognition & Emotion, 6,* 169–200.

Elias, N. (1978). *The history of manners: Vol. 1. The civilizing process* (E. Jephcott, Trans.). New York: Pantheon Books. (Original work published 1939)

Fallon, A. E., Rozin, P., & Pliner, P. (1984). The child's conception of food: The development of food rejections with special reference to disgust and contamination sensitivity. *Child Development, 55,* 566–575.

Faulkner, J., Schaller, M., Park, J. H., & Duncan, L. A. (2004). Evolved disease-avoidance mechanisms and contemporary xenophobic attitudes. *Group Processes and Intergroup Relations, 7,* 333–353.

Ferenczi, S. (1952). The ontogenesis of the interest in money. In S. Ferenczi (Ed.) & E. Jones (Trans.), *First contributions to psychoanalysis* (pp. 319–331). London: Hogarth Press. (Original work published 1914)

Fessler, D. M. T., & Haley, K. J. (2006). Guarding the perimeter: The outside-inside dichotomy in disgust and bodily experience. *Cognition & Emotion, 20,* 3–19.

Fine, G. A. (1988). Good children and dirty play. *Play and Culture, 1,* 43–56.

Fiske, S. T., Cuddy, A. J. C., Glick, P., & Xu, J. (2002). A model of (often mixed) stereotype content: Competence and warmth. *Journal of Personality and Social Psychology, 82,* 878–902.

Goldenberg, J. L., Pyszczynski, T., Greenberg, J., Solomon, S., Kluck, B., & Cornwell, R. (2001). I am not an animal: Mortality salience, disgust, and the denial of human creatureliness. *Journal of Experimental Psychology: General, 130,* 427–435.

Gray, J. M., Young, A. W., Barker, W. A., Curtis, A., & Gibson, D. (1997). Impaired recognition of disgust in Huntington's disease gene carriers. *Brain, 1120,* 2029–2038.

Greenberg, J., Pyszczynski, T., & Solomon, S. (1986). The causes and consequences of a need for self-esteem: A terror management theory. In R. F. Baumeister (Ed.), *Public self and private self* (pp. 189–212). New York: Springer-Verlag.

Grunfeld, D. I. (1982). *The Jewish dietary laws: Vol. 1. Dietary laws regarding forbidden and permitted foods, with particular reference to meat and meat products* (3rd ed.). London: Soncino Press.

Haidt, J. (2001). The emotional dog and its rational tail: A social intuitionist approach to moral judgment. *Psychological Review, 108,* 814–834.

Haidt, J., & Bjorklund, F. (2008). Social intuitionists answer six questions about morality. In W. Sinnott-Armstrong (Ed.), *Moral psychology, Vol. 2: The cognitive science of morality* (pp. 181–217). Cambridge, MA: MIT Press.

Haidt, J., Koller, S., & Dias, M. (1993). Affect, culture, and morality, or is it wrong to eat your dog? *Journal of Personality and Social Psychology, 65*, 613–628.

Haidt, J., McCauley, C. R., & Rozin, P. (1994). A scale to measure disgust sensitivity. *Personality and Individual Differences, 16*, 701–713.

Haslam, N. (2006). Dehumanization: An integrative review. *Personality and Social Psychology Review, 10*, 252–264.

Hejmadi, A., Rozin, P., & Siegal, M. (2004). Once in contact, always in contact: Contagious essence and conceptions of purification in American and Hindu Indian children. *Developmental Psychology, 40*, 467–476.

Hemenover, S. H., & Schimmack, U. (2007). That's disgusting! . . . , but very amusing: Mixed feelings of amusement and disgust. *Cognition & Emotion, 21*, 1102–1113.

Hodson, G., & Costello, K. (2007). Interpersonal disgust, ideological orientations and dehumanization as predictors of intergroup attitudes. *Psychological Science, 18*, 691–698.

Husted, D. S., Shapira, N. A., & Goodman, W. K. (2006). The neurocircuitry of obsessive–compulsive disorder and disgust. *Progress in NeuroPsychopharmacology and Biological Psychiatry, 30*, 389–399.

Inbar, Y., Pizarro, D. A., & Bloom, P. (in press). Conservatives are more easily disgusted than liberals. *Cognition & Emotion.*

Izard, C. E. (1977). *Human emotions.* New York: Plenum Press.

James, W. (1950). *The principles of psychology.* New York: Dover. (Original work published 1890)

Kass, L. (1994). *The hungry soul.* New York: Free Press.

Lazarus, R. S. (1991). *Emotion and adaptation.* New York: Oxford University Press.

Levenson, R. W. (1992). Autonomic nervous system differences among emotions. *Psychological Science, 3*, 23–27.

Marzillier, S., & Davey, G. C. L. (2005). Anxiety and disgust: Evidence for a unidirectional relationship. *Cognition & Emotion, 19*, 729–750.

Matchett, G., & Davey, G. C. L. (1991). A test of a disease-avoidance model of animal phobias. *Behaviour Research and Therapy, 29*, 91–94.

McCauley, C. (1998). When screen violence is not attractive. In J. Goldstein (Ed.), *Why we watch: The attractions of violent entertainment* (pp. 144–162). New York: Oxford University Press.

McKay, D. (2002). Introduction to the special issue: The role of disgust in anxiety disorders. *Journal of Anxiety Disorders, 16*, 475–476.

Miller, S. B. (2004). *Disgust: The gatekeeper emotion.* Hillsdale, NJ: Analytic Press.

Miller, W. I. (1997). *The anatomy of disgust.* Cambridge, MA: Harvard University Press.

Moll, J., deOliveira-Souza, R., Moll, F. T., Ignacio, F. A., Bramati, I. E., & Caparelli, D. E. M. (2005). The moral affiliations of disgust: A functional MRI study. *Cognitive and Behavioral Neurology, 8*, 68–78.

Navarette, C. D., & Fessler, D. M. T. (2006). Disease avoidance and ethnocentrism: The effects of disease vulnerability and disgust sensitivity on intergroup attitudes. *Evolution and Human Behavior, 27*, 270–282.

Nemeroff, C., & Rozin, P. (1992). Sympathetic magical beliefs and kosher dietary practice: The interaction of rules and feelings. *Ethos: The Journal of Psychological Anthropology, 20*, 96–115.

Nemeroff, C., & Rozin, P. (1994). The contagion concept in adult thinking in the United States: Transmission of germs and interpersonal influence. *Ethos: The Journal of Psychological Anthropology, 22*, 158–186.

Olatunji, B. O., Lohr, J. M., Sawchuk, C. N., & Tolin, D. F. (2007). Multimodal assessment of disgust in contamination-related obsessive–compulsive disorder. *Behaviour Research and Therapy, 45*, 263–276.

Olatunji, B. O., & McKay, D. (2006). Introduction to the special series: Disgust sensitivity in anxiety disorders. *Journal of Behavior Therapy and Experimental Psychiatry, 37*, 1–3.

Olatunji, B. O., & Sawchuk, C. N. (2005). Disgust: Characteristic features, social manifestations, and clinical implications. *Journal of Social and Clinical Psychology, 24*, 932–962.

Olatunji, B. O., Williams, N. L., Lohr, J. M., & Sawchuk, C. N. (2005). The structure of disgust: Domain specificity in relation to contamination ideation and excessive washing. *Behaviour Research and Therapy, 43*, 1069–1086.

Olatunji, B. O., Williams, N. L., Tolin, D. F., Abramowitz, J. S., Sawchuk, C. N., Lohr, J. M., et al. (2007). The Disgust Scale: Item analysis, factor structure, and suggestions for refinement. *Psychological Assessment, 19*, 281–297.

Pelham, B. W., Mirenberg, M. C., & Jones, J. K. (2002). Why Susie sells seashells by the seashore: Implicit egotism and major life decisions. *Journal of Personality and Social Psychology, 82*, 469–487.

Phillips, M. L., Young, A. W., Senior, C., Brammer, M., Andrews, C., Calder, A. J., et al. (1997, October 2). A specific neural substrate for perceiving facial expressions of disgust. *Nature, 389*, 495–498.

Pinker, S. (1997). *How the mind works*. New York: Norton.

Plutchik, R. (1980). *Emotion: A psychoevolutionary synthesis*. New York: Harper & Row.

Power, M., & Dalgleish, T. (1997). *Cognition and emotion: From order to disorder*. East Sussex, England: Psychology Press.

Rosen, A., & Rozin, P. (1993). Now you see it. . . . now you don't: The preschool child's conception of invisible particles in the context of dissolving. *Developmental Psychology, 29*, 300–311.

Rozin, P. (1990). Getting to like the burn of chili pepper: Biological, psychological and cultural perspectives. In B. G. Green, J. R. Mason, & M. R. Kare (Eds.), *Chemical senses, Volume 2: Irritation* (pp. 231–269). New York: Marcel Dekker.

Rozin, P. (1997). Moralization. In A. Brandt & P. Rozin (Eds.), *Morality and health* (pp. 379–401). New York: Routledge.

Rozin, P. (2006). Domain denigration and process preference in academic psychology. *Perspectives on Psychological Science, 1*, 365–376.

Rozin, P. (2007). Exploring the landscape of modern academic psychology: Finding and filling the holes. *American Psychologist, 62*, 754–766.

Rozin, P. (2008). Specific habituation to disgust/death elicitors as a result of dissecting a cadaver. *Judgment and Decision Making, 3*, 191–194.

Rozin, P., & Fallon, A. E. (1987). A perspective on disgust. *Psychological Review, 94*, 23–41.

Rozin, P., Fallon, A. E., & Mandell, R. (1984). Family resemblance in attitudes to food. *Developmental Psychology, 20*, 309–314.

Rozin, P., Haidt, J., & McCauley, C. R. (1993). Disgust. In M. Lewis & J. M. Haviland (Eds.), *Handbook of emotions* (pp. 575–594). New York: Guilford Press.

Rozin, P., Haidt, J., & McCauley, C. R. (2000). Disgust. In M. Lewis & J. M. Haviland-Jones (Eds.), *Handbook of emotions* (2nd ed., pp. 637–653). New York: Guilford Press.

Rozin, P., Haidt, J., McCauley, C. R., Dunlop, L., & Ashmore, M. (1999). Individual differences in disgust sensitivity: Comparisons and evaluations of paper-and-pencil versus behavioral measures. *Journal of Research in Personality, 33*, 330–351.

Rozin, P., Haidt, J., McCauley, C. R., & Imada, S. (1997). The cultural evolution of disgust. In H. M. Macbeth (Ed.), *Food preferences and taste: Continuity and change* (pp. 65–82). Oxford, England: Berghahn.

Rozin, P., Lowery, L., Imada, S., & Haidt, J. (1999). The CAD triad hypothesis: A mapping between three moral emotions (contempt, anger, disgust) and three moral codes (community, autonomy, divinity). *Journal of Personality and Social Psychology, 76*, 574–586.

Rozin, P., Millman, L., & Nemeroff, C. (1986). Operation of the laws of sympathetic magic in disgust and other domains. *Journal of Personality and Social Psychology, 50*, 703–712.

Rozin, P., & Nemeroff, C. (1990). The laws of sympathetic magic: A psychological analysis of similarity and contagion. In J. Stigler, G. Herdt, & R. A. Shweder (Eds.), *Cultural psychology: Essays on comparative human development* (pp. 205–232). Cambridge, England: Cambridge University Press.

Rozin, P., Nemeroff, C., Horowitz, M., Gordon, B., & Voet, W. (1995). The borders of the self: Contamination sensitivity and potency of the mouth, other apertures and body parts. *Journal of Research in Personality, 29*, 318–340.

Rozin, P., & Schiller, D. (1980). The nature and acquisition of a preference for chili pepper by humans. *Motivation & Emotion, 4*, 77–101.

Rozin, P., & Singh, L. (1999). The moralization of cigarette smoking in America. *Journal of Consumer Behavior, 8*, 321–337.

Schaller, M., & Neuberg, S. (2007). *The nature in prejudice(s)*. Manuscript submitted for publication.

Scherer, K. R., & Wallbott, H. G. (1994). Evidence for universality and cultural variation of differential emotion response patterning. *Journal of Personality and Social Psychology, 66*, 310–328.

Schienle, A., Schafer, A., Stark, R., Walter, B., Franz, M., & Vaitl, D. (2003). Disgust sensitivity in psychiatric disorders: A questionnaire study. *Journal of Nervous and Mental Disease, 191*, 831–834.

Shweder, R. A., Much, N. C., Mahapatra, M., & Park, L. (1997). The "big three" of morality (autonomy, community, divinity), and the "big three" explanations of suffering. In A. Brandt & P. Rozin (Eds.), *Morality and health* (pp. 119–169). New York: Routledge.

Siegal, M. (1988). Children's knowledge of contagion and contamination as causes of illness. *Child Development, 59*, 1353–1359.

Solomon, S., Greenberg, J., & Pyszczynski, T. (1991). A terror management theory of social behavior: The psychological functions of self-esteem and cultural worldviews. In M. P. Zanna (Ed.), *Advances in experimental social psychology* (Vol. 24, pp. 93–159). New York: Academic Press.

Sprengelmeyer, R., Young, A. W., Calder, A. J., Karnat, A., Lange, H., Homberg, V., et al. (1996). Loss of disgust: Perception of faces and emotions in Huntington's disease. *Brain, 119*, 1647–1665.

Stark, R., Walter, B., Schienle, A., & Vaitl, D. (2005). Psychophysiological correlates of disgust and disgust sensitivity. *Journal of Psychophysiology, 19*, 50–60.

Thomas, K. (1983). *Man and the natural world. Changing attitudes in England 1500–1800.* London: Penguin.

Tomkins, S. S. (1963). *Affect imagery consciousness: Vol. 2. The negative affects.* New York: Springer Publishing Company.

Wheatley, T., & Haidt, J. (2005). Hypnotically induced disgust makes moral judgments more severe. *Psychological Science, 16*, 780–784

Woody, S. R., & Teachman, B. A. (2000). Intersection of disgust and fear: Normative and pathological views. *Clinical Psychology: Science and Practice, 7*, 291–311.

Zhong, C.-B., & Liljenquist, K. (2006, September 8). Washing away your sins: Threatened morality and physical cleansing. *Science, 313*, 1451–1452.

2

DISGUST SENSITIVITY: PSYCHOMETRIC OVERVIEW AND OPERATIONAL DEFINITION

BUNMI O. OLATUNJI AND JOSH M. CISLER

Initially described as the *forgotten emotion* in the experimental psychopathology literature (Phillips, Senior, Fahy, & David, 1998), disgust is now an important emotion for consideration in the etiology of various psychological disorders, including spider phobia, blood-injection-injury (BII) phobia, contamination-based obsessive–compulsive disorder (OCD), eating disorders, and sexual dysfunction, as subsequent chapters in this volume highlight. Accordingly, it has been proposed that *disgust sensitivity*, the tendency to experience disgust toward a wide range of aversive stimuli (Tolin, Sawchuk, & Lee, 1999), may operate as a vulnerability factor for certain disorders (Olatunji & Sawchuk, 2005).

Enhancing our understanding of the nature of individual differences in disgust sensitivity requires the development of reliable and valid measures of the construct. Indeed, the measurement of disgust sensitivity has undergone substantial refinement over the past 2 decades. Although disgust sensitivity was originally conceptualized in the context of contaminated foods (Rozin, Fallon, & Mandell, 1984), research efforts have since extended the application of the disgust sensitivity construct to include a broader range of contextual elicitors (Haidt, McCauley, & Rozin, 1994; Kleinknecht, Kleinknecht, & Thorndike, 1997). More recent work has also resulted in the development of a measure that assesses disgust sensitivity independently of specific contextual elicitors (Cavanagh & Davey, 2000; van Overveld, de Jong, Peters, Cavanagh, & Davey, 2006). Currently available measures of disgust sensitivity differ with regard to content, coverage, and format. However, these differing assessment instruments may be evaluated with regard to their psychometric properties. This chapter presents a critical analysis of current self-report measures of disgust sensitivity. This analysis largely focuses on the psychometric properties of the measures with emphasis on the validity of the different instruments as measures of the disgust sensitivity construct. We also discuss future research directions that may better inform the development and refinement of better measures.

DISGUST ASSESSMENT INSTRUMENTS

Theoretical advances in the conceptualization of disgust have facilitated the development of several self-report measures of disgust. These measures include the Disgust and Contamination Sensitivity Questionnaire (DQ; Rozin et al., 1984), the Disgust Scale (DS; Haidt et al., 1994), the Disgust Emotion Scale (DES; Walls & Kleinknecht, 1996), the Looming of Disgust Questionnaire (LODQ; Williams, Olatunji, Elwood, Connolly, & Lohr, 2006), and the Disgust Propensity and Sensitivity Scale (DPSS; Cavanaugh & Davey, 2000). Each has been instrumental in highlighting the potential role that disgust may play in various clinical and social contexts (Olatunji & Sawchuk, 2005). The measures converge to assess disgust response; however, there are important conceptual differences in the thematic organization of the items in each measure. The differences in the content of these measures may have important research implications.

The Disgust and Contamination Sensitivity Questionnaire

The first measure of disgust sensitivity to appear in the research literature was the DQ (Rozin et al., 1984). The DQ was initially developed to assess similarities and differences between children and parents in attitudes toward certain foods. In its original form, the DQ was embedded in a larger measure that included three sections: food preferences, disgust sensitivity, and miscellaneous (e.g., culinary knowledge). The disgust sensitivity section contained 24 items, each rated on a 9-point Likert hedonic scale (e.g., 1 = *do not want to eat at all*, 9 = *would like to eat very much*). Illustrative examples of the items of the DQ are "How disgusting would you find it to eat your favorite soup from a soup bowl after it had been stirred by a thoroughly washed fly swatter?" "How disgusting would you find it to drink your favorite lemonade when a nontoxic leaf from a houseplant falls into your glass and goes to the bottom?" and "How disgusting would you find it to eat your favorite cookie after a bite had been taken by a waiter in a restaurant?" Scores on each item are summed to yield a total DQ score (ranging from 24–216; low score = high disgust sensitivity).

There is a paucity of published studies directly examining the psychometric properties of the DQ. However, Table 2.1 shows that there is some evidence that the DQ is an internally consistent measure of disgust sensitivity

TABLE 2.1
Internal Consistency of Self-Report Measures of Disgust Sensitivity

Measure	Study	Sample	Alpha coefficient
Disgust and Contamination Sensitivity Questionnaire	Merckelbach et al. (1999)	166 undergraduate students	.96
	Merckelbach et al. (1999)	44 undergraduate students	.94
	Merckelbach et al. (1999)	36 patients with blood-injection-injury phobia	.97
	Muris et al. (1999)	189 children (M age = 9.67)	.91
	Muris et al. (2000)	173 undergraduate students	.95
	Exeter-Kent & Page (2006)	44 undergraduate students	.96
	van Overveld et al. (2006)	967 undergraduate students	.72
Disgust Scale	Haidt et al. (1994)	454 undergraduates and physical plant/food process workers	.84
	Haidt et al. (1994)	251 undergraduate students	.81
	Quigley et al. (1997)	149 undergraduate students	.86
	Druschel & Sherman (1999)	149 undergraduate students	.87
	Olatunji, Tolin, Huppert, & Lohr (2005)	100 undergraduate students	.86
	Tolin et al. (2006)	1,005 undergraduate students	.83
	Olatunji, Lohr, Sawchuk, & Tolin (2007)	30 contamination-fearful and 30 nonfearful participants	.91
	Olatunji, Smits, et al. (2007)	22 injection-fearful participants	.74
Disgust Emotional Scale	Olatunji (2006)	22 spider-fearful and 28 nonfearful participants	.93
	Olatunji, Lohr, et al. (2006)	30 contamination-fearful and 30 nonfearful participants	.93
	Olatunji, Sawchuk, et al. (2007)	260 undergraduate students	.90
	Olatunji, Sawchuk, et al. (2007)	307 undergraduate students	.91
	Olatunji, Smits, et al. (2007)	22 injection-fearful participants	.95

Note. M = mean.

toward contaminated foods. Studies have also examined the test–retest reliability of the DQ. For example, Merckelbach, de Jong, Arntz, and Schouten (1993) administered the DQ before treatment and several (between 2 and 6) months after treatment in a sample of 28 spider phobic participants. Mean scores on the DQ were found to be stable, 123.7 ($SD = 31.8$) and 120.5 ($SD = 36.5$), respectively, with a Pearson correlation of .84. Mulkens, de Jong, and Merckelbach (1996) examined the test–retest reliability of the DQ in a sample of female undergraduates ($N = 22$) who completed the measure on two occasions, 4 weeks apart. The reliability of the DQ was satisfactory ($r = .80$) in this sample with mean scores of 131.2 ($SD = 28.4$) and 135.2 ($SD = 28.6$), respectively.

Examinations of the validity of the DQ are largely limited to studies examining the relation between disgust sensitivity and specific phobias. Indeed, such studies have reported significant relations between the DQ and measures of animal fears (i.e., Arrindell, Mulkens, Kok, & Vollenbroek, 1999; Mulkens et al., 1996) and BII fears (i.e., Merckelbach, Muris, de Jong, & de Jongh, 1999). However, the positive association between the DQ and specific phobias has not been a consistent finding in the literature (de Jong & Merckelbach, 1998; Thorpe & Salkovskis, 1998). Some studies have also examined the validity of the DQ with regard to its relation with other self-report indexes of disgust. For example, de Jong and Merckelbach (1998) found a significant correlation between the DS and disgust responses to a wide range of stimuli including small animals, foods, and hygiene concerns. The DQ is also moderately correlated with trait anxiety ($r = .35$; Muris, Merckelbach, Schmidt, & Tierney, 1999) but not depression ($r = .10$; Muris et al., 2000). These early findings suggest that disgust sensitivity, as assessed by the DQ, may reflect a stable individual difference personality characteristic that may be important for consideration in the etiology of certain disorders.

The Disgust Scale

Theoretical accounts suggest that elicitors of disgust consist of a wide range of stimuli that extends beyond contaminated foods (Rozin, Haidt, & McCauley, 1993). Indeed, it has been noted that the exclusive focus of the DQ on contaminated foods limits its utility for investigation in other research domains (i.e., in anxiety disorder research; Olatunji & Sawchuk, 2005). To address the content limitations of the DQ, Haidt et al. (1994) developed the DS. The DS is described as a measure of disgust sensitivity across eight domains: (a) *food* that has spoiled, is culturally unacceptable, or has been fouled in some way; (b) *animals* that are slimy or live in dirty conditions; (c) *body products*, including body odors, feces, and mucus; (d) *body envelope violations*, or mutilation of the body; (e) *death* and dead bodies; (f) *sex*, involving culturally deviant sexual behavior; (g) *hygiene*, or violations of culturally expected hygiene practices; and (h) *sympathetic magic*, which involves stimuli without infectious qualities that either resemble contaminants (e.g., feces-shaped candy) or were once in contact with contaminants (e.g., a sweater worn by an ill person).

The DS consists of 32 items and is broken down into two sections. The first section (16 items) is designed to assess avoidance behaviors as well as emotional reactions to potential disgust elicitors without any reference to the word disgust (true–false format). For example, "It would bother me to see a rat run across my path in a park" *True/False*. Scoring the first section of the DS consists of adding up the number of "true" responses (along with the three reversed scored items). The second section (16 items) consists of actual disgust scenarios in which participants are asked to rate according to the severity of disgust experienced. Each question in the second section is rated on a 3-point Likert-type scale, ranging from 0 (*not disgusting at all*) to 2 (*very disgusting*). An example item reads, "You see a man with his intestines exposed after an accident." Scoring of the second section consists of adding up all of the responses and dividing them by 2. Total DS scores are derived by summing the scores from the two sections. Scores on the DS range from 0 to 32, with higher scores indicating greater disgust sensitivity.

The DS is currently regarded as the measure of choice for assessing the disgust sensitivity construct (Olatunji & Sawchuk, 2005). In fact, the measure has been translated into several languages (i.e., Swedish, Japanese, German). However, there is an absence of a comprehensive examination of the measurement properties of the DS. In fact, Haidt et al. (1994) provided the only comprehensive examination of the factor structure and psychometric properties of the original English version of the DS. As shown in Table 2.1, Haidt et al. (1994) reported adequate internal consistency for the DS total score. However, poor coefficient alpha estimates were found for each of the eight subscales in two independent samples (ranging from .27–.63). Numerous studies have reported adequate internal consistency estimates for the DS total score since the initial measurement validation study. However, the internal consistencies for the eight subscales continue to be problematic. For example, Tolin, Woods, and Abramowitz (2006) found internal consistencies for the eight DS subscales ranging from .36 to .65, and van Overveld et al. (2006) found that alphas for all eight DS subscales were below .43. Schienle, Stark, Walter, and Vaitl (2003) found internal consistencies ranging from .26 to .64 for the eight subscales in the German translation of the DS, and Björklund and Hursti (2004) found a mean subscale internal consistency of .43 for the Swedish translation of the DS.

Examinations of the test–retest reliability of the DS are limited. However, one study revealed that DS total scores among injection phobic participants remained unchanged over a 1-week period with mean scores of 21.40 (*SD* = 3.82) and 21.18 (*SD* = 3.48), respectively (Olatunji, Smits, Connolly, Willems, & Lohr, 2007). The validity of the DS has also been examined in relation with anxiety disorder symptoms and other psychopathology. The DS has been shown to be related to measures of spider phobia (de Jong & Muris, 2002), BII phobia (Olatunji, Williams, Sawchuk, & Lohr, 2006), OCD (Mancini, Gragnani, & D'Olimpio, 2001; Olatunji, Sawchuk, Lohr, & de Jong, 2004), and eating disorders (Troop, Murphy, Bramon, & Treasure, 2000). Haidt et al. (1994) provided additional evidence for the convergent validity of the DS with significant correlations with measures of thrill seeking scale ($r = -.47$) and experience seeking ($r = -.49$). The DS has also demonstrated significant correlations with anxiety ($r = .20$; Thorpe, Patel, & Simonds, 2003) and neuroticism ($r = .45$; Druschel & Sherman, 1999) as well as schizoid and dependent personality traits (Quigley, Sherman, & Sherman, 1997). Positive correlations with measures of food neophobia ($r = .30$) and nausea frequency ($r_s = .28$) have also been reported as evidence of the convergent validity of the DS (Björklund & Hursti, 2004).

There is an absence of evidence of the convergent validity of the DS in psychophysiological studies. For example, Stark, Walter, Schienle, and Vaitl (2005) found that elevated DS scores were not significantly related to physiological parameters of heart rate, skin conductance response, and electromyographic activity of the musculus levator labii during exposure to disgust-relevant images. However, the convergent validity of the DS is supported by significant positive correlations with other self-report and behavioral measures of disgust sensitivity. For example, de Jong, Peters, and Vanderhallen (2002) found significant correlations between the DS and the DQ in a sample of spider fearful and nonfearful women ($r = -.33$). Rozin, Haidt, McCauley, Dunlop, and Ashmore (1999) also demonstrated a relatively strong relationship ($r = .51$) between the DS and disgust behavior across a set of 32 behavioral tasks. Björklund and Hursti (2004) also found a behavioral measure of the willingness to touch, hold, and taste disgusting food objects correlated negatively with the DS ($r = -.46$).

Evidence for the divergent validity of the DS is provided by Haidt et al. (1994), who reported the absence of a correlation between the DS and extroversion ($r = -.06$), a finding that has since been replicated (Druschel & Sherman, 1999). DS has also been reported to have modest correlations with depression ($r = .17$; Tolin, Woods, & Abramowitz, 2006). In addition, some research has shown relatively low correlations (i.e., $r = .17$) between the DS and anxiety sensitivity (i.e., Cisler, Reardon, Williams, & Lohr, 2007; Valentiner, Hood, & Hawkins, 2005), suggesting that disgust sensitivity, as assessed by the DS, may not overlap conceptually with anxiety sensitivity, the belief that interoceptive manifestations of fear signal imminent physical harm or loss of cognitive and/or affective control (Reiss & McNally, 1985). However, some reports have questioned the divergent validity of the DS. For example, Davey and Bond (2006) found significant positive correlations between the DS and measures of "disgust-irrelevant" anxiety symptoms such as claustrophobia ($rs = .51, .44$) and height phobia ($rs = .42, .41$).

Although the DS has facilitated research efforts dedicated to better understanding the experience of disgust toward a wide range of stimuli, the measure is clearly not without psychometric limitations. In fact, one study suggests that seven items (i.e., Items 2, 7, 8, 21, 23, 24, and 25) should be considered for removal from the DS (Olatunji, Williams, et al., 2007). Furthermore, the DS subscales yield a limited range of response scaling (0–4), which could result in ceiling effects that may reduce the scales' sensitivity to detect meaningful relations between variables of interest (Olatunji, Sawchuk, de Jong, & Lohr, 2007). However, the most problematic limitation of the DS is the poor internal consistency of its eight subscales. This problematic aspect of the DS is not particularly surprising, however, because the factor analyses reported by Haidt et al. (1994) did not unequivocally support the eight subscales. Haidt et al. (1994) reported that an initial principal-components analysis of the matrix of intercorrelations of the DS items actually yielded 10 factors, with a relatively large first factor and 9 smaller factors. A second principal-components analysis yielded 11 factors, and varimax rotation failed to produce fully interpretable factors. In a psychometric evaluation of a Swedish version of the DS, confirmatory factor analysis of the eight-factor model of the DS provided satisfactory fit to the data and was significantly better than alternative one-factor or five-factor models (Björklund & Hursti, 2004). However, the validity of the eight DS subscales is yet to be evaluated in the original English version of the measure. Another possible explanation for the low internal consistency of the DS subscales is the small number of items for each subscale (four items each). Therefore, a more comprehensive measure that assesses multiple disgust domains would be a psychometric improvement.

The Disgust Emotion Scale

Given the poor internal consistency of the DS subscales, Walls and Kleinknecht (1996) developed the DES. The DES is a 30-item scale that measures disgust sensitivity across five domains: animals, injections and blood draws, mutilation and death, rotting foods, and smells. Participants are asked to rate their degree of disgust or repugnance if they were to be exposed to each item, using a 5-point Likert-type scale, ranging from 0 (*no disgust or repugnance at all*) to 4 (*extreme disgust or repugnance*). Thus, the DES topographically differs from the DS in two notable ways. First, the DES asks participants to respond on the basis of a 5-point Likert-type scale. This is in contrast with the true–false and 3-point Likert format of the DS. Second, the DES measures only five domains of disgust compared with the eight domains of disgust on the DS. Moreover, each subscale of the DES contains six items, compared with four items per subscale in the DS. Thus, the DES subscales yield a much wider range (0–30) than the DS, potentially allowing for more sensitive detection of individual differences in disgust sensitivity.

Studies have shown that the DES total score demonstrates excellent internal consistency (see Table 2.1). The five subscales have also been shown to be internally consistent. For example, Kleinknecht, Kleinknecht, and Thorndike (1997) found alpha coefficients for the five DES subscales, ranging from .80 to .90; and Sawchuk, Lohr, Tolin, Lee, and Kleinknecht (2000) reported that the alpha coefficient for the five DES subscales ranged from .73 to .87. Olatunji, Williams, et al. (2006) provided more conservative estimates of the internal consistency of the DES subscales with alpha coefficients, ranging from .63 to .89. Despite the psychometric improvements of the DES relative to the DS, few reports have examined the validity of its proposed five-factor structure. Olatunji, Sawchuk, et al. (2007) reported the only extensive psychometric evaluation of the DES. Exploratory and confirmatory factor analyses of the DES provided supportive evidence for the five-factor structure. However, there was some indication of item overlap within some of the DES subscales. Furthermore, the authors found adequate alphas for each of the five subscales (.67–.89, .58–.89) in two independent nonclinical samples. Supportive evidence was also found for the DES as its subscales correlated significantly with the DS total score (rs ranged from .28–.55).

Supportive evidence of the convergent validity of the DES can also be revealed in studies that examine the relation between disgust sensitivity and anxiety symptoms. For example, Sawchuk et al. (2000) found that the DES total score was significantly positively correlated with measures of BII phobia ($r = .68$), spider phobia ($r = .24$), and contamination-based OCD ($r = .43$). Kleinknecht et al. (1997) also found that a latent disgust experiences variable consisting of the subscales of the DES was significantly correlated ($r = .56$) with a latent trait anxiety variable. No study to date has examined the convergent validity of the DES in relation to behavioral or physiological measures of disgust. However, more recent studies have examined the relationship between scores on the DES and pictorial ratings. For example, Olatunji (2006) found that the DES was significantly correlated with fear and disgust ratings of spider pictures ($rs = .42$ and .56, respectively) as well as fear and disgust ratings of pictures of rotting foods and body products ($rs = .60$ and .53, respectively) in a sample of spider fearful and nonfearful participants. In a similar study, Olatunji, Lohr, Willems, and Sawchuk (2006) found that the DES was significantly correlated with fear and disgust ratings of pictures of threatening stimuli (rs ranged from .46–.53, respectively) as well as fear and disgust ratings of pictures of rotting foods and body products (rs ranged from .46–.78) in a sample of contamination fearful and nonfearful participants.

The Looming of Disgust Questionnaire

Several potential cognitive biases may have implications for understanding the relationship between disgust sensitivity and anxiety disorder symptoms. For example, Teachman (2006) argued that biased secondary appraisals of disgust-relevant situations may be critical to the development and maintenance of pathological disgust reactions. One cognitive bias that may be particularly relevant to disgust is looming vulnerability (Riskind, 1997). *Looming vulnerability*, broadly construed, pertains to the tendency to construct dynamic mental scenarios that involve the perceived movement, approach, spread, or escalation in risk or danger of potentially threatening, disgusting, or fear-provoking stimuli. A number of studies have shown that looming vulnerability is uniquely related to a wide range of anxiety disorder symptoms (e.g., specific phobia, OCD, generalized anxiety disorder; Riskind & Williams, 2005). To examine how looming vulnerability may relate to disgust, Williams et al. (2006) developed the LODQ.

The LODQ is a measure of the tendency to view potentially disgusting situations as rapidly rising in threat value. Participants are instructed to read and "vividly imagine" themselves in eight brief vignettes that describe potentially disgusting situations that correspond to different disgust domains (rotting foods and body products, contaminated foods, death and envelope violations, small animals). Participants then complete six questions for each vignette by using a 5-point Likert scale. A total score for cognitive vulnerability to disgust (LOD total) is calculated by aggregating responses to five items across the vignettes (e.g., LOD threat: "To what extent is the level of threat or danger to you increasing as the scene unfolds?"; LOD sick: "To what extent is the threat of your becoming nauseous or sick increasing as the scene unfolds?"; LOD disgust: "To what extent is your level of disgust increasing as the scene unfolds?"; LOD spread: "How quickly is [the disgust stimulus approaching, spreading, or moving] in the scene that you imagine?"; and, LOD ds: "How disgusted do you feel imagining yourself in this situation?"). Item subscales are calculated by aggregating scores for that item across the vignettes. A total score for secondary appraisals of disgust (LOD cope) is also calculated by aggregating responses to item six across the vignettes (e.g., "As the scene unfolds, to what extent do you imagine yourself being able to cope with the situation?").

Estimates of the internal consistency of the LOD total score, factor scores, and item subscales appear to be adequate (alphas ranged from .96 for the total score to a low estimate of .80 for the LOD cope score; Williams et al., 2006). The LOD total score has strong positive correlations with the cognitive vulnerability to disgust and disgust sensitivity factor scores and item subscales. The LOD total score, factor scores, and item subscales are also reported to be negatively correlated with the LOD cope subscale score, suggesting that to the extent that participants believed that they would be able to cope with the disgust scenario, they reported imagining less spread or movement of disgust stimuli; less increasing threat value, sickness or nausea, and disgust; and being less disgusted by the scenarios. The LOD total score was also moderately correlated with the DS total score ($r = .58$, $p <.001$). The secondary appraisals of disgust score (LOD cope) was negatively related to overall DS disgust sensitivity, suggesting that the perceived ability to cope with a disgust eliciting scenario is associated with less disgust sensitivity, and the LOD subscale that assesses the perceived movement, approach, or spread of a disgust stimulus was associated with greater disgust sensitivity on the DS.

Group differences between nonanxious control participants (NACs), anxious control participants (ACs), and contamination-related OCD participants (OCDs) on the LOD were also assessed by Williams et al. (2006). Results showed that OCDs scored significantly higher than ACs, who in turn scored higher than NACs. Examination of group differences on the five-item subscales that compose the LOD total score revealed that all item subscales were successful at discriminating the NACs from the OCDs and ACs, but only the item subscale that assesses the movement, approach, or spread of the disgust stimulus discriminated between the ACs and the OCDs. Examination of the factor scores revealed a similar pattern in that the four context driven factors were successfully able to discriminate the NACs from the OCDs and ACs, but only the secondary appraisals of disgust (LOD cope) score were successful at discriminating the ACs from the OCDs.

Summary Analysis of the DQ, DS, DES, and LODQ

Development of the DQ, DS, and DES has facilitated studies showing that the experience of disgust may contribute to a wide range of psychopathology symptoms (Olatunji & Sawchuk, 2005). The more recent development of the LODQ will likely contribute to new research that examines cognitive appraisals related to disgust in various disorders. Although these measures (total scores) generally demonstrate good reliability, they are limited in several aspects. First, they assess disgust sensitivity in response to specific contextual disgust elicitors. That is, each assesses disgust responses to a specific stimuli or situation. As such, the assessment of disgust sensitivity offered by these three measures may be limited to the types of elicitors assessed, as opposed to a more general assessment of the degree to which, or frequency with which one experiences disgust sensitivity. Moreover, the item content of disgust measures has substantial overlap with symptoms of specific anxiety disorders (e.g., DS item, "I never let any part of my body touch the toilet seat in public restrooms" = contamination symptoms of OCD). Thus, findings that patients with various disorders are characterized by higher disgust sensitivity levels may partially reflect shared item content between measures of disgust sensitivity and psychopathological symptoms.

The DQ, DS, DES, and LODQ also aim to assess disgust sensitivity without clearly differentiating *disgust sensitivity* from *disgust propensity*. The term "disgust sensitivity" emerged from Rozin and colleagues' early research, investigating disgust and the acquisition of food likes and dislikes (e.g., Rozin et al., 1993; Rozin, Fallon, & Augustoni-Ziskind, 1984). In this context, Rozin and colleagues referred to disgust and contamination sensitivity as the degree or propensity to respond to stimuli with disgust. However, the meaning of "sensitivity" in relation to disgust has been confused with the meaning of "sensitivity" in other domains, such as anxiety sensitivity (e.g., see Taylor, 1999). Disgust sensitivity as defined by the work of Rozin and colleagues refers to a heightened propensity to respond with disgust, but anxiety sensitivity does not refer to a heightened propensity to respond with anxiety. Similarly, anxiety sensitivity refers to responding with fear to interoceptive manifestations of fear, but Rozin and colleagues' conceptualization of disgust sensitivity does not refer to responding with disgust to interoceptive manifestations of disgust. Use of the same term to refer to different processes appears to have contributed to the confusion and imprecise communication of the operational definition of disgust sensitivity. Accordingly, perhaps a more face-valid definition of disgust sensitivity as currently assessed by the DQ, DS, DES, and LODQ is disgust propensity, or the degree to which an individual experiences disgust. Disgust sensitivity could be conceptualized as the degree to which an individual's experience of disgust is aversive or having strong disgust reactions for very minor disgust-relevant events (i.e., watching people spit out toothpaste after brushing their teeth). The most recently developed measure of disgust sensitivity appears to improve on the limitations of the DQ, DS, DES, and LODQ in broadening the conceptual parameters of the assessment of disgust sensitivity.

The Disgust Propensity and Sensitivity Scale

Cavanaugh and Davey (2000) developed the DPSS to (a) remove contextual elicitors from confounding the assessment of disgust and (b) differentiate disgust sensitivity from disgust propensity. Although this distinction is not without controversy (i.e., Lilienfeld, 1996), the differentiation of disgust sensitivity from disgust propensity is akin to the differentiation of the degree to which an individual experiences anxiety (i.e., trait anxiety) from the degree to which an individual's experience of anxiety is aversive (i.e., anxiety sensitivity). The DPSS is a 32-item measure designed to assess the frequency of experiencing disgust (propensity; 16 items) as well as the emotional effect of those symptoms (sensitivity; 16 items). Prior psychometric evaluation of the DPSS has revealed that the measure demonstrates good internal consistency with and alpha coefficient of .92 for the DPSS total score (Davey & Bond, 2006). The DPSS Disgust Propensity and Disgust Sensitivity subscales have also been shown to demonstrate good internal consistency with alpha coefficients of .89 and .87, respectively (Cavanagh & Davey, 2000). The DPSS Disgust Propensity and Disgust Sensitivity subscales have also demonstrated good convergent validity with significant correlations with measures of hypochondriasis (e.g., Davey & Bond, 2006).

Given the potential utility of the DPSS in advancing research on the relationship between disgust experiences and symptoms of psychopathology, van Overveld et al. (2006) examined the psychometric properties of the DPSS in a large Dutch sample ($N = 967$). Selection of items based on theory- and data-driven considerations resulted in a revised DPSS (DPSS–R) that consisted of only 16 items. CFA of the DPSS–R yielded support for a two-factor model that consisted of disgust propensity (alpha coefficient = .78; test–retest reliability = 0.69) and disgust sensitivity (alpha coefficient = 0.77; test–retest reliability = 0.77). Examination for the convergent validity of the DPSS–R revealed that the Disgust Propensity and Disgust Sensitivity subscales were significantly correlated with each other ($r = .54$) and with measures of spider ($r = .20, r = .16$, respectively) and BII ($r = .35, r = .35$, respectively) fear. The Disgust Propensity and Disgust Sensitivity subscales were also found to be significantly correlated with the DQ ($r = -.21, r = -.16$, respectively) and the DS ($r = .37, r = .29$, respectively).

Olatunji, Cisler, Deacon, Connolly, and Lohr (2007) sought to examine the psychometric properties of the DPSS–R in an American sample ($N = 340$). Consistent with the findings of van Overveld et al. (2006), principal-components analysis of the DPSS–R revealed a two-factor structure that consisted of Disgust Propensity and Disgust Sensitivity. Although the two-factor structure converged well with that of van Overveld et al., four of the DPSS–R items did not load on the predicted factor. However, good reliability was found for the DPSS–R total score, Disgust Propensity subscale, and the Disgust Sensitivity subscale (alpha coefficients = .90, .84, and .83, respectively). Examination of convergent validity indicated that the Disgust Propensity and Disgust Sensitivity subscales were highly correlated with the DPSS–R total score ($r = .84$ and .83, respectively). The two subscales were also highly correlated with each other ($r = .66$). The DPSS–R total score, Disgust Propensity subscale, and Disgust Sensitivity subscale were also significantly correlated with measures of spider fear (*rs* ranged from .32–.34), injection fear (*rs* ranged from .25–.34), contamination fear (*rs* ranged from .32–.37), and negative affect (*rs* ranged from .37–.38). The DPSS–R and its subscales also demonstrated good divergent validity with negligible correlations with positive affect (*rs* ranged from −.02– −.09).

Although the DQ, DS, and DES appear to be better suited for studies in which the assessment of specific disgust stimuli or a range of stimuli that elicit disgust is central to the study hypothesis, and the LODQ may facilitate research on disgust-based appraisals, the DPSS–R appears to be a more useful instrument for examining disgust sensitivity as it relates to various disorders. However, additional studies dedicated to the refinement of the DPSS–R items will be necessary. Specifically, the items that compose the disgust propensity and disgust sensitivity factors must demonstrate stability across cultures. Future research is also needed to examine whether the factor structure of the DPSS–R varies between and within different samples. Indeed, no currently available data speak to the psychometric properties of the DPSS–R in a clinical sample. Although convenient, the exclusive use of undergraduate samples to examine the psychometric properties of the DPSS–R may constrain its generalizability. Future research that examines the factor structure of the DPSS–R in community and clinical samples may help to reconcile some of its current item-level inconsistencies. Given the unique strengths of the DPSS–R, future research may underscore the utility of this measure in clinical research.

BEHAVIORAL ASSESSMENT OF DISGUST SENSITIVITY

Development of the DQ, DS, DES, and DPSS–R has facilitated a growing body of research on the role of disgust sensitivity in clinical disorders (Olatunji & Sawchuk, 2005). However, studies that rely exclusively on the use of self-report measures of disgust sensitivity are limiting. For example, causal inferences are often difficult to make with the exclusive use of self-report instruments depending on the experimental design (i.e., correlational studies). It is more important to note that relationships between measures of disgust and study variables may also be inflated as a result of questionnaire-specific method variance. Experimentally, disgust is relatively easy to elicit under controlled laboratory settings without risking significant ethical concerns (Rozin, Lowery, & Ebert, 1994). Furthermore, if disgust sensitivity is important in the etiological and maintenance of specific psychological conditions, then differences that emerge on self-report measures should also be observed on behavioral measures.

Rozin et al. (1999) offered perhaps the most comprehensive evaluation of behavioral measures of disgust sensitivity. In their study, 68 undergraduate students were exposed to 32 behavioral tasks. These tasks assessed the participant-determined degree of exposure (looking at, picking up, touching, and in some cases eating) to objects such as a cockroach, cremated ashes, and a freshly killed pig's head and to disgusting video clips (seconds watching). Participants were also exposed to disgust-irrelevant control tasks, such as imitating a chicken or holding one's hand in ice water. Analysis of the intercorrelations of the behavioral tasks revealed four factors: food-related disgust, body violation-and-death-related disgust, compliance motivation, and embarrassability. Only the two behavioral disgust factors correlated significantly with the DS total score; a combination of the two correlated .58 with DS scores obtained months before the laboratory assessment and correlated .71 with scores obtained immediately after behavioral assessment.

Studies on clinical disorders have also used behavioral measures of disgust sensitivity. For example, Mulkens et al. (1996) asked spider phobic and nonphobic women to eat a cookie after a spider had walked across it. Only

25% of the phobic women ate the cookie compared with 71% of the non-phobic women who ate the cookie. The two groups of women were also exposed to a disgust-relevant behavioral measure in which participants were asked to participate in a tea-tasting task. In the task, the taste and flavor of a cup of tea had to be judged (how much do you like the taste of this tea?) three times using 100-millimeter visual analogue scales. Two of the three cups that contained the tea were clean, and one cup was dirty (all cups were identical as was the tea in each cup). Although participants took more time before drinking from the dirty cup relative to the control cups, no significant group differences were found between phobic and nonphobic women on delay in drinking from the dirty cup. Participants also drank more tea from the clean than from the control cups. However, no significant group differences were found between phobic and nonphobic participants in the amount of tea drunk from the dirty cup.

Woody and Tolin (2002) also examined disgust sensitivity in spider fearful individuals with behavioral measures. As outlined in Table 2.2, the behavioral measures included stimuli from four domains of disgust: food, animals, body products, and envelope violations. Findings indicated that the animals task evoked the most avoidance, with only 58% of the participants fully completing the task. Although a majority of participants completed each task, only 39% of the participants fully completed every task. Anxiety and disgust ratings for each task were highly correlated (rs ranged from .61–.85). However, each task evoked significantly more disgust than anxiety. Logistic regression was then used to examine the degree to which the DS total score incremented the prediction of avoidance on each disgust behavioral task over and above self-reported disgust during the task and the behavioral task-relevant DS subscale. The results showed that the DS total score significantly predicted avoidance on only the animals task. The body products task evoked the most disgust and the animals task evoked the most anxiety. Furthermore, high spider fearful participants reported experiencing more disgust and anxiety than the low spider group across all tasks. However, no group differences were observed on avoidance on the behavioral tasks.

Behavioral assessment of disgust sensitivity has also been used in studies on BII phobia. Koch, O'Neil, Sawchuk, and Connolly (2002) examined differences between BII fearful and nonfearful participants across disgust domains of food, blood, mutilation, and animal (see Table 2.2). BII phobic participants rated the blood and mutilation stimuli as more fearful and disgusting than did nonphobic participants. However, BII phobic participants rated the blood and mutilation stimuli significantly more disgusting than fearful. No group differences emerged on fear and disgust ratings for the animal behavioral task. Analyses of behavioral responding revealed that BII phobic participants were less willing to perform all tasks that involved blood and mutilation stimuli and less willing to complete the later stages of tasks involving animal stimuli. BII phobic participants were less likely than nonphobic participants to eat a

TABLE 2.2

Sample Tasks for Behavioral Assessment
of Disgust Sensitivity Across Multiple Domains

Study	Disgust domain	Behavioral task description
Woody & Tolin (2002)	Foods	Participants chose whether to consume a cookie served with a new plastic flyswatter (with original packaging evident), fruit juice stirred with a different new flyswatter (without packaging), juice stirred with a used (washed and sterilized) hair comb, and juice served in a glass with a large plastic cockroach floating in it.
	Animals	Participants were presented with a transparent covered glass bowl that was two-thirds full of live earthworms and asked to complete a series of steps that involved closer contact with the worms. The most challenging step of the series was to immerse a whole hand into the bowl of worms for 3 seconds.
	Body products	Participants were asked to complete a series of steps including examining and sniffing a basin that contained a vomit-like mixture. The imitation vomit included common food ingredients (i.e., cottage cheese, tomato soup, apple juice, soy sauce, bits of vegetables) with a vomit-like odor that was simulated with several drops of a 1% solution of isovaleric and butyric acids. The most challenging part of the task was to run a finger around the inside of the basin.
	Envelope violations	Participants viewed progressively graphic video footage of a 3-minute segment of heart reduction surgery. The footage consisted of an initial incision and continued with surgical procedures to open the chest cavity, culminating with a surgical saw used to cut through the breastbone.
Koch et al. (2002)	Blood	Participants were asked about their willingness to look at and touch (with and without latex gloves) a 4-inch × 4-inch square of surgical gauze with theatrical blood on it.
	Mutilation	Participants were asked about their willingness to look at and touch (with and without latex gloves) a 15-inch severed deer leg with fur and hoof intact.
	Animal	Participants were asked about their willingness to look at, touch, pick up, and hold in hand (with and without latex gloves) a dead mounted American cockroach and a dead mounted 2-centimeter earthworm.
	Food	Participants were asked about their willingness to eat a cookie that was placed in contact for approximately 5 seconds with the stimuli in the blood, mutilation, and animal tasks (participants were required to eat the cookie if they reported a willingness to do so).
Tsao & McKay (2004)	Food	Participants were offered five miniature chocolate chip cookies served on an unused rat trap.
	Animal	Participants were presented with a thoroughly cleaned but live earthworm resting on a plastic lid. The participants were then asked to hold the earthworm for as long as they could.

(continues)

TABLE 2.2
Sample Tasks for Behavioral Assessment
of Disgust Sensitivity Across Multiple Domains *(Continued)*

Study	Disgust domain	Behavioral task description
	Body products	Participants were presented with a piece of fake vomit on a clean ceramic plate and asked to hold the fake vomit in their hands for as long as they could.
	Envelope violations	Participants were presented with an uncovered box of chocolates. All chocolates in the box were the same, but the center chocolate in the array was replaced with a fake human eyeball. Participants were told they could select and eat any one chocolate they liked.
	Death	Participants were presented with an ornamented black vase that looked similar to an urn. The open top of the vase was lined with enough cigarette ash to be easily noticed. Each participant was told that the urn had ashes in it, but that they had been dumped out. Then, the participants were asked to place their hand into the opening of the urn for as long as they could.
	Sympathetic magic	Participants were presented with 200 milliliters of water in a Styrofoam cup with the label "saliva" turned toward them. The participants were told that there was plain water in the cup and that they were free to drink as much or as little of the water as they liked.
Olatunji, Lohr, Sawchuk, & Tolin (2007)	Smells	Participants were asked to approach a shirt that was placed in a zip-locked bag. Participants were told that the shirt had been in a dog kennel for a couple of days and had accumulated residuals of animal feces and urine. Participants were instructed to open the bag and smell the shirt.
	Food	Participants were asked to approach and touch mold that was growing on a rotting orange.
	Animals	Participants were asked to approach and pick up a live green earthworm that was resting on a plastic container.
	Body products	Participants were instructed to put on protective gloves, approach a bedpan with urine in it (the substance was actually apple juice), and touch the inside of the bedpan.
	Death	Participants were instructed to approach an urn with human remains inside (actually regular ashes). They were instructed to open the urn and touch the inside.
	Hygiene	Participants were asked to approach a pair of stained underwear (brown pudding was used to resemble feces) and pick it up.
	Envelope violation	Participants were instructed to approach a tray with cow eyeballs and inject one of the eyeballs with a hypodermic needle.
	Sympathetic magic	Participants were instructed to approach and pick up a pencil that they were told had to be thoroughly sanitized because it was dropped in a toilet.

cookie after it had come into contact with the animal stimuli. No significant differences emerged between BII phobic and nonphobic participants on consumption of the cookie after it had come into contact with the blood and mutilation stimuli.

More recent research on contamination fear, a subtype of OCD, has begun to incorporate behavioral measures into the assessment of disgust sensitivity. In one such study, Tsao and McKay (2004) exposed contamination fearful, high-trait anxiety, and low-trait anxiety participants to six different behavioral tasks, corresponding with food, animals, body products, envelope violations, death, and sympathetic magic domains of disgust (see Table 2.2). The results of this study showed significant differences between the contamination fearful group and the high-trait anxiety group on the animal and sympathetic magic task. Significant differences on the food, animal, envelope violations, and death tasks were also found between the contamination fearful group and the low-trait anxious group.

Olatunji, Lohr, Sawchuk, and Tolin (2007) exposed contamination fearful and nonfearful participants to the eight different behavioral tasks outlined in Table 2.2. The results of this study showed that contamination fearful participants were less willing than the nonfearful participants to comply with the disgust-relevant tasks, with the exception of the envelope violation task. Contamination fearful participants were also less likely than the nonfearful participants to approach the disgust stimuli in the tasks (measured in feet), with the exception of stimuli in the animal task. Contamination fearful participants reported significantly more fear and disgust to the behavioral tasks than did nonfearful participants. However, disgust ratings were significantly higher than fear ratings for the behavioral tasks among contamination fearful participants. Fear and disgust ratings for the eight tasks were also significantly correlated among contamination fearful (rs ranged from .68–.93) and nonfearful participants (rs ranged from .48–.91).

Behavioral assessment of disgust sensitivity is a useful complement to self-report because it can potentially more sensitively assess the same processes as those targeted by self-report disgust measures as well as corroborate findings from self-report. Furthermore, behavioral assessment of disgust may capture unique components of treatment outcome not captured by self-report. However, the behavioral measures of disgust sensitivity should meet the psychometric criteria that are commonly applied to self-report measures. Perhaps the most critical psychometric issue involves reliability, construct validity, and the establishment of linkages between behavioral measures of disgust sensitivity and other psychological processes.

If behavioral measures or disgust sensitivity truly assesses individual differences, one would expect high levels of test–retest stability. Despite its importance, the test–retest reliability of behavioral measures of disgust sensitivity is rarely assessed or reported. The dissociation that has been observed between behavioral measures of disgust sensitivity and self-report measures of disgust sensitivity also suggests that construct validity may be problematic. For example, Olatunji, Lohr, et al. (2007) found that a behavioral measure of envelope violation disgust sensitivity was not significantly correlated with self-reported measures of disgust sensitivity toward animal, death, hygiene, and sex stimuli. Furthermore, Woody and Tolin (2002) found that DS total scores significantly predicted avoidance on only one of four behavioral measure of disgust sensitivity (animals). Perhaps some of the difficulty in determining the construct validity is the variability in the content of behavioral measures of disgust sensitivity across studies. For example, many of the behavioral measures of disgust developed by Rozin et al. (1999) were so objectionable that the majority of the participants did not comply with the tasks (i.e., only 9% compliance for touching a mealworm to one's lip). Thus, subsequent studies were more inclined to use less objectionable behavioral measures. The construct validity of behavioral measures of disgust sensitivity is also further completed by differences in the actual dependent variable (i.e., compliance and willingness, duration in contact with disgust stimuli, physical distance from disgust stimuli). Future research on disgust and disgust sensitivity would greatly benefit from the development and validation of a psychometrically standardized set of behavioral tasks that assess sensitivity to disgust across multiple domains.

A standardized behavioral assessment battery for disgust sensitivity will ultimately facilitate attempts to link disgust sensitivity (as a vulnerability factor) to specific psychological processes. Indeed, some research has highlighted the importance of behavioral assessment of disgust in the treatment of psychological disorders. For example, McKay (2006) used behavioral exposure to the following disgust items (were identified as disgust evoking and not anxiety evoking) in the treatment of contamination-based OCD: used garbage cans, dumpster trash receptacles, sticky and/or greasy food, cigarette ashes, dirty water (a mix of soil and water). Although the use of behavioral exposure to disgust stimuli in this study represents an important advancement in the literature, the psychometric properties of the behavioral measures of disgust were not assessed. Researchers should devote more attention to the systematic assessment of reliability, stability, and generalizability of behavioral measures of disgust sensitivity. Standardized behavioral assessment of disgust may resolve inconsistencies between studies as well as allow for stronger inferences to be made with regard to the role of disgust sensitivity in various psychological disorders.

IS DISGUST SENSITIVITY A UNIQUE CLINICAL CONSTRUCT?

There is currently some debate with regard to the uniqueness of the disgust sensitivity construct in the context of psychological disorders. It has been argued that disgust sensitivity may be an amplified component of neuroticism or negative affectivity, as opposed to a unique and independent clinical construct (Thorpe & Salkovskis, 1998). Indeed, studies have shown that disgust sensitivity is significantly correlated with neuroticism and negative affectivity (Haidt et al., 1994; Olatunji, 2006; Quigley et al., 1997). However, studies have consistently shown that disgust sensitivity remains significantly related to measures of specific phobia (i.e., Olatunji, 2006) and contamination-based OCD (Mulkens et al., 1996; Olatunji, Lohr, et al., 2007) even after controlling for negative affective states. The rather modest relationships with anxiety sensitivity also suggest that disgust sensitivity is a distinct construct (Cisler et al., 2007), and it is not likely to be redundant with variables that correlate highly with anxiety sensitivity, such as trait anxiety (Valentiner et al., 2005). In fact, there is now clear evidence that trait anxiety and disgust sensitivity are independent constructs each of which has relationships with anxiety disorder symptoms over and above the effect of the other (Davey & Bond, 2006). These findings suggest that disgust sensitivity is unique and independently functional in the acquisition, maintenance, or intensity of some disorders.

The experience of disgust appears to be distinct from that of fear (Page, 1994). However, it has been suggested that the feeling of disgust is potentiated in the presence of fear (Thorpe & Salkovskis, 1998), representing an epiphenomenon rather than a functional relationship (Woody & Tolin, 2002). Indeed, studies have shown that self-reported fear and disgust are highly correlated ($r = .83$; Sawchuk, Lohr, Westendorf, Meunier, & Tolin, 2002). The problematic overlap between self-reported fear and disgust is also well articulated in the imprecise emotional labels model advanced by Woody and Teachman (2000). With this model, Woody and Teachman (2000) argued that participants may confuse fear and disgust when the emotional experience is of mild or moderate intensity. This renders interpretations of the unique role of disgust in various disorders difficult as the majority of the current research findings are based on nonclinical (mild disgust) and analogue (moderate disgust) samples with very few studies examining disgust in clinical samples that may be expected to experience disgust at an intense level thus facilitating its differentiation from fear (Olatunji & Sawchuk, 2005).

The confusion between fear and disgust may also reflect imitations of current self-report measures. For example, measures such as the DS assess only disgust reactions to specific stimuli and situations. Similarly, measures such as the Fear Survey Schedule (FSS; Geer, 1965) assess only fear reactions. Currently available self-report measures are based on the notion that disgust and fear (a) are the opposites of one another and (b) cannot coexist. Thus, the measures only allow for one kind of response. For example, on the DS, if a participant wants to communicate their dislike of a stimulus, they have no choice but to rate it as "disgusting," although they may actually be experiencing fear. Future research may benefit from the development of dimensional self-report instruments that conceptualize disgust and fear as intersecting emotions. As depicted

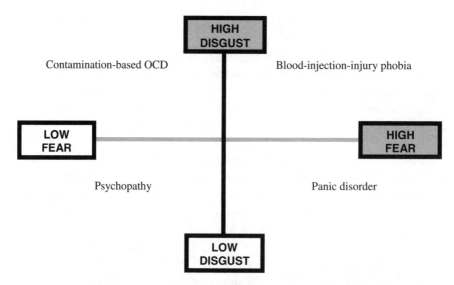

Figure 2.1. A schematic of a dimensional approach to the assessment of fear and disgust in the context of specific disorders. OCD = obsessive–compulsive disorder.

in Figure 2.1, such a measure would be consistent with a diagnostic taxonomy by which various disorders could be categorized based on emotion responses to disorder-relevant stimuli (e.g., Berenbaum, Raghavan, Le, Vernon, & Gomez, 2003). Development of dimensional self-report instruments may also address some of the problems outlined by the imprecise emotional labels model. By pursuing the assessment of both fear and disgust in response to a given stimuli, participants may be more likely to consider the differences between the two emotions resulting in more precise and accurate self-reporting of emotional reactions.

CONCLUSION

Given the proposed relevance of disgust in specific disorders, it is crucial that researchers attend more to critical psychometric issues in the assessment of disgust sensitivity. Future systematic examination of the reliability, temporal stability, and generalizability of self-report and behavioral measures of disgust sensitivity may ultimately help to improve our understanding of the role of disgust in various disorders. However, more consistent articulation of the operational definition of disgust sensitivity must first be pursued. It has been suggested that meaningful distinctions may be made between *state* disgust (the emotion elicited by disgusting stimuli) versus *trait* disgust (disgust sensitivity, or a general tendency to become disgusted; Woody & Tolin, 2002). Measures such as the DQ, DS, DES, and LODQ appear to be better conceptualized as measures of state disgust, whereas the DPSS–R more closely approximates a measure of trait disgust (see Table 2.3 for sample items). In theory, individual differences in disgust sensitivity should relate to the experiencing of disgust in various situations. Indeed, a review of the psychometrics of available disgust measures suggest that state and trait disgust do overlap, with individuals high in trait disgust showing stronger state disgust responses. However, it remains unclear whether state and trait disgust are truly different constructs, or the same construct on an aversion (versus anxiety) continuum.

Although disgust sensitivity may play a role in some disorders, currently available evidence is based largely on correlational studies. Thus, it is possible that the relationship between measures of disgust sensitivity and measures of psychological disorders may simply reflect the possibility that disgust is experienced as a consequence of psychological disorders. Advancing methodological rigor with regard to psychometric validation of the disgust sensitivity construct will be crucial in providing prospective and longitudinal evidence on the directionality of the disgust sensitivity–psychological disorder relationship. The disparity in the programs of research between disgust

TABLE 2.3
Sample Items for Self-Report Assessment
of Disgust Sensitivity Across Multiple Domains

Measure	Domain	Item
Disgust Scale	Food	You see someone put ketchup on vanilla ice cream and eat it.
	Animals	It would bother me to see a rat run across my path in a park.
	Body products	If I see someone vomit, it makes me sick to my stomach.
	Sex	I think homosexual activities are immoral.
	Envelope violations	You see a man with his intestines exposed after an accident.
	Death	It would bother me tremendously to touch a dead body.
	Hygiene	You discover that a friend of yours changes underwear only once a week.
	Magic	A friend offers you a piece of chocolate shaped like dog feces.
Disgust Emotion Scale	Foods	A glass of spoiled milk
	Blood and injection	A bottle of your blood
	Smells	The smell of urine
	Mutilation and death	A dead person unknown to you
	Animals	A sewer rat
Disgust Propensity and Sensitivity Scale—Revised	Disgust sensitivity	It scares me when I feel nauseous.
	Disgust propensity	I screw up my face in disgust.

sensitivity and other psychological vulnerabilities (i.e., anxiety sensitivity) clearly suggests that current research is lacking on disgust sensitivity. This disparity is largely a function of limited research on the psychometrics of the disgust sensitivity construct. If the processes by which disgust sensitivity affects the development, maintenance, and treatment of various disorders are to be predicted and controlled, it is necessary to broaden the current psychometric knowledge base of the disgust sensitivity construct.

REFERENCES

Arrindell, W. A., Mulkens, S., Kok, J., & Vollenbroek, J. (1999). Disgust and the sex difference in fears to common indigenous animals. *Behaviour Research and Therapy, 37*, 273–280.

Berenbaum, H., Raghavan, C., Le, H.-N., Vernon, L., & Gomez, J. (2003). A taxonomy of emotional disturbances. *Clinical Psychology: Science and Practice, 10*, 206–226.

Björklund, F., & Hursti, T. J. (2004). A Swedish translation and validation of the Disgust scale: A measure of disgust sensitivity. *Scandinavian Journal of Psychology, 45*, 279–284.

Cavanagh, K., & Davey, G. C. L. (2000, October). *The development of a measure of individual differences in disgust.* Paper presented at the meeting of the British Psychological Society, Winchester, England.

Charash, M., & McKay, D. (2002). Attention bias for disgust. *Anxiety Disorders, 16*, 529–541.

Cisler, J., Reardon, J., Williams, N., & Lohr, J. M. (2007). Anxiety sensitivity and disgust sensitivity interact to predict contamination fears. *Personality and Individual Differences, 42*, 935–946.

Davey, G. C. L., & Bond, N. (2006). Using controlled comparisons in disgust psychopathology research: The case of disgust, hypochondriasis and health anxiety. *Journal of Behavior Therapy and Experimental Psychiatry, 37*, 4–15.

de Jong, P. J., Andrea, H., & Muris, P. (1997). Spider phobia in children: Disgust and fear before and after treatment. *Behaviour Research and Therapy, 35*, 559–562.

de Jong, P. J., & Merckelbach, H. (1998). Blood-injection-injury phobia and fear of spiders: Domain specific individual differences in disgust sensitivity. *Personality and Individual Differences, 24*, 153–158.

de Jong, P. J., & Muris, P. (2002). Spider phobia: Interaction of disgust and perceived likelihood of involuntary physical contact. *Journal of Anxiety Disorders, 16*, 51–65.

de Jong, P. J., Peters, M., & Vanderhallen, I. (2002). Disgust and disgust sensitivity in spider phobia: Facial EMG in response to spider and oral disgust imagery. *Journal of Anxiety Disorders, 16*, 477–493.

Druschel, B. A., & Sherman, M. F. (1999). Disgust sensitivity as a function of the Big Five and gender. *Personality and Individual Differences, 26*, 739–748.

Exeter-Kent, H. A., & Page, A. (2006). The role of cognitions, trait anxiety and disgust sensitivity in generating faintness around blood–injury phobic stimuli. *Journal of Behavior Therapy and Experimental Psychiatry, 37*, 41–52.

Geer, J. (1965). The development of a scale to measure fear. *Behaviour Research and Therapy, 3*, 45–53.

Haidt, J., McCauley, C., & Rozin, P. (1994). Individual differences in sensitivity to disgust: A scale sampling seven domains of disgust elicitors. *Personality and Individual Differences, 16*, 701–713.

Harvey, T., Troop, N. A., Treasure, J. L., & Murphy, T. (2002). Fear, disgust, and abnormal eating attitudes: A preliminary study. *International Journal of Eating Disorders, 32*, 213–218.

Kleinknecht, R. A., Kleinknecht, E. E., & Thorndike, R. M. (1997). The role of disgust and fear in blood and injection-related fainting symptoms: A structural equation model. *Behaviour Research and Therapy, 35*, 1075–1087.

Koch, M., O'Neil, K., Sawchuk, C., & Connolly, K. (2002). Domain-specific and generalized disgust sensitivity in blood-injection-injury phobia: The application of behavioral approach/avoidance tasks. *Journal of Anxiety Disorders, 16*, 511–527.

Lilienfeld, S. O. (1996). Anxiety sensitivity is not distinct from trait anxiety. In R. Rapee (Ed.), *Current controversies in the anxiety disorders* (pp. 228–244). New York: Guilford Press.

Mancini, F., Gragnani, A., & D'Olimpio, F. (2001). The connection between disgust and obsessions and compulsions in a non-clinical sample. *Personality and Individual Differences, 31*, 1173–1180.

McKay, D. (2006). Treating disgust reactions in contamination-based obsessive–compulsive disorder. *Journal of Behavior Therapy and Experimental Psychiatry, 37*, 53–59.

McNally, R. J. (2002). Disgust has arrived. *Journal of Anxiety Disorders, 16*, 561–566.

Merckelbach, H., de Jong, P. J., Arntz, A., & Schouten, E. (1993). The role of evaluative learning and disgust sensitivity in the etiology and treatment of spider phobia. *Advances in Behaviour Research and Therapy, 15*, 243–255.

Merckelbach, H., Muris, P., de Jong, P. J., & de Jongh, A. (1999). Disgust sensitivity, blood-injection-injury fear, and dental anxiety. *Clinical Psychology and Psychotherapy, 6*, 279–285.

Mulkens, S. A., de Jong, P. J., & Merckelbach, H. (1996). Disgust and spider phobia. *Journal of Abnormal Psychology, 105*, 464–468.

Muris, P., Merckelbach, H., Nederkoorn, S., Rassin, E., Candel, I., & Horselenberg, R. (2000). Disgust and psychopathological symptoms in a nonclinical sample. *Personality and Individual Differences, 29*, 1163–1167.

Muris, P., Merckelbach, H., Schmidt, H., & Tierney, S. (1999). Disgust sensitivity, trait anxiety and anxiety disorders symptoms in normal children. *Behaviour Research and Therapy, 37*, 953–961.

Olatunji, B. O. (2006). Evaluative learning and emotional responding to fearful and disgusting stimuli in spider phobia. *Journal of Anxiety Disorders, 20*, 858–876.

Olatunji, B. O., Cisler, J. M., Deacon, B., Connolly, K., & Lohr, J. M. (2007). The Disgust Propensity and Sensitivity Scale—Revised: Psychometric properties and specificity in relation to anxiety disorder symptoms. *Journal of Anxiety Disorders, 21*, 918–930.

Olatunji, B. O., Lohr, J. M., Sawchuk, C. N., & Tolin, D. F. (2007). Multimodal assessment of disgust in contamination-related obsessive–compulsive disorder. *Behaviour Research and Therapy, 45*, 263–276.

Olatunji, B. O., Lohr, J., Willems, J., & Sawchuk, C. N. (2006). Expectancy bias for disgust and emotional responding in contamination-related obsessive–compulsive disorder. *Anxiety, Stress, & Coping, 19*, 383–396.

Olatunji, B. O., & Sawchuk, C. N. (2005). Disgust: Characteristic features, social manifestations, and clinical implications. *Journal of Social and Clinical Psychology, 27*, 932–962.

Olatunji, B. O., Sawchuk, C. N., Arrindell, W., & Lohr, J. M. (2005). Disgust sensitivity as a mediator of the sex differences in contamination fears. *Personality and Individual Differences, 38*, 713–722.

Olatunji, B. O., Sawchuk, C. N., de Jong, P. J., & Lohr, J. M. (2007). Disgust sensitivity and anxiety disorder symptoms: Psychometric properties of the Disgust Emotion Scale. *Journal of Psychopathology and Behavioral Assessment, 29*, 115–124.

Olatunji, B. O., Sawchuk, C. N., Lohr, J. M., & de Jong, P. J. (2004). Disgust domains in the prediction of contamination fear. *Behaviour Research and Therapy, 42*, 93–104.

Olatunji, B. O., Smits, J. A., Connolly, K. M., Willems, J., & Lohr, J. M. (2007). Examination of the rate of decline in fear and disgust during exposure to threat-relevant stimuli in blood-injection-injury phobia. *Journal of Anxiety Disorders, 21*, 445–455.

Olatunji, B. O., Tolin, D. F., Huppert, J., & Lohr, J. M. (2005). The relation between fearfulness, disgust sensitivity and religious obsessions in a non-clinical sample. *Personality and Individual Differences, 38*, 891–902.

Olatunji, B. O., Williams, N. L., Lohr, J. M., & Sawchuk, C. N. (2005). The structure of disgust: Domain specificity in relation to contamination ideation and excessive washing. *Behaviour Research and Therapy, 43*, 1069–1086.

Olatunji, B. O., Williams, N. L., Sawchuk, C. N., & Lohr, J. M. (2006). Disgust, anxiety, and fainting symptoms in blood-injection-injury fears: A structural model. *Journal of Anxiety Disorders, 20*, 23–41.

Olatunji, B. O., Williams, N. L., Tolin, D. F., Sawchuk, C. N., Abramowitz, J. S., Lohr, J. M., et al. (2007). The Disgust scale: Item analysis, factor structure, and suggestions for refinement. *Psychological Assessment, 19*, 281–297.

Page, A. C. (1994). Blood-injury phobia. *Clinical Psychology Review, 14*, 443–461.

Phillips, M. L., Senior, C., Fahy, T., & David, A. S. (1998). Disgust—the forgotten emotion of psychiatry. *British Journal of Psychiatry, 173*, 373–375.

Power, M., & Dalgleish, T. (1997). *Cognition and emotion: From order to disorder.* East Sussex, England: Psychology Press.

Quigley, J., Sherman, M., & Sherman, N. (1997). Personality disorder symptoms, gender, and age as predictors of adolescent disgust sensitivity. *Personality and Individual Differences, 22,* 661–667.

Reiss, S., & McNally, R. J. (1985). Expectancy model of fear. In S. Reiss & R. R. Bootzin (Eds.), *Theoretical issues in behavior therapy* (pp. 107–121). San Diego, CA: Academic Press.

Riskind, J. H. (1997). Looming vulnerability to threat: A cognitive paradigm for anxiety. *Behaviour Research and Therapy, 35,* 793–802.

Riskind, J. H., & Williams, N. L. (2005). A unique vulnerability common to all anxiety disorders: The looming maladaptive style. In L. B. Alloy & J. H. Riskind (Eds.), *Cognitive Vulnerability to Emotional Disorders* (pp. 175–206). New York: Erlbaum.

Rozin, P., Fallon, A. E., & Augustoni-Ziskind, M. L. (1984). The child's conception of food: The development of contamination sensitivity to "disgusting" substances. *Developmental Psychology, 21,* 1075–1079.

Rozin, P., Fallon, A. E., & Mandell, R. (1984). Family resemblance in attitudes to food. *Developmental Psychology, 20,* 309–314.

Rozin, P., Haidt, J., & McCauley, C. R. (1993). Disgust. In M. Lewis & J. M. Haviland (Eds.), *Handbook of emotions* (pp. 575–594). New York: Guilford Press.

Rozin, P., Haidt, J., McCauley, C., Dunlop, L., & Ashmore, M. (1999). Individual differences in disgust sensitivity: Comparisons and evaluations of paper-and-pencil versus behavioral measures. *Journal of Research in Personality, 33,* 330–351.

Rozin, P., Lowery, L., & Ebert, R. (1994). Varieties of disgust faces and the structure of disgust. *Journal of Personality and Social Psychology, 66,* 870–881.

Sawchuk, C. N., Lohr, J. M., Tolin, D. F., Lee, T. C., & Kleinknecht, R. A. (2000). Disgust sensitivity and contamination fears in spider and blood-injection-injury phobias. *Behaviour Research and Therapy, 38,* 753–762.

Sawchuk, C. N., Lohr, J. M., Westendorf, D. A., Meunier, S. A., & Tolin, D. F. (2002). Emotional responding to fearful and disgusting stimuli in specific phobia. *Behaviour Research and Therapy, 40,* 1031–1046.

Schienle, A., Stark, R., Walter, B., & Vaitl, D. (2003). The connection between disgust sensitivity and blood-related fears, faintness symptoms, and obsessive–compulsiveness in a non-clinical sample. *Anxiety, Stress, & Coping, 16,* 185–193.

Stark, R., Walter, B., Schienle, A., & Vaitl, D. (2005). Psychophysiological correlates of disgust and disgust sensitivity. *Journal of Psychophysiology, 19,* 50–60.

Taylor, S. (Ed.). (1999). *Anxiety sensitivity: Theory, research, and treatment of the fear of anxiety.* Mahwah, NJ: Erlbaum.

Teachman, B. A. (2006). Pathological disgust: In the thoughts, not the eye, of the beholder. *Anxiety, Stress, & Coping, 19,* 335–351.

Thorpe, S. J., Patel, S. P., & Simonds, L. M. (2003). The relationship between disgust sensitivity, anxiety, and obsessions. *Behaviour Research and Therapy, 41,* 1397–1409.

Thorpe, S. J., & Salkovskis, P. M. (1998). Studies on the role of disgust in the acquisition and maintenance of specific phobias. *Behaviour Research and Therapy, 36,* 877–893.

Tolin, D. F., Lohr, J. M., Sawchuk, C. N., & Lee, T. C. (1997). Disgust and disgust sensitivity in blood-injection-injury and spider phobia. *Behaviour Research and Therapy, 10,* 949–953.

Tolin, D. F., Sawchuk, C. N., & Lee, T. C. (1999). The role of disgust in blood-injection-injury phobia. *The Behavior Therapist, 22,* 96–99.

Tolin, D. F., Woods, C. M., & Abramowitz, J. S. (2006). Disgust sensitivity and obsessive–compulsive symptoms in a non-clinical sample. *Journal of Behavior Therapy and Experimental Psychiatry, 37,* 30–40.

Troop, N. A., Murphy, F., Bramon, E., & Treasure, J. L. (2000). Disgust sensitivity in eating disorders: A preliminary investigation. *International Journal of Eating Disorders, 27,* 446–451.

Tsao, S. D., & McKay, D. (2004). Behavioral avoidance tests and disgust in contamination fears: Distinctions from trait anxiety. *Behaviour Research and Therapy, 42,* 207–216.

Valentiner, D., Hood, J., & Hawkins, A. (2005). Fainting history, disgust sensitivity, and reactions to disgust-eliciting film stimuli. *Personality and Individual Differences, 38,* 1329–1339.

van Overveld, W. J. M., de Jong, P. J., Peters, M. L., Cavanagh, K., & Davey, G. C. L. (2006). Disgust propensity and disgust sensitivity: Separate constructs that are differentially related to specific fears. *Personality and Individual Differences, 41,* 1241–1252.

Walls, M. M., & Kleinknecht, R. A. (1996, April). *Disgust factors as predictors of blood-injury fear and fainting.* Paper presented at the annual meeting of the Western Psychological Association, San Jose, CA.

Williams, N. L., Olatunji, B. O., Elwood, L., Connolly, K., & Lohr, J. (2006). Cognitive vulnerability to disgust: Development and validation of the Looming of Disgust Questionnaire. *Anxiety, Stress, & Coping, 19,* 365–382.

Woody, S. R., & Teachman, B. A. (2000). Intersection of disgust and fear: Normative and pathological views. *Clinical Psychology: Science and Practice, 7,* 291–311.

Woody, S. R., & Tolin, D. F. (2002). The relationship between disgust sensitivity and avoidant behavior: Studies of clinical and nonclinical samples. *Journal of Anxiety Disorders, 16,* 543–559.

3

DISGUST: A COGNITIVE APPROACH

NATHAN L. WILLIAMS, KEVIN M. CONNOLLY, JOSH M. CISLER,
LISA S. ELWOOD, JEFFREY L. WILLEMS, AND JEFFREY M. LOHR

As a basic emotion, disgust is proposed to have unique physiological, behavioral, subjective, and cognitive correlates and consequences (Izard, 1992, 1993). As noted in chapter 1 of this volume, considerable research over the past decade has examined the distinct subjective, behavioral, and physiological components of disgust (cf. Olatunji & Sawchuk, 2005; Woody & Teachman, 2000). At the same time, there has been a paucity of research that has examined the cognitive components or information-processing biases involved in disgust, or the cognitive mechanisms by which adaptive disgust reactions may become pathological. This chapter reviews the extant research examining the cognitive characteristics of disgust.

A cognitive approach to disgust refers to both of the following: (a) examining the appraisals and beliefs associated with disgust, and (b) examining the information-processing biases associated with disgust. Cognitive processes have received considerable empirical attention in the anxiety disorders, with research typically demonstrating biases in attention, interpretation, and implicit memory (Williams, Watts, MacLeod, & Mathews, 1997). Given the role of disgust in anxiety and related disorders, it is hypothesized that disgust will be associated with unique cognitive processes and information-processing biases that may either work in tandem with fear-related biases associated with anxiety or that may constitute unique effects. Prior to reviewing the extant literature on information processing and disgust we first discuss the cognitive biases, appraisals, and beliefs that may be implicated in the experience of disgust.

Disgust and fear may interact through several pathways to influence the development and maintenance of specific phobias and contamination-related obsessive–compulsive disorder (OCD). Some have suggested that disgust may operate in an interactive or additive manner with fear as an amplified component of negative affectivity (e.g., Sawchuk, Lohr, Westendorf, Meunier, & Tolin, 2002; Thorpe & Salkovskis, 1998; Woody & Teachman, 2000). In contrast, others have proposed that disgust and fear may share a similar disease-avoidance function in particular anxiety disorders—the prevention of contamination (e.g., Tolin, Worhunsky, & Maltby, 2004; Woody & Teachman, 2000). Along these lines, Woody and Teachman (2000) suggested that appraisals focused on the threat of contagion are common to both fear and disgust and that elevated disgust sensitivity or biased cognitive processes may lead to the overestimation of this threat as well as exaggerated perceptions of harm resultant from exposure to disgusting stimuli (see also Teachman, 2006).

COGNITIVE BIASES AND DISGUST

Several potential cognitive biases have implications for understanding the relationship between disgust and some anxiety disorders. Teachman (2006) provided an interesting analysis of appraisal processes in disgust. Primary appraisals refer to an individual's beliefs about the likelihood of danger. Primary disgust appraisals may reflect an individual's beliefs about the possibility of contamination (Teachman, 2006). Secondary appraisals refer to an individual's beliefs about the ability to cope with possible danger. Secondary disgust appraisals may refer to an individual's beliefs about the ability to cope when there is a possibility for disgust or contagion. Teachman (2006) related these processes to pathological processes: "While the majority of individuals will report some level of disgust in response to a [disgusting stimulus], it is those individuals who believe that becoming disgusted is in some way dangerous or meaningful whose disgust responses will increase and interfere with their functioning" (p. 337). For example, if individuals believe that they would be able to successfully cope with the threat of contamination in a disgust-relevant situation, then they would not be predicted to be vulnerable to contamination-related OCD or specific phobias.

Rozin and Fallon (1987) and Rozin and Nemeroff (1990) posited that *sympathetic magic* is integral to the relation between disgust and contamination. Sympathetic magic represents a set of implausible beliefs about the transmission of contagion resulting from either real or imagined contact with a contaminated object (Nemeroff & Rozin, 1994). The "law of contagion" in sympathetic magic beliefs refers to the belief of "once in contact, always contaminated." For example, if a fly lands in someone's drink, that drink may be rendered permanently contaminated even after the fly has been removed. The "law of similarity" in sympathetic magic beliefs refers to the belief that benign objects resembling foul objects are also foul. For example, fudge shaped into dog excrement may cause an individual to refuse to eat the fudge. Interpretations based on the laws of sympathetic magic (Rozin & Nemeroff, 1990) may explain some individuals' aversion to veridically harmless objects that are believed to be contaminated (i.e., the law of contagion) or that resemble contaminated or disgusting objects (i.e., the law of similarity). Tolin et al. (2004) provided evidence through an experimental "chain of contagion" task (i.e., the perceived transfer of contamination from a disgust object to new pencils across a series of removals from the original noxious object) that individuals with OCD evidence greater sympathetic magic than either socially phobic or nonanxious control participants. Specifically, individuals with OCD did not perceive a reduction in contamination across successive points of removal from contact with a disgusting index stimulus.

Another potential cognitive bias that is relevant to disgust is looming vulnerability to threat (Riskind, 1997; Riskind & Williams, 2006). Looming vulnerability, broadly construed, pertains to the tendency to construct dynamic mental scenarios involving the perceived movement, approach, spread, or escalation in risk or danger of potentially threatening, disgusting, or fear-provoking stimuli. The "looming vulnerability" model of anxiety posits that the distinct cognitive phenomenology of anxiety and anxiety disorders involves mental representations of dynamically intensifying danger and rapidly rising risk (Riskind, 1997; Riskind & Williams, 2006; Riskind, Williams, Gessner, Chrosniak, & Cortina, 2000). For example, a person with a looming interpretation bias may perceive a spider in the corner of a room as rapidly approaching, whereas a person without the looming interpretation bias may perceive the same spider as just a static spider in the corner of the room.

Of potential interest here is the link between looming vulnerability (i.e., the perception of a potential contagion as spreading, approaching the person, and increasing in threat value) and disgust or contamination concerns. Indeed, students with subclinical OCD symptoms have evidenced a looming vulnerability bias to imagine scenes of contamination as actively spreading, moving, and rising in risk (Riskind, Abreu, Strauss, & Holt, 1997). Furthermore, contamination fearful students who were asked to imagine a contamination scene as looming showed greater aversive responses than did students asked to imagine the scene as static (Riskind, Wheeler, & Picerno, 1997). Tolin et al. (2004) provided additional support for the role of looming vulnerability in contamination fears. In their study, the extent to which a contaminated object was rated as looming (i.e., spreading, changing, or approaching the person) mediated the degree to which contamination was perceived as indefinitely transmitted.

Looming vulnerability may be a cognitive vulnerability for the development of pathological disgust through its biasing effects on the perceived threat of contamination. We contend that if disgust appraisals focus on the threat of contamination (Woody & Teachman, 2000) and potential contagions that are perceived as moving, spreading, or approaching the person (i.e., looming) are associated with greater contamination fears (e.g., Tolin et al., 2004), then potentially disgusting objects or scenarios that are perceived as looming should be associated with greater disgust. Consistent with the disease-avoidance model of specific phobias (Matchett & Davey, 1991), disgust reactions would only be predicted to occur to the extent that disgusting objects are perceived as capable of reaching and contaminating the individual. To this end, disgust sensitive individuals have been shown to appraise potentially disgusting stimuli as rapidly approaching, spreading, or increasing in threat value, while subsequently underestimating their ability to cope with such disgust stimuli (e.g., Williams, Olatunji, Elwood, Connolly, & Lohr, 2006).

DISGUST AND INFORMATION PROCESSING

A second aspect of a cognitive approach to disgust involves evaluating the extent to which disgust is associated with biased information processing in the areas of attention, interpretation, and memory. Information processing allows for the accurate interpretation of our external environment for the purpose of behaving in a manner likely to maintain life functions. Avenues of information processing are directly applicable in our understanding of how anxiety or fear can be acquired and maintained.

Information-processing theory predicts that individuals have a cognitive network that guides the interpretation of environmental stimuli (Lang, 1977). Foa and Kozak (1986) argued that individuals with information-processing biases do not process new information that is inconsistent with their cognitive fear network. This hypothesis focuses primarily on the constructs of fear and anxiety, whereas the emotion of disgust has been relatively uninvestigated (Woody & Teachman, 2000). Disgust is a distinct emotion; therefore, it is expected that the emotion of disgust may exhibit a unique information-processing pattern.

Attentional Bias

Attention refers to several kinds of mental processes, ranging from concentration on a specific task, to the selection of competing stimuli for further processing, or to the exclusion of interfering stimuli (e.g., Shapiro, 1994). Our attentional system promotes awareness of the external environment, facilitates adaptive and effective responding, and provides an early detection system for potential threat or danger (e.g., Williams, Mathews, & MacLeod, 1996). Attentional allocation is theorized to be influenced by the extent to which a given stimulus is recognized as pertinent, or relevant, to the organism (e.g., Bundesen, Habekost, & Kyllingsbaek, 2005). The term *attentional bias* refers to the tendency to preferentially allocate attentional resources to potentially threatening or dangerous stimuli relative to more neutrally valenced stimuli (e.g., McNally, 1996). Attentional biases are theorized to be a process by which anxiety is developed and maintained (Beck & Clark, 1997; MacLeod, Rutherford, Campbell, Ebsworthy, & Holker, 2002; Mogg & Bradley, 1998). Attentional biases have been observed across anxiety disorders, including posttraumatic stress disorder (Bryant & Harvey, 1995; McNally, Kaspi, Bradley, & Zeitlin, 1990), generalized anxiety disorder (Bradley, Mogg, Millar, & White, 1995), social phobia (Becker, Rinck, Margraf, & Roth, 2001), snake phobia (Wikstrom, Lundh, Westerlund, & Hogman, 2004), and panic disorder (Buckley, Blanchard, & Hickling, 2002).

Whereas a substantial amount of research has investigated attentional biases toward fear-relevant threat, few studies have investigated attentional biases toward disgust-relevant threat. The extant research that assesses attention toward disgust yields tentative evidence of an attentional bias toward disgust-relevant threat. Charash and McKay (2002) investigated Stroop task performance for disgusting, generally threatening, and neutral words among nonclinical participants. The Stroop task (Stroop, 1935) presents words displayed in varying colors. The participant's task is to detect the color while ignoring the semantic content of the word. Longer latencies to report the color of disgust words compared with neutral words suggests difficulty in ignoring the semantic content of disgust words relative to neutral words, thus suggesting biased attention toward disgust stimuli (Cisler, Bacon, & Williams, in press). Charash and McKay found longer latencies toward disgust words compared with neutral words, thus suggesting an attentional bias for disgust. Additionally, disgust sensitivity correlated with the attentional bias for disgust among participants who received a disgust prime (i.e., hearing a story about a cockroach crawling into your mouth), thus suggesting a linear relation between the experience of disgust and a disgust-related attentional bias. Results from Charash and McKay suggest that there is an attentional bias toward disgust-relevant threat regardless of clinical anxiety status.

Despite evidence for a normative attentional bias toward disgust stimuli, there is currently no evidence that an attentional bias toward disgust is integral in any of the disgust-related anxiety disorders (i.e., spider phobia, blood-injection-injury [BII] phobia, contamination-related OCD). Individuals with spider phobia display an attentional bias toward spider-related stimuli (Miltner, Krieschel, Hecht, Trippe, & Weiss, 2004; Öhman, Flykt, & Esteves, 2001; Rinck,

Reinecke, Ellwart, Heuer, & Becker, 2005; Thorpe & Salkovskis, 1997; van den Hout, Tenney, Huygens, & de Jong, 1997) on a variety of different experimental tasks designed to measure attentional biases. However, Thorpe and Salkvoskis (1998) demonstrated that spider phobic individuals display an attentional bias only for spider stimuli and not for disgust stimuli. Similarly, Sawchuk, Lohr, Lee, and Tolin (1999) found that the attentional bias for disgust stimuli among individuals with BII fear did not differ from the attentional bias for disgust stimuli among individuals with low BII fear. Thus, BII phobia does not appear to be characterized by an attentional bias for disgust. For contamination-related OCD, prior research demonstrates an attention bias for disorder-relevant stimuli (i.e., contamination-related stimuli; Foa, Ilai, McCarthy, Shoyer, & Murdock, 1993; Tata, Leibowitz, Prunty, Cameron, & Pickering, 1996), but there have been no studies that examine an attentional bias to disgust stimuli specifically.

In sum, the available evidence suggests that (a) a normative attentional bias for disgust stimuli (Charash & McKay, 2002; Sawchuk et al., 1999) and (b) spider phobia, BII phobia, and contamination-related OCD are not associated with an attentional bias for disgust. The literature on attentional biases toward disgust is in its infancy. Indeed, evidence of a normative attentional bias toward disgust is limited to two studies, both of which used the same experimental attentional bias task. Replication by use of different experimental attentional bias tasks is necessary. Future research should also focus on elucidating the phenomenological characteristics of attentional biases for disgust. For example, are attentional biases toward disgust characterized by an exaggerated difficulty removing attention from disgusting stimuli, an exaggerated vigilance toward detecting disgusting stimuli, or both? Answers to these basic questions about attentional processes in disgust may reveal the cognitive mechanisms mediating avoidance of and discomfort with disgusting stimuli.

Interpretive Biases

Interpretation bias is the propensity to interpret ambiguous stimuli in a threatening manner and has been implicated in the etiology and maintenance of anxiety disorders (Clark, Salkovskis, Ost, & Breitholtz, 1997; Huppert, Foa, Furr, Filip, & Mathews, 2003). The misinterpretation of ambiguous stimuli may act to maintain abnormal levels of disgust through behavioral avoidance, such that avoiding certain situations may prevent an individual from learning that the misinterpretation is incorrect.

In one study (Davey, Bickerstaffe, & MacDonald, 2006), four groups of participants experienced disgust, anxiety, happy or a neutral mood induction and then heard homophones presented through headphones. These homophones had neutral and threatening meanings. For example, *dye* and *die* are pronounced identically but have meanings that differ in valence. Participants were then asked to spell the homophones. An interpretation bias would be demonstrated by increased threat spellings (e.g., die) compared with neutral spellings (e.g., dye). Both the disgust and anxiety groups interpreted significantly more threat and neutral homophones as threat than both the happy and neutral groups. These findings highlight the possibility that the experience of disgust causes a negative interpretational bias that is similar to that reported for fear and anxiety.

Two other types of interpretation bias are covariation biases and expectancy biases. Covariation bias refers to one's propensity to perceive either a relationship between two nonrelated events or an inaccurate relationship between two related events. For example, visiting a new city during bad weather may lead to the possibly erroneous belief that the city always has bad weather. The preparedness theory (Seligman, 1971) proposes that humans are predispositioned to learn to associate aversive events with stimuli that were evolutionary advantageous to avoid. Research has supported this theory by demonstrating that learned associations between phobic stimuli (e.g., spiders and snakes) and aversive stimuli are more difficult to extinguish and are less affected by verbal instructions than associations between nonphobic stimuli and aversive stimuli. For example, it may be easier to associate spiders with pain compared with associating a mushroom with pain. Tomarken, Mineka, and Cook (1989) suggested that covariation biases may lead to enhanced conditioning and the development of phobias, such that covariation biases may lead an individual to overinterpret a single negative experience with a stimulus (e.g., "a spider jumped out at me in kitchen, so spiders will always be lurking in the kitchen!"). Expectancy biases reflect a nondata driven cognitive bias for predicting aversive outcomes following the presentation of threat-relevant stimuli. That is, whereas covariation biases represent biased memory for how often two types of stimuli have co-occurred in the past, expectancy biases represent biased a priori expectations about what is likely to occur in the future. It has been suggested that covariation biases reflect a continuation of expectancy biases that occur following the presentation of data (e.g., picture–outcome pairings). If covariation estimates were a continuation of preexisting expectancy biases, then one would predict a congruent pattern of expectancy biases and covariation biases between phobic and nonphobic individuals.

Pictures of neutral stimuli (e.g., rabbits) or disgust stimuli (e.g., pictures of blood donations) were presented to BII-phobic individuals and nonphobic individuals by de Jong and Peters (2007a). Presentation of these pictures was followed by one of three possible outcomes: a shock, drinking a disgusting fluid, or nothing. For example, a picture of a rabbit could be followed by a shock; a picture of a blood donation could be followed by having to drink a disgusting fluid. Each outcome had an equal probability of following each type of picture. Prior to beginning the experiment, participants were asked how often they expected the different types of stimuli to occur with the different types of outcomes. An expectancy bias would be demonstrated by expecting more outcomes with a particular type of stimulus compared with other stimulus-outcome pairings. Following presentation of the stimulus-outcome pairings, participants were asked to recall how often the outcomes occurred with the stimuli. Participants would demonstrate a covariation bias by remembering more outcomes for a particular picture type than actually occurred (e.g., remembering more disgust outcomes with blood-donation pictures compared with nothing as the outcome). Results revealed that both high- and low-BII phobic individuals expected greater pairings of blood-donation pictures with aversive outcomes compared with nothing. There was no difference in the type of aversive outcome expected to occur with the blood-donation pictures: Participants expected disgust outcomes to occur with blood-donation pictures as often as they expected shock outcomes to occur with blood-donation pictures. In contrast, the results failed to reveal a covariation bias: Neither the high- nor low-BII phobic individuals remembered an exaggerated number of disgust outcomes occurring with blood-donation pictures. Similarly, neither group remembered an exaggerated number of shock outcomes that occurred with blood-donation pictures. This study demonstrates normative expectancy biases, such that all participants regardless of BII fear level expected aversive outcomes to occur with blood-donation pictures. The results failed to reveal a normative covariation bias. Additionally, the results failed to show a difference between fear- and disgust-outcome expectancies. This is somewhat surprising, given that the blood-donation pictures are ostensibly related to mutilation-related disgust elicitors.

A similar experimental design was used by de Jong and Peters (2007b) with high- and low-spider-phobic individuals. The stimuli of relevance were pictures of spiders, and the outcomes were drinking a disgusting fluid, a shock, or nothing. Results revealed that although both high- and low-spider-phobic individuals expected shock outcomes to occur with spider pictures, only the high-phobic individuals expected disgust outcomes to occur with spiders. As with the other de Jong and Peters (2007a) study, results failed to suggest a covariation bias between spiders and either disgust or shock outcomes among both the high- and low-phobic groups. That low-spider-fearful individuals expect fear outcomes, and not disgust outcomes, to occur with spiders suggests that at the normative level spiders are not interpreted as disgusting. Among high-spider-fearful individuals, however, spiders appear to be associated with disgust, but not fear, outcomes. Similar results were found by Olatunji, Cisler, Meunier, Connolly, and Lohr (2008), when high-spider-fearful individuals demonstrated an expectancy bias for spider pictures to be paired with disgust facial-expression outcomes, whereas low-spider-fearful individuals expected spider pictures to be paired with fear facial-expression outcomes.

It is difficult to draw conclusions from only three studies, but a few speculations from these data are warranted. First, that only high-spider-fearful individuals expect disgust outcomes with spider stimuli suggests that disgust may be an integral component of spider phobia. The biased expectations for disgust may reflect either exaggerated beliefs about the disgusting nature of spiders (i.e., primary appraisals; Teachman, 2006) or exaggerated beliefs about the inability to cope with feeling disgusted in response to a spider. Second, disgust outcomes are expected to occur with blood stimuli as often as fear outcomes in both high- and low-BII-fearful individuals. This suggests that both fear and disgust may be associated with blood stimuli (cf. Sawchuk, Lohr, et al., 2002). That there were no differences in high- and low-BII-fearful individuals suggests that disgust expectancies may not be an integral component of BII fears. This does not necessarily suggest that disgust is not integral to BII fear but just that disgust expectancies are not a significant maintaining factor. Third, that no covariation biases for disgust outcomes to occur with either spider or blood stimuli when expectancies biases were first present suggests that covariation biases for disgust are susceptible to refutation. That is, disgust-expectancy biases do not appear to be stable and resistant to change. It may be the case that whereas fears are encapsulated from cognitive control (Öhman & Mineka, 2001), disgust, at least disgust expectancy biases, is more amenable to cognitive restructuring.

Memory Biases

Memory bias within the realm of anxiety, fear, and disgust has been assessed using a variety of methods, including noise-rating tasks (Foa, Amir, & Gershuny, 1997), word-stem completion tasks (McCabe, 1999), facial (Foa, Gilboa-Schechtman, Amir, & Freshman, 2000) and sentence recognition tasks (Foa et al., 1997), signal detection tasks (Sawchuk, Meunier, Lohr, & Westendorf, 2002), and lexical decision paradigms (MacLeod & Mathews, 1991). Implicit memory is commonly thought of as the examination of memory functions located outside of conscious processing, whereas explicit memory is regarded as the examination of memory functions within the realm of conscious thought. Given that there is very limited research on memory biases in disgust, we also review studies of contamination-related OCD given that contamination fear is robustly correlated with disgust and that contamination-relevant stimuli (e.g., germs, dirty toilets) closely resemble normative disgust elicitors.

To date, only two experimental studies have examined implicit-memory biases in contamination fear and disgust (Foa et al., 1997; Sawchuk et al., 1999). Foa et al. used a noise-rating paradigm in which participants were first presented with neutral sentences and contamination-related sentences. The sentences were then presented again but this time accompanied by varying levels of noise, and participants were asked to rate the volume of noise paired with either contamination sentences or neutral sentences. Implicit-memory bias would be demonstrated by participants who were rating the noise paired with contamination sentences as softer than noise paired with neutral sentences. Softer noise ratings demonstrate an implicit memory bias in that the noise is less distracting for sentences that are better recognized, thus it is rated as softer compared with the noise accompanying unrecognized sentences. Foa et al. found that the noise paired with the contamination fear stimuli was rated louder than the neutral stimuli by both OCD individuals and a nonanxious control group. Overall, this study failed to support the hypothesis that OCD patients exhibit biases in implicit-memory function compared with nonpatients.

Sawchuk et al. (1999) presented BII-phobic and nonphobic individuals with one of two videos: disgust or neutral. They then completed the Stroop task with four categories of words: medical, disgust, negative, and neutral. A word-stem completion test was then administered by using the words from the Stroop task. An implicit-memory bias would be demonstrated by more word-stem completions for a particular word category (e.g., disgust) compared with neutral word stems. The BII-phobic group completed significantly more medical and disgust words in the word-stem completion test than the non-phobic individuals. This suggests an implicit bias for disgust words, but only among highly BII-fearful individuals.

In contrast to studies of implicit-memory biases, studies of explicit-memory biases reveal a more consistent effect. Radomsky and Rachman (1999) found support for memory biases in individuals with OCD (contamination fear) compared with anxious and nonanxious control groups. In this study the participants witnessed the experimenter either contaminate several objects (i.e., compact disc) or viewed the experimenter just touch the objects without the act of contamination. The participants were then asked to identify the objects touched by the experimenter. The OCD participants recalled the contaminated objects better than the noncontaminated objects. This study supports the prediction that contamination-fearful-OCD individuals exhibit an explicit-memory bias toward threat relevant stimuli.

Ceschi, Van der Linden, Dunker, Perroud, and Bredart (2003) replicated the previous study, using more specific control groups (i.e., OCD washers, socially anxious individuals, and nonanxious individuals). The results failed to support the findings of Radomsky and Rachman (1999). The OCD washers group was not significantly different from the control groups in terms of this memory ability. However, the OCD washers had better recall for the source (dirty or clean tissue) of the contaminated objects compared with the clean objects. This response pattern was different from the patterns of each control group. This result was described as a memory bias for threatening information within contextually primed situations.

Explicit-memory bias for disgust was also examined by Charash and McKay (2002), using an unselected student sample. Participants were first given one of three priming stories (e.g., disgust, fear, and neutral). They then participated in the Stroop Color-Naming Task (Stroop, 1935). The participants then engaged in a recall task in which they were instructed to remember as many items in the Stroop Color-Naming Task as possible. There was a positive correlation found between disgust sensitivity, as measured by the Disgust Sensitivity Questionnaire, and the quantity of disgust words recalled. This correlation suggests a relationship between disgust sensitivity and memory for disgust stimuli.

The only conflicting evidence for explicit-memory biases was provided by Foa et al. (1997). These researchers examined explicit recognition of contamination versus neutral sentences between an OCD (contamination fears) group and a control group by using a sentence recognition task. The findings failed to support the hypothesis that OCD individuals differ from non-OCD individuals in explicit memory for contamination stimuli. OCD and control participants both identified a lower number of contamination stimuli compared with the neutral stimuli.

In sum, the only evidence for implicit-memory bias comes from one study finding greater word-stem completion for disgust words among high-BII-phobic individuals compared with low-BII-phobic individuals. It was not reported whether the low-BII group completed greater disgust word stems compared with neutral; therefore it cannot be determined whether nonanxious individuals exhibit a normative implicit-memory bias for disgust words. Using a different paradigm, Foa et al. (1997) failed to find evidence of implicit-memory biases for contamination-related stimuli among either the OCD or the control group. It is difficult to draw conclusions from these two studies given all of the differences between them, but it may be the case that word-stem completion tasks are more sensitive to implicit memory compared with the noise-rating task. One study of explicit-memory biases specifically for disgust revealed greater recall for disgust words among individuals with greater disgust sensitivity, thus suggesting that individual differences in disgust moderate the explicit-memory bias effect. Studies of contamination fears have generally found evidence for explicit-memory bias; however, the effect may be specific for source memory. Additionally, the effect is specific for highly contamination fearful individuals. Given that both fear and disgust are implicated in contamination fears (Rachman, 2004), it is difficult to interpret the unique effect that disgust plays in these memory biases.

GENERAL SUMMARY OF INFORMATION-PROCESSING EMPIRICAL FINDINGS

The primary aim of this chapter was to critically review and summarize the experimental psychopathology literature in the area of information-processing biases within contamination fears and disgust. Results of this relatively limited research generally support an attention bias for disgust; however, there is very limited evidence that disgust-related anxiety disorders are characterized by heightened attentional biases for disgust. Limited memory-bias research has found mixed results for implicit biases and generally positive results for explicit-memory biases. Future research may benefit from using different methodologies to assess implicit- and explicit-memory biases. Expectancy and covariation bias research have yielded conflicting results. The controversy over whether covariation bias is merely a continuation of expectancy biases is a current topic of investigation (Amin & Lovibond, 1997). Some researchers hypothesize that the covariation-bias phenomenon is a continuation of a preexisting expectancy (Davey, 1995). Others believe that covariation bias is a unique and separate phenomenon from expectancy bias (Amin & Lovibond, 1997). Amin and Lovibond (1997) contended that covariation bias is an occurrence in which an anxious individual is unable to use new information to modify existing expectancies, whereas nonanxious individuals are able to use this corrective information. Future research should examine this discrepancy in disgust.

FUTURE DIRECTIONS IN DISGUST-RELATED INFORMATION-PROCESSING STUDIES

Rather than trying to draw any conclusions or offer any explanations from the very limited amount of extant research, it seems best to provide suggestions for future research in this area. First, research effort should be dedicated to examining normative cognitive processes in disgust. Knowledge of normative processes may then provide a basis from which to examine possible pathological disgust-cognitive processes in disgust-related disorders (e.g., BII phobia). Second, research on cognitive processes in disgust should specifically examine cognitive characteristics that are unique to disgust compared with fear. For example, research from our lab has demonstrated that disgust attentional biases may be characterized by an exaggerated difficulty in disengaging attention from disgust stimuli compared with fear attentional biases (Cisler, Olatunji, Lohr, & Williams, in press). Future research that reveals cognitive aspects of disgust that are unique from fear may shed light on how disgust-related cognitive processes contribute to the development or maintenance of disorders. Third, research that examines cognitive processes unique to disgust compared with fear will need to control possible differences between disgust and fear in arousal and valence. That is, information processing can be affected by both arousal and valence. Given that disgust- and fear-related stimuli likely differ in regard to arousal and valence, researchers will have to control for these differences when examining cognitive processes unique to disgust. Fourth, future interpretive-bias investigations will likely benefit from continued examinations of both expectancy and covariation biases for disgust stimuli. This line of research may shed some light on the current debate whether expectancy and covariation biases are really the same phenomena or if they possess unique attributes. Finally, the phenomenon of looming has yet to be experimentally examined in disgust. Given the overlap between sympathetic magic beliefs in disgust and the looming construct, laboratory-based studies of looming in disgust seems prudent.

CONCLUSION

In the present chapter we have attempted to synthesize relevant research on a cognitive approach to understanding disgust. This approach consists of evaluating both (a) the unique appraisals, beliefs, and cognitive biases associated with disgust; and (b) extent to which disgust is associated with distinct information-processing effects in the areas of attention, interpretation, and memory. Consistent with Rozin, Haidt, and McCauley (2000), we view disgust as a multidimensional construct that centers around the unifying theme of ideational content related to potential contamination of the body, soul, and broad social order. It is likely that cognitive appraisals, beliefs, and biases play a different role depending on the type of disgust assessed, with more basic forms of disgust that involve less conscious cognitive processes and more evolved forms of disgust, consisting of a much stronger cognitive and cultural emphasis.

REFERENCES

Amin, J. M., & Lovibond, P. F. (1997). Dissociations between covariation bias and expectancy bias for fear-relevant stimuli. *Cognition & Emotion, 11*, 273–289.

Beck, A. T., & Clark, D. A. (1997). An information processing model of anxiety: Automatic and strategic processes. *Behaviour Research and Therapy, 35*, 49–58.

Becker, E. S., Rinck, M., Margraf, J., & Roth, W. T. (2001). The emotional Stroop effect in anxiety disorders: General emotionality or disorder specificity? *Journal of Anxiety Disorders, 15*, 147–159.

Bradley, B. P., Mogg, K., Millar, N., & White, J. (1995). Selective processing of negative information: Effects of clinical anxiety, concurrent depression, and awareness. *Journal of Abnormal Psychology, 104*, 532–536.

Bryant, R. A., & Harvey, A. G. (1995). Processing threatening information in posttraumatic stress disorder. *Journal of Abnormal Psychology, 104*, 537–541.

Buckley, T. C., Blanchard, E. B., & Hickling, E. J. (2002). Automatic and strategic processing of threat stimuli: a comparison between PTSD, panic disorder, and non-anxiety controls. *Cognitive Therapy and Research, 26*, 97–115.

Bundesen, C., Habekost, T., & Kyllingsbaek, S. (2005). A neural theory of visual attention: Bridging cognition and neurophysiology. *Psychological Review, 112*, 291–328.

Ceschi, C., Van der Linden, M., Dunker, D., Perroud, A., & Bredart, S. (2003). Further exploration memory bias in compulsive washers. *Behaviour Research and Therapy, 41*, 737–748.

Charash, M., & McKay, D. (2002). Attention bias for disgust. *Anxiety Disorders, 16*, 529–541.

Cisler, J. M., Bacon, A. K., & Williams, N. L. (in press). Phenomenological characteristics of attentional biases towards threat: a critical review. *Cognitive Therapy and Research*.

Cisler, J. M., Olatunji, B. O., Lohr, J. M., & Williams, N. L. (in press). Attentional bias differences between disgust and fear: Implications for the role of disgust in anxiety disorders. *Cognition & Emotion*.

Clark, D. M., Salkovskis, P. M., Ost, L. G., & Breitholtz, E. (1997). Misinterpretation of body sensations in panic disorder. *Journal of Consulting and Clinical Psychology, 65*, 203–213.

Davey, G. C. L. (1995). Preparedness and phobias: Specific evolved associations or a generalized expectancy bias. *Behavioral Brain Sciences, 18*, 289–325.

Davey, G. C. L., Bickerstaffe, S., & MacDonald, B. (2006). Experienced disgust causes a negative interpretation bias: A causal role for disgust in anxious psychopathology. *Behaviour Research and Therapy, 44*, 1375–1384.

de Jong, P. J., & Peters, M. L. (2007a). Blood-injection-injury fears: Harm- vs. disgust-relevant selective outcomes associations. *Journal of Behavior Therapy and Experimental Psychiatry, 38*, 263–274.

de Jong, P. J., & Peters, M. L. (2007b). Contamination vs. harm-relevant outcome expectancies and covariation bias in spider phobia. *Behaviour Research and Therapy, 45*, 1271–1284.

Foa, E. B., Amir, N., & Gershuny, B. (1997). Implicit and explicit memory in obsessive–compulsive disorder. *Journal of Anxiety Disorders, 11*, 119–129.

Foa, E. B., Gilboa-Schechtman, E., Amir, N., & Freshman, M. (2000). Memory bias in generalized social phobia: Remembering negative emotional expressions. *Journal of Anxiety Disorders, 14*, 501–519.

Foa, E. B., Ilai, D., McCarthy, P. R., Shoyer, B., & Murdock, T. (1993). Information processing in obsessive–compulsive disorder. *Cognitive Therapy and Research, 17*, 173–189.

Foa, E. B., & Kozak, M. J. (1986). Emotional processing of fear: Exposure to corrective information. *Psychological Bulletin, 99*, 20–35.

Huppert, J. D., Foa, E. B., Furr, J. M., Filip, J. C., & Mathews, A. (2003). Interpretation bias in social anxiety: A dimensional perspective. *Cognitive Therapy and Research, 27*, 569–577.

Izard, C. E. (1992). Basic emotions, relations among emotions, and emotion-cognition relations. *Psychological Review, 99*, 561–565.

Izard, C. E. (1993). Four systems for emotion activation: Cognitive and noncognitive processes. *Psychological Review, 100*, 68–90.

Lang, P. G. (1977). Imagery in therapy: An information processing analysis of fear. *Behavior Therapy, 8*, 862–886.

MacLeod, C., & Mathews, A. (1991). Biased cognitive operations in anxiety: Accessibility of information or assignment of processing priorities? *Behaviour Research and Therapy, 29*, 599–610.

MacLeod, C., Rutherford, E., Campbell, L., Ebsworthy, G., & Holker, L. (2002). Selective attention and emotional vulnerability: Assessing the causal basis of their association through the experimental manipulation of attentional bias. *Journal of Abnormal Psychology, 111*, 107–123.

Matchett, G., & Davey, G. C. L. (1991). A test of a disease-avoidance model of animal phobias. *Behaviour Research and Therapy, 29*, 91–93.

McCabe, R. E. (1999). Implicit and explicit memory for threat words in high and low anxiety sensitive participants. *Cognitive Therapy and Research, 23*, 21–38.

McNally, R. J. (1996). Cognitive bias in the anxiety disorders. In D. A. Hope (Ed.), *Nebraska Symposium on Motivation: Vol. 43. Perspectives on anxiety, panic, and fear* (pp. 211–250). Lincoln: University of Nebraska Press.

McNally, R. J., Kaspi, S. P., Bradley, C. R., & Zeitlin, S. B. (1990). Selective processing of threat cues in posttraumatic stress disorder. *Journal of Abnormal Psychology, 99*, 398–402.

Miltner, W. H., Krieschel, S., Hecht, H., Trippe, R., & Weiss, T. (2004). Eye movements and behavioral responses to threatening and nonthreatening stimuli during visual search in phobic and nonphobic subjects. *Emotion, 4*, 323–339.

Mogg, K., & Bradley, B. P. (1998). A cognitive-motivational analysis of anxiety. *Behaviour Research and Therapy, 36*, 809–848.

Nemeroff, C., & Rozin, P. (1994). The contagion concept in adult thinking in the United States: Transmission of germs and of interpersonal influence. *Ethos, 22*, 158–186.

Öhman, A., Flykt, A., & Esteves, F. (2001). Emotion drives attention: Detecting the snake in the grass. *Journal of Experimental Psychology: General, 130*, 466–478.

Öhman, A., & Mineka, S. (2001). Fears, phobias, and preparedness: Toward an evolved module of fear and fear learning. *Psychological Review, 108*, 483–522.

Olatunji, B. O., Cisler, J. M., Meunier, S., Connolly, K., & Lohr, J. M. (2008). Expectancy bias for fear and disgust and behavioral avoidance in spider fearful individuals. *Cognitive Therapy and Research, 32*, 460–469.

Olatunji, B. O., & Sawchuk, C. N. (2005). Disgust: Characteristic features, social manifestations, and clinical implications. *Journal of Social and Clinical Psychology, 24*, 932–962.

Rachman, S. (2004). Fear of contamination. *Behaviour Research and Therapy, 42*, 1227–1255.

Radomsky, A. S., & Rachman, S. (1999). Memory bias in obsessive–compulsive disorder (OCD). *Behaviour Research and Therapy, 37*, 605–618.

Rinck, M., Reinecke, A., Ellwart, T., Heuer, K., & Becker, E. S. (2005). Speeded detection and increased distraction in fear of spiders: Evidence from eye movements. *Journal of Abnormal Psychology, 114*, 235–248.

Riskind, J. H. (1997). Looming vulnerability to threat: A cognitive paradigm for anxiety. *Behaviour Research and Therapy, 35*, 685–702.

Riskind, J. H., Abreu, K., Strauss, M., & Holt, R. (1997). Looming vulnerability to spreading contamination in subclinical OCD. *Behaviour Research and Therapy, 35*, 405–414.

Riskind, J. H., Wheeler, D. J., & Picerno, M. R. (1997). Using mental imagery with subclinical OCD to "freeze" contamination in its place: Evidence for looming vulnerability theory. *Behaviour Research and Therapy, 8*, 757–768.

Riskind, J. H., & Williams, N. L. (2006). A unique vulnerability common to all anxiety disorders: The looming maladaptive style. In L. B. Alloy & J. H. Riskind (Eds.), *Cognitive vulnerability to emotional disorders* (pp. 175–206). New York: Erlbaum.

Riskind, J. H., Williams, N. L., Gessner, T. L., Chrosniak, L. K., & Cortina, J. M. (2000). The looming maladaptive style: Anxiety, danger, and schematic processing. *Journal of Personality and Social Psychology, 79*, 837–852.

Rozin, P., & Fallon, A. E. (1987). A perspective on disgust. *Psychological Review, 94*, 23–41.

Rozin, P., Haidt, J., & McCauley, C. R. (2000). Disgust. In M. Lewis & J. M. Haviland (Eds.), *Handbook of emotions* (2nd ed., pp. 637–653). New York: Guilford Press.

Rozin, P., & Nemeroff, C. (1990). The laws of sympathetic magic: A psychological analysis of similarity and contagion. In J. W. Stigler, R. A. Shweder, & G. Herdt (Eds.), *Cultural psychology: Essays on comparative human development* (pp. 205–232). New York: Cambridge University Press.

Sawchuk, C. N., Lohr, J. M., Lee, T. C., & Tolin, D. F. (1999). Exposure to disgust-evoking imagery and information processing biases in blood-injection-injury phobia. *Behaviour Research and Therapy, 37*, 249–257.

Sawchuk, C. N., Lohr, J. M., Westendorf, D. H., Meunier, S. A., & Tolin, D. F. (2002). Emotional responding to fearful and disgusting stimuli in specific phobia. *Behaviour Research and Therapy, 40*, 1031–1046.

Sawchuk, C. N., Meunier, S. A., Lohr, J. M., & Westendorf, D. H. (2002). Fear, disgust, and information processing in specific phobia: the application of signal detection theory. *Journal of Anxiety Disorders, 16*, 495–510.

Seligman, M. E. (1971). Phobias and preparedness. *Behavior Therapy, 2*, 307–320.

Shapiro, K. L. (1994). The attentional blink: The brain's 'eyeblink.' *Current Directions in Psychological Science, 3*, 86–89.

Stroop, J. R. (1935). Studies of interference in serial verbal reactions. *Journal of Experimental Psychology, 18*, 643–662.

Tata, P. R., Leibowitz, J. A., Prunty, M. J., Cameron, M., & Pickering, A. D. (1996). Attentional bias in obsessional compulsive disorder. *Behaviour Research and Therapy, 34*, 53–60.

Teachman, B. A. (2006). Pathological disgust: In the thoughts, not the eye, of the beholder. *Anxiety, Stress, & Coping, 19*, 335–351.

Thorpe, S. J., & Salkovskis, P. M. (1997). Information processing in spider phobics: The Stroop colour naming task may indicate strategic but not automatic attentional bias. *Behaviour Research and Therapy, 35*, 131–144.

Thorpe, S. J., & Salkovskis, P. M. (1998). Studies on the role of disgust in the acquisition and maintenance of specific phobias. *Behaviour Research and Therapy, 36*, 877–893.

Tolin, D. F., Worhunsky, P., & Maltby, N. (2004). Sympathetic magic in contamination-related OCD. *Journal of Behavior Therapy and Experimental Psychiatry, 35*, 193–205.

Tomarken, A. J., Mineka, S., & Cook, M. (1989). Fear-relevant selective associations and covariation bias. *Journal of Abnormal Psychology, 98*, 381–394.

van den Hout, M., Tenney, N., Huygens, K., & de Jong, P. (1997). Preconscious processing of bias in specific phobia. *Behaviour Research and Therapy, 35*, 29–34.

Wikstrom, J., Lundh, L., Westerlund, J., & Hogman, L. (2004). Preattentive bias for snake words in snake phobia? *Behaviour Research and Therapy, 42*, 949–970.

Williams, J. M. G., Mathews, A., & MacLeod, C. (1996). The emotional Stroop task and psychopathology. *Psychological Bulletin, 120*, 3–24.

Williams, J. M. G., Watts, F. N., MacLeod, C., & Mathews, A. (1997). *Cognitive psychology and the emotional disorders* (2nd ed.). Chichester, England: Wiley.

Williams, N. L., Olatunji, B. O., Elwood, L. S., Connolly, K. M., & Lohr, J. M. (2006). Cognitive vulnerability to disgust: Development and validation of the Looming of Disgust Questionnaire. *Anxiety, Stress, & Coping, 19*, 365–382.

Woody, S. R., & Teachman, B. A. (2000). Intersection of disgust and fear: Normative and pathological views. *Clinical Psychology: Science and Practice, 7*, 291–311.

II

RESPONSE PATTERNS

4

THE ACQUISITION AND MAINTENANCE OF DISGUST: DEVELOPMENTAL AND LEARNING PERSPECTIVES

CRAIG N. SAWCHUK

Disgust is one of the basic human emotions with reliable physiological, expressive, and behavioral responses that are universally recognized across cultures. The emergence of a well-defined innate disgust response early in human life has clear adaptive value for our species. Specific learning experiences and sociocultural influences, however, shape the scope and intensity of the disgust response over the life span. I begin this chapter by summarizing the developmental features of disgust from infancy to old age. Next, I consider learning, cognitive, biological, and sociocultural factors that combine to influence the acquisition of disgust. Finally, I review key learning concepts that maintain disgust reactivity across time.

DISGUST ACROSS THE LIFE SPAN

Disgust is readily identifiable at birth and present across the life span (Rozin & Fallon, 1987; Rozin, Haidt, & McCauley, 2000; Sullivan & Lewis, 2003). Although widely regarded as one of the basic human emotions, disgust is remarkably complex, durable, and dynamic. As humans develop, neurological mechanisms and environmental interactions contribute in shaping the disgust response. Significant changes also occur in the range of stimuli and circumstances capable of evoking this emotion, evolving from biologically prepared basic taste aversions early in life to higher order appraisals of ethics and morality in adulthood.

Disgust in Infancy

Facial expressions associated with discrete emotions can be readily observed shortly after birth (Camaras, Holland, & Patterson, 1993). Before offering a more detailed description of the disgust response in infancy, the functional value of studying facial expressions must first be considered. The careful investigation of facial expressions in the early stages of life is valuable in two respects (Sullivan & Lewis, 2003). First, facial expressions, oftentimes integrated with bodily movements and vocalizations, provide basic information in regard to an infant's status and functioning. In the absence of formal language and other means for communication at this stage, facial expressions can be used to gauge the infant's needs, arousal level, and quality of the response to environmental stimuli. Caregivers rely heavily on such expressions to guide their own responses when interacting with infants. Furthermore, they serve as a developmentally appropriate building block for other highly influential learning processes across the life span, such as social modeling. Interactions between infants and caregivers form an early basis for emotional expression, emotional regulation, and subsequent language development (Mundy & Willoughby, 1996; Walden & Knieps, 1996).

Second, the examination of facial expressions offers insights into the neurocognitive functioning of the developing infant. As the brain matures, innate expressions generated at the subcortical level become increasingly complex as other higher order sensory, cognitive, and motivational systems become involved throughout childhood (Sullivan & Lewis, 2003). Even among neurologically damaged or developmentally delayed infants, the basic repertoire of human facial expression remains largely intact, especially the facial expression of disgust (Steiner, 1979). Thus, increased sophistication of emotional expression represents a general index by which to monitor an infant's transition through and achievement of developmental milestones.

Considerable advances have been made over the last 3 decades in the methodological assessment and coding of facial expressions in infants and young children (e.g., Izard, 1982; Oster, 1978). In the absence of other forms of communication that develop later in childhood, facial coding represents an essential means by which to identify emotions early in life. Facial expressions of disgust are clearly observable in newborns (Soussignan, Schaal, Marlier, & Jiang, 1997). In a manner similar across the life span (Ekman, Friesen, & Ancoli, 1980; Izard, 1971; Levenson, 1992), the full disgust facial expression among newborns and infants involves gaping of the mouth, drooping of the lower lip, wrinkling of the nose, and retracting the upper lip (Rosenstein & Oster, 1988). At this early stage of development, however, disgust reactions are provoked only through gustatory and olfactory stimulation. For instance, bitter tasting substances, such as quinine, elicit the characteristic facial response of disgust, with more intense concentrations resulting in an action tendency for the infant to turn away from the "noxious" stimulant (Ganchrow, Steiner, & Daher, 1983; Rosenstein & Oster, 1988; Steiner, 1979). Facial features of the disgust response at the start of the life span offer support for its primary functional value as a means for protecting against further entry and incorporation of substances into the gustatory or olfactory apertures (Plutchik, 1980; Rozin et al., 2000; Rozin & Fallon, 1987).

Less intense facial reactions are elicited when one examines responses to sour-tasting substances (Sullivan & Lewis, 2003). The disgust expression under these circumstances may be slightly more delayed, involve pursing of the lips, and may not necessarily involve turning away from the substance. Increased variability in responses to milder sour tastes becomes even more prominent at 4 months of age, as some infants may exhibit a more positive, approach-oriented response such as smiling, following exposure (Bennett, 2002). Such variability in orientation to sour stimuli may represent an early manifestation of individual food preferences.

In sum, the study of disgust in newborns and infants offers a unique developmental window of time by which to observe this emotion in its most innate, purest, and noncognitive form. Facial expressions of disgust in infancy, as brief and fleeting as they might be, are remarkably similar in form and function across the life span. Even among infants with neurocognitive, sensory, and developmental disabilities, the characteristic facial expression of disgust remains largely intact. Gustatory and olfactory responses to a small range of disgust elicitors offer support for the notion that certain disgust stimuli are more biologically prepared.

Disgust in Childhood and Adolescence

Childhood is a time of considerable physical, neurocognitive, and social development. Basic taste and smell aversions continue to dominate the repertoire of the disgust response during the early stages of childhood. Children below the age of 8 years tend not to show aversion toward or rejection of higher order representations of disgust (Rozin & Fallon, 1987; Rozin, Fallon, & Augustoni-Ziskind, 1986). For instance, younger children are quite willing to eat chocolate shaped like dog feces and drink from a glass of juice that had been stirred with a fly swatter. Much to the dismay of their parents and caregivers, bodily products (e.g., feces, urine, mucus, vomit) and certain animals (e.g., worms, slugs, spiders) may entice approach behavior and actually become the focus of play. Evaluative and interpretative judgments of contagion appear largely absent during this period. Although children as young as 4 years old may show signs of rejection because of perceptions of contamination (Siegal & Share, 1990), this response may be better accounted for by parental modeling as opposed to internally driven concerns over threat value and disease acquisition (Rozin & Fallon, 1987).

In a series of clever experiments with children between the ages of 3.5 and 12 years, Fallon, Rozin, and Pilner (1984) were able to generate both quantitative and qualitative information about developmental changes in food rejections and contamination ideation. A large picture book was presented to the children as the experimenter narrated scenarios that involved potential contamination threat. The scenarios assessed their willingness to drink a desired beverage as objects of varying degrees of contamination threat (candy, hot dog, distasteful food, leaf, grasshopper, poison, feces) came into variable proximity with the drink (contacting the outside rim of the glass; submerged in the bottom of the glass; submerged in the glass but then removed with a spoon; following removal, refilling with the same beverage; following removal, washing the glass thoroughly and refilling with the same beverage). Results showed increasing differentiation in contamination sensitivity with increasing age. Specifically, the youngest age cohort (3.9–6.1 years) showed little differentiation across the contaminating substances and would consume the beverage after the substance had been removed with the spoon. The middle age group (6.4–7.8 years) similarly showed little difference in response to the contaminants but were likely to consume the beverage only after the glass was refilled after the substance was removed. The oldest age cohort (8.2–11.11 years) showed much clearer differentiation in contaminants, with more negative ratings of the grasshopper, poison, and fecal stimuli. Furthermore, this age group would only consume the beverage after the glass had been washed and refilled, signifying the emergence of beliefs about the durability of potentially contaminating substances and the necessity for sanitization prior to consumption. It is interesting to note that when an adult sample was exposed to the same series of tasks, even washing was insufficient to promote consumption of the beverage that had been contacted by the grasshopper, poison, and feces.

A subsequent study conducted in Japan sought to further understand the developmental processes involved in contamination appraisal (Toyama, 1999). By using a similar narration-picture methodology as did Fallon et al. (1984), Toyama (1999) conducted a series of three experiments with Japanese children age 4 to 7 years and undergraduate adults. Whereas the Fallon et al. (1984) studies assessed whether the participants themselves would consume the target substance, the Toyama (1999) experiments introduced a fictional character as the consumer of the target substance. The studies placed disgust (feces), dangerous (poison), and taste (sugar) contaminants either inside (contact), beside an open (proximity), or beside a covered (noncontact) glass of water. Results indicated that 7-year-old and adult participants display similar reasoning styles in appraising probable contamination: Disgust and dangerous substances need to come into direct or proximal contact with the water to render it contaminated. The 4-year-old participants generally assumed a more liberal view that all three substances were potential contaminants. Furthermore, even noncontact scenarios were more likely to be perceived as being contaminated in comparison to their older counterparts. Finally, when a colored dye was added to the water to change its physical appearance following the contact, proximal, and noncontact scenarios, the perceptions of contamination by the 4-year-old children were amplified. Such visual changes had little impact on the contamination appraisals of the 7-year-old and adult cohorts.

Thus, older children and preteens, similar to adults, may display similar appraisal styles over which stimuli are deemed to be potential carriers of contagion; however, as people age, perceptions over the durability of contaminants (and likely concerns over the consequences of physical contact) strengthen. Late childhood may therefore represent the period in which the *laws of sympathetic magic* (Rozin & Nemeroff, 1990) begin to form. Although younger children also appear to demonstrate a level of contamination appraisal, they may rely more so on the presence of concrete visual cues as evidence of infection or spoilage.

The increase in cognitive sophistication and abstraction among children marks their ability to learn from previous experience and anticipate future consequences. Furthermore, personal experiences, social modeling, and cultural influences gain considerable momentum in shaping the disgust response through later childhood, preteen, and adolescence. As noted earlier, older children start showing finer distinctions among stimuli in regard to their contamination threat value. Likewise, they begin to require a greater degree of perceived safety (or cleanliness) before approaching and contacting substances that they perceive to have been "tainted." Ideational representations of disgusting objects (e.g., chocolate shaped like feces) become increasingly capable of inducing repugnance. Language development promotes emotional labeling and an expansion of their disgust vocabulary (e.g., gross, sick, yucky). Overt behavioral action tendencies indicative of rejection, such as pushing away, gaze aversion, and contact avoidance, become core aspects of the disgust response repertoire. Finally, among older children, facial expressions of disgust are now more stable and representative of its presentation across the life span.

Unfortunately, little empirical information exists in regard to age-related changes to different classes of disgust elicitors in later childhood and adolescence. Exclusive gustatory and olfactory cues of disgust in infancy and early childhood are now augmented by visual (e.g., seeing a decayed animal), auditory (e.g., hearing someone vomit), and tactile (e.g., touching a slimy insect) sensory modalities in older children. Extrapolating from research with infants and younger children (Sullivan & Lewis, 2003), the domains capable of eliciting disgust clearly expand beyond those involved with simple food rejection. Bodily products, small animals, hygiene, interpersonal, and social–moral areas increasingly gain the propensity to become associated with disgust and rejection. More abstract representations of disgust, such as those in the interpersonal and social–moral realm, are more likely to develop during the teenage years. Adolescence marks a critical period in which peer groups and cultural expectations exert stronger influences over attitudes, values, beliefs, and behaviors (Remschmidt, 1994). Adult sex differences in reactivity to various classes of disgust elicitors likely have their roots in this developmental stage. Advances in abstract thinking, introspection, and the ability to take the perspective of others (Remschmidt, 1994) allows for more complex emotional manifestations that involve disgust, such as contempt, anger, embarrassment, guilt, and shame (McNally, 2002; Power & Dalgleish, 1997; Rozin, Lowery, Imada, & Haidt, 1999).

Disgust in Adulthood

The majority of descriptive and experimental disgust research has been conducted with college-aged and young adults. Self-report studies that use a variety of measures to assess disgust have uniformly found robust sex differences, with women generally endorsing greater disgust sensitivity than men (Arrindell, Mulkens, Kok, & Vollenbroek, 1999; Haidt, McCauley, & Rozin, 1994; Olatunji, Sawchuk, Arrindell, & Lohr, 2005; Templer, King, Brooner, & Corgiat, 1984; Tucker & Bond, 1997; Wronska, 1990). Additional research also suggests that women score higher than men on obsessive–compulsive measures of contamination fear, offering converging support for sex differences in contagion-related concerns (Mancini, Gragnani, & D'Olimpio, 2001; Olatunji et al., 2005; van Oppen, 1992). Although self-reported disgust is higher among the female population, neuroimaging studies suggest that men and women show comparable degrees of brain activation when processing disgust-related stimuli (Schienle, Schafer, Stark, Walter, & Vaitl, 2005).

Rozin and Fallon (1987) argued that the combination of facial expression, nausea, ideational rejection, and contamination are the key features in differentiating disgust in adulthood from earlier developmental stages. As noted earlier with adolescents, a dramatic gap is apparent in the disgust literature in regard to age-related changes in disgust sensitivity through adulthood, especially among the geriatric population. It is feasible that differing age cohorts may be characterized by variable levels of disgust reactivity to specific classes of disgust stimuli. For instance, younger adults may find certain types of envelope violations, such as body piercing, to be less disgusting than older adults. Furthermore, with advancing age comes greater cumulative experience and perspective taking with bodily functions, illness, and death, and thus older age groups may regard such stimuli as less disgust evoking than younger adults. Although it is possible that interpersonal and moral domains of disgust may gain prominence over time, social and moral reasoning in later life appears to be influenced by several factors, such as health, education, and social support (Pratt, Diessner, Pratt, Hunsberger, & Pancer, 1996). Several lines of additional research are needed to clarify whether different age cohorts are in fact characterized by differences in sensitivity to various disgust domains, as well as to determine whether the robust sex differences in disgust sensitivity remain stable at later points in the life span.

The extent of disgust-related research in the geriatric population is limited to neuroimaging and facial recognition studies, many of which are hampered by small sample sizes. In one study, healthy participants between the ages of 55 and 78 were exposed to films depicting happiness, disgust, and fear–disgust. Results indicated that cerebral blood flow increased to limbic and paralimbic brain structures across all emotional states, with disgust showing even greater activation in the thalamic region relative to the other emotions (Paradiso et al., 1997). Facial recognition studies also support territorial-specific processing of different emotional cues, with disgust expressions being characterized by greater activation in the insula and basal ganglia brain structures (Phillips et al., 1998; Sprengelmeyer, Rausch, Eysel, & Przuntek, 1998). Furthermore, diseases that target the basal ganglia region, such as Huntington's disease, have been found to profoundly affect the ability to process disgust-related facial expressions (Gray, Young, Barker, Curtis, & Gibson, 1997; Sprengelmeyer et al., 1996). Given that normal aging tends to be associated with gradual declines in various aspects of cognitive functioning, a small body of research has investigated whether age-related changes occur in the processing of different emotional states. In a cross-sectional study of participants between the ages of 18 and 30, and 58 and 70 years, increased age was associated with decrements in the processing of fear and anger faces, whereas the processing of disgust slightly improved across the life span (Calder et al., 2003). Converging data are therefore suggestive that the neurobiological processing of disgust, in contrast with other basic emotions, may be more durable across time.

PROCESSES INVOLVED IN DISGUST ACQUISITION

Disgust is an emotion that is easily learned and not easily forgotten. The sum of the theoretical literature suggests multiple mechanisms are involved in the acquisition of disgust, including learned experiences, cognitive processes, biological mechanisms, and sociocultural influences (Rozin et al., 2000; Rozin & Fallon, 1987; Woody & Teachman, 2000).

Learned Experiences and Associative Conditioning

Although not as well articulated in the disgust literature, the three pathways model to fear acquisition (Rachman, 1977) represents a useful framework by which to describe how certain disgust responses are learned through associative or conditioning processes. The first pathway involves direct classical conditioning in which a previously neutral or benign object (conditioned stimulus; e.g., eggs) becomes associated with another stimulus (unconditioned stimulus; e.g., food poisoning, flu virus) that naturally elicits feelings of disgust (unconditioned response; e.g., nausea, gagging, vomiting). Through the process of spatial and temporal contiguity, the previously neutral object becomes able to elicit disgust (conditioned response) independent of the original unconditioned stimulus. Rozin and Zellner (1985) clearly articulated this process of *Pavlovian conditioning* to explain human and animal food preferences and avoidances. At its essence, disgust is a food-related rejection mechanism that is evolutionarily designed to promote survival. Thus, it is not surprising that food-related aversions can be experimentally induced in a short amount of time across various animal species (Garcia & Koelling, 1966; Goudie, Stolerman, Demellweek, & D'Mello, 1982).

In humans, research with patients with cancer who are receiving chemotherapy and radiation has demonstrated the rapid acquisition of food aversions because of their association with nausea resulting from treatment (Andresen, Birch, & Johnson, 1990; Bernstein, 1978; Bernstein & Treneer, 1985; Bernstein & Webster, 1980; Carrell, Cannon, Best, & Stone, 1986; Okifuji & Friedman, 1992; Schafe & Bernstein, 1996; Schwartz, Jacobsen, & Bovbjerg, 1996). Some authors have specifically highlighted the differential outcomes of chemotherapy-induced nausea on affective and behavioral responses toward food. For instance, Schwartz et al. (1996) noted that nausea following chemotherapy infusion more strongly influenced affective ratings of food, yet exerted less influence over behavioral consumption as several other medical factors may influence postinfusion eating patterns.

Although considerable individual variability exists in the range and number of conditioned food aversions (de Silva & Rachman, 1987; Mattes, 1991), few efforts have been made to identify those factors that might be responsible for mediating these individual differences. One such study revealed that self-reported motion sickness did in fact correlate with total number of conditioned food aversions, although this relationship was only significant among female participants (Fessler & Arguello, 2004). Patients undergoing chemotherapy for the first time provide a unique opportunity to investigate a variety of potential vulnerability factors (e.g., disgust sensitivity, anxiety sensitivity, temperament, number of prechemotherapy food aversions) that may place individuals at increased risk for developing postchemotherapy food aversions. Furthermore, subsequent monitoring of this population across time may also allow for a longitudinal investigation of those factors that might predict the speed by which these conditioned food aversions are resolved.

Beyond food aversions, limited attention has been paid to studying other domains that may become the focus of classically conditioned disgust responses. Approximately 47% of individuals with blood-injection-injury and small animal phobias reported direct classical conditioning experiences in the onset of their phobic concerns (Öst, 1989). Although disgust may be involved in both of these phobia subtypes (Matchett & Davey, 1991; Page, 1994), it is challenging to separate out the independent influences of disgust and fear, especially given the methodological limitations of recall studies. Woody and Teachman (2000) aptly noted that unconditioned disgust-evoking stimuli primarily involve basic sensory stimuli, such as odors, as opposed to moral and ideational domains that are more directly shaped by cultural norms and belief systems. Thus, certain contexts, situations, objects, animals, and individuals may develop the capacity to elicit disgust through traditional classical-conditioning processes, especially when they become associated with malodors, putrid tastes, or aversive visual features.

Problems with traditional classical-conditioning accounts and the observation that fears could be acquired in the absence of direct experience suggested the involvement of two other indirect learning mechanisms: observational modeling and the transfer of negative information (Rachman, 1977). The acquisition of disgust may also be conditioned through these two vicarious routes. In observational modeling, observing another person reacting in a disgusting manner (e.g., facial cues, rejection, vomiting) to specific stimuli is sufficient for an observer to acquire the same response (Rozin & Fallon, 1987). Rozin and Zellner (1985) argued that many food aversions can be acquired through social-modeling processes. For instance, young children learn to reject and avoid certain foods and substances from observing facial expressions and behavioral reactions in their caregivers (Rozin, Hammer, Oster, Horowitz, & Marmora, 1986), as opposed to basing it on aversive characteristics of the stimulus, perceptions of contamination threat value, or their own negative experiences. It is not surprising that parents and children share very similar food aversions, which may involve a combination of genetic loading and modeled experiences (Fallon et al., 1984). It is also conceivable that a much broader range of disgust elicitors can also become conditioned through social-modeling processes, including bodily products, blood, small animals, hygiene, sex, interpersonal, and moral domains. Individual and cultural differences in disgust-related attitudes toward these various elicitors may be accounted for in large part by these social cues. Watching certain television programs or exploring various Internet domains may serve as additional vehicles for observational transmission of disgust. NBC's *Fear Factor*, for instance, routinely depicts graphic and intense disgust provocations (e.g., being trapped in a glass box and covered with worms, stink beetles,

cockroaches, and maggots; eating cow intestines) and associated participant reactions (e.g., facial aversion, gagging, vomiting). There are also several Web sites, such as "ratemyvomit.com," that are fairly self-explanatory
in their objective.

Disgust may also be acquired through the receipt of negative information. Similar to social modeling, the transmission of negative information from
others or the media may be sufficient to affect food aversions and avoidances
(Fallon et al., 1984; Rozin & Zellner, 1985). Rozin and Fallon (1987) have
suggested that this route of disgust acquisition is primarily cognitive, as
opposed to affective, in nature. Evaluative-conditioning processes, as discussed
in further detail in the next section, is one such avenue through which individuals make a basic judgment about the acceptability or unacceptability of a
particular disgust stimulus. Once a judgment is made, additional cognitive
elaborations about physical features, origination, degree of approachability,
and infectious potential may ensue to solidify one's impressions and guide
future behavior. At the level of ideation, learning about the origins or contents of certain objects (e.g., a piece of steak that is found out to be dog meat)
may render it unacceptable and repulsive. Furthermore, media reports about
potential contamination threats (e.g., mad cow disease, SARS, HIV) may
affect rejection and disgust-mediated avoidance tendencies. Information
transfer is a key process by which disgust becomes recruited in shaping social
morality and order (Rozin et al., 1999, 2000). Once widely accepted behaviors may become "demoralized" by linking them with disgust-evoking characteristics. Cigarette smoking (Rozin et al., 1999; Rozin & Singh, 1999),
vegetarianism (Fessler, Arguello, Mekdara, & Macias, 2003; Rozin et al.,
1999), and homophobia (Olatunji & Sawchuk, 2005) are some examples
through which social morals evolve through their association with disgust-
evoking characteristics or ideals.

Cognitive Processes

Cognitive processes, such as evaluative learning, may also be applied to
traditional conditioning models to further describe how disgust reactions are
acquired. Evaluative learning simply involves a "hedonistic" judgment over
liking or disliking a particular stimulus (Levey & Martin, 1987). Although
an efficient way to process information, making such a judgment can bias
subsequent elaborations, which in turn will further solidify one's initial
impressions. Maggots, as an example, are creatures that few people express
an initial fondness toward. Challenging an individual to directly handle a
maggot may provoke further elaboration of its disgust-evoking characteristics (e.g., slimy, parasitic, disease carrier, associated with decomposition).
Although the mechanisms governing evaluative learning are not well understood (Rozin, Wrzcsniewski, & Byrnes, 1998), such evaluations are resistant

to extinction (Baeyens, Crombez, van den Bergh, & Eelen, 1988) and are viewed as an important process in mediating disgust acquisition (Woody & Teachman, 2000).

Biological Mechanisms

Biological diathesis factors, such as preparedness and genetics, may partially account for similarities and differences across individuals (and possibly cultures) in their reactivity to disgust cues. Preparedness theory was proposed to account for the nonrandom distribution of human fears (Seligman, 1971), especially those that preclude any evidence of direct or indirect conditioning experiences. Such theorists argue that a narrow range of stimuli are naturally capable of readily eliciting fearful behavior, are slow to extinguish once acquired, and are essentially noncognitive. Furthermore, prepared stimuli are often species specific and believed to be evolutionarily adaptive to the survival of that species' ancestry, thereby suggestive of underlying genetic diatheses (Seligman, 1971). Empirical testing of preparedness theory's tenets in the acquisition and durability of human fears has received equivocal support at best (cf. McNally, 1987). Although stronger support has been generated for the resistance to extinction and noncognitive nature of biologically prepared phobias, hypotheses regarding the selectively rapid acquisition of such fears have not been substantiated (McNally, 1987).

Disgust reactions to the range of potential elicitors also demonstrate preparedness features. The primary function of disgust is to maintain sanitation and protect the organism from contaminant infection (Rozin et al., 2000). Aversive rejection behaviors (e.g., nausea, vomiting) reflect an evolutionary adaptive function against oral incorporation of stimuli deemed to be carrying harmful agents (Rozin & Fallon, 1987). Basic taste aversions in both human (Bernstein, 1978) and animal species (Garcia & Koelling, 1966) conform to the preparedness tenets of rapid acquisition, slow extinction, and noncognitive processes. Although a vast array of stimuli may become targets of disgust among humans, not all disgust elicitors are created equal. Certain classes of disgust elicitors do appear to show a nonrandom distribution pattern, with more frequent aversions toward foods, small animals, and body products, in contrast to those categories that appear to be more socially constructed (e.g., interpersonal and moral domains). Furthermore, small animal phobias, which have garnered perhaps the strongest support for preparedness features (McNally, 1987; Skre et al., 2000), can involve a blending of both fearful and disgusting characteristics. However, the utility of preparedness theory as a framework for describing selective onset and maintenance processes for disgust-specific stimuli is premature as such hypotheses have not been systematically investigated.

Although genetic factors are likely involved in disgust, its contribution is more speculative given the nature–nurture confound inherent in available studies, which are admittedly sparse. Parents and children show moderate correlations in regard to food preferences and disgust–contamination sensitivity (Rozin et al., 2000). A twin study of contamination sensitivity revealed only slightly higher associations among monozygotic ($r = .29$) in comparison with dizygotic ($r = .24$) twins (Rozin & Millman, 1987).

Does a biological predisposition toward disgust sensitivity exist? Both the search and debate will no doubt continue. At a conceptual level, a generalized disgust proneness or some temperamental feature holds promise as an underlying vulnerability factor to partially explain individual differences in disgust reactivity. However, from an empirical standpoint, progress in this area has been limited. Although the construct of disgust sensitivity has been framed in a manner analogous to anxiety sensitivity, the actual assessment of anxiety sensitivity has been approached in a more unitary way (Taylor & Cox, 1998), focusing on the basic "fear of fear-related symptoms" notion (Reiss, Peterson, Gursky, & McNally, 1986). Disgust sensitivity measurement, conversely, has focused almost exclusively on aversion intensity toward either food or a diverse range of disgust stimuli (Haidt et al., 1994; Olatunji & Sawchuk, 2005). In addition to refinements in how disgust sensitivity is operationalized and assessed, future investigations will need to further articulate exactly which outcomes disgust sensitivity is designed to predict to justify its continued empirical attention.

Sociocultural Influences

Although articulated in greater detail in chapter 7 of this volume, culture plays a substantial role in shaping disgust acquisition processes. Regarded as a universal human emotion, the overt facial expression of disgust demonstrates remarkable similarity across different cultures (Ekman et al., 1987). Sociocultural differences emerge in regulating the intensity of emotional expression and shaping specific categories of disgust elicitors (Haidt et al., 1994; Olatunji & Sawchuk, 2005; Rozin & Fallon, 1987), especially those in interpersonal and moral domains (Rozin et al., 2000). Just as the microculture of the family profoundly influences disgust in children, the macroculture of larger groups, societies, and nations establishes influence over its members. A number of theorists have further speculated that social influences of disgust are probably more important to the development of avoidance and rejection tendencies in humans than its evolutionary preparedness value (Haidt et al., 1994; Rozin et al., 2000). Sociocultural influences not only provide a basic building block for defining the boundaries and experience of disgust in humans but also profoundly mediate this emotion over the life span.

PROCESSES INVOLVED IN DISGUST MAINTENANCE

Negative reinforcement, stimulus generalization, and expectancy learning are all potential contributors to maintaining disgust across time. Furthermore, these concepts also help explain individual differences in disgust-related functional impairment. Negative reinforcement occurs when specific behaviors increase over time because of their effectiveness in reducing or preventing discomfort in an individual. In regard to disgust, reactive and proactive behaviors can develop to reduce sensations of nausea, stench, and feelings of dirtiness and contamination. These behaviors, therefore, hold negatively reinforcing properties. Reactive behaviors involve actions such as washing, cleaning, and overt escape that emerge following actual or perceived contact with a disgusting stimulus. They serve a fundamentally protective function to maintain safety and sanitation by either neutralizing the threat itself (e.g., washing) or creating physical distance between oneself and the threat-relevant stimulus. Proactive behaviors involve those actions that are designed to preempt any situation or circumstance in which confrontation with a disgusting stimulus is likely. Avoiding a city dump, sewage treatment plant, or butcher shop would be examples of more overt action tendencies. Subtle avoidance behaviors, such as averting one's eyes away from a disheveled homeless person or a television program depicting surgery, may also have some degree of negatively reinforcing value. Avoidance of being associated with certain people, organizations, groups, and ideals may also have negatively reinforcing properties at the interpersonal and social–moral level of disgust.

Although escape or avoidance responding may look similar between fear and disgust, these behaviors may be somewhat less effective in providing reassurance when exposed to disgust-relevant stimuli. For those who come into contact with spiders and are afraid of being bitten, escaping the situation and creating physical distance between themselves and the spider is an effective means for providing safety and reassurance that they will not be attacked and harmed. For those who come into contact with spiders and are concerned about being contaminated, it may be harder to dispel disgust-relevant concerns even after successfully escaping the situation and creating distance between oneself and the spider. The locus of threat here is not the spider per se but rather its representation as a carrier of disease. Given the microscopic size of germs and bacteria, visual assurance of threat avoidance is not possible. Furthermore, contaminants may also have an "incubating quality" in that the full consequence of exposure to the threat (e.g., illness, disease) may not be realized until a later time. The disgust–contamination relationship may therefore be mediated by beliefs that brief contact with dirt and germs results in rapid, growing, and spreading infection (Riskind, Abreu, Strauss, & Holt, 1997) and permanent transfer of the disgust object's infectious properties

(Nemeroff & Rozin, 1994). These beliefs, therefore, can serve to maintain disgust-related responding.

Ample evidence suggests that stimulus generalization can maintain disgust and more important, expand the range of stimuli that become associated with this emotion (Rozin & Fallon, 1987). Generalization can occur through shared physical characteristics and ideational processes (Rozin & Fallon, 1987). In regard to physical properties, an object may become associated with disgust because of its structural resemblance to another existing disgust-evoking stimulus. Gooey, oozing substances that are completely benign may be avoided because of their resemblance to human or animal mucus. From an ideational perspective, animals can be avoided because of their association with or proximity to environments that are perceived to be dirty and unclean. The disease-avoidance model highlights how generalized physical characteristics and ideational processes can influence the development of small animal fears (Matchett & Davey, 1991). This model postulates that certain harmless animals are avoided because of either their physical resemblance to disgusting objects (e.g., slugs, feces) or concerns over their potential as carriers of disease (e.g., rats).

Expectancy evaluations allow the individual to develop predictive information over conditioned associations and their outcomes as a result of repeated experience. Although expectancies have not been directly applied to learning models of disgust, relevant extrapolations can be drawn from the fear and anxiety literature. Anxious individuals tend to overestimate the likelihood of confrontation with feared stimuli, their degree of fear upon exposure, and the intensity of the negative consequences, while at the same time, underestimate their ability to cope with adverse circumstances (Arntz, Hildebrand, & van den Hout, 1994; Rachman, 1994; Thorpe & Salkovskis, 1995). It is conceivable that similar cognitive processes are operating in disgust-related avoidance behavior, especially in regard to concerns over contamination.

These mechanisms responsible for maintaining disgust can help explain individual differences in disgust sensitivity and provide useful dimensions to describe how disgust can become functionally impairing. Learning involves a dynamic interplay between the individual and the environment in shaping expectancies, beliefs, physical reactions, and action tendencies. Initial escape-related responding to disgust cues can result in predominant avoidance behavior as individuals learn to anticipate situations that may provoke uncomfortable and not so easily dispelled sensations of disgust. Perceptions of heightened personal vulnerability to infection coupled with exaggerated appraisals in regard to the "virulent" nature of objects, situations, individuals, and ideals can create a system of beliefs that may be resistant to disconfirmation. These circumstances place individuals under objective vulnerability for impairments in personal, social, and occupational roles and responsibilities.

CAN DISGUST BE UNLEARNED?

Extinction, habituation, and changes in cognitive processing are prominent concepts used to describe the effectiveness of exposure-based therapies to reduce fear (Lang, Craske, & Bjork, 1999). Early treatments that describe the process of phobic fear reduction relied largely on the participant's verbal report of generalized subjective distress. Participants were neither specifically oriented to report the emotion of fear per se, nor focus on other discrete emotional states, including disgust. In fact, only recently has disgust been more formally separated out and studied independently from fear over the course of exposure therapy (e.g., Smits, Telch, & Randall, 2002).

Especially in regard to extinction, it is now widely accepted that repeated exposure to varying gradients of the conditioned stimulus does not simply overwrite or destroy original fear learning (Bouton, Garcia-Gutierrez, Zilski, & Moody, 2006; Rescorla, 2001). Although individuals may learn new meanings of the fear cue (Lang et al., 1999), perhaps what people really learn is how to tolerate, inhibit, or suppress the action tendency of fear itself (Bouton, 2002; Bouton et al., 2006). The strength of this new "inhibition learning" can be maximized under conditions in which the treatment context promotes the learning of multiple retrieval cues for coping (Bouton, 2002). To date, almost no information exists on treating maladaptive disgust responses. However, adapting the principles of inhibition learning from traditional fear-based exposure treatments may have direct implications for how to approach managing disgust in a therapeutic context.

SUMMARY AND FUTURE IMPLICATIONS

From early reflexive responses to gustatory stimuli in infancy to higher order cognitive appraisals of contagion in adulthood, disgust is both a simple and complex human emotion. Given that the preponderance of research has been conducted with infants, young children, and college-aged adults, additional research is clearly needed with other populations along the age continuum. An unfortunate void exists in the study of disgust in adolescents, middle-aged adults, and geriatric populations. Research with these other age cohorts can help specify important developmental periods that shape the expression of disgust and how it becomes blended with other emotions to form more complex affective representations. Technological advances in neuroimaging procedures may also prove to be particularly useful in better understanding the neurobiological processing of disgust and its affiliated emotions across the life span. Furthermore, research with adolescents and older adults would clarify the developmental trajectory of age-related changes in reactivity to the expansive range of disgust-related elicitors.

Although traditional learning and cognitive theories of fear acquisition extrapolate well to disgust, additional research accounting for biological and sociocultural factors is needed to clarify individual differences in disgust proneness. A novel area of research would be to study individuals or populations who display relatively little reactivity to disgust-related cues (e.g., waste management workers). Understanding dispositional and experiential features that may "inoculate" certain individuals to the effects of disgust and perceived contagion may hold unique clinical applications for treating phobic disorders or aversions in which disgust plays a prominent role.

REFERENCES

Andresen, G. V., Birch, L. L., & Johnson, P. A. (1990). The scapegoat effect on food aversions after chemotherapy. *Cancer, 66,* 1649–1653.

Arntz, A., Hildebrand, M., & van den Hout, M. (1994). Overprediction of anxiety, and disconfirmatory processes, in anxiety disorders. *Behaviour Research and Therapy, 32,* 709–722.

Arrindell, W. A., Mulkens, S., Kok, J., & Vollenbroek, J. (1999). Disgust and sex differences in fears to common indigenous animals. *Behaviour Research and Therapy, 37,* 273–280.

Baeyens, F., Crombez, G., van den Bergh, O., & Eelen, P. (1988). Once in contact always in contact: Evaluative conditioning is resistant to extinction. *Advances in Behaviour Research and Therapy, 10,* 179–199.

Bennett, D. (2002). Facial expressivity at 4 months: A context by expression analysis. *Infancy, 3,* 97–114.

Bernstein, I. L. (1978, June 16). Learned taste aversions in children receiving chemotherapy. *Science, 200,* 1302–1303.

Bernstein, I. L., & Treneer, C. M. (1985). Learned food aversions and tumor anorexia. In T. G. Burish, S. M. Levy, & B. E. Meyerowitz (Eds.), *Cancer, nutrition, and eating behavior: A biobehavioral perspective* (pp. 65–75). Hillsdale, NJ: Erlbaum.

Bernstein, I. L., & Webster, M. M. (1980). Learned taste aversion in humans. *Physiology & Behavior, 25,* 363–366.

Bouton, M. E. (2002). Context, ambiguity, and unlearning: Sources of relapse after behavioral extinction. *Society of Biological Psychiatry, 52,* 976–986.

Bouton, M. E., Garcia-Gutierrez, A., Zilski, J., & Moody, E. W. (2006). Extinction in multiple contexts does not necessarily make extinction less vulnerable to relapse. *Behaviour Research and Therapy, 44,* 983–994.

Calder, A. J., Keane, J., Manly, T., Sprengelmeyer, R., Scott, S., Nimmo-Smith, I., et al. (2003). Facial expression recognition across the adult lifespan. *Neuropsychologia, 41,* 195–202.

Camaras, L., Holland, E. A., & Patterson, M. J. (1993). Facial expressions. In M. Lewis & J. M. Haviland (Eds.), *Handbook of emotions* (pp. 199–208). New York: Guilford Press.

Carrell, L. E., Cannon, D. S., Best, M. R., & Stone, M. J. (1986). Nausea and radiation-induced taste aversions in cancer patients. *Appetite, 7*, 203–208.

de Silva, P., & Rachman, S. (1987). Human food aversions: Nature and acquisition. *Behaviour Research and Therapy, 25*, 457–468.

Ekman, P., Friesen, W. V., & Ancoli, S. (1980). Facial signs of the emotional experience. *Journal of Personality and Social Psychology, 39*, 1125–1134.

Ekman, P., Friesen, W. V., O'Sullivan, M., Chan, A., Diacoyanni-Tarlatzis, I., Heider, K., et al. (1987). Universals and cultural differences in the judgments of facial expressions of emotion. *Journal of Personality and Social Psychology, 53*, 712–717.

Fallon, A. E., Rozin, P., & Pilner, P. (1984). The child's conception of food: The development of food rejections with special reference to disgust and contamination sensitivity. *Child Development, 55*, 566–575.

Fessler, D. M. T., & Arguello, A. P. (2004). The relationship between susceptibility to nausea and vomiting and the possession of conditioned food aversions. *Appetite, 43*, 331–334.

Fessler, D. M. T., Arguello, A. P., Mekdara, J. M., & Macias, R. (2003). Disgust sensitivity and meat consumption: A test of an emotivist account of moral vegetarianism. *Appetite, 41*, 31–41.

Ganchrow, J. R., Steiner, J. E., & Daher, M. (1983). Neonatal facial expression in response to different qualities and intensities of gustatory stimuli. *Infant Behavior and Development, 6*, 473–484.

Garcia, J., & Koelling, R. A. (1966). Relation of cue to consequence in avoidance learning. *Psychonomic Science, 4*, 123–124.

Goudie, A. J., Stolerman, I. P., Demellweek, C., & D'Mello, G. D. (1982). Does conditioned nausea mediate drug-induced conditioned taste aversion? *Psychopharmacology, 78*, 277–281.

Gray, J. M., Young, A. W., Barker, W. A., Curtis, A., & Gibson, D. (1997). Impaired recognition of disgust in Huntington's disease genetic carriers. *Brain, 120*, 2029–2038.

Haidt, J., McCauley, C., & Rozin, P. (1994). Individual differences in sensitivity to disgust: A scale sampling seven domains of disgust elicitors. *Personality and Individual Differences, 16*, 701–713.

Izard, C. E. (1971). *The face of emotion*. New York: Appleton-Century-Crofts.

Izard, C. E. (1982). *A system for identifying affect expressions by holistic judgments (AFFEX)*. Newark, DE: Instructional Resources Center.

Lang, A. J., Craske, M. G., & Bjork, R. A. (1999). Implications of a new theory of disuse for the treatment of emotional disorders. *Clinical Psychology: Science and Practice, 6*, 80–94.

Levenson, R. W. (1992). Autonomic nervous system differences among emotions. *Psychological Science, 3*, 23–27.

Levey, A. B., & Martin, I. (1987). Evaluative conditioning: A case for hedonistic transfer. In H. J. Eysenck & I. Martin (Eds.), *Theoretical foundations of behavior therapy* (pp. 113–131). New York: Plenum Press.

Mancini, F., Gragnani, A., & D'Olimpio, F. (2001). The connection between disgust and obsessions and compulsions in a non-clinical sample. *Personality and Individual Differences, 31,* 1173–1180.

Matchett, G., & Davey, G. C. (1991). A test of a disease-avoidance model of animal phobias. *Behaviour Research and Therapy, 29,* 91–94.

Mattes, R. D. (1991). Learned food aversions: A family study. *Physiology & Behavior, 50,* 499–504.

McNally, R. J. (1987). Preparedness and phobias: A review. *Psychological Bulletin, 101,* 283–303.

McNally, R. J. (2002). Disgust has arrived. *Journal of Anxiety Disorders, 16,* 561–566.

Mundy, P., & Willoughby, J. (1996). Nonverbal communication, joint attention and early socioemotional development. In M. Lewis & M. W. Sullivan (Eds.), *Emotional development in atypical children* (pp. 65–88). Mahwah, NJ: Erlbaum.

Nemeroff, C., & Rozin, P. (1994). The contagion concept in adult thinking in the United States: Transmission of germs and of interpersonal influence. *Ethos, 22,* 158–186.

Okifuji, A., & Friedman, A. G. (1992). Experimentally induced taste aversions in humans: Effects of overshadowing on acquisition. *Behaviour Research and Therapy, 30,* 23–32.

Olatunji, B. O., & Sawchuk, C. N. (2005). Disgust: Characteristic features, social manifestations, and clinical implications. *Journal of Social and Clinical Psychology, 24,* 932–962.

Olatunji, B. O., Sawchuk, C. N., Arrindell, W. A., & Lohr, J. M. (2005). Disgust sensitivity, anxiety symptoms, and the biological sex difference in contamination fears. *Personality and Individual Differences, 38,* 713–722.

Öst, L. G. (1989). One session treatment for specific phobias. *Behaviour Research and Therapy, 27,* 1–7.

Oster, H. (1978). Facial expression and affect development. In M. Lewis & L. Rosenbaum (Eds.), *The development of affect* (pp. 43–75). New York: Plenum Press.

Page, A. C. (1994). Blood-injection-injury phobia. *Clinical Psychology Review, 14,* 443–461.

Paradiso, S., Robinson, R. G., Andreasen, N. C., Downhill, J. E., Davidson, R. J., Kirchner, P. T., et al. (1997). Emotional activation of limbic circuitry in elderly normal subjects in a PET study. *American Journal of Psychiatry, 154,* 384–389.

Phillips, M. L., Young, A. W., Scott, S. K., Calder, A. J., Andrew, C., Giampietro, V., et al. (1998). Neural responses to facial and vocal expressions of fear and disgust. *Proceedings of the Royal Society of London Series B—Biological Sciences, 265,* 1809–1817.

Plutchik, R. (1980). *Emotion: A psychoevolutionary synthesis.* New York: Harper & Row.

Power, M., & Dalgleish, T. (1997). *Cognition and emotion: From order to disorder.* East Sussex, England: Psychology Press.

Pratt, M. W., Diessner, R., Pratt, A., Hunsberger, B., & Pancer, S. M. (1996). Moral and social reasoning and perspective taking in later life: A longitudinal study. *Psychology and Aging, 11*, 66–73.

Rachman, S. (1977). The conditioning theory of fear acquisition: A critical examination. *Behaviour Research and Therapy, 15*, 375–387.

Rachman, S. (1994). The overprediction of fear: A review. *Behaviour Research and Therapy, 32*, 83–690.

Reiss, S., Peterson, R. A., Gursky, D. M., & McNally, R. J. (1986). Anxiety sensitivity, anxiety frequency, and the prediction of fearfulness. *Behaviour Research and Therapy, 24*, 1–8.

Remschmidt, H. (1994). Psychosocial milestones in normal puberty and adolescence. *Hormone Research, 41*, 19–29.

Rescorla, R. A. (2001). Retraining of extinguished Pavlovian stimuli. *Journal of Experimental Psychology: Animal Behavior Processes, 27*, 115–124.

Riskind, J. H., Abreu, K., Strauss, M., & Holt, R. (1997). Looming vulnerability and spreading contamination in subclinical OCD. *Behaviour Research and Therapy, 35*, 405–414.

Rosenstein, D., & Oster, H. (1988). Differential response to four basic tastes in newborns. *Child Development, 59*, 1555–1568.

Rozin, P., & Fallon, A. E. (1987). A perspective on disgust. *Psychological Review, 94*, 23–41.

Rozin, P., Fallon, A. E., & Augustoni-Ziskind, M. (1986). The child's conception of food: Development of categories of accepted and rejected substances. *Journal of Nutritional Education, 18*, 75–81.

Rozin, P., Haidt, J., & McCauley, C. R. (2000). Disgust. In M. Lewis & J. Haviland (Eds.), *Handbook of emotions* (2nd ed., pp. 637–653). New York: Guilford Press.

Rozin, P., Hammer, L., Oster, H., Horowitz, T., & Marmora, V. (1986). The child's conception of food differentiation of categories of rejected substances in the 16 months to 5 year age range. *Appetite, 7*, 141–151.

Rozin, P., Lowery, L., Imada, S., & Haidt, J. (1999). The CAD triad hypothesis: A mapping between three moral emotions (contempt, anger, disgust) and three moral codes (community, autonomy, divinity). *Journal of Personality and Social Psychology, 76*, 574–586.

Rozin, P., & Millman, L. (1987). Family environment, not heredity, accounts for family resemblances in food preferences and attitudes: A twin study. *Appetite, 8*, 125–134.

Rozin, P., & Nemeroff, C. (1990). The laws of sympathetic magic: A psychological analysis of similarity and contagion. In J. W. Stigler, R. A. Shweder, & G. Herdt (Eds.), *Cultural psychology: Essays on comparative human development* (pp. 205–232). New York: Cambridge University Press.

Rozin, P., & Singh, L. (1999). The moralization of cigarette smoking in America. *Journal of Consumer Behavior, 8*, 321–337.

Rozin, P., Wrzcsniewski, A., & Byrnes, D. (1998). The elusiveness of evaluative conditioning. *Learning and Motivation, 29*, 397–415.

Rozin, P., & Zellner, D. A. (1985). The role of Pavlovian conditioning in the acquisition of food likes and dislikes. *Annals of the New York Academy of Science, 443*, 189–202.

Schafe, G. E., & Bernstein, I. L. (1996). Taste aversion learning. In E. D. Capaldi (Ed.), *Why we eat what we eat: The psychology of eating* (pp. 31–51). Washington, DC: American Psychological Association.

Schienle, A., Schafer, A., Stark, R., Walter, B., & Vaitl, D. (2005). Gender differences in the processing of disgust- and fear-inducing pictures: An fMRI study. *Neuroreport, 16*, 277–280.

Schwartz, M. D., Jacobsen, P. B., & Bovbjerg, D. H. (1996). Role of nausea in the development of aversions to a beverage paired with chemotherapy treatment in cancer patients. *Physiology & Behavior, 59*, 659–663.

Seligman, M. E. P. (1971). Phobias and preparedness. *Behavior Therapy, 2*, 307–320.

Siegal, M. S., & Share, D. L. (1990). Contamination sensitivity in young children. *Developmental Psychology, 26*, 455–458.

Skre, I., Onstad, S., Torgersen, S., Philos, D. R., Lygren, S., & Kringlen, E. (2000). The heritability of common phobic fear: A twin study of a clinical sample. *Journal of Anxiety Disorders, 14*, 549–562.

Smits, J. A., Telch, M. J., & Randall, P. K. (2002). An examination of the decline in fear and disgust during exposure-based treatment. *Behaviour Research and Therapy, 40*, 1243–1253.

Soussignan, R., Schaal, B., Marlier, L., & Jiang, T. (1997). Facial and autonomic responses to biological and artificial olfactory stimuli in human neonates: Re-examining early hedonistic discrimination of odors. *Physiology & Behavior, 62*, 745–758.

Sprengelmeyer, R., Rausch, M., Eysel, U. T., & Przuntek, H. (1998). Neural structures associated with recognition of facial expressions of basic emotions. *Proceedings of the Royal Society of London Series B—Biological Sciences, 265*, 1927–1931.

Sprengelmeyer, R., Young, A. W., Calder, A. J., Karnat, A., Lange, H., Homberg, V., et al. (1996). Loss of disgust-perception of faces and emotions in Huntington's disease. *Brain, 119*, 1647–1665.

Steiner, J. E. (1979). Human facial expressions in response to taste and smell stimulation. *Advances in Child Development and Behavior, 13*, 257–296.

Sullivan, M. W., & Lewis, M. (2003). Emotional expressions of young infants and children: A practitioner's primer. *Infants and Young Children, 16*, 120–142.

Taylor, S., & Cox, B. J. (1998). Anxiety sensitivity: Multiple dimensions and hierarchical structure. *Behaviour Research and Therapy, 36*, 37–51.

Templer, D. I., King, F. L., Brooner, R. K., & Corgiat, M. (1984). Assessment of body elimination attitude. *Journal of Clinical Psychology, 40*, 754–759.

Thorpe, S. J., & Salkovskis, P. M. (1995). Phobic beliefs: Do cognitive factors play a role in specific phobias? *Behaviour Research and Therapy, 33*, 805–816.

Toyama, N. (1999). Developmental changes in the basis of associational contamination thinking. *Cognitive Development, 14,* 343–361.

Tucker, M., & Bond, N. W. (1997). The role of gender, sex role, and disgust in fear of animals. *Personality and Individual Differences, 22,* 135–138.

van Oppen, P. (1992). Obsessions and compulsions: Dimensional structure, reliability, convergent and divergent validity of the Padua Inventory. *Behaviour Research and Therapy, 30,* 631–637.

Walden, T., & Knieps, L. (1996). Reading and responding to social signals. In M. Lewis & M. W. Sullivan (Eds.), *Emotional development in atypical children* (pp. 29–42). Mahwah, NJ: Erlbaum.

Woody, S. R., & Teachman, B. A. (2000). Intersection of disgust and fear: Normative and pathological views. *Clinical Psychology: Science and Practice, 7,* 291–311.

Wronska, J. (1990). Disgust in relation to emotionality, extraversion, psychoticism and imagery abilities. In P. J. D. Drenth, J. A. Sergeant, & R. J. Takens (Eds.), *European perspectives in psychology* (Vol. 1, pp. 125–138). Chichester, England: Wiley.

5

A CROSS-CULTURAL PERSPECTIVE ON DISGUST

LISA S. ELWOOD AND BUNMI O. OLATUNJI

Observation, theory, and empirical support have led to the proposition that several innate, universal emotions exist (Darwin 1872/1965; Ekman, 1992, 1999; Izard, 1991, 1992; Tomkins & McCarter, 1964). Proponents of the universal theories of emotion suggest that individuals are born hard-wired to experience the basic emotions (Ekman, Levenson, & Friesen, 1983; Tomkins & McCarter, 1964). Although the emotions are expected to be similar across individuals, some of the emotion components are believed to be susceptible to influence by the environment and experiences of the individual (Abe & Izard, 1999). The facial expressions associated with the various emotions are typically expected to be consistent, but it has been suggested that culture influences the evoking stimuli, linked affects, display rules, and behavioral consequences (Ekman, 1994; Ekman, Sorenson, & Friesen, 1969).

Traditional lists of basic emotions include disgust, anger, fear, surprise, happiness, and sadness (Ekman et al., 1969, 1983; Ekman & Friesen, 1971). Empirical studies have tested the universality hypothesis by examining the reactions of members of different cultures, infants, and animals to similar contexts that may evoke the basic emotions, and there is some evidence that some degree of universality of emotions exists (Ekman, 1992, 1994). Although there is a consensus that there are some similarities in emotional experience across

99

cultures, theories differ on the proposed importance of the influence of culture on the experience and/or expression of emotion (Russell, 1995). Universality research has been accused of using methods that enhance the similarities between cultures and ignoring alternative explanations of findings. For example, Russell (1994) suggested that the previous results are consistent with several interpretations, including initial interpretation of the expressions into culture specific categories that are later paired with the most similar provided emotion, bipolar dimensions of expressions, situation-specific responses, and instrumental actions, in addition to the universality explanation.

DISGUST AS A BASIC EMOTION

Research and theory have focused on identifying the signal, physiological response, theme of antecedent events, and function unique to disgust to support its classification as a basic emotion. Disgust was originally conceptualized as a protective mechanism designed to prevent the oral ingestion of inappropriate objects (Darwin, 1872/1965). The original function of disgust, to aid in disease avoidance and food selection, is most consistent with what is currently termed *core disgust*. Core disgust elicitors are items that could be ingested and are potentially harmful, such as certain types of food, animals, and body products (Haidt, Rozin, McCauley, & Imada, 1997; Rozin, Haidt, McCauley, 2000). Rozin et al. (2000) suggested that the original oral rejection function of disgust has since been accompanied by a denial of mortality and a protection of the body, soul, and social order (Rozin et al., 2000). Current conceptualizations of disgust have added three additional categories of disgust elicitors: animal–nature (i.e., sex, death, hygiene, envelope violations), interpersonal (i.e., direct or nondirect contact with strangers or undesirables), and moral (i.e., moral offenses; Rozin et al., 2000).

THE FACE OF DISGUST

Consistent with the original function of disgust, to avoid ingestion of inappropriate objects, signals associated with disgust focus on the face, and more specifically the mouth. Early conceptualizations of the disgust facial expression differed somewhat in their emphasis. Darwin's (1872/1965) initial description of the facial expression of disgust emphasized the gape (i.e., mouth held open widely) but also mentioned a raised upper lip and a nose wrinkle. Izard's (1971) description of the portrayal of disgust included a raised upper lip, the mouth corners drawn and back, and the tongue moved forward and may be slightly protruding. As depicted in Figure 5.1, Ekman and Friesen's (1975) description of the disgust expression consists of a lip retraction, a

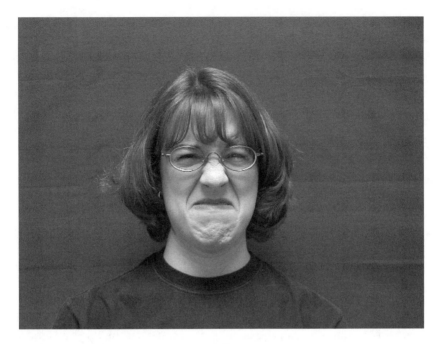

Figure 5.1. Prototypical disgust expression.

raised lower lip, and a wrinkled nose. This facial expression often signals the experience of nausea, increased salivation and parasympathetic responding and functions to protect the body from the ingestion of an object (Levenson, 1992; Levenson, Ekman, & Friesen, 1990; Rozin et al., 2000).

CROSS-CULTURAL STUDIES ON DISGUST

Contemporary conceptualizations of disgust have been largely based on findings of studies conducted in Western countries. If disgust is a universal emotion, then similar characteristics should be associated with the expression and experience of disgust across cultures. For disgust to be considered a universal emotion, cross-cultural studies need to reveal similarities in the signal, physiological response, antecedents, and function of disgust.

Facial Recognition of Emotion

The most common method used for testing the universality theory is to ask participants from different cultures to match emotional facial expressions with emotion labels (Ekman et al., 1969). This standard facial expression identification task preselects photographs that depict the basic emotions. For example, photographs are often of posed expressions, in which the individual was either asked to display a specific emotion or instructed to present facial muscles in a specific manner. The facial expressions are then briefly presented to a participant, and he or she is asked to select the emotional label that is consistent with the facial expression from a list of other emotional labels (Ekman et al., 1969). The percentage of correct responses is then compared with the base rate, chance percentages, and/or across groups. Facial expression recognition tasks have been conducted using a variety of samples including Western, non-Western, and preliterate cultures. The most common approach to the cross-cultural examination of emotions is to obtain participants in at least one Western and one non-Western sample and compare the responses and accuracy rates on the recognition task. Findings of similar high rates of accuracy of the identification of the disgust expression on these recognition tasks would provide support for the universal experience of disgust.

Accuracy

The basic facial expression recognition task assesses the accuracy with which various samples label the facial expression with the targeted emotion chosen from a list of emotions. This basic form of the recognition task has been administered to participants from a large number of samples. As would be expected, on the basis of the fact that the majority of the studies have been conducted by American researchers and used photographs of American individuals displaying the facial expression, participants from the United States have consistently succeeded at identifying disgust with accuracy ranging from 60% (on one expression) to 96% (Biehl et al., 1997; Ekman et al., 1969, 1987; Haidt & Keltner, 1999; Matsumoto, 1992; Matsumoto & Ekman, 1989). Japan is the second most frequent sample to be included in facial expression recognition studies. Japanese participants generally produced lower accuracy rates than U.S. participants, with correct identification ranging from 30% to 82% (Biehl et al., 1997; Ekman et al., 1969, 1987; Izard, 1971; Matsumoto, 1992; Matsumoto & Ekman, 1989; Yik & Russell, 1999).

The percentage of accurate identification for the disgust expression across all non-U.S. samples ranges from 29% (New Guinea Pidgin) to 98% (Malaysia; Biehl et al., 1997; Ekman et al., 1969, 1987; Haidt & Keltner, 1999). The reported accuracy rates for recognition studies that have included disgust are depicted in Table 5.1. Several patterns emerge when examining accuracy rates across samples. First, the majority of the samples achieved accuracy rates above 50%. The only groups to yield scores below 50% were New Guinea Fore and Pidgin and Japan in one study (accuracy rates were above 50% in the other six studies including Japanese samples). Some variation appeared in the samples that scored above 50%. The United States, most European countries, and the South American countries typically received

TABLE 5.1

Percentage of Accurate Identification of Disgust Expressions,
Using Forced-Choice and Free-Response Methods
in Past Cross-Cultural Studies

Study	Country (% correct identification)	Stimuli used
Forced choice		
Biehl et al., 1997	United States (81), Japan (75), Sumatra (76), Vietnam (57), Poland (83), Hungary (84)	JACFEE
Boucher & Carlson, 1980	American stimuli: United States (87), Malay (67) Malay stimuli: United States (57), Malay (52)	American stimuli: coded using FACS; Malay stimuli: created for study chosen by poser & experimenter
Ducci et al., 1982	Ethiopia (55)	Obtained from Ekman & Friesen, coded using FACS
Ekman, 1972	United States (86), Brazil (86), Chile (85), Argentina (79), Japan (82), New Guinea Dani (91), New Guinea Fore (85)	New Guinea participants used emotion story task; all others standard. Selected using the facial action scoring technique
Ekman & Friesen, 1971	New Guinea Fore adults (77, 89); children (95, 78)	Emotion story
Ekman et al., 1969	United States (82), Brazil (86), Japan (82), New Guinea Pidgin (29), New Guinea Fore (44), Borneo (not highest response)	Chosen for study
Ekman et al., 1987	Estonia (71), Germany (61), Greece (77), Hong Kong (65), Italy (89), Japan (60), Scotland (79), Sumatra (70), Turkey (74), US (86)	Chosen for study using FACS
Haidt & Keltner, 1999[a]	United States (78), India (83)	Chosen for study using FACS
Hejmadi et al., 2000[a]	United States (96, 60, 92), India (65, 57, 52)	Created emotion portrayals based on classic Indian dance texts
Huang et al., 2001	Chinese (50); compared with past U.S. results	JACFEE
Izard, 1971	United States (83), English (85), German (73), Swedish (88), French (79), Swiss (78), Greek (88), Japanese (56), African (55)	Chosen for study
Matsumoto, 1992	United States (91), Japan (75)	Same as Matsumoto & Ekman, 1989
Matsumoto & Ekman, 1989	United States (78), Japan (68)	Created for study using FACS
McAndrew, 1986	Malaysia (98)	From Ekman & Friesen (1975)
Yik & Russell, 1999	Canada (57), Chinese (57), Japan (30)	From Ekman & Friesen (1976)

(*continues*)

TABLE 5.1

Percentage of Accurate Identification of Disgust Expressions,
Using Forced-Choice and Free-Response Methods
in Past Cross-Cultural Studies   *(Continued)*

Study	Country (% correct identification)	Stimuli used
Free Response		
Haidt & Keltner, 1999[a]	United States (64), India (82)	Chosen for study using FACS
Hejmadi et al., 2000[a]	United States (83, 65, 74), India (67, 54, 71)	Created emotion portrayals based on classic Indian dance texts
Russell et al., 1993	Narrow criteria: Canada (62), Greece (68), Japan (50) Broad criteria: Canada (66), Greece (68), Japan (56)	JACFEE

Note. JACFEE = Japanese and Caucasian Facial Expressions of Emotion (Matsumoto & Ekman, 1988); FACS = Facial Action Coding System (Ekman & Friesen, 1978).
[a]Two studies included both forced-choice and free-response conditions in their studies. Results for each type of method are presented in the corresponding section.

accuracy ratings above 75%. Canada and Germany produced lower accuracy scores than their neighboring countries and did not produce accuracy scores above 75%. The samples from Asia and Africa tended to fall in the 50% to 75% accuracy range. In sum, these findings suggest that the Western and South American cultures tended to be more accurate in their identification of the disgust expression than non-Western cultures. As the majority of the studies used Western posers and language (as the original word), this may suggest that culture and/or language may have some influence on the recognition of facial expressions.

Isolated Cultures

Although the majority of the facial expression recognition studies have used participants from either Western or Western-influenced cultures, some research has been done using participants from isolated cultures. Ekman and Friesen (1971) recruited participants from the Fore linguistic cultural group of New Guinea. Participants with both minimal and some contact with Western culture were recruited and selected for participation. Participants were read a brief story designed to depict a particular emotion and then asked to pick the appropriate reaction from photographs that depicted facial expressions associated with various emotions. Although New Guinea participants yielded low accuracy scores on the traditional facial recognition task in a previous study (Ekman et al., 1969), the accuracy ratings were much higher with this modified method. The disgust facial expression was identified the majority of the time and significantly more often than the other facial expressions presented in both disgust stories by both adults ("smell story," 77% correct; "dislike story," 89% correct) and children ("smell story," 95% correct; "dislike story," 78% correct; Ekman & Friesen, 1971). There were no significant differences in accuracy between the more Western-influenced and the less Western-influenced groups. In a similar study, Ekman (1972) had participants from New Guinea's Fore and Dani groups complete the emotion story task described earlier. The disgust expression was the most frequent expression associated with the disgust story by both groups (Fore, 85% accuracy; Dani, 91% accuracy). The finding that the accuracy rates for members of isolated cultures were similar to past findings using college students from Western or Western-influenced cultures was interpreted as support for the notion that disgust is a universal emotion with a clearly identifiable facial expression.

In addition to examining the accuracy of the recognition of the disgust expression, the production of the disgust expression has also been tested with members of isolated cultures. Ekman (1972) conducted an emotion expression production study using members of the New Guinea Fore culture that did not participate in the recognition task. Participants were read the emotion stories used in the recognition task and asked to make the facial expression that would appear if they were in that situation. U.S. college students were later asked to identify the emotion depicted in the Fore facial expressions, and they accurately identified the Fore disgust expressions 46% of the time (Ekman, 1972). This was considered an accurate judgment of the disgust expression and interpreted as further support for the universality of the disgust expression.

Free Response

One criticism of the standard emotion recognition task is its use of forced-choice response options, and it has been suggested that this method exaggerates the similarity of emotions between cultures (Russell, 1994). Although the forced-choice method provides a list of emotions as options for the participant to choose from, free-response methods require the participants to answer without any form of guidance. The participants are instead allowed to select the emotion they feel fits the expression best. For example, a participant may see a picture of a positive expression and think the expression represents excitement. When the free-response method is used, the participant is able to provide excitement as the perceived emotion. On the contrary, if the forced-choice method is used, then participants' options are limited. In that case, participants are likely to choose the answer that is the closest to their chosen emotion. Thus, if asked to choose from happiness, anger, sadness, and disgust participants' final answer is likely to be happiness rather than their original response of excitement. Two studies that compared free responses provided by participants from America with those from India reported disgust as the most frequent response provided for the disgust expression (Haidt & Keltner, 1999; Hejmadi, Davidson, & Rozin, 2000). Moreover, whereas some of the percentages were lower than what is typically reported, using the forced-choice method, all samples identified disgust at a rate above 50% (Haidt & Keltner, 1999; Hejmadi et al., 2000). A third study that allowed participants to provide their own response recruited participants from Canada, Greece, and Japan (Russell, Suzuki, & Ishida, 1993). Disgust was the modal response to the disgust expression and was provided by 50% or greater of the participants in all three samples (Russell et al., 1993). Table 5.1 depicts the percentage of participants that provide disgust as the correct response for the disgust expression in the free-response studies. These studies suggest that although the percentage of correct identification may be lower by using free-response methods compared with fixed-choice methods, participants still accurately identify the disgust emotion the majority of the time.

Additional Emotions

The standard facial recognition task has also been criticized for instructing participants to choose only one of a list of emotions, which could give the illusion that emotions are more discrete and the cultures are more similar than they are in reality (Russell, 1994). Two studies have varied the standard emotion recognition task to allow participants to list multiple emotions as being portrayed in the emotion expression. In both of the studies, the disgust label was the most frequently listed emotion for the disgust expression (Ekman et al., 1987; Yrizarry, Matsumoto, & Wilson-Cohn, 1998). However, analyses done by Yrizarry et al. (1998) revealed that the amount of variance accounted for by the disgust response that predicted the disgust photograph in their study was 44% in the American sample and 15% in the Japanese sample. Both studies indicated that contempt was listed as a secondary emotion to disgust (Ekman et al., 1987; Yrizarry et al., 1998), and one reported anger as an emotion frequently listed along with disgust (Yrizarry et al., 1998). Yrizarry et al. (1998) concluded that the finding of additional nontarget emotions does not contradict the universality thesis as long as the target emotion was rated as most salient.

Social Message

Facial expressions of emotion also function to convey information to others (Fridlund, 1994). In addition to the standard selection of the appropriate emotion, Yik and Russell (1999) asked Canadian, Cantonese-speaking Chinese, and Japanese-speaking Japanese participants to identify the social message conveyed by photographs of facial expressions. The disgust emotion was correctly identified at a rate higher than base rate in all three cultures. Whereas disgust was the highest endorsed emotion statement ("I'm feeling disgusted") for the disgust expression in the Canadian and Chinese samples, anger ("I'm really mad") was the highest endorsed emotion statement for the disgust expression by the Japanese sample (Yik & Russell, 1999). The disgust-relevant social message ("That stinks!") was the highest endorsed social message for the disgust expression in all three samples (Yik & Russell, 1999).

The association among disgust, anger, and contempt found in the studies conducted by Yrizarry and colleagues (1998) and Yik and Russell (1999) can be explained by the contempt, anger, and disgust (CAD) triad hypothesis, which suggests that CAD are critical and related moral emotions (Rozin, Lowery, Imada, & Haidt, 1999) that are elicited by specific sociocultural norm violations. The violations are classified into one of three ethics used by various cultures: community (communal codes, including hierarchy), autonomy (individual rights), and divinity (purity–sanctity; Shweder, Much, Mahapatra, & Park, 1997). Contempt is proposed to be related to community violations, anger to autonomy violations, and disgust to divinity violations. Rozin et al. examined the cross-cultural validity of the CAD hypothesis by recruiting participants from the United States and Japan to participate in a series of studies. Participants in both samples assigned the hypothesized emotion label and facial expression to the corresponding violation the majority of the time. When asked to produce a facial expression appropriate to a situation, U.S. participants (Japanese participants were not included in this study) produced facial expressions consistent with the emotion proposed to be evoked by each situation. According to the CAD triad hypotheses, the emotions of contempt, anger, and disgust may cluster together in a functional manner to maintain social order across cultures.

Alternative Methods

Extending beyond the labeling of emotion methodology, two cross-cultural studies used the relived emotion task to examine cross-cultural manifestations of disgust. The relived emotion task examines the production of facial expressions in participants when remembering situations in which they experienced specific emotions (Hmong Americans vs. European Americans: Tsai & Chentsova-Dutton, 2003; Scandinavian Americans vs. Irish Americans: Tsai, Chentsova-Dutton, Freire-Bebeau, & Przymus, 2002). The facial muscles AU4, AU9, and AU10 (using the FACS, Ekman & Friesen, 1978) were found to be more associated with disgust than other emotions in all cultural groups (Tsai & Chentsova-Dutton, 2003; Tsai et al., 2002).

In an attempt to assess the natural expression of emotion, Ekman (1972) videotaped American and Japanese participants as they watched neutral and stress-inducing film clips. The researchers observed the facial expressions displayed by the participants while watching the film clips and recorded the frequency of the emotion expressions displayed. Both Japanese and American participants displayed disgust reactions while viewing the stress-inducing clip (the frequency of disgust expressions was 48 and 61, respectively). The author noted that disgust was the expression that differed in frequency the most between the neutral and stressful clips. These findings suggest that disgust is a natural response to negative stimuli in both the United States and Japan.

Another variation on the standard facial emotion expression recognition task used expressions displayed in dance from classic Hindu texts that provide a theory of emotion and a detailed account of how classic emotions should be expressed (Hejmadi et al., 2000). The photographs in the recognition task place an emphasis on the hands in addition to the face. American and Indian participants were assigned to either the free-response or fixed-response condition, and three disgust portrayals were presented in each condition. Disgust was the most common response to the disgust emotion portrayals in all pictures and conditions. Percentage of correct recognition ranged from 60% to 96% in the fixed-response condition and from 65% to 83% in the free-response condition (Hejmadi et al., 2000). The study provided support for the universality of disgust while using stimuli derived from a non-Western culture.

Intensity

Although facial expression identification is an important component, the examination of multiple emotion dimensions is needed to achieve a clearer conceptualization of the universality of the disgust emotion. Several studies have looked at estimates of the intensity of expressions across cultures. Results across studies have not consistently supported differences or lack of differences between cultures in the perceived intensity of disgust facial expressions. Two studies compared intensity ratings between Japanese and American participants. Although Matsumoto and Ekman (1989) did not find any significant differences in intensity ratings, Matsumoto, Kasri, and Kooken (1999) found differences between American and Japanese participants in both the perceived expression and the experience of disgust. The authors suggested that participants may differentiate between the perceived intensity of the external display of the expression (i.e., the intensity of the other person's portrayal of the emotion) and the intensity of the experience at the time the expression is being displayed (i.e., the intensity of the person's internal experience when displaying the emotion). Whereas the American participants rated the expression as more intense than the Japanese participants, the Japanese participants rated the experience as more intense than the American participants (Matsumoto et al., 1999). Within-group examination of the relation between experience and expression revealed that American participants rated the expression as more intense than the experience, whereas the Japanese rated expression and experience as equally intense.

Several studies examined perceived intensity in American participants with various cultural identifications. Matsumoto (1993) found that American participants that identified themselves as Black rated photographs of facial expressions of disgust as more intense than participants that identified themselves as Caucasian or Asian. Tsai and colleagues (2002) provided participants with an emotion and corresponding description then asked them to recall a time when they felt the emotion very strongly, focus on the moment when they felt the emotion, and relive the emotion. No differences were found between Hmong Americans and European Americans in displayed or perceived intensity during the relived emotion tasks. Similarly, Tsai and Chentsova-Dutton (2003) reported no significant differences in the displayed intensity of the disgust expression between American participants with Scandinavian and Irish ancestors.

Two studies used a larger number of culturally diverse samples to examine perceived intensity. Biehl et al. (1997) examined participants from six countries: Hungary, Japan, Poland, Sumatra, the United States, and Vietnam; they later classified the countries as Western (United States, Poland, and Hungary) or non-Western (Japan, Vietnam, and Sumatra) for analyses. Results indicated that the Western countries rated half (four out of eight) of the disgust photographs as more intense than the non-Western countries, but there were no significant differences in the intensity ratings of the other disgust photographs (Biehl et al., 1997). In one of the more comprehensive cross-cultural studies of emotion to date, Ekman et al. (1987) recruited participants from 10 countries: Estonia, Germany, Greece, Hong Kong, Italy, Japan, Scotland, Sumatra, Turkey, and the United States. The perceived intensity ratings obtained revealed significant differences between countries on perceived intensity but failed to find a pattern underlying the differences (Ekman et al., 1987). Although cross-cultural studies that examine differences in perceived emotion have not consistently indicated differences in perceived emotion between cultures, the studies that have found differences suggest that culture is likely to have an influence on the intensity of perception and possibly experience of the emotion.

Physiology

The universality hypotheses would predict that the physiological characteristics of disgust should be similar across cultures. However, cross-cultural comparisons of the physiological responses of disgust are rare. Two studies examining physiological patterns between specific cultures when reliving disgust experiences reported no differences in skin conductance levels (Hmong Americans vs. European Americans: Tsai & Chentsova-Dutton, 2003; Scandinavian Americans vs. Irish Americans: Tsai et al., 2002).

In a more comprehensive assessment of physiology, Levenson, Ekman, Heider, and Friesen (1992) recruited male participants from the Minangkabau culture of West Sumatra to participate in a directed facial action task. The Minangkabau culture is a matrilineal, Muslim, agrarian culture with strong beliefs about the inappropriateness of public displays of negative emotion. Findings in Minangkabau culture were compared with previous findings obtained in the United States. To create the disgust facial expression, participants were instructed to wrinkle their noses while opening the mouth, pull the lower lip down, and move the tongue forward without sticking it out (Levenson et al., 1992). Overall, the disgust configuration was associated with less heart-rate acceleration, less finger pulse transmission time, less finger pulse amplitude (actually showing a decrease in amplitude), a shortening of respiratory period, and less deepening of respiration. Disgust displayed significantly less heart-rate acceleration than anger, fear, and sadness (with happiness in between). Disgust and happiness showed significantly greater shortening of finger pulse transmission time than sadness (with anger and fear in between). Disgust and fear were associated with significantly more shortening of respiratory period than happiness (with anger and sadness in between). Finally, disgust was associated with significantly less respiratory depth than happiness (with the other emotions in between). The Culture × Emotion interaction was nonsignificant for all of the physiological measures except for respiratory depth, suggesting that the differences between emotions were not different across the cultures. Although the Minangkabau participants displayed facial configurations of a lower quality than American participants on most emotions, the two samples did not display significantly different levels of quality of the disgust configuration. However, the Minangkabau participants rated the creation of the facial configuration as more difficult than the American participants and were less likely to report experiencing disgust while maintaining the facial configuration.

Elicitors of Disgust

One characteristic of disgust that has been theorized as likely influenced by culture is the common elicitor of the emotion (Ekman, 1994). The standard method of assessing elicitors of disgust is to ask the participants to list stimuli that evoke the emotion. However, studies have varied on how they have classified and reported the participants' responses. Some researchers have reported general themes of responses. Results suggest that Hmong Americans, European Americans, Scandinavian Americans, and Irish Americans typically listed events that revolved around another's person's actions as elicitors of disgust (Tsai & Chentsova-Dutton, 2003; Tsai et al., 2002). The Hmong American and European American samples also frequently listed nonhuman organisms or objects as elicitors of disgust (Tsai et al., 2002).

Curtis and Biran (2001) examined disgust elicitors provided by participants in previous studies. The samples included participants that were recruited from India, Burkina Faso, the Netherlands, the United Kingdom, and an international airport sample (included individuals from Europe, Greece, the United States, the Middle East, and Africa). As shown in Table 5.2, many similarities in disgust elicitors were provided across samples. For example, feces appear to be salient disgust stimuli for humans across cultures. After reviewing the participants' responses, the authors provided five categories of disgust elicitors that best captured the cross-cultural data: (a) bodily excretions and body parts, (b) decay and spoiled food, (c) particular living creatures, (d) certain categories of "other people," and (e) violations of moral or social norms (Curtis & Biran, 2001). The authors concluded that the provided elicitors supported a disease avoidance model of disgust and provided examples of pathogens related to each common elicitor (e.g., feces are related to infectious intestinal diseases caused by pathogens such as salmonella).

Other studies have classified the disgust elicitors by using preselected, theoretically derived dimensions. Haidt and Keltner (1999) presented pictures of facial expressions to participants who were asked to provide a description of an event that may have happened to the person to cause them to feel that way. The provided situations were classified into one of five general domains: other-critical, self-conscious, negative, positive, cognitive. These domains were then split in to a total of 15 subcodes (other-wrong, unpleasant-social, self-wrong, social exposure, failure, loss, unpleasant physical, danger, success, pleasant social, pleasant physical, comedy, unexpected, confused, and thinking). For example, the negative domain was split into four subcodes: failure, loss, unpleasant-physical, and danger. The authors described disgust as "taking in or being too close to an indigestible object or idea" (Haidt & Keltner, 1999, p. 249). On the basis of this conceptualization, it was predicted that situations provided

TABLE 5.2
Examples of Disgust Elicitors Provided in Five Culturally Diverse Samples

Country	Common disgust elicitors
India	Feces, urine, toilets, worn clothes, flies, insects, dead rats, dead crickets in food, rotting flesh
Burkina Faso, West Africa	Feces, unswept yard, flies on food, dirty latrine, diarrhea, sores, dirty food, worms, impure substances associated with birth
Netherlands	Feces, hairs, vermin, cats, dogs, rotten waste, aphids in lettuce, pollution, drug users
United Kingdom	Feces, vomit, wounds, stained kitchen, flies, rotten food, dirty hotel, drunks, rude people
International airport	Feces, animal saliva, spitting, sweat, vomit, rotten food, bad smells, insects, mucus

Note. Data from Curtis and Biran (2001).

as elicitors of the disgust facial expression would fall into the general negative category and the more specific unpleasant-physical category. Events with negative implications for the self's goals, attachments, and hedonics were assigned to the negative category. Events that fall in the unpleasant-physical category described exposure to things that are physically unpleasant. Results indicated that participants' provided elicitors of disgust were primarily in line with the predictions, with 73% of the U.S. responses and 93% of the Indian responses in the negative domain and 58% of the U.S. responses and 59% of the Indian responses classified as unpleasant-physical. Therefore, the majority of participants in both the United States and India made associations between situations and the expression of disgust consistent with predictions, suggesting that the disgust facial expression was interpreted similarly by both groups.

Galati et al. (2005) asked participants from Italy, Spain, and Cuba to describe events that elicit strong emotions but did not specify which emotion experiences to describe. After the identification of the situation, participants were asked to rate the eliciting event on the following dimensions: novelty, pleasantness, goal relevance, coping potential, and compatibility with social and individual norms. Unfortunately, the free-response method used resulted in a small number of disgust events described ($n = 9$), and no analyses of between-group differences in antecedent events were conducted. When the events were considered across groups, the events provided suggested that antecedents to the experience of disgust were novel, unpleasant, not goal conducive, not controllable, often attributed to another person, compatible with individual norms, and not compatible with social norms (Galati et al., 2005).

Scherer and colleagues (Scherer, 1997; Scherer & Wallbott, 1994) examined emotion-eliciting events and event appraisals by recruiting participants from 37 countries to recall and provide information about events that elicited various emotions. The researchers found that although some variation between cultures existed, the similarities outweighed the differences. Emotion profiles were created summing across the countries, rather than describing the profiles for each country or region individually. Results indicated that disgust is an emotion that is experienced frequently, as most of the participants were able to remember recent experiences that elicited the emotions (Scherer & Wallbott, 1994). In addition, disgust was described as a short-lived emotion, with most of the experiences described lasting between a few minutes and an hour. Taken together, the participants' responses suggested that disgust was low in intensity, relatively freely expressed, accompanied by low physiological responses, and related to withdrawal behaviors (Scherer & Wallbott, 1994). The participants' responses also suggested that disgust had negative effects on relationships, was accompanied by little nonverbal behavior, and often resulted in short utterances (Scherer & Wallbott, 1994).

Participants' responses were also used to examine the qualities and universality of the emotion-eliciting events (Scherer, 1997). Results suggested that disgust-eliciting events are often unexpected, unpleasant, highly immoral, and unfair (Scherer, 1997). The responses also suggested that disgust did not have a clear causality and typically did not function as a hindrance to a goal. However, the disgust profile based on the chosen dimensions was weaker than some of the other emotion profiles, such as joy, anger, and guilt, and it often resulted in the misclassification of disgust-eliciting events as anger-eliciting events. Immorality was the dimension that best discriminated disgust from the other emotions. When the emotion profiles were compared across the culture regions, the disgust profiles were intercorrelated with $r = .61$. However, this intercorrelation was the lowest of the included emotions (joy, anger, fear, sadness, guilt, and shame), indicating that the profiles showed some variation between cultures (Scherer, 1997). The authors did note that the lower correlation could be partly due to the lack of a clear and distinct profile for disgust. The overall pattern of correlation of emotion profiles suggested that Latin American and African profiles were less similar to the other regions (North/Central Europe, the Mediterranean Basin, the New World, and Asia).

Haidt et al. (1997) obtained information about disgust elicitors by interviewing nonnative English speakers living in the United States about disgust-equivalent words in other languages. Words that linked bodily concerns and social and moral concerns were found in most languages, but the types of social and moral concerns described across cultures revealed some differences. For example, American sociomoral disgust is typically elicited by perceived character flaws of others, such as violations of basic dignities of other human beings or the possession of offensive beliefs or attitudes. Japanese descriptions of sociomoral disgust typically referred to everyday social interactions in which other people failed to meet the individual's needs or expectations or the individual failed to meet his or her own standards. The authors concluded that moral disgust is often experienced when their basic assumptions or expectations about the order of society are not met. Using this approach, the American and Japanese differences described earlier can be explained by the individualistic and collectivist natures of the countries. This conceptualization allows for variation between cultures and suggests that the similarity of these disgust elicitors should be related to the similarity of the culture's morals and social natures.

Certain foods are also regarded as elicitors of disgust (Haidt, McCauley, & Rozin, 1994), and there are cross-cultural differences in the degree to which foods are regarded as disgusting. Indeed, it has been noted that in the United States, there is a particular association between the experience of disgust and food, whereas in Hindu India, the experience of disgust is more often associated with interpersonal and moral violations (Rozin, 1999). Although spiders are often appraised as disgusting in Western cultures, in many other areas of the world (i.e., Indo-China, the Caribbean, and Africa) spiders are frequently eaten as a delicacy (Bristowe, 1932, 1945). A belief common in many cultures, perhaps more so in Western cultures, is "you are what you eat" (Rozin, 1990). This belief suggests that an individual takes on some of the physical, behavioral, and intentional properties of the consumed item (Rozin & Nemeroff, 1990). A disgust response to a food item can therefore be a reaction to either the item itself or to someone or something the item was in contact with prior to consumption. Rozin (1990) suggested that these beliefs explain some cultural practices related to food, such as refusing to eat food prepared by an enemy or someone of a lower class.

Fears

Disgust has been linked with the development and maintenance of several anxiety symptoms and disorders, including small animal phobia, blood-injection-injury (BII) phobia, and obsessive–compulsive disorder (OCD; Olatunji & Sawchuk, 2005). However, cross-cultural findings that link disgust and anxiety disorder symptoms are very limited. Davey et al. (1998) did examine animal fears in seven countries (i.e., Hong Kong, Japan, India, Korea, the Netherlands, United Kingdom, and United States). Participants rated their level of fear toward 51 animals. Factor analyses revealed that a three-factor structure was supported in all samples. The three factors represented animals that were fear irrelevant (generally not responded to with fear; e.g., rabbit, sheep), fear relevant (considered fierce; e.g., lion, tiger), disgust relevant (associated with dirt, disease, and contagion; cockroach, spider). The authors reported that the animals that loaded on the disgust relevant factor were fairly consistent across cultures, with cockroach, spider, worm, leech, bat, lizard, and rat significantly loading on the disgust relevant factor across all seven countries. Differences between the countries did emerge, however; Indian participants reported lower levels of fear to the disgust relevant animals than did all other countries, and Japanese participants reported significantly higher levels of fear toward disgust-relevant animals than did participants from India, United Kingdom, United States, Korea, and Hong Kong. Similarly, the Indian disgust relevant fear factor contained fewer animals than the other countries, whereas the Japanese disgust-relevant fear factor contained more animals than all other countries. Although some differences did emerge, disgust-related animal fears appeared to be more similar than different across countries.

Olatunji, Sawchuk, de Jong, and Lohr (2006) examined the relation between disgust sensitivity and BII fears in U.S. and Dutch samples. U.S. participants reported higher levels of disgust toward foods, sex, envelope violations (i.e., injections), hygiene, death, and sympathetic magic (stimuli without infection qualities of their own that either resemble contaminants or were once in contact with contaminants) domains. No differences emerged between the U.S. and Dutch participants on disgust toward small animals and body products domains. However, the samples did differ in their levels of BII fears, with U.S. participants reporting greater fears of injections and blood draws, and Dutch participants reporting greater fears of mutilations. Disgust sensitivity and level of BII fears were correlated in both samples, but the correlation was stronger in the U.S. sample (medium to large) than in the Dutch sample (small to medium). However, the hypothesized relations between disgust and BII fears were found in both samples. The findings suggest that the frequency and strength of disgust sensitivity may vary by culture but that some basic relations between disgust sensitivity and phobic fears are likely to exist.

Sawchuk, Olatunji, and de Jong (2006) examined differences in the relation between disgust and contamination-based OCD in U.S. and Dutch samples. Stepwise regression analyses revealed that disgust toward injections and blood draws, hygiene, and smells reliably predicted contamination fear scores in both samples. However, disgust toward injections and blood draws was the dominant predictor in the Dutch sample, whereas disgust toward hygiene concerns was the dominant predictor in the U.S. sample. Furthermore, although female gender was a significant, independent predictor in the U.S. sample, this variable did not successfully predict contamination concerns in the Dutch sample. Subsequent comparisons of core and animal reminder disgust domains suggested that contamination fear in the Dutch sample is best predicted by a combination of core and animal reminder disgust elicitors, whereas contamination fear in the U.S. sample was best predicted by only core disgust domains.

Emotion Language

One challenge in cross-cultural research is overcoming the language barrier. To compare results across countries, it is essential that participants in all countries are participating in the same study. This requires that instructions, questions, and answers be similar across cultures. In emotion recognition studies, it is essential that the words chosen to represent specific emotions have the same meaning in all languages. Complicating the translation process, all of the proposed basic emotions are represented by single words in the English language, whereas other languages may not have an appropriate word to represent the emotion, may not differentiate between two of them, or include emotions important to that culture that do not have an English translation (Haidt & Keltner, 1999; Russell, 1991).

Cross-cultural research typically relies on translation and back translation to ensure that words are equivalent across languages. To achieve this, one translator is asked to translate a word from its original language into the new language. A second translator is then asked to translate the word in the new language back to the original language. The production of the original word in the back translation is interpreted to mean that the chosen word in the new language is the correct interpretation of the original word. However, little research has examined the effectiveness of this process. What research does exist has cast some doubt on the appropriateness of this procedure. Russell and Sato (1995) compared the original English word with the equivalent words in Japanese and Chinese identified through the back translation process for 14 emotion words, including disgust. Instead of asking the participants to identify the emotion portrayed in a photograph of a facial expression, the participants were asked to "judge (on a seven point scale) how good each face shown was as an expression of someone who feels X, where X was one of the emotion words" (Russell & Sato, 1995). The authors then examined the correlations between samples. Twelve of the 14 emotion words were designated as good translations after yielding high correlations. However, disgust was one of the problem words. The Japanese word for disgust was dissimilar to the English and Chinese words (which were similar to each other). The Japanese word for disgust was correlated at .18 with the English word and at .09 with the Chinese word (the English and Chinese words were correlated at .83; Russell & Sato, 1995). When the words were depicted in a two-dimensional space, with valence and arousal as the dimensions, the Chinese and English disgust words fell in a similar area on the plot near angry and scared. The Japanese word fell in a different area of the plot, near the words related to sadness. These results suggest that traditional methods for identifying appropriate translations of disgust may not be as effective as was formerly believed.

CONCLUSION

Disgust is a basic human emotion that may be characterized by a unique signal, physiological response, and theme of antecedent events (Ekman, 1999). Cross-cultural studies of disgust have examined each characteristic. The signal that has received the most attention is the facial expression associated with disgust (i.e., upturned upper lip, wrinkled nose, and dropping of the mouth corners). This facial expression has been associated with the emotion of disgust at rates higher than predicted by chance in numerous studies, using varied methodologies and samples (Biehl et al., 1997; Ekman et al., 1969, 1987; Ekman & Friesen, 1971; Haidt & Keltner, 1999; Hejmadi et al., 2000; Huang, Tang, Helmseste, Shiori, & Someya, 2001; Matsumoto, 1992; Matsumoto & Ekman, 1989; Russell et al., 1993; Yik & Russell, 1997). In forced choice studies, disgust was reported as the emotion most commonly associated with the disgust photograph in all but two cases (Ekman et al., 1969; Yik & Russell, 1997). Findings have revealed that the modification of the basic identification task to allow participants to provide their own emotion has only slightly reduced the percentage of participants labeling the disgust expression with the disgust emotion and has consistently resulted in 50% or greater correct identification (Haidt & Keltner, 1999; Hejmadi et al., 2000; Russell et al., 1993). However, Western cultures have somewhat consistently yielded higher accuracy scores than non-Western cultures (Ekman et al., 1969; Matsumoto, 1992; Matsumoto & Ekman, 1989).

The examination of disgust recognition in isolated cultures has produced mixed findings, with participants producing higher accuracy rates when asked to pair a face with an emotional story as opposed to the typical pairing of the emotion word with the facial expression (Ekman et al., 1969; Ekman & Friesen, 1971). Despite these differences, participants across cultures have consistently paired the disgust emotion with the disgust facial expression, which provides support for the universal experience of the disgust emotion. Providing additional support for the universality of the disgust emotion, the few studies comparing the physiology related to disgust between cultures have suggested that the physiological reaction is similar across cultures (Tsai & Chentosva-Dutton, 2003; Tsai et al., 2002; Levenson et al., 1992).

Although findings suggest that the presence of disgust appears across cultures, some of the characteristics of disgust may be vulnerable to cultural influence. Several studies that examined the perceived intensity of facial expressions of disgust revealed significant differences across cultures (Biehl et al., 1997; Ekman et al., 1987; Matsumoto, 1993; Matsumoto et al., 1999). Although general themes of disgust elicitors appear to be consistent across cultures, some variation appears in the specific elicitors provided by participants from different cultures (Haidt et al., 1997; Haidt & Keltner, 1999; Scherer, 1997; Scherer & Wallbott, 1994; Tsai & Chentsova-Dutton, 2003; Tsai et al., 2002). Taken together, the extant research suggests that disgust is a universal emotion. However, cultural variations may influence the experience and elicitors of disgust.

Additional cross-cultural research on disgust is needed to clarify inconsistencies between past findings and to address questions that have thus far remained unanswered. Russell and Sato's (1995) findings related to the accuracy of the back-translation process have some dire implications for both future and past research. Past research has typically relied on the back translation process to validate their methods. Additional research assessing more advanced ways of ensuring the meanings of words across languages is needed. Another limitation of the reviewed research is that disgust has predominantly been studied along with other emotions. Studies that examine disgust independent of other emotions would be able to obtain information specific to disgust and allow for a more detailed inspection of the emotion, likely identifying more subtle differences between cultures.

The progression of cross-cultural work has been described, using a series of phases that evolve from noticing differences to explaining differences (Matsumoto & Yoo, 2006). Phase one studies included examinations of cross-cultural comparisons that document differences between studies without providing information about the source of the differences. Phase two of cross-cultural research consists of the identification of meaningful dimensions of cultural variability. These dimensions describe ways that cultures might differ from each other, such as the individualism versus collectivism distinction. Phase three identifies ways to predict and explain these differences in the individuals within the culture. Matsumoto and Yoo (2006) suggested that the majority of previous cross-cultural research has fallen into one of the previous three phases. However, a new phase of cross-cultural research that consists of linkage studies are desperately needed (Matsumoto & Yoo, 2006). Linkage studies are described as empirical tests of the link between the observed differences and the cultural sources proposed to explain the differences. Linkage studies should assess and empirically test all of the assumptions in proposed mediational models. For example, if researchers hypothesized that differences in trait anxiety between Culture A and Culture B led to the differences in disgust between the two cultures, a corresponding linkage study would have to empirically test the differences trait anxiety and disgust in the two countries along with the relation between trait anxiety and disgust. The majority of the studies that examine disgust cross-culturally have been Phase one studies that simply assess and report differences between cultures. The most common variable that has been theorized to be related to disgust differences is individualism-collectivism (e.g., Haidt et al., 1997; Matsumoto, 1992; Matsumoto et al., 1999). As research that examines the experience of disgust continues to move forward, it is suggested that future cross-cultural research focus on assessing differences in disgust in less studied areas (e.g., the development of disgust, the relation between disgust and psychopathology) with emphasis on offering theoretical models that can explain differences that may exist.

REFERENCES

Abe, J. A., & Izard, C. E. (1999). The developmental function of emotions: An analysis in terms of differential emotions theory. *Cognition & Emotion, 13,* 523–549.

Biehl, M., Matsumoto, D., Ekman, P., Hearn, V., Heider, K., Kudoh, T., & Ton, V. (1997). Matsumoto and Ekman's Japanese and Caucasian facial expressions of emotion (JACFEE): Reliability data and cross-national differences. *Journal of Nonverbal Behavior, 21,* 3–21.

Boucher, J. D., & Carlson, G. E. (1980). Recognition of facial expression in three cultures. *Journal of Cross-Cultural Psychology, 11,* 263–280.

Bristowe, W. S. (1932). Insects and other invertebrates for human consumption in Siam. *Transactions of the Entymological Society of London, 80*, 387–404.

Bristowe, W. S. (1945). Spider superstitions and folklore. *Transactions of the Connecticut Academy for Arts and Science, 36*, 53–90.

Curtis, V., & Biran, A. (2001). Dirt, disgust, and disease. *Perspectives in Biology and Medicine, 44*, 17–31.

Darwin, C. (1965). *The expression of the emotions in man and animals*. Chicago: University of Chicago Press. (Original work published 1872)

Davey, G. C. L., McDonald, A. S., Hirisave, U., Prabhu, G. G., Iwawaki, S., Jim, C. I., et al. (1998). A cross-cultural study of animal fears. *Behavior Research and Therapy, 36*, 735–750.

Ducci, L., Arcuri, L., Georgis, T. W., & Sineshaw, T. (1982). Emotion recognition in Ethiopia: The effect of familiarity with Western culture on accuracy of recognition. *Journal of Cross-Cultural Psychology, 13*, 340–351.

Ekman, P. (1972). Universals and cultural differences in facial expressions of emotion. In J. K. Cole (Ed.), *Nebraska symposium on motivation: Vol. 19. Cultural psychology* (pp. 207–283). Lincoln: University of Nebraska Press.

Ekman, P. (1992). An argument for basic emotions. *Cognition & Emotion, 6*, 169–200.

Ekman, P. (1994). Strong evidence for universals in facial expressions: A reply to Russell's mistaken critique. *Psychological Bulletin, 115*, 268–287.

Ekman, P. (1999). Basic emotions. In T. Dalgleish & M. Power (Eds.), *Handbook of cognition and emotion* (pp. 45–60). New York: Wiley.

Ekman, P., & Friesen, W. V. (1971). Constants across cultures in the face and emotion. *Journal of Personality and Social Psychology, 17*, 124–129.

Ekman, P., & Friesen, W. V. (1975). *Unmasking the face: A guide to recognizing emotions from facial clues*. Englewood Cliffs, NJ: Prentice Hall.

Ekman, P., & Friesen, W. V. (1978). *Facial Action Coding System: A technique for the measurement of facial movement*. Palo Alto, CA: Consulting Psychologists Press.

Ekman, P., & Friesen, W. V. (1986). A new pan-cultural facial expression of emotion. *Motivation & Emotion, 10*, 159–168.

Ekman, P., Friesen, W. V., O'Sullivan, M., Chan, A., Diacoyanni-Tarlatzis, I., Heider, K., et al. (1987). Universals and cultural differences in the judgments of facial expressions of emotion. *Journal of Personality and Social Psychology, 53*, 712–717.

Ekman, P., Levenson, R. W., & Friesen, W. V. (1983, September 16). Autonomic nervous system activity distinguishes among emotions. *Science, 221*, 1208–1210.

Ekman, P., Sorenson, E. R., & Friesen, W. V. (1969, April 4). Pan-cultural elements in facial displays of emotion. *Science, 164*, 86–88.

Fridlund, A. J. (1994). *Human facial expression: An evolutionary view*. San Diego, CA: Academic Press.

Galati, D., Schmidt, S., Sini, B., Tinti, C., Manzano, M., Roca, M., et al. (2005). Emotional experience in Italy, Spain, and Cuba: A cross-cultural comparison. *Psychologia, 48*, 268–287.

Haidt, J., & Keltner, D. (1999). Culture and facial expression: Open-ended methods find more expressions and a gradient of recognition. *Cognition & Emotion, 13*, 225–266.

Haidt, J., McCauley, C., & Rozin, P. (1994). Individual differences in sensitivity to disgust: A scale sampling seven domains of disgust elicitors. *Personality and Individual Differences, 16*, 701–713.

Haidt, J., Rozin, P., McCauley, C., & Imada, S. (1997). Body, psyche, and culture: The relationship between disgust and morality. *Psychology and Developing Societies, 9*, 107–131.

Hejmadi, A., Davidson, R. J., & Rozin, P. (2000). Exploring Hindu Indian emotion expressions: Evidence for accurate recognition by Americans and Indians. *Psychological Science, 11*, 183–187.

Huang, Y., Tang, S., Helmeste, D., Shioiri, T., & Someya, S. (2001). Differential judgment of static facial expressions of emotions in three cultures. *Psychiatry and Clinical Neurosciences, 55*, 479–483.

Izard, C. E. (1971). *The face of emotion.* East Norwalk, CT: Appleton-Century-Crofts.

Izard, C. E. (1991). *The psychology of emotions.* New York: Plenum.

Izard, C. E. (1992). Basic emotions, relations among emotions, and emotion–cognition relations. *Psychological Review, 99*, 561–565.

Levenson, R. W. (1992). Autonomic nervous system differences among emotions. *Psychological Science, 3*, 23–27.

Levenson, R. W., Ekman, P., & Friesen, W. V. (1990). Voluntary facial action generates emotion-specific autonomic nervous system activity. *Psychophysiology, 27*, 363–384.

Levenson, R. W., Ekman, P., Heider, K., & Friesen, W. V. (1992). Emotion and autonomic nervous system activity in the Minangkabau of West Sumatra. *Journal of Personality and Social Psychology, 62*, 972–988.

Matsumoto, D. (1992). American-Japanese cultural differences in the recognition of universal facial expressions. *Journal of Cross-Cultural Psychology, 23*, 72–84.

Matsumoto, D. (1993). Ethnic differences in affect intensity, emotion judgments, display rules, and self-reported emotional expression in an American sample. *Motivation & Emotion, 17*, 107–123.

Matsumoto, D., & Ekman, P. (1988). *Japanese and Caucasian facial expressions of emotion (JACFEE)* [Slides]. San Francisco, CA: Intercultural and Emotion Research Laboratory, Department of Psychology, San Francisco State University.

Matsumoto, D., & Ekman, P. (1989). American-Japanese cultural differences in intensity ratings of facial expressions of emotion. *Motivation & Emotion, 13*, 143–157.

Matsumoto, D., Kasri, F., & Kooken, K. (1999). American-Japanese cultural differences in judgments of expression intensity and subjective experience. *Cognition & Emotion, 13*, 201–218.

Matsumoto, D., & Yoo, S. H. (2006). Toward a new generation of cross-cultural research. *Perspectives on Psychological Science, 1*, 234–250.

McAndrew, F. T. (1986). A cross-cultural study of facial recognition thresholds for facial expressions of emotion. *Journal of Cross-Cultural Psychology, 17,* 211–224.

Olatunji, B. O., & Sawchuk, C. N. (2005). Disgust: Characteristic features, social implications, and clinical manifestations. *Journal of Social and Clinical Psychology, 24,* 932–962.

Olatunji, B. O., Sawchuk, C. N., de Jong, P. J., & Lohr, J. M. (2006). The structural relation between disgust sensitivity and blood-injury-injection fears: A cross-cultural comparison of US and Dutch data. *Journal of Behavior Therapy and Experimental Psychiatry, 37,* 16–29.

Rozin, P. (1990). Social and moral aspects of food and eating. In I. Rock (Ed.), *The legacy of Somolon Asch: Essays in cognition and social psychology* (pp. 97–110). Hillsdale, NJ: Erlbaum.

Rozin, P. (1999). Food is fundamental, fun, frightening, and far-reaching. *Social Research, 66,* 9–30.

Rozin, P., Haidt, J., & McCauley, C. R. (2000). Disgust. In M. Lewis & J. M. Haviland-Jones (Eds.), *Handbook of emotions* (2nd ed., pp. 637–653). New York: Guilford Press.

Rozin, P., Lowery, L., Imada, S., & Haidt, J. (1999). The CAD triad hypothesis: A mapping between three moral emotions (contempt, anger, disgust) and three moral codes (community, autonomy, divinity). *Journal of Personality and Social Psychology, 76,* 574–586.

Rozin, P., & Nemeroff, C. J. (1990). The laws of sympathetic magic: A psychological analysis of similarity and contagion. In J. Stigler, G. Herdt, & R. A. Shweder (Eds.), *Cultural psychology: The Chicago symposia on human development* (pp. 205-233). New York: Cambridge University Press.

Russell, J. A. (1991). Culture and categorization of emotions. *Psychological Bulletin, 110,* 426–250.

Russell, J. A. (1994). Is there universal recognition of emotion from facial expression? A review of the cross-cultural studies. *Psychological Bulletin, 115,* 102–141.

Russell, J. A. (1995). Facial expressions of emotion: What lies beyond minimal universality? *Psychological Bulletin, 118,* 379–391.

Russell, J. A., & Sato, K. (1995). Comparing emotion words between languages. *Journal of Cross-Cultural Psychology, 26,* 384–391.

Russell, J. A., Suzuki, N., & Ishida, N. (1993). Canadian, Greek, and Japanese freely produced emotion labels for facial expressions. *Motivation & Emotion, 17,* 337–351.

Sawchuk, C. N., Olatunji, B. O., & de Jong, P. J. (2006). Disgust domains in the prediction of contamination fear: A comparison of Dutch and US samples. *Anxiety, Stress, & Coping, 19,* 397–407.

Scherer, K. R. (1997). Profiles of emotion-antecedent appraisal: Testing the theoretical predictions across cultures. *Cognition & Emotion, 11,* 113–150.

Scherer, K. R., & Wallbott, H. G. (1994). Evidence for universality and cultural variation of differential emotion response patterning. *Journal of Personality and Social Psychology, 66*, 310–328.

Shweder, R. A., Much, N. C., Mahapatra, M., & Park, L. (1997). The "Big Three" of morality (autonomy, community, divinity) and the "Big Three" explanations of suffering. In A. M. Brandt & P. Rozin (Eds.), *Morality and health* (pp. 119–169). New York: Routledge.

Tomkins, S. S., & McCarter, R. (1964). What and where are the primary affects? Some evidence for a theory. *Perceptual and Motor Skills, 18*, 119–158.

Tsai, J. L., & Chentsova-Dutton, Y. (2003). Variation among European Americans in emotional expression. *Journal of Cross-Cultural Psychology, 6*, 650–657.

Tsai, J. L., Chentsova-Dutton, Y., Freire-Bebeau, L., & Przymus, D. E. (2002). Emotional expression and physiology in European Americans and Hmong Americans. *Emotion, 2*, 380–397.

Yik, M. S. M., & Russell, J. A. (1999). Interpretation of faces: A cross-cultural study of a prediction from Fridlund's theory. *Cognition & Emotion, 13*, 93–104.

Yrizarry, N., Matsumoto, D., & Wilson-Cohn, C. (1998). American-Japanese differences in multiscalar intensity ratings of universal facial expressions of emotions. *Motivation & Emotion, 22*, 315–327.

6

THE PSYCHOPHYSIOLOGY OF DISGUST: MOTIVATION, ACTION, AND AUTONOMIC SUPPORT

SCOTT R. VRANA

A major theme of this text is that the study of disgust has been largely ignored until fairly recently. This is certainly true in the literature on the psychophysiology of emotion. The emotion categories that have received the most attention from psychophysiological researchers are those in which psychophysiological phenomena have the most direct implications for psychopathology and physical health: fear, with its implications for diagnosis and treatment of anxiety disorders (Lang, 1968), and anger, with implications for Type A personality and cardiovascular disease (al'Absi & Bongard, 2006). This lack of attention has been unfortunate for progress on psychopathology, particularly anxiety disorders, as noted in other chapters. In addition, semantic overlap between disgust and anger gives investigations of the psychophysiology of disgust the potential to contribute to the study of cardiovascular disorders and makes it uniquely suited to answer some important questions about basic issues in emotion. This chapter reviews findings on the psychophysiology of disgust and its implications for basic research on emotion. First, however, an approach to emotion is described that will allow the research on disgust to be put in context.

AN APPROACH TO THE PSYCHOPHYSIOLOGY OF EMOTION

Emotions are generally considered to be action dispositions that organize and direct behavior, and prepare the body for action (Lang, 1979, 1995). They are typically investigated in the laboratory through measurement of self-reported affect, physiological response, and behavior. These three systems of emotion are loosely organized; that is, each system is multiply determined and to some extent separately determined and are only moderately correlated with each other (Lang, 1968).

Many theorists organize the emotional terrain into a small set of primary or fundamental emotions, usually including (at least) joy, sadness, anger, fear, and disgust. Although there is variation in each of the three systems across these fundamental emotion categories, many theorists believe that emotion can be most profitably organized around two dimensions. The primary dimension is *valence* (Mehrabian, 1970; Russell, 1980). This dimension provides the motivational direction (approach–avoidance) for behavior. The second dimension, *arousal*, instantiates the vigor of activity required for the behavior. In addition to being organized along these dimensions, all emotional phenomena also involve context-specific tactical behaviors that are determined by the needs of the specific emotional situation. Very often the specific emotion categories are best defined by the context-specific behaviors associated with them: The prototypical fear behavior is flight; the prototypical anger behavior is fighting. However, sometimes these tactical behaviors are very different for the same basic emotion, depending on the situational context; for example, fear may involve headlong flight or immobile freezing, and anger may elicit a warning scowl or an appeasing smile.

The psychophysiology of an emotional situation is dependent on (at least) the motivational system (appetitive–aversive), the vigor of activation required for the emotional behavior (high or low arousal), and the specific tactical behavioral requirements of the situation. The implications of each aspect for the psychophysiology of disgust are reviewed in detail in later sections, but briefly: Much work over the last 15 years (reviewed in Bradley, Cuthbert, & Lang, 1999) has showed that the startle reflex response indexes emotional aversiveness; in addition, facial expression, particularly activity at the corrugator muscle, is a robust measure of negative valence (Witvliet & Vrana, 1995). Arousal or activation is measured through activity in the autonomic nervous system (Witvliet & Vrana, 1995), most commonly using heart rate (HR) or skin conductance, an index of skin sweat activity; in addition, significant activation also affects general somatic muscle activity.

The tactical behavioral output, or readiness for specific behavioral response, can be seen in multiple psychophysiological channels. The energy requirements for the specific behavioral dispositions prompted by the situation often are evident in the autonomic nervous system as the organism prepares for vigorous action; in addition, specific muscle movements (measured through electromyography [EMG]) in the face or limbs may also be part of the context-specific emotional action pattern or facial-expressive display. Social signaling as part of an emotional action pattern (e.g., a sneer and furrowing of the brow to signal the intention to attack) may also be measured in facial EMG (Fridlund, 1992). As already noted, these behavioral requirements and their attendant physiological profile may differ within the same emotion category. For example, the psychophysiology of fear might be significant HR and muscle tension increase preparatory to flight for an animal phobic but might involve little heart-rate change for a social phobic when the behavioral disposition is hypervigilant scanning for negative evaluation in social situations (McNeil, Vrana, Melamed, Cuthbert, & Lang, 1993). Thus, the psychophysiology of emotion is dependent on preparation for the specific action appropriate to the situation in which the emotion occurs.

To measure its psychophysiology effects, emotion must be evoked in the laboratory through some internal or external stimulus such as imagery, still pictures, video, music, smell, social interaction, or an in vivo presentation. These methods of emotional evocation engage perceptual and cognitive processes, and perceptual and cognitive processes have their own psychophysiological effects. The most common distinction found in research on the psychophysiology of perceptual and cognitive processes is between the intake of stimulus information from the environment as opposed to rejection of information from the environment during effortful cognitive processing (Lacey, 1967). Stimulus intake evokes the orienting response, one component of which is HR deceleration. The orienting response, and consequent HR decrease, is larger with more interesting, complex, or meaningful stimuli. Conversely, stimulus rejection to process information internally results in HR acceleration, with greater HR acceleration associated with more effortful information processing (Panayiotou & Vrana, 1998). Fear-eliciting pictures (e.g., of snakes, guns, attacking dogs, angry faces) are typically more interesting and meaningful than neutral pictures (e.g., household objects, neutral faces). Consequently, for all but the most fearful individuals, viewing fear pictures results in larger HR decreases than viewing neutral pictures (Hamm, Cuthbert, Globisch, & Vaitl, 1997). However, internally generated imagery of these same fear contents results in larger HR increases than imagining a neutral scenario.

In sum, the psychophysiological response to an emotional situation can be largely accounted for through the motivational dimension (aversive vs. appetitive) of the emotional situation, the behavioral/energetic requirements of the emotional context, the specific tactical actions required in the situation, and the perceptual and cognitive requirements of the emotional processing task. From this perspective, asking the question, "What is the psychophysiology of emotion?" is not a particularly fruitful inquiry. Also, "What is the psychophysiological response to disgust?" is too broad a question unless one takes into consideration the perceptual, cognitive, and behavioral requirements of the specific situation. That is, there is no one particular psychophysiological profile of disgust. Rather, there is a response to perceiving and processing significant information from the environment, evaluating it, and then developing and carrying out an adaptive response to the situation. Different response output channels (e.g., HR, skin sweat activity, facial expression) can have consistent or different responses to activation of disgust, depending on the task requirements.

DISGUST AND THE BASIC ISSUES OF EMOTION

This chapter reviews data on the psychophysiology of disgust as a function of the motivational dimension of disgust, the vigor of the behavioral requirements of the disgust context, the specific behaviors required in the situation, and the perceptual and cognitive requirements of the task. It has already been noted that, as a fundamental emotion, disgust has been significantly understudied. However, as other chapters in this volume make clear, many facets of anxiety disorders have been newly examined in light of recent theorizing about disgust, and these new approaches can be used to reexamine old data for their relevance to disgust. For example, studies of psychophysiology have often used common phobic stimuli such as animals or insects; more recent thinking on phobia (Davey, Cavanagh, & Lamb, 2003) has made the distinction between phobic processes associated with danger (e.g., large dogs, lions) and those associated with disgust related to contamination and disease (e.g., rats, cockroaches).

Throughout the 1990s the most common stimuli used in studies of the psychophysiology and neurobiology of emotion have been slides from the International Affective Picture Set (IAPS; Lang, Bradley, & Cuthbert, 1995), a set of over 500 still pictures spanning an extraordinarily wide range of contents and emotional qualities. A common design in studies that use the IAPS is to combine a variety of picture contents into the affective categories of positive (e.g., pictures of opposite-sex nudes, appetizing food, children), neutral (e.g., pictures of household objects, faces of people displaying neutral expressions), and negative to examine the influence of the affective dimension of valence on psychophysiological response. In most studies the negative category includes fear-inducing pictures (attacking animals, angry faces) as well as common disgust themes such as contamination-related animals and mutilated bodies and faces. In fact, pictures that depict mutilation are among the most powerfully aversive contents (Bradley, Codispoti, Cuthbert, & Lang, 2001). Unfortunately, in most studies the specific content of the pictures was subsumed under the overall negative affect category, and therefore the specific effect of disgust cannot be ascertained; however, more recent studies have investigated the specific effects of picture contents such as mutilation, illness, and pollution (e.g., Bradley et al., 2001) so that the effect of disgust-related themes can be examined. Thus, although it has only recently received explicit attention, disgust has played an important and underappreciated role in basic studies of psychophysiological response to aversive emotional content, often in the guise of "negative" or "fear" stimulus categories.

Disgust is also important to the study of basic emotion because of the light it can shed on the desynchrony between the different systems of emotional expression. The approach to emotion taken in this chapter is that one's verbal report of emotional experience in a situation can be considered another response output channel; one that, like psychophysiological responses, is multiply determined by the perceptual, cognitive, and behavioral context of the specific situation. To a great extent, the report of emotional experience can be considered a semantic evaluation task that is largely determined by the meaning of emotional words in the participant's language and culture (Vrana, Cuthbert, & Lang, 1986), whereas the expressive physiology may derive from the fundamental action disposition involved in the emotional context (Lang, 1979); for example, fighting or fleeting in contexts labeled *anger* or *fear*.

In this view, when consistency between verbal report of emotion and physiological response is found (typically in the $r = .30$ range), it is because of consistency between the semantic labels for a situation and the action required in that situation, not because the verbal report and physiology are the result of an emotional experience. That is, the report of fear and higher HR co-occur because the sort of situations we label as "fear" are situations in which we are disposed to run away, and the act of running requires cardiovascular mobilization to support the energy needs of this vigorous behavior. This suggests that synchrony between verbal report and physiological measures of emotion will not occur when the judged semantic meaning of the situation is not consistent with the fundamental action disposition. For example, social phobics may label their social concerns as *fear* without showing accelerated HR, if their primary behavioral disposition in a social context is passive worry or hypervigilant search for signs of negative evaluation, rather than active flight. Synchrony and desynchrony between verbal, physiological, and behavioral expressions of emotion have long been of interest to clinical psychologists and emotion researchers (Lang, 1968; Rachman & Hodgson, 1974), who have found increased synchrony to be a reliable predictor of exposure treatment outcome (Beckham, Vrana, May, Gustafson, & Smith, 1990).

The emotion of disgust provides a particularly interesting perspective on desynchrony. When considered as a primary or fundamental emotion (e.g., Ekman & Friesen, 1975; Izard, 1971; Plutchik, 1980; Tomkins, 1963), disgust is typically defined as "Revulsion at the prospect of (oral) incorporation of an offensive object" (Rozin & Fallon, 1987, p. 23). Using this definition, the initiating stimulus (some offensive or contaminating material) and the adaptive action disposition (avoiding or expelling the material) are clear. However, another English-language definition of disgust incorporates a sense of moral disapproval of another's actions or appearance (Ekman & Friesen, 1975); a typical dictionary definition of this version of disgust is "a strong feeling of dislike, finding a thing very unpleasant, or against one's principles" (*Oxford American Dictionary*, 1980). Using this definition, one can report disgust with someone's moral behavior, political viewpoint, or even, to quote one memorable journal article title, "Disgust with life in general" (Finlay-Jones, 1983). Moreover, more often than not, it is this moral sense of the word that people point to when asked what disgusts them (Haidt, Rozin, McCauley, & Imada, 1997), resulting in a kind of desynchrony between the most prevalent common-language definition of disgust and the scientific definition of disgust as a fundamental emotion. However, it seems that the initiating stimulus for this common-usage sort of disgust varies widely across people, and the typical action disposition associated with this type of disgust is not at all clear. Thus, one could imagine someone reporting equally intense disgust at the possibility of drinking sour milk or listening to Rush Limbaugh (or Al Franken), yet the psychophysiological response would be quite different in these two cases.

THE MOTIVATIONAL SUBSTRATE OF DISGUST

Lang (1995), starting with a dimensional view of emotion, described emotion as being organized around two motivational systems: an appetitive system that involves approach toward objects that promote survival and a defensive–aversive system that involves avoidance or withdrawal from objects that threaten survival. As noted earlier, there may be significant variability in the semantic definition of disgust, and the psychophysiological profile attendant in the perceptual, cognitive, and behavioral tasks involved in the elicitation of disgust in the laboratory. However, one clearly agreed-on aspect of disgust is its place on the defensive–aversive dimension of emotion. Regardless of whether the disgust is elicited by four-legged vermin or a political ideology; irrespective of the specific behavior prompted by the object of disgust, the emotion is always negative in valence, and the basic motivational direction involves avoidance or escape. At least two psychophysiological measures have been consistently associated with the defensive–aversive motivational dimension: potentiation of the startle reflex response and increased activity at the corrugator supercilli facial muscle region.

Startle Reflex Response

More than a decade of research (reviewed in Bradley et al., 1999) has revealed the startle reflex response to be a robust index of the defensive motivational system. The startle reflex is elicited by an intense, sudden-onset stimulus (e.g., a loud noise or a bright flash of light). The response in human beings is initially a full-body contractile response that quickly habituates, leaving an eyeblink response that is typically measured in laboratory studies as the change in muscle tension at the orbicularis oculi, the muscle that circles the eye and tenses to shut the eye (Graham, 1975). The magnitude of the startle reflex is enhanced, and the onset latency of the reflex is shortened when a startling stimulus is presented while an aversive stimulus is being processed. Startle response augmentation has been found with a wide variety of methods that elicit aversive processing, including viewing negative pictures from IAPS (Vrana, Spence, & Lang, 1988), fear imagery (Vrana & Lang, 1990), noxious smells (Miltner, Matjak, Braun, Diekmann, & Brody, 1994), aversive conditioning (Hamm, Greenwald, Bradley, & Lang, 1993), and threat of shock (Grillon, Ameli, Woods, Merikangas, & Davis, 1991).

In the first study to specifically examine the startle reflex response to disgust material (Vrana, 1994), undergraduate participants memorized brief sentences describing disgusting (e.g., "As I chew on a mouthful of salad, I watch a cockroach scatter from my salad plate onto the table"), anger-inducing (e.g., "I sit helplessly in traffic as an old junker rear-ends my new car, then cuts into the wrong lane; I look as hard as I can but it gets away before I get the license plate number"), and neutral (e.g., "At the end of a long day of studying I am sitting on the couch watching a documentary on TV") situations. After memorization to a criterion, participants were instructed to imagine actively participating in the scenes when cued by tones of different pitches that indicated which scene to imagine. Ninety-five dB(A) white noise (50-milliseconds long) startling stimuli were presented during imagery periods and relaxation periods. Startle reflex responses were greater when elicited during disgust or anger imagery than during neutral imagery, and responses during disgust and anger imagery did not differ in their magnitude.

As noted earlier, most studies using the IAPS slides to investigate the effects of affective valence on psychophysiological response included mutilation pictures, which could be considered related to disgust in the negative category. The large majority of studies have found robust response augmentation when the startling stimulus is presented while a participant is viewing negative affective pictures, compared with positive or neutral pictures. Hamm et al. (1997) were the first to examine mutilation pictures as a separate category, and they found that viewing these pictures augmented the magnitude of the startle reflex response to a startling auditory stimulus compared with the startle response elicited while viewing affectively neutral slides, particularly among mutilation-fearful participants. Yartz and Hawk (2002) elicited the startle response while participants viewed fearful, neutral, pleasant, disgust/blood, or disgust/other pictures and found that the startle response was augmented while viewing negatively valent pictures compared with pleasant pictures with no difference in startle magnitude between the two different disgust-relevant categories. Mean startle responses during disgust pictures were nonsignificantly larger than during fear pictures overall; although among women, startle responses were significantly larger during disgust than during fear pictures.

Bradley et al. (2001) have taken the most finely grained look at the effect of specific IAPS slide contents on the startle reflex response, including five negatively valent picture contents potentially relevant to disgust (mutilation, accidents, contamination, illness, and pollution), as well as three other negative contents (human attack, animal attack, and loss), and seven positively valent picture contents (opposite sex nudes, erotic couples, adventure, food, nature, sports, and family). Overall, the startle responses to a 95-dB(A), white-noise probe were larger while viewing negative compared with positive pictures. Within the negative stimulus contents, the mean content differences generally tracked the rated aversiveness of the content, and the statistical comparisons between categories of negative pictures were generally not significant. Similarly, Stanley and Knight (2004) found that startle responses were larger while viewing disgust pictures than when viewing positive pictures, and startle responses during disgust pictures did not differ from startle responses while viewing either neutral or threat pictures. Like Stanley and Knight (2004), Balaban and Taussig (1994) did not find a difference between startle reflex responses elicited during disgust and neutral pictures; unlike the other studies described here, this study found that startle responses elicited during disgust pictures were significantly smaller in magnitude than startle responses elicited during threat pictures. The balance of findings, however, support the contention that viewing disgust pictures results in startle reflex magnitude augmentation at a level similar to other negative, high-arousal emotional contents.

The startle reflex response is also modified by negative affect induced by unpleasant odors. The studies that have been completed in this area have primarily described their odor manipulations as eliciting negative affect, although one might surmise that unpleasant odors would more frequently be associated with disgust than with other negative emotion categories such as fear, anger, or sadness. In fact, one study that asked for specific emotional reactions to unpleasant odors found that the most frequently named emotion was disgust (Alaoui-Ismaili, Robin, Rada, Dittmar, & Vernet-Maury, 1997). Additionally, it seems that olfactory stimulation intuitively would be more effective in eliciting disgust than most other emotion elicitation methods; even imagining the odors used in these studies (e.g., hydrogen sulfide, limburger cheese, and smoked cigar butts) evokes a response. The four studies that have investigated startle reflex modification by odor (Ehrlichman, Brown, Zhu, & Warrenburg, 1995, 1997; Kaviani, Wilson, Checkley, Kumari, & Gray, 1998; Miltner et al., 1994) have all found that the startle reflex response was augmented during exposure to unpleasant odors compared with a neutral or no-odor condition.

Given the success of the odor manipulation in activating the defensive–aversive system as indexed by startle reflex modification, and the evident connection between odor and disgust, the use of odor as a disgust elicitor is a promising area for future research.

Corrugator Supercilii EMG

Another reliable index of negative affect processing is EMG activity at the corrugator supercilii muscle region. The corrugator muscle is above the eye, and activity in this area furrows the brow in a frown. Many studies (see Dimberg, 1990, and Fridlund & Izard, 1983, for early reviews) have found increases in corrugator EMG while processing a variety of negative emotions and decreases in activity at the corrugator EMG during positive emotion processing, regardless of the method used to induce emotion. Consistent with findings using other negative emotions, disgust increases corrugator EMG activity compared with neutral and positive emotional processing during viewing of IAPS pictures (Bradley et al., 2001; Hamm et al., 1997; Yartz & Hawk, 2002) or imagining disgusting scenarios (Vrana, 1993, 1994). In fact, Yartz and Hawk (2002) found greater corrugator activity while participants viewed disgusting compared with fear-inducing images, and two other studies (Bradley et al., 2001; Hamm et al., 1997) that presented pictures in multiple categories revealed greater corrugator activity while viewing mutilation pictures compared with all other picture categories.

SPECIFIC BEHAVIORAL DISPOSITIONS IN DISGUST

It is clear that disgust is part of the defensive–aversive motivational system, as indexed by consistently augmented startle reflex responses and increased corrugator (frown) muscle activity during disgust processing. Complementary to falling along the defensive–aversive motivational system, the specific function of disgust is the avoidance or expelling of noxious or offensive substances from the mouth. The typical behaviors engaged to accomplish this function include a characteristic facial expression, recognized by Darwin (1872), involving closing off the nostrils to avoid an unpleasant odor and opening the mouth to either passively or actively expel disgusting contents. As a fundamental emotion, this facial expression of disgust is found across cultures (Ekman, 1973) and in human neonates (Steiner, 1979). This expression is also found across species; for example, in rats exposed to bitter tastes (Grill & Norgren, 1978). In human beings, this facial expression can be measured as EMG activity at the levator labii (superioris and alesque nasi), a muscle that lies alongside the nose and when tensed wrinkles the nose to close the nostrils and raises the upper lip to open the mouth.

In the first study to evaluate the hypothesis that levator labii EMG activity is specifically sensitive to disgust (Vrana, 1993), participants imagined disgusting, anger-inducing, joyful (positive and highly arousing), and pleasantly relaxing scenarios described in single, evocative sentences, with imagery cued by tones of different frequencies. Results showed that EMG at the levator labii muscle region was significantly greater during disgust imagery than during anger or pleasure imagery. Replicating many previous results, EMG activity at the corrugator supercilli muscle region differentiated negative from positive imagery, and EMG activity at the zygomaticus major muscle region (which pulls the corners of the mouth back into a smile) were greatest during joy imagery (joy imagery produced a high level of activity at the levator labii as well, but this was demonstrated to be due to cross-talk with zygomaticus activity). This study is important as the first demonstration of a specific pattern of facial EMG activity during disgust, and it is one of the few studies that have shown a reliable difference in EMG activity between two negative emotions in a large group of unselected participants.

These results were replicated in a subsequent imagery study (Vrana, 1994). Later studies have revealed that EMG activity at the levator labii increases while viewing disgusting pictures from the IAPS. Yartz and Hawk (2002) found that levator labii activity was greater during disgust compared with fear-picture viewing, a result that held regardless of picture valence or arousal or interest level, disgust subtype (blood or other), or participant gender. Schienle, Stark, and Vaitl (2001) found greater levator labii activity to disgust pictures than to neutral or pleasant pictures specifically among disgust-sensitive and blood-fearful participants. The same research group (Stark, Walter, Schienle, & Vaitl, 2005) later found increased levator labii while viewing general disgust (like poor hygiene or perished food) and disgust/mutilation pictures compared with the viewing of neutral pictures.

Several notable features of the Vrana (1993) study bear mentioning. First, even though, as predicted, participants rated themselves as feeling high levels of disgust during the anger images, participants displayed high levels of levator labii during disgust images but not during anger images. That each participant imagined several different disgust and anger scenarios was used to test the limits of this effect, by comparing each participant's anger image rated as most disgusting and each participant's disgust image rated as least disgusting. In this way, a set of anger and disgust images was created that was *matched on self-reported disgust* (actually, the anger images in this set were rated as nonsignificantly more disgusting, and significantly more negative, than the disgust images). Levator labii was significantly greater during disgust than anger imagery, even with this matched set of images. This represents a dramatic demonstration of a desynchrony between the self-reported experience of disgust and the facial expressive pattern characteristic of disgust, and it illustrates the general principle that semantic meaning of the emotion word is at variance with the specific behavioral requirements of the emotional situation.

A second notable feature of this study is a demonstration that the facial expression of disgust is specifically associated with the functional behaviors (expelling noxious substances from the mouth) relevant to the situation. Some of the disgust scenarios in this study involved expelling noxious orally ingested stimuli (e.g., "Waking up drowsily, I feel a slimy movement on my upper lip; slowly I grab for it but I was too slow—the slug had already moved into my mouth"), and some scenarios did not (e.g., "I listen as the obese man in the next booth lets out a riveting belch; the smell of the fried foods he just binged on churns my stomach").[1] Levator labii activity was found to be greater during imagery that involved orally expelling stimuli than for nonoral disgust imagery, despite these images having nearly identical disgust, valence, arousal, and vividness ratings. Thus, the facial expression of disgust seems specifically related to the functional behavioral action pattern particular to the emotion—it is found to a much lesser extent during anger imagery and during disgust situations not requiring that behavioral action, even though the self-reported experience of disgust was equal in these different situations. This desynchrony between the self-reported experience of disgust and the facial expression is hard to reconcile with theories of emotion that assert that emotional report and facial expression are both reflections of an internal emotional experience. However, these data are consistent with the idea that verbal report and facial expression are differently determined; the former by a semantic judgment about the meaning of the situation and the latter by the behavioral demands of the emotional situation.

This is not to say that the behavioral demands of the situation are the only cause of an emotional response. Although levator labii activity was largest in disgust contexts that required oral expulsion, there was some activity in the other disgust images. When a noxious or disgusting stimulus is encountered, the full range of behavioral dispositions may be activated (including oral expulsion and gross motor avoidance), with only the context-relevant behaviors proceeding to completion. This phenomenon has been called a "Darwinian algorithm," in that animals err on the side of false positives in identifying and acting on situations with potential survival implications (Cosmides & Tooby, 1987). In addition, facial expressions do have social communicative functions as well as defensive or appetitive functions (Fridlund, 1992), and one might activate the levator labii intentionally to wrinkle one's nose in communication of disgust over a moral transgression or political idea.

---

[1] If one wants to know how to create stimuli like these, the answer is to ask male college freshmen for help.

Areas for Future Research

At least two other potential functions of disgust have implications for measurement of specific behavioral dispositions. Similar to the function of opening the mouth to empty noxious substances, vomiting can serve the function of expelling noxious substances that have already been consumed. The electrogastrogram (EGG) measures gastric myoelectrical activity, and increases in the spectral power of the EGG have been associated with motion sickness, feelings of nausea, and vomiting (Hu, McChesney, Player, Buchanan, & Scozzafava, 1999). Thus, it may be sensitive to disgust. One study looked at the effect of emotional stimuli on the EGG (Vianna & Tranel, 2006). This study found that increases in EGG spectral power were related to self-reported arousal while participants viewed film clips that evoked happiness, disgust, fear, and sadness. The effect was not specific to disgust; nevertheless, given the connection between disgust and gastrointestinal upset, additional research on disgust and EGG activity is warranted.

A second relevant function, particularly salient in the face of mutilation or bodily injury, is fainting to prevent blood loss. Fainting has been linked to disgust (e.g., Olatunji, Williams, Sawchuk, & Lohr, 2006). A diphasic vaso-vagal response, involving an initial, brief increase in HR and blood pressure followed by a swift and sustained drop and, occasionally, fainting, has been found in people with blood and injury phobia (Öst, Sterner, & Lindahl, 1984). Thus, research that examines cardiovascular response to disgust stimuli on a second-by-second basis may be useful in developing an autonomic "signature" of disgust, particularly to blood- or injury-related stimuli.

Finally, it should be emphasized that the full range of behavioral dispositions associated with disgust, and the final action pattern, may only emerge in the presence of exceptionally evocative stimuli. Thus, pictures and imagery may be at best only moderately effective ways to study the full disgust response. In this respect, research that examines the effect of unpleasant odors on levator labii EMG activity or the EGG would be an enlightening and important extension of the present literature.

THE AUTONOMIC PSYCHOPHYSIOLOGY OF DISGUST

The response of the autonomic nervous system to disgust is multidetermined. As we have seen, it can be affected by the specific behavioral requirements in the disgust situation; that is, if disgust is caused by a bodily injury, there might be a vasovagal response resulting in a reduction in HR and blood pressure designed to stem blood loss. In addition, the autonomic response of any emotional situation may involve a general cardiovascular mobilization to support the energy demands of the required behaviors. For example, preparation for a swift escape or vigorous fight would require increased HR, blood pressure, and respiratory activity to satisfy the energy demands of the body. As already described, the typical behavioral demands of disgust involve avoiding or expelling noxious substances. Thus, depending on the behavioral and energetic demands of the disgust situation, the cardiovascular response can vary from significant HR and blood pressure increase supporting active and violent expulsion of offending material, to no change (during passive avoidance of noxious substances), to significant HR and blood pressure decreases from a vasovagal response caused by bodily injury.

Finally, the perceptual–cognitive demands of the emotion-induction task affect the autonomic response in a research study. Taking in a stimulus (say, viewing a picture or a video) evokes an orienting response resulting in HR decrease, with greater orienting (i.e., greater decrease) for information that is novel, interesting, and/or meaningful, which is to say emotional. Conversely, shutting out the environment to process information cognitively (say, completing an imagery task) results in HR increase, with more effortful processing resulting in greater HR increase. The skin conductance response (SCR), which measures skin sweat activity, usually on the hand, is considered a good measure of sympathetic nervous system activity and is reactive to novel, interesting, and/or meaningful information from the environment (Boucsein, 1992). We need to keep these myriad influences on the autonomic system in mind when interpreting the research data. Because of the important cognitive–perceptual effects on the autonomic nervous system, the results are organized here by the method used to elicit disgust.

Production of Facial Expressions

Some of the earliest data on the autonomic physiology of disgust came from studies that involve the production of emotional facial expressions (Ekman, Levenson, & Friesen, 1983; Levenson, Carstensen, Friesen, & Ekman, 1991; Levenson, Ekman, & Friesen, 1990). This method involves having the participant produce an expression on his or her face through instructed movement of specific muscles, without labeling the expression as involving a particular emotion. This approach has been used as a test of the link between facial expression of emotion and other physiological and experiential components of an emotional response. In these studies, production of a disgust facial expression resulted in smaller HR increase and equivalent SCR compared with anger, fear, or sad facial expressions. Moving and holding facial muscles to produce these expressions can be seen as a physically effortful task with its own energy requirements, and a subsequent study found that these HR results can be largely accounted for by the effort required to produce the expressions (Boiten, 1996), although the original authors later disputed this interpretation of their results (Levenson & Ekman, 2002).

Picture Viewing

More recent studies have used pictures from the IAPS set or video clips to elicit disgust and have found data that are consistent with the framework described earlier. Scheinle et al. (2001) found lower HR, although no differences in blood pressure, while viewing disgust pictures than while viewing neutral or pleasant pictures. A later study by this group (Stark et al., 2005) found that orienting (i.e., HR decrease) to the disgust slides was greater with increased self-reported experience of disgust. Bradley et al. (2001) similarly found HR deceleration during pictures that depict a range of disgust-related contents (mutilation, pollution, illness, and contamination). Johnsen, Thayer, and Hugdahl (1995) found greater HR decrease while participants viewed slides from the Ekman and Friesen (1975) slide set that depict people making disgust or anger expressions than while viewing people making fear expressions. Hamm et al. (1997) found HR increase during a 6-s viewing of mutilation slides among mutilation-fearful women; however, this occurred only to the first trial, and on subsequent viewings of mutilation slides the typical cardiac deceleration was found. Similarly, Page (2003) found blood pressure increases among disgust-sensitive participants to a slide of a needle and of blood, but only one trial of each was presented. Many studies (Bradley et al., 2001; Hamm et al., 1997; Johnsen et al., 1995; Scheinle et al., 2001; Stanley & Knight, 2004; Stark et al., 2005) have measured the SCR to onset of the pictures. As would be expected on the basis of its sensitivity to interesting stimuli from the environment, all of these studies found that SCR increase was greater to disgusting pictures than to neutral, or less arousing, stimuli.

Film Viewing

Video that depicts disgust scenes, especially involving bodily mutilation or surgical procedures, have quite powerful physiological and psychological effects and are often used to manipulate emotional reaction when researchers are interested in studying the effects studies of emotional regulation. Thus, most of the studies described here have some other research agenda beyond studying the psychophysiology of disgust, and the results of interest here were abstracted from the overall results. Gross (1998; Gross & Levenson, 1993) has found HR decrease while people watch films depicting burn victims or surgical procedures. Similarly, Demeree et al. (2006) found decreased HR but also found increased respiration rate and skin conductance while participants watched a video from an animal slaughterhouse compared with watching a neutral video. Leshner, Miles, Bolls, and Thomas (2006), in an applied study, found that HR decreased while participants watched antismoking advertisements that were high in fear or disgust. Sherman, Haidt, and Coan (2006) found that HR decreased from baseline when participants watched a "moral disgust video" (depicting neo-Nazis, skinheads, and the KKK).

Imagery

One early study (Levenson et al., 1991) found that asking participants to relive a disgust experience resulted in smaller HR increases compared with anger, fear, or sadness imagery. Two subsequent studies (Vrana, 1993, 1994) found that the HR increase during disgust imagery was equal to or greater than other arousing imagery contents, including anger and joy. The difference in results in these studies may be in the content of the material. Vrana (1993, 1994) gave participants specific disgust scenarios to imagine that involved the need to orally expel or actively avoid contact with noxious substances. These scenes involved an active and arousing action set consistent with the definition of disgust as a fundamental (cross-species and cross-culture) emotion. Levenson et al.'s (1991) "relive" instruction allowed participants to relive a past emotional experience without providing a specific situational context. The relived disgust situations may have involved the sense of disgust as a strong feeling of dislike or finding something against one's principles, which is the sense of the word people more often than not identify (Haidt et al., 1997). This sort of scenario does not involve action that would require a high level of cardiovascular mobilization to support.

Odor

Several studies have examined the specific emotional qualities and autonomic responses to pleasant and unpleasant odors. Alaoui-Ismaili, Robin, et al. (1997) found that unpleasant odors were described as eliciting disgust more than any other emotion (about 60% of the time), with the second-most likely responses being anger (about 15% of the time) and surprise (about 10% of the time). This group found a response profile characteristic of the unpleasant, disgusting odors, including instantaneous HR increase, a long-lasting SCR, and high skin blood-flow responses (Alaoui-Ismaili, Robin, et al., 1997; Alaoui-Ismaili, Vernet-Maury, Dittmar, Delhomme, & Chanel, 1997). A study that measured HR and skin conductance during unpleasant and pleasant odors found the same pattern of data, although contrasts were not significant (Miltner et al., 1994). Yet another study that measured HR during unpleasant odors found *greater* HR during unpleasant odors compared with a no-odor control condition (Ehrlichman et al., 1997). There were numerous methodological differences between these studies, however, and more research is needed before any firm conclusion on the reasons for the discrepant findings can be reached.

CONCLUSION

The results of research on the psychophysiology of disgust fit nicely within the context of the research literature on the psychophysiology of emotion. The startle reflex response modification and corrugator supercilii EMG findings place disgust clearly as a negatively valent emotion and part of the defensive–aversive motivational system. The function of disgust (avoiding or expelling noxious substances) produces a specific facial expression in the presence of stimuli that activate this behavioral disposition (e.g., in the presence of noxious substances). Cardiovascular mobilization is needed to provide energy to the body to support the behaviors that are activated. In addition, the autonomic nervous system is acutely responsive to the perceptual and cognitive processing that takes place whenever emotion is evoked by external stimulus or internal cognitive activity.

The psychophysiology of disgust has been understudied compared with other fundamental emotions, at least under its own name—many studies, for example, have used videotape or still pictures that depict mutilation or surgical procedures to study emotional regulation or have used pictures of roaches or rats to study the physiology of fear. The emotion categories that have received the most attention from psychophysiological researchers, fear and anger, are those with the most direct implications for psychopathology and physical health. Disgust, as we have seen, is related in an important way to both other negative emotions, and increased attention to the psychophysiology of disgust will have implications for knowledge about psychopathology and emotion.

For example, study of phobic fear has only recently made the distinction between fear of danger and fear of contamination. Contamination fear may be more usefully conceptualized as disgust, which can have a completely different psychophysiological profile than an active avoidance response to danger. Making the distinction between fear of danger and fear of disgust or contamination in future studies could bring important conceptual and empirical clarity to a number of issues, including psychophysiological response to exposure therapy and synchrony between psychophysiology and verbal response during exposure therapy, both of which have been shown to predict treatment outcome (Beckham et al., 1990; Foa & Kozak, 1986).

Similarly, there is an overlap between the semantic use of the words *anger* and *disgust* in describing certain negative states that involve disapproval of another's actions; however, the cardiovascular profile of anger and disgust can differ significantly. Making the distinction between anger and disgust in studies of Type A behavior can increase our knowledge about the relationship between emotional response, personality, and heart disease; furthermore, making this distinction can shed light on basic issues of synchrony and desynchrony between self-reported emotion and psychophysiological response. Thus, the study the psychophysiology of disgust promises significant discoveries, and with the increasing awareness of the importance of disgust to various forms of psychopathology, it is anticipated that this literature will grow.

REFERENCES

al'Absi, M., & Bongard, S. (2006). Neuroendocrine and behavioral mechanisms mediating the relationship between anger expression and cardiovascular risk: Assessment considerations and improvements. *Journal of Behavioral Medicine, 29*, 573–591.

Alaoui-Ismaili, O., Robin, O., Rada, H., Dittmar, A., & Vernet-Maury, E. (1997). Basic emotions evoked by odorants: Comparison between autonomic responses and self-evaluation. *Physiology & Behavior, 62*, 713–720.

Alaoui-Ismaili, O., Vernet-Maury, E., Dittmar, A., Delhomme, G., & Chanel, J. (1997). Odor hedonics: Connection with emotional response estimated by autonomic parameters. *Chemical Senses, 22*, 237–248.

Balaban, M. T., & Taussig, H. N. (1994). Salience of fear/treat in the affective modulation of the human startle blink. *Biological Psychology, 38*, 117–131.

Beckham, J. C., Vrana, S. R., May, J. G., Gustafson, D. J., & Smith, G. R. (1990). Emotional processing and fear measurement synchrony as indicators of treatment outcome in fear of flying. *Journal of Behavior Therapy and Experimental Psychiatry, 21*, 153–162.

Boiten, F. (1996). Autonomic response patterns during voluntary facial action. *Psychophysiology, 33*, 123–131.

Boucsein, W. (1992). *Electrodermal activity.* New York: Plenum Press.

Bradley, M. M., Codispoti, M., Cuthbert, B. N., & Lang, P. J. (2001). Emotion and motivation. I: Defensive and appetitive reactions in picture processing. *Emotion, 1*, 276–298.

Bradley, M. M., Cuthbert, B. N., & Lang, P. J. (1999). Affect and the startle reflex. In M. E. Dawson, A. M. Schell, & A. H. Bohmelt (Eds.), *Startle modification: Implications for neuroscience, cognitive science, and clinical science* (pp. 157–183). New York: Cambridge University Press.

Cosmides, L., & Tooby, J. (1987). From evolution to behavior: Evolutionary psychology as the missing link. In J. Dupré (Ed.), *The latest on the best: Essays on evolution and optimality* (pp. 276–306). Cambridge, MA: The MIT Press.

Darwin, C. (1872). *The expression of the emotions in man and animals.* London: Murray.

Davey, G. C. L., Cavanagh, K., & Lamb, A. (2003). Differential aversive outcome expectancies for high- and low-predation fear-relevant animals. *Journal of Behavior Therapy and Experimental Psychiatry, 34*, 117–128.

Demeree, H. A., Schmeichel, B. J., Robinson, J. L., Pu, J., Everhart, D. E., & Berntson, G. G. (2006). Up- and down-regulating facial disgust: Affective, vagal, sympathetic, and respiratory consequences. *Biological Psychology, 71*, 90–99.

Dimberg, U. (1990). Facial electromyographic reactions and autonomic activity to auditory stimuli. *Biological Psychology, 31*, 137–147.

Ehrlichman, H., Brown, S., Zhu, J., & Warrenburg, S. (1995). Startle reflex modulation during exposure to pleasant and unpleasant odors. *Psychophysiology, 32*, 150–154.

Ehrlichman, H., Brown, S., Zhu, J., & Warrenburg, S. (1997). Startle reflex modulation by pleasant and unpleasant odors in a between-subjects design. *Psychophysiology, 34*, 726–729.

Ekman, P. (1973). *Darwin and facial expression: A century of research in review*. Oxford, England: Academic Press.

Ekman, P., & Friesen, W. (1975). *Unmasking the face: A guide to recognizing emotions from facial clues*. Oxford, England: Prentice-Hall.

Ekman, P., Levenson, R. W., & Friesen, W. V. (1983, September 16). Autonomic nervous system activity distinguishes among emotions. *Science, 221*, 1208–1210.

Finlay-Jones, R. A. (1983). Disgust with life in general. *Australian and New Zealand Journal of Psychiatry, 17*, 149–152.

Foa, E. B., & Kozak, M. J. (1986). Emotional processing of fear: Exposure to corrective information. *Psychological Bulletin, 99*, 20–35.

Fridlund, A. J. (1992). Darwin's anti-Darwinism in the expression of the emotions in man and animals. In K. T. Strongman (Ed.), *International review of studies on emotion* (Vol. 2, pp. 117–137). Oxford, England: Wiley.

Fridlund, A. J., & Izard, C. E. (1983). Electromyographic studies of facial expressions of emotions and patterns of emotions. In J. T. Cacioppo & R. E. Petty (Eds.), *Social psychophysiology: A sourcebook* (pp. 243–286). New York: Guilford Press.

Graham, F. K. (1975). The more or less startling effects of weak prestimulation. *Psychophysiology, 12*, 238–248.

Grill, H. J., & Norgren, R. (1978). Mimetic responses to gustatory stimuli in neurologically normal rats. *Brain Research, 143*, 263–279.

Grillon, C., Ameli, R., Woods, S. W., Merikangas, K., & Davis, M. (1991). Fear-potentiated startle in humans: Effects of anticipatory anxiety on the acoustic blink reflex. *Psychophysiology, 28*, 588–595.

Gross, J. (1998). Antecedent- and response-focused emotion regulation: Divergent consequences for experience, expression, and physiology. *Journal of Personality and Social Psychology, 2*, 224–237.

Gross, J., & Levenson, R. (1993). Emotional suppression: Physiology, self-report, and expressive behavior. *Journal of Personality and Social Psychology, 64*, 970–986.

Haidt, J., Rozin, P., McCauley, C., & Imada, S. (1997). Body, psyche, and culture: The relationship between disgust and morality. *Psychology and Developing Societies, 9*, 107–131.

Hamm, A. O., Cuthbert, B., Globisch, J., & Vaitl, D. (1997). Fear and the startle reflex: Blink modulation and autonomic response patterns in animal and mutilation fearful subjects. *Psychophysiology, 34*, 97–107.

Hamm, A. O., Greenwald, M. K., Bradley, M. M., & Lang, P. J. (1993). Emotional learning, hedonic change, and the startle probe. *Journal of Abnormal Psychology*, *102*, 453–465.

Hu, S., McChesney, K. A., Player, A. B., Buchanan, J. B., & Scozzafava, J. E. (1999). Systematic investigation of physiological correlates of motion sickness induced by viewing an optokinetic rotating drum. *Aviation, Space, and Environmental Medicine*, *70*, 759–765.

Izard, C. E. (1971). *The face of emotion*. East Norwalk, CT: Appleton-Century-Crofts.

Johnsen, B. H., Thayer, J. F., & Hugdahl, K. (1995). Affective judgment of the Ekman faces: A dimensional approach. *Journal of Psychophysiology*, *9*, 193–202.

Kaviani, H., Wilson, G. D., Checkley, S. A., Kumari, V., & Gray, J. A. (1998). Modulation of the human acoustic startle reflex by pleasant and unpleasant odors. *Journal of Psychophysiology*, *12*, 353–361.

Lacey, J. I. (1967). Somatic response patterning and stress: Some revisions of activation theory. In M. H. Appley & R. Trumbull (Eds.), *Psychological stress: Issues in research* (pp. 14–42). New York: Appleton-Century-Crofts.

Lang, P. J. (1968). Fear reduction and fear behavior: Problems in treating a construct. In J. M. Shlien (Ed.), *Research in psychotherapy* (Vol. 1, 90–202). Washington, DC: American Psychological Association.

Lang, P. J. (1979). A bio-informational theory of emotional imagery. *Psychophysiology*, *16*, 495–512.

Lang, P. J. (1995). The emotion probe: Studies of motivation and attention. *American Psychologist*, *50*, 372–385.

Lang, P. J., Bradley, M. M., & Cuthbert, B. N. (1995). The international affective picture system (IAPS): *Technical manual and affective ratings*. Gainesville: Center for Research in Psychophysiology, University of Florida.

Leshner, G., Miles, S., Bolls, P. D., & Thomas, E. (2006). Yuck: The effect of fear appeal and disgust images on processing anti-smoking ads. *Psychophysiology*, *43*, S59.

Levenson, R. W., Carstensen, L. L., Friesen, W. V., & Ekman, P. (1991). Emotion, physiology, and expression in old age. *Psychology and Aging*, *6*, 28–35.

Levenson, R. W., & Ekman, P. (2002). Difficulty does not account for emotion-specific heart rate changes in the directed facial action task. *Psychophysiology*, *39*, 397–405.

Levenson, R. W., Ekman, P., & Friesen, W. V. (1990). Voluntary facial action generates emotion-specific autonomic nervous system activity. *Psychophysiology*, *27*, 363–384.

McNeil, D. W., Vrana, S. R., Melamed, B. G., Cuthbert, B. N., & Lang, P. J. (1993). Emotional imagery in simple and social phobia: Fear versus anxiety. *Journal of Abnormal Psychology*, *102*, 212–225.

Mehrabian, A. (1970). A semantic space for nonverbal behavior. *Journal of Consulting and Clinical Psychology*, *35*, 248–257.

Miltner, W., Matjak, M., Braun, C., Diekmann, H., & Brody, S. (1994). Emotional qualities of odors and their influence on the startle reflex in humans. *Psychophysiology*, *31*, 107–110.

Olatunji, B. O., Williams, N. L., Sawchuk, C. N., & Lohr, J. M. (2006). Disgust, anxiety and fainting symptoms associated with blood-injection-injury fears: A structural model. *Journal of Anxiety Disorders*, *20*, 23–41.

Öst, L., Sterner, U., & Lindahl, I. (1984). Physiological responses in blood phobics. *Behaviour Research and Therapy*, *22*, 109–117.

Oxford American Dictionary. (1980). New York: Oxford University Press.

Page, A. C. (2003). The role of disgust in faintness elicited by blood and injection stimuli. *Journal of Anxiety Disorders*, *17*, 45–58.

Panayiotou, G., & Vrana, S. R. (1998). Performance and physiological effects of self-focused attention among socially anxious and nonanxious individuals. *Psychophysiology*, *35*, 328–336.

Plutchik, R. (1980). A general psychoevolutionary theory of emotion. In R. Plutchik & H. Kellerman (Eds.), *Emotion: Theory, research, and experience: Vol. 1. Theories of emotion* (pp. 3–33). New York: Academic Press.

Rachman, S., & Hodgson, R. (1974). I. Synchrony and desynchrony in fear and avoidance. *Behaviour Research and Therapy*, *12*, 311–318.

Rozin, P., & Fallon, A. E. (1987). A perspective on disgust. *Psychological Review*, *94*, 23–41.

Russell, J. A. (1980). A circumplex model of affect. *Journal of Personality and Social Psychology*, *39*, 1161–1178.

Schienle, A., Stark, R., & Vaitl, D. (2001). Evaluative conditioning: A possible explanation for the acquisition of disgust responses? *Learning and Motivation*, *32*, 65–83.

Sherman, G. D., Haidt, J., & Coan, J. A. (2006). Is immorality disgusting? Sociomoral disgust, throat tightness, and heart rate deceleration. *Psychophysiology*, *43*, S89.

Stanley, J., & Knight, R. G. (2004). Emotional specificity of startle potentiation during the early stages of picture viewing. *Psychophysiology*, *41*, 935–940.

Stark, R., Walter, B., Schienle, A., & Vaitl, D. (2005). Psychophysiological correlates of disgust and disgust sensitivity. *Journal of Psychophysiology*, *19*, 50–60.

Steiner, J. E. (1979). Human facial expressions in response to taste and smell stimulation. In H. W. Reese & L. P. Lipsitt (Eds.), *Advances in child development and behavior* (Vol. 13, pp. 257–295). New York: Academic Press.

Tomkins, S. S. (1963). *Affect, imagery, and consciousness: Vol. 2. The negative affects*. New York: Springer Publishing Company.

Vianna, E. P. M., & Tranel, D. (2006). Gastric myoelectrical activity as an index of emotional arousal. *International Journal of Psychophysiology*, *61*, 70–76.

Vrana, S. R. (1993). The psychophysiology of disgust: Differentiating negative emotional contexts with facial EMG. *Psychophysiology*, *30*, 279–286.

Vrana, S. R. (1994). Startle reflex response during sensory modality specific disgust, anger, and neutral imagery. *Journal of Psychophysiology, 8,* 211–218.

Vrana, S. R., Cuthbert, B. N., & Lang, P. J. (1986). Fear imagery and text processing. *Psychophysiology, 23,* 247–253.

Vrana, S. R., & Lang, P. J. (1990). Fear imagery and the startle-probe reflex. *Journal of Abnormal Psychology, 99,* 189–197.

Vrana, S. R., Spence, E. L., & Lang, P. J. (1988). The startle probe response: A new measure of emotion? *Journal of Abnormal Psychology, 97,* 487–491.

Witvliet, C. V., & Vrana, S. R. (1995). Psychophysiological responses as indices of affective dimensions. *Psychophysiology, 32,* 436–443.

Yartz, A. R., & Hawk, L. W. (2002). Addressing the specificity of affective startle modulation: fear versus disgust. *Biological Psychology, 59,* 55–68.

7

THE FUNCTIONAL NEUROANATOMY OF DISGUST

ANNE SCHIENLE

As mentioned in previous chapters in this volume, disgust is considered a basic emotion in the majority of classification systems (e.g., Ekman, 1992; Izard, 1999; Plutchik, 1980). One key assumption associated with this conceptualization of primary or prototypical emotions holds that disgust has a specific evolutionary history in which an adaptive role has developed to help the organism to deal with a particular class of stimuli critical for survival. This role most likely has its origin in the phylogenetically more primitive sensation of distaste, which is triggered by bad-tasting or spoiled food and leads to food rejection. As such, distaste, and the next psychoevolutionary stage, disgust, aim at the prevention of disease by facilitating the rejection or discharge of harmful substances from the mouth and the stomach (Rozin & Fallon, 1987; Rozin, Haidt, & McCauley, 2000). Accordingly, disgust has a basic bioregulatory function and is directly related to a particular motivational system: hunger/aversion.

If one accepts the premise that there is indeed a bioevolutionary history of disgust, then it would also seem highly probable that a system for the decoding of disgust stimuli and the initiation of adequate response strategies has evolved and would be represented in the brain. Such a neural system would be responsible for regulating the three response components of disgust, which are comprised of characteristic physiological changes (e.g., nausea), overt behaviors (e.g., open mouth with protruded tongue), and a specific subjective state that constitutes the human disgust response (e.g., feelings of repugnance, revulsion, and loathing).

Altogether, each mentioned response component of disgust (subjective, expressional, somatic) points to its roots as a revulsion response and as a basic biological motivational system that would be integrated into the brain's functions. However, what would such a central representation look like? Recent advances in the development of brain imaging technologies, such as functional magnetic resonance imaging (fMRI) and positron emission tomography (PET), coupled with greater accessibility to such apparatuses for research purposes, have helped the scientific community to establish initial insights about how the neural circuitry that underlies disgust processing functions.

At this point it should be noted that both fMRI and PET are only indirect measures of neural activity. The so-called blood oxygenation level dependent response is the most common fMRI signal. Blood oxygenation level dependent changes are a result of the fact that "working" neurons have an increased demand for oxygen. The vascular system responds to this need with an increase in cerebral blood flow to activated brain regions. As a consequence, the absolute amount of deoxygenated hemoglobin is reduced, which in turn leads to MR signal increase. Two important assets of fMRI are its high structural resolution (in the range of some millimeters) and that it is noninvasive. PET, however, is invasive and has a lower temporal resolution than fMRI. It uses radioactive substances with a short half-life (e.g., radioactive glucose) that are usually injected in the blood cycle. The molecules become concentrated in the activated brain area. When they decay, radiation is emitted, which can be detected by the scanning device.

It is my hope that this chapter presents the reader with an overview of the use of neuroimaging techniques (fMRI, PET) and how they can assist in making inferences about neural disgust correlates in the human brain. The chapter focuses on two central disgust processes: the perception of disgust and the feeling of disgust. In two consecutive sections, I review studies covering disgust elicitation and disgust decoding in healthy individuals. In a subsequent section, I consider investigations on mental and neuropsychiatric disorders that are characterized by dysfunctions in disgust processing. Those individuals suffering from these disorders can be described as being afflicted by either the experience of excessive feelings of disgust or by selective deficits in the correct classification of disgust signals. The study of both types of aberrant disgust processes seems to be a helpful approach to better understand the neural basis of this primary emotion. The last section of this chapter presents a brief summary and conclusion as well as a short indication of possible paths that future research on central disgust correlates may take.

Before the aforementioned disgust-related topics are addressed, an opening section attempts to broaden the view by looking at the functional neuroanatomy of affective processes in general. As readers will see, although modern brain imaging techniques have helped to identify some key puzzle pieces that begin to explain how the emotional brain works, a truly detailed picture that provides a comprehensive and conclusive overview of the exact mechanisms that underpin this complex system has not yet emerged. It is important to note that at present there is no general agreement on how affective processing in the brain is organized. There is, for example, disagreement about the degree of *function specificity* of emotion processors in the brain. Whereas some researchers claim that certain brain regions work highly emotion specific, others favor an integrative approach. Namely, *specific emotion processor models* postulate that certain affective experiences are mediated by specific central affect programs initiated in localized brain regions. In the narrowest sense, this would imply that these areas would be activated by one particular emotive signal or signal class but not by any other. In neuropsychological terms one would refer to a double dissociation.

Integrative multisystem models, however, are more closely connected with dimensional accounts of emotions. The core assumption holds that all emotions can be described by a small number of dimensions such as valence (positive vs. negative), motivated behavior (approach vs. withdrawal), and intensity or arousal (calm vs. excited). Accordingly, during the experiencing of different feelings certain elements of an affective brain circuitry are shared.

In the following section four influential biological theories that vary in the degree of assumed functional specificity of emotion-relevant brain systems are briefly described: (a) LeDoux (1996), (b) Rolls (1999), (c) Davidson (2001), and (d) Damasio (1999). LeDoux (1996) can be considered a proponent of the *specific emotion processor model*. Others (Davidson, 2001; Rolls, 1999) are rather sceptical of the idea that basic emotion processes are tied to very circumscribed brain areas. They favor *integrative multisystem models*. Finally, the concept by Damasio (1999) combines specificity-oriented and integration-oriented views.

NEUROBIOLOGICAL THEORIES OF HUMAN EMOTIONS

A concept of how the emotional brain works that describes (relative) emotion specificity has been put forward by LeDoux (1996, 2000). The model centers on a distinct brain structure involved in the processing of threat stimuli: the amygdala. When this brain region receives information from the sensory organs through the thalamus, a quick but also rudimentary decision is made about whether a stimulus possesses aversive qualities. It is an automatic response modus that enables the initiation of fight-or-flight responses and could therefore, by nature, be considered part of an effective emotional early warning system. This type of response is accomplished by the central amygdala, which connects with many other brain areas that control the motor and somatic components of the fear response.

Conscious feelings of fear are thought to arise from a second, slower pathway that travels first from the sensory input to the higher cortex and then afterward to the amygdala. Here, the frightening stimulus is analyzed in detail, using information from many other parts of the brain. This second pathway enables the individual to generate complex avoidance strategies in a specific threatening situation and thus helps to optimize the defense response. In summary, LeDoux's (1996) concept ascribed the amygdala a key function in a central fear circuit: "The amygdala seems to do the same thing—take care of fear responses—in all species that have an amygdala. This is not the only function of the amygdala, but it is certainly an important one" (p. 174).

Edmund Rolls (1999), who is known for his integrative neurobiological model, defined emotions as states elicited by positive and negative reinforcers. He described a two-dimensional system for the categorization of affective states, with one dimension being the presence and the other one being the absence of a reward or punishment in the environment of the individual. The elicitation of a specific emotion depends on further factors aside from the reinforcement contingency; for instance, on the intensity of the stimulus or the possibility of an individual to show an active or passive behavioral response. This implies that the omission of a reward may lead to the feeling of anger when active coping strategies are available, whereas sadness will be experienced when only passive responses are at hand. The neural pathways that are involved in this type of emotional processing are sensory cortices, which send their information to the amygdala, the insula, and the orbitofrontal cortex (OFC). Especially the amygdala and the OFC are concerned with the evaluation of the reward and punishment value of stimuli. These brain regions do not work emotion specific, but emotion integrative. Relative to this work, Rolls (1999) wrote, "Thus I suggest caution in interpreting human studies as showing that the amygdala (or orbitofrontal cortex) are involved only in certain emotions" (p. 111).

The third biological approach covers the concept of integrated and lateralized processing of emotion-relevant stimuli, and it was termed the *valence asymmetry model* by Davidson (2001). He postulated that feelings that motivate approach behavior (e.g., happiness) lead to relatively increased activation of the left prefrontal cortex (PFC). The complementary right-hemispheric PFC response pattern will be evoked when the withdrawal system becomes involved, which is the case for the emotions fear, disgust, and sadness. The model has been primarily supported by experiments that use electroencephalography, whereas in neuroimaging studies proper tests of asymmetry effects are sparse and have produced heterogeneous results. The approach by Davidson and colleagues (Davidson & Irwin, 1999; Davidson et al., 2000) has been extended by stating that not only affective states but also affective styles, that is, temporally stable response tendencies of individuals to experience certain emotions, are also based on functional frontal asymmetries. Neural traits like this could explain why a person is prone to recurrent experiences of withdrawal emotions or to the development of affective syndromes such as depression.

The following statement on neuroanatomical emotion specificity comes from Antonio Damasio (1999, p. 62): "The amygdala is necessary for fear conditioning . . . ; however, has little interest in recognizing or learning about disgust. . . ." Damasio further described that emotional experiences correlate with the activation of several brain regions that are involved in the representation or the regulation of the organism's current state. Damasio (1999) claimed that the aim of emotions is maintaining the homeostasis of the organism, which requires *subcortical* (e.g., hypothalamus, brain stem) as well as *cortical* areas (e.g., anterior cingulate cortex [ACC], insula, secondary somatosensory cortices). These regions receive signals from the viscera, the musculosceletal system, and from the internal milieu. In addition, brain areas such as the insula and the ACC also generate regulatory signals. Specific states of emotions arise through the interaction of the described brain regions, by which distinct perceptual landscapes of the organism's internal state are formed. Top-down modulations of these states are possible by means of influences executed, for example, by the OFC. Accordingly, the concept by Damasio and colleagues (Damasio, 1999; Damasio et al., 2000) holds emotion-specific assumptions that are incorporated in the concept of an integrative overall system. The described neurobiological models on emotions, or better said, on the experience of affective states, point to a fundamental conceptual problem not yet resolved and revolve around the question of whether emotion-relevant brain functions can be localized in discrete areas of the brain or whether they are represented in distributed or lateralized networks that span a number of brain regions.

A similar problem becomes apparent when looking at another process: the recognition of emotions. Typical emotive signals in the environment of humans include facial expressions. Their quick and correct identification is an important aspect of interpersonal communication and thus crucial for social interaction. Theories that address the neural basis underlying facial emotion perception are heterogeneous and can also be labeled as rather emotion specific or integrative. Haxby, Hoffmann, and Gobbini (2000) described a core brain system as well as an extended system involved in the processing of facial expressions. According to this model, their recognition relies on the inferior occipital gyrus, the lateral fusiform gyrus, and the superior temporal sulcus (STS), which together form the fundamental network. Whereas the processing of face identity can be ascribed to the fusiform face area, dynamic facial aspects are decoded in the STS. Adolphs (2002) characterized the extended system in greater detail. This system is involved in the processing of affective face components. Adolphs (2002) proposed that the recognition of facial emotion relies on a distributed network of brain structures including the occipitotemporal cortex, the amygdala, the OFC, and parietal areas. It is within this system that distinct neural circuitries may subserve individual emotions (for a review, see Calder, Lawrence, & Young, 2001).

The issues concerning the neural correlates of emotion recognition and the elicitation of affective states become even more complicated when one considers that the two processes are in fact not completely independent from one another. It is still open to debate whether the decoding of a specific emotion displayed by a sender is accompanied by the generation of the associated affective state in the receiver. Some authors have put forward the thesis that emotional facial expressions are "contagious," which would imply that both processes accompany each other (e.g., Hatfield, Cacioppo, & Rapson, 1994). According to Adolphs (2002), this would suggest that the perception of an emotion in a conspecific involves simulation of the emotional state within the relevant cortical circuitry of the observer. If this is indeed the case, then certain brain regions may in fact be relevant for more than one process. Both the amygdala and the insula, for example, may be important for the identification of emotive signals, as well as for the generation of affective states (Phillips, Drevets, Rauch, & Lane, 2003).

It is hoped that the following section will help the reader to gain an overview of how the use of fMRI and PET can assist in making inferences about the neural correlates of disgust perception and disgust feelings. To facilitate a comparison between these two domains, the section focuses on the processing of visual disgust elicitors.

THE FUNCTIONAL NEUROANATOMY OF DISGUST

The study of the functional neuroanatomy of disgust is, as of this writing, a very young research area. In contrast to another basic emotion, fear, the investigation of neural disgust correlates had been neglected for a long time in the field of affective neuroscience, until around the late 1990s, when the first fMRI experiments were conducted on the topic of disgust recognition (Phillips et al., 1997, 1998; Sprengelmeyer, Rausch, Eysel, & Przuntek, 1998). Since then, the research area has been expanded, and researchers have also started to investigate the neural substrates of disgust experiences.

Disgust Perception

The standard paradigm for the investigation of disgust perception in humans consists of the presentation of affective facial expressions. The participants are asked to look at a series of pictures of individuals whose facial mimics depict a typical expression of disgust. Concurrent with the viewing, brain activation is recorded through fMRI or PET. The responses are then compared with neutral faces, other affective expressions (e.g., fear expressions), or a fixation condition.

Phillips et al. (1997) exposed participants to pictures that show faces with disgust and fear expressions in an fMRI study. Compared with neutral faces, fear led to amygdala activation, whereas disgust stimulated the anterior insula and a set of other brain regions (the medial frontal cortex, the cingulate gyrus, the dorsolateral PFC, visual cortices, the middle and superior temporal gyrus, the thalamus and the putamen). This finding was replicated in a subsequent study (Phillips et al., 1998), in which the viewing of prototypical faces displaying disgust provoked activation in the anterior insula, striatal structures (caudate nucleus, putamen, pallidus), and occipital and temporal visual areas. The viewing of fear expressions triggered amygdala activation. Similar observations were made by Sprengelmeyer et al. (1998), who detected activation of the insula, the OFC, and the putamen during participants' perception of disgusted facial expressions, whereas fearful faces stimulated the fusiform gyrus, the dorsolateral, and the inferior frontal cortex.

As expected, these first fMRI experiments were in line with the assumption that the amygdala is implicated in the perception of fear and the insula in disgust. A specialization of the insular cortex in the recognition of disgust-relevant signals has also been derived from studies that use other neurobiological methods in humans and animals (for a summary, see Augustine, 1996). Here, it could be shown that in primates, parts of the insula take over functions of the gustatory cortex, which contain taste-sensitive neurons. Furthermore, insular tumors and lesions have been connected with pathological vomiting. Altogether, there seems to be a fairly good amount of evidence reinforcing the concept of a connection between disgust as an originally food-related emotion and the observed insular activation.

A specific insular involvement during disgust recognition has also been reported in more recent fMRI experiments (Phillips et al., 2004; Schroeder et al., 2004; Wicker et al., 2003; Williams et al., 2005). Relative to neutral and surprised facial expressions, disgust was associated with the activation of the insula, the inferior frontal gyrus, the postcentral gyrus, inferior and middle occipital gyri as well as the cuneus (Schroeder et al., 2004). In the study by Wicker et al. (2003), participants were presented with a video clip in which an individual was leaning forward to smell the content of a glass and then afterward displayed a facial expression with typical disgust characteristics. Relative to clips in which the smelling was associated with a neutral face, disgust triggered activation of the anterior insula together with the involvement of occipitotemporal and frontal regions, as well as of the cingulate gyrus. Phillips et al. (2004) compared the brain activation in response to overt and covert presentations of facial expressions of fear and disgust. Within the overt condition, stimuli were presented long enough (170 ms) to be consciously perceived and correctly classified by the participants. In the covert (non-conscious) condition, each picture was shown for only 30 ms, which made it impossible to label the displayed expression. The consciously perceived stimuli were associated with emotion-specific activation patterns in which fear led to significant responses of the amygdala and in which disgust led to significant insular involvement. The direct comparison of both conditions (overt disgust vs. overt fear) failed, however, to provide statistical support for greater insular activation during disgust recognition relative to fear. The analysis of the nonconscious conditions showed neither a specific insular nor amygdalar activation for the target emotions. Williams et al. (2005) simultaneously recorded fMRI and skin conductance responses to pictures showing fearful, disgusted, and angry facial expressions. Fearful versus neutral faces elicited amygdala responses together with activation maxima, for example, in the hippocampus, the ACC, the visual association cortex, the putamen, and the thalamus. Disgust expressions relative to neutral ones were associated with insular involvement. Additional activation occurred in the amygdala-hippocampal complex, the ACC, the lateral PFC and occipitotemporal regions. When only those stimuli that were able to elicit electrodermal responses were analyzed, fear led to increased activation in the amygdala and disgust in the insula, as well as in the basal ganglia (putamen). Findings from the direct comparison of the fear with the disgust condition were not reported.

There are also studies that were not able to replicate the specific insular engagement in disgust perception (Anderson, Christoff, Panitz, de Rosa, & Gabrieli, 2003; Gorno-Tempini et al., 2001; Surguladze et al., 2003; Winston, O'Doherty, & Dolan, 2003). Winston et al. (2003) performed an fMRI study in which participants viewed emotional faces displaying low or high intensities of disgust. The responses were compared with fearful, happy, and sad expressions. The results indicated that the anterior insula was not specifically involved in disgust but that the amygdala and the visual association cortex were activated in all high-intensity conditions. This underlines, according to Winston et al. (2003), the general role of these brain regions in the decoding of emotionally salient stimuli. Moreover, Winston et al. (2003) assessed the effects of the experimental task and compared direct and incidental processing of the stimulus material. The participants were presented with a picture of two faces on the screen and had to decide which face was more male (implicit task) or more emotional (explicit task). Relative to the gender task, focusing on the emotionality provoked activation in different brain areas including the insula. The authors hypothesized that this activation may be a result of the simulation of the emotional display in the observer leading to an affective experience and its corresponding neural correlates. Surguladze et al. (2003) presented participants with mild and intense expressions of four emotions (disgust, fear, happiness, sadness) in a comparable experimental procedure by using fMRI. Both disgust intensities provoked activation in the visual association cortex when contrasted with the neutral condition—more specifically in the fusiform gyrus. Strong disgust expressions were said to involve the posterior cingulate cortex as well. Significant amygdala activity occurred in the high-intensity fear and the low-intensity sadness condition. Subsequently computed trend analyses indicated that with increasing intensities of disgust there was a significant linear activation augmentation in the anterior insula. Such a trend was not present in the amygdala for increasing fear intensities.

Gorno-Tempini et al. (2001) examined the effects of explicit and implicit processing of facial disgust expressions, in comparison with happy ones, in an fMRI study. The participants were requested to either decide about the gender of a face or about the expressed emotion. When the participants made emotion judgments, disgust activated the amygdala, whereas the insular cortex was responsive to both emotions. Gur et al. (2002) reported similar findings. The participants viewed facial displays of disgust, happiness, sadness, anger, and fear. Their task alternated between deciding whether posers displayed a negative or positive emotion and whether they were young or old. In this study, the amygdala response was greater during the emotion task than the age discrimination task, and this was the case across all facial expressions. Variations of the experimental task were also the focus of an fMRI study by Anderson et al. (2003). The authors used an attentional manipulation in which the participants were either instructed to focus on a facial expression (neutral, fearful, or disgusted) or on a picture of a building superimposed on the face. When the participants were attending to the faces, a comparison of the disgust relative to the other conditions resulted in enhanced insular activation. This effect disappeared during distraction in which the disgust and fear conditions were characterized by comparable insular responses. Moreover, there was significant amygdala activation during the unattended relative to the attended disgust condition. Here, the amygdala response was even marginally stronger in the disgust than in the fear condition.

Disgust Feelings

Typical visual provocation methods in fMRI and PET studies for disgust induction include the presentation of emotion-relevant scenes or of video clips. The recorded brain activation during their viewing is most commonly compared with an affectively neutral condition or with other emotions.

One of the first neuroimaging studies on the induction of disgust feelings was a PET experiment by Paradiso et al. (1997). The participants were presented with soundless video excerpts that provoked either disgust or a mixture of fear and disgust. The disgust/fear clip showed a rat crawling into the mouth of a man and the disgust clip portrayed how a man finds a decapitated horse head in his bed. Relative to a neutral condition (fire in a fireplace), the disgust film provoked an increased blood flow in the thalamus, the cerebellum, and in occipitotemporal regions. The fear/disgust condition was associated with activation in the OFC and occipitotemporal cortex. In a similar PET study, Lane, Reiman, Ahern, Schwartz, and Davidson (1997) used three silent film clips to generate the target emotions disgust, sadness, and happiness. The disgust clip that depicted a rat crawling on a sleeping man provoked increased activation in the dorsolateral PFC, the thalamus, and in anterior temporal regions. This pattern, however, was not specific for disgust but also occurred during the other emotions. In addition, disgust triggered increased blood flow in the midbrain, the cerebellum, and the visual association cortex. The tests on activation asymmetries were nonsignificant for all conditions.

A set of disgust-evoking scenes from different disgust categories including body products (e.g., excrements), bodily deviations (e.g., deformed legs, warts), repulsive animals (e.g., maggots, worms), and unusual food (e.g., a man eating a grasshopper) formed the stimulus material of an fMRI investigation by Schienle, Stark, et al. (2002). The participants were scanned while viewing alternating blocks of disgust-inducing, fear-inducing, and affectively neutral pictures. The disgust pictures, rated as highly repulsive, induced activation in the insula, the amygdala, the OFC, and occipitotemporal cortex. Because the insula was comparably active in the fear condition, the findings did not fit into the concept that the insula is a specific disgust processor. This conclusion was also derived from an fMRI study by Stark et al. (2003), who applied the same stimulus set with longer presentation times for the individual pictures (10 s instead of 1.5 s). Again, the target emotions could be elicited specifically, and the valence as well as the arousal ratings did not differ between the disgust and fear conditions. Relative to neutral pictures, disgust provoked activation in the amygdala, the thalamus, and prefrontal and occipitotemporal regions. The contrasting of the fear with the disgust condition did not reveal any statistically significant difference in the activation patterns. Also, none of the tests investigating hemispheric asymmetries and gender differences yielded statistical significance. The main results of this study were replicated in an experiment by the same authors (Stark, Schienle, Girod, et al., 2005). This experiment focused on the differences in brain activation of participants who were viewing erotic and disgust-inducing pictures. Here again, disgust was associated with amygdala (and not with insula) activation.

The research group around Schienle (Schienle, Schäfer, Stark, Walter, & Vaitl, 2005a; Schienle, Schäfer, Walter, Stark, & Vaitl, 2005; Stark et al., 2004; Stark, Schienle, Girod, et al., 2005) also applied their standard disgust picture set (Schienle, Stark, et al., 2002), depicting body products, repulsive animals, and food to study moderating factors of disgust processing. The list of influences on the neural responses that were analyzed included gender, disgust sensitivity of the participants, stimulus repetition, and the stimulus type (disgust faces vs. disgust scenes).

An unexpected finding of the fMRI study by Schienle et al. (2005a) was the failure to detect gender differences in brain activation to disgust-inducing pictures. A substantial sample of 51 men and 41 women had been scanned while looking at repulsive scenes (e.g., spoiled food, poor hygiene). According to the affective ratings, the elicited disgust was stronger in women, which is in line with many previous self-report studies that point to greater disgust sensitivity in women than in men (Rozin & Fallon, 1987). It should be noted, however, that the brain activation pattern was similar in both genders.

The disgust sensitivity of the participants, however, turned out to be an important factor in the modulation of brain activation to disgust-inducing stimuli (Schienle et al., 2005b; Stark, Schienle, Sarlo, et al., 2005). This personality trait had been assessed with the Questionnaire for the Assessment of Disgust Sensitivity (QADS; Schienle, Walter, Stark, & Vaitl, 2002), a German extended version of the Disgust Scale by Haidt, McCauley, and Rozin (1994). This self-report measure describes five different disgust domains (death/deformation, body secretions, spoilage, poor hygiene, and oral rejection), and the participants are asked to indicate how disgust-inducing a particular situation would be for them. The QADS sum score was positively correlated with the amygdala activation during disgust induction (Schienle et al., 2005b). Stark, Schienle, Sarlo, et al. (2005) also observed a positive relationship between the degree of disgust sensitivity and amygdala activation. The stimulus material of this experiment consisted of a disgust-inducing film clip, which showed hundreds of crawling cockroaches.

Different aspects of the experimental design and their influences on brain activation were the focal points of two fMRI experiments (Stark et al., 2004; Schäfer, Schienle, & Vaitl, 2005). When the same disgust pictures were repeatedly shown in two different scanning sessions, a significant deactivation occurred in the amygdala, the insula, the hippocampus, and the visual association cortex in the second session. This was the case even though the affective ratings of the participants had not changed. The study by Schäfer et al. (2005) is among the few investigations in which the hemodynamic effects of two different types of disgust stimuli (faces vs. scenes) were directly compared with each other. It is interesting to note that this study showed that facial expressions of disgust lost their capacity to induce significant brain activation when they were presented after a disgust-inducing scene.

Taken together, the described studies that used static and moving visual disgust pictures give little indication of specific insula importance. One of the few exceptions was reported by Wright, He, Shapira, Goodman, and Liu (2004), who investigated fMRI responses to depictions of two different disgust contents (mutilation and contamination), as well as to fear-inducing scenes (attacks). The anterior insula was activated in both disgust conditions but not in the fear condition. A limitation of this study was that activation patterns for the contrasts mutilation/contamination versus fear were not reported. Such contrasts were formed in a study by Schienle et al. (2006), who were not able to replicate insula-specific activation for mutilation or contamination.

The Functional Neuroanatomy of Disgust and Its Disorders

Individuals who experience intense and uncontrollable feelings of disgust as well as those with specific deficits in the decoding of disgust signals have been repeatedly investigated to better understand the underlying neural circuitry of this basic emotion. Changes in disgust reactivity can be seen in different mental and neuropsychiatric disorders, such as obsessive–compulsive disorder (OCD), Huntington's disease, and specific phobias, which have also been investigated in brain-imaging studies. The majority of the experiments applied a so-called symptom provocation design in which the patients were exposed to disorder-relevant material. Less often, generally disgust-evoking stimuli were used for the investigation of participants' overall disgust sensitivity.

OCD is an anxiety disorder, which is characterized by recurrent and intrusive thoughts (obsessions), as well as repetitive behaviors (compulsions). One commonly presented symptom cluster revolves around washing compulsions. The patients are afraid to be contaminated or to contaminate another person. This concern in turn triggers excessive cleaning and washing rituals in order to try to prevent possible harmful consequences (e.g., infection, disease). Thus, the connection between this OCD subtype and disgust would seem to be obvious. Disgust irrelevance is assumed for the second main OCD type with checking compulsions. Individuals with OCD execute control behaviors (e.g., of locks, electrical appliances) in an attempt to prevent burglary and accidents.

Breiter et al. (1996) examined patients who were suffering primarily from either washing compulsions or sexual obsessions. The brain activation was compared between two conditions. The patients were exposed to a contaminated item (e.g., a tissue soaked in toilet water) during symptom provocation, whereas the neutral control condition consisted of the presentation of a comparable innocuous stimulus (e.g., a tissue soaked in tap water). The elicitation of OCD symptoms triggered activation of the insula together with the OFC, the ACC, the basal ganglia, and the amygdala. Patients with washing compulsions ("washers") and checking compulsion ("checkers"), as well as healthy controls, were studied in an fMRI experiment by Phillips et al. (2000). They had been presented with pictures, which are generally considered to be disgusting and washer-relevant scenes (rated as more disgusting by washers than by healthy controls and checkers). Whereas the patients suffering from washing compulsions showed insula activation during both conditions, the insula involvement was restricted to the disorder-irrelevant disgust pictures in both checkers and the healthy controls. Additional activation in the patients with washing compulsions could be seen in the OFC, the ACC, and parietal brain regions. Similar findings have been reported by Shapira et al. (2003), who investigated fMRI responses to generally disgust-inducing pictures of patients suffering from contamination and illness fears. The clinical group displayed a greater involvement of the insula, the parahippocampal region, and of the OFC than with the healthy controls.

There are also null findings with regard to insula engagement in OCD (Adler et al., 2000; McGuire et al., 1994; Rauch et al., 1994). The symptom provocation applied within these PET and fMRI studies consistently provoked activation in the OFC and in the basal ganglia (caudate nucleus), but not in the insular cortex. Also not in line with the insula specificity hypothesis is the investigation conducted by Schienle, Schäfer, Walter, et al. (2005). They exposed OCD patients to individually disorder-relevant, generally disgust- and fear-inducing pictures and found insula activation in all three conditions.

The studies on Huntington's disease focused on the deficits of this patient group in disgust recognition. The syndrome is dominantly inherited and leads to neurodegenerative processes primarily affecting the basal ganglia—a second brain region besides the insula that is discussed as being significant in disgust processing. Using functional MRI, Hennenlotter et al. (2004) studied a group of Huntington's disease gene carriers, who did not yet display manifest symptoms. The patient group showed reduced anterior insula activity when viewing disgusted facial expressions relative to healthy controls. This response pattern was accompanied by a reduced identification performance for disgust faces, which did not apply to other expressions (happiness, surprise, fear, sadness, anger).

Looking at the third disorder type, specific phobias, several brain-imaging studies addressed the effects of symptom provocation and disgust elicitation in the respective patient groups. For those individuals suffering from spider- or blood-injection-injury phobia it has been put forward that disgust may at least be an equally important emotion for the origin and maintenance of these disorders (see chaps. 8 and 9, this volume). Findings in regard to insula involvement in spider phobia are again heterogeneous. Whereas two provocation studies reported activation of the insula (Dilger et al., 2003; Rauch et al., 1995), others described an activation pattern that included the visual association cortex (Dilger et al., 2003; Fredrikson, Wik, Annas, Ericson, & Stone-Elander, 1995; Paquette et al., 2003; Schienle, Schäfer, Walter, et al., 2005), the OFC and dorsolateral PFC (Dilger et al., 2003; Fredrikson et al., 1995; Johanson et al., 1998; Paquette et al., 2003; Rauch et al., 1995; Schienle, Schäfer, Walter, et al., 2005), the hippocampus/parahippocampal region (Fredrikson et al., 1995; Paquette et al., 2003), and the amygdala (Dilger et al., 2003; Schienle, Schäfer, Walter, et al., 2005), but none of these studies reported activation of the insula.

A single investigation on blood-phobic participants revealed stronger activation of the visual association cortex relative to healthy controls when viewing disorder-irrelevant disgust pictures (Schienle et al., 2003). This response difference was interpreted as an arousal effect reflecting greater selective attention for disgust-evoking stimuli in blood-phobic compared with nonphobic individuals.

CRITICAL ASPECTS AND FUTURE PERSPECTIVES

This chapter reviewed findings from PET and fMRI studies on the processing of two types of visual disgust stimuli: pictures of facial disgust expressions and depictions of repulsive contents. Depending on the stimulus class under investigation and the underlying theoretical approach of the authors, different activation patterns have been described. The proponents of the specificity model conducted for the most part studies that provided support for the central role of the insula for the identification of displays of disgust (Anderson et al., 2003; Phillips et al., 1997, 1998, 2004; Schroeder et al., 2004; Sprengelmeyer et al., 1998; Wicker et al., 2003; Williams et al., 2005). Figure 7.1 (top panel) shows the activation maxima in the left and right insular cortex for disgusted relative to neutral faces as reported in the aforementioned eight investigations with a total of 86 participants (50 males, 36 females). It is interesting to note that the activation was not always directly located in the insula but in brain regions in close vicinity, such as the operculum, frontal gyri, or the basal ganglia. Moreover, activation was not restricted to dorsal insular regions with gustatory functions and is therefore difficult to bring in line with the idea of disgust as a primarily food-related emotion. Thus, the proposed specificity of localization is not as great as often portrayed.

The specificity concept can be further questioned by addressing a methodological issue. In the majority of emotion perception studies, results were reported for the contrasts disgust versus neutral and fear versus neutral. A significant activation of the insula for the first contrast and a nonsignificant one for the second contrast was then interpreted to mirror a disgust-specific engagement of this brain area (e.g., Phillips et al., 1997; Sprengelmeyer et al., 1998; Williams et al., 2005). However, such a conclusion is not valid without further statistical analysis, namely, a direct comparison of disgust with another emotion condition. Such contrasts have been computed with different outcomes. Whereas Schroeder et al. (2004) observed a more pronounced insular involvement during the processing of disgusted relative to surprised faces, the direct comparison of the disgust and fear condition in the study by Phillips et al. (2004) showed no statistically significant difference in insular responses. The specificity concept has finally been challenged by a meta-analysis of the functional neuroanatomy of emotions, in which no specific

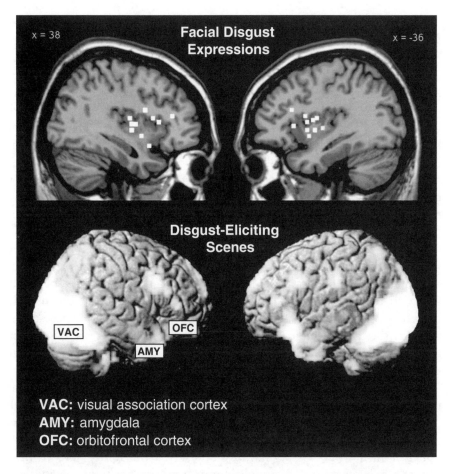

Figure 7.1. Brain activation while viewing facial expressions of disgust and disgust-eliciting scenes. Top panel: Activation maxima in the insular cortex while processing disgusted facial expressions (as reported in eight investigations; Anderson et al., 2003; Phillips et al., 1997, 1998, 2004; Schroeder et al., 2004; Sprengelmeyer et al., 1998; Wicker et al., 2003; Williams et al., 2005; $n = 86$; contrast disgust > neutral). Bottom panel: Activation while processing disgust-evoking scenes ($n = 92$; Schienle et al., 2005a; contrast: disgust > neutral).

association between the insula (or the basal ganglia) and disgust could be revealed (Phan, Wager, Taylor, & Liberzon, 2002).

The integrative neural network approach supports the assertion that combined activation of different brain regions occurs during processing of basic emotions (i.e., disgust). Figure 7.1 (bottom panel) depicts activation recorded during the exposure to disgust-evoking scenes in a sample of 92 participants (51 men, 41 women; Schienle et al., 2005a). The involved central regions included the visual association cortex, the amygdala, and the OFC. As mentioned before, these regions have been consistently identified in studies on the production of disgust states. Each brain area has important functions for the decoding of the salience of environmental information. It belongs to one of the most replicated findings in the field of affective neuroscience that emotion-relevant signals, relative to neutral signals, lead to stronger and more extended functional activity in visual brain areas (Phan et al., 2002). This response pattern has been interpreted to reflect "motivated attention," which would imply that the processing of salient, survival-relevant stimuli is facilitated by enhanced visual cortex responses (Bradley et al., 2003). A role in directing defensive, as well as appetitive motivational engagement, has also been ascribed to the amygdala, which has reciprocal connections with the visual association cortex (Rolls, 1999). The resulting loop may help to maintain attention and to facilitate the fast discrimination of emotive stimuli. Hereto, the OFC cortex, the amygdala, and also the insula are connected with each other through a substantial bilateral information exchange. Accordingly, the interplay between these areas may be the basis for the decoding of the emotional significance of stimuli and the elicitation of feelings. Thus, in contrast to the specificity approach, the integrative model assigns more general functions to the insula in the representation of emotional states. Augustine (1996), for example, described this brain area as a "limbic integration cortex." This concept is in line with a multitude of identified functions of the insula, such as pain perception, emotional recall, and imagery (Augustine, 1996; Phan et al., 2002).

The most critical aspect of the integrative model is that neuroimaging researchers who have adopted this approach usually describe a set of simultaneously activated brain loci and then imply that these loci work together and form a functional network (e.g., Schienle, Stark, et al., 2002). Such a conclusion, however, is premature because it is primarily derived from other data sources (e.g., lesion studies) and is not based on brain imaging data. Within the area of neuroimaging research on disgust, it still needs to be elucidated whether activated brain regions affect each other and in what way they exert their effects. Thus, both the specificity approach and the integration approach appear to be too simplistic as yet to describe the complexity of emotion processes in general and disgust processes in particular.

This conclusion leads directly to a new promising method for the analysis of neuroimaging data, known as the *functional and effective connectivity approach* (Friston & Büchel, 2004). The underlying idea holds that the coordination of activity between different neural assemblies is necessary for the generation of complex cognitive and affective states. Accordingly, one either looks at the undirected association (functional connectivity) between the activation in different brain areas (i.e., the correlation between two or more fMRI time series recorded from distributed brain regions) or at the effective connectivity. The latter approach goes beyond the first one by describing the directed influence of one brain region on the functional state of another one. Finally, realistically complex models of brain functional integration may include nonlinear interactions. Here, for example, it is assumed that the influence of one brain region on another is modulated by input from a third region.

The analysis of such moderating factors, in particular, seems to be very useful for understanding the complexity of neural disgust processing. As outlined before, different moderating factors exert considerable influence on disgust-associated brain activation, such as the experimental task (e.g., implicit vs. explicit processing), the stimulus context (e.g., the number and type of emotion conditions), or individual differences (e.g., personality traits, age of the participants). It had a great impact on the observed activation pattern whether participants were asked to focus on or to distract from the displayed emotion, or whether they were characterized by high or low disgust sensitivity (Anderson et al., 2003; Schienle et al., 2005b). Thus, analyzing the effects of such moderating factors and their neural correlates in more detail would seem to be a promising approach for future investigations.

In summary, the description of patterns of interactions will add to the information derived from activation analyses of discrete regions and distributed neural regions. Such descriptions might help to bring the specificity and the integrative approach together to form a comprehensive neurobiological model of disgust processing.

REFERENCES

Adler, C. M., McDonough-Ryan, P., Sax, K. W., Holland, S. K., Arndt, S., & Starkowski, S. M. (2000). fMRI of neuronal activation with symptom provocation in unmedicated patients with obsessive compulsive disorder. *Journal of Psychiatric Research, 34,* 317–324.

Adolphs, R. (2002). Neural systems for recognizing emotions. *Current Opinion in Neurobiology, 11,* 231–239.

Anderson, A. K., Christoff, K., Panitz, D., de Rosa, E., & Gabrieli, J. D. E. (2003). Neural correlates of the automatic processing of facial signals. *The Journal of Neuroscience, 23,* 5627–5633.

Augustine, J. R. (1996). Circuitry and functional aspects of the insular lobe in primates including humans. *Brain Research Reviews, 22,* 229–244.

Bradley, M. M., Sabatinelli, D., Lang, P. J., Fitzsimmons, J. R., King, W., & Desai, P. (2003). Activation of the visual cortex in motivated attention. *Behavioral Neuroscience, 117,* 369–380.

Breiter, H., Rauch, S. L., Kwong, K. K., Baker, J. R., Weisskoff, R. M., Kennedy, D. N., et al. (1996). Functional magnetic resonance imaging of symptom provocation in obsessive-compulsive disorder. *Archives of General Psychiatry, 53,* 595–606.

Calder, A. J., Lawrence, A. D., & Young, A. W. (2001). The neuropsychology of fear and loathing. *Nature Reviews Neuroscience, 2,* 352–363.

Damasio, A. R. (1999). *The feeling of what happens. Body and emotion in the making of consciousness*. New York: Harcourt Brace.

Damasio, A. R., Grabowski, T. J., & Bechara, A. (2000). Subcortical and cortical brain activity during the feeling of self-generated emotions. *Nature Neuroscience, 3*, 1049–1056.

Davidson, R. J. (2001). Toward a biology of personality and emotion. *Annals of the New York Academy of Sciences, 935*, 191–207.

Davidson, R. J., & Irwin, W. (1999). The functional neuroanatomy of emotion and affective style. *Trends in Cognitive Science, 3*, 11–21.

Davidson, R. J., Jackson, D. C., & Kalin, N. H. (2000). Emotion, plasticity, context, and regulation: Perspectives from affective neuroscience. *Psychological Bulletin, 126*, 890–909.

Dilger, S., Straube, T., Mentzel, H. J., Fitzek, C., Reichenbach, J., Hecht, H., et al. (2003). Brain activation to phobia-related pictures in spider phobic humans: An event-related functional magnetic resonance imaging study. *Neuroscience Letters, 248*, 29–32.

Ekman, P. (1992). An argument for basic emotions. *Cognition & Emotion, 6*, 169–200.

Fredrikson, M., Wik, G., Annas, P., Ericson, K., & Stone-Elander, S. (1995). Functional neuroanatomy of visually elicited simple phobic fear: Additional data and theoretical analysis. *Psychophysiology, 32*, 43–48.

Friston, K. J., & Büchel, C. (2004). Functional connectivity: Eigenimages and multivariate analyses. In R. S. J. Frackowiak, K. J. Friston, C. D. Frith, R. J. Dolan, C. J. Price, J. T. Ashburner, et al. (Eds.), *Human brain function* (2nd ed., pp. 999–1018). San Diego, CA: Academic Press.

Gorno-Tempini, M. L., Pradelli, S., Serafini, M., Pagnoni, G., Baraldi, P., Porro, C., et al. (2001). Explicit and incidental facial expression processing: An fMRI study. *Neuroimage, 14*, 465–473.

Gur, R. C., Schroeder, L., Turner, T., McGrath, C., Chan, R. M., Turetsky, B. I., et al. (2002). Brain activation during facial emotion processing. *Neuroimage, 16*, 651–662.

Haidt, J., McCauley, C. R., & Rozin, P. (1994). Individual differences in sensitivity to disgust: A scale sampling seven domains of disgust elicitors. *Personality and Individual Differences, 16*, 701–713.

Hatfield, E., Cacioppo, J. T., & Rapson, R. L. (1994). *Emotional contagion*. Cambridge, England: Cambridge University Press.

Haxby, J. V., Hoffmann, E. A., & Gobbini, M. I. (2000). The distributed human neural system for face perception. *Trends in Cognitive Sciences, 4*, 223–233.

Hennenlotter, A., Schroeder, U., Erhard, P., Haslinger, B., Stzahl, R., Weindl, A., et al. (2004). Neural correlates associated with impaired disgust processing in pre-symptomatic Huntington's disease. *Brain, 127*, 1446–1453.

Izard, C. E. (1999). *Die Emotionen des Menschen*. Weinheim, Germany: Beltz.

Johanson, A., Gustafson, L., Passant, U., Risberg, J., Smith, G., Warkentin, S., et al. (1998). Brain function in spider phobia. *Psychiatry Research Neuroimaging, 84,* 101–111.

Lane, R. D., Reiman, E. M., Ahern, G. L., Schwartz, G. E., & Davidson, R. J. (1997). Neuroanatomical correlates of happiness, sadness and disgust. *American Journal of Psychiatry, 154,* 926–933.

LeDoux, J. E. (1996). *The emotional brain: The mysterious underpinnings of emotional life.* New York: Simon & Schuster.

LeDoux, J. E. (2000). Emotion circuits in the brain. *Annual Reviews in Neuroscience 23,* 155–184

McGuire, P. K., Bench, C. J., Frith, S. D., Marks, I. M., Frackowiak, R. S. J., & Dolan, R. J. (1994). Functional anatomy of obsessive–compulsive phenomena. *British Journal of Psychiatry, 164,* 459–468.

Paquette, V., Lévesque, J., Mensour, B., Leroux, J. M., Beaudoin, G., Bourgouin, P., et al. (2003). "Change the mind and you change the brain": Effects of cognitive–behavioral therapy on the neural correlates of spider phobia. *Neuroimage, 18,* 401–409.

Paradiso, S., Robinson, R. G., Andreasen, N. C., Downhill, J. E., Davidson, R. J., Kirchner, P. T., et al. (1997). Emotional activation of limbic circuitry in elderly normal subjects in a PET study. *American Journal of Psychiatry, 1154,* 384–389.

Phan, K. L., Wager, T., Taylor, S. F., & Liberzon, I. (2002). Functional neuroanatomy of emotion: A meta-analysis of emotion activation studies in PET and fMRI. *Neuroimage, 16,* 331–348.

Phillips, M. L., Drevets, W. C., Rauch, S. L., & Lane, R. (2003). Neurobiology of emotion perception. I: The neural basis of normal emotion perception. *Biological Psychiatry, 54,* 504–514.

Phillips, M. L., Marks, I. M., Senior, C., Lythgoe, D., O'Dwyer, A. M., Meehan, O., et al. (2000). A differential response in obsessive–compulsive disorder patients with washing compared with checking symptoms to disgust. *Psychological Medicine, 30,* 1037–1050.

Phillips, M. L., Williams, L. M., Heining, M., Herba, C. M., Russell, T., Andrew, C., et al. (2004). Differential neural responses to overt and covert presentations of facial expressions of fear and disgust. *Neuroimage, 21,* 1484–1496.

Phillips, M. L., Young, A. W., Scott, S. K., Calder, A. J., Andrew, C., Giampietro, V., et al. (1998). Neural responses to facial and vocal expressions of fear and disgust. *Proceedings of the Royal Society of London, 265,* 1809–1817.

Phillips, M. L., Young, A. W., Senior, C., Brammer, M., Andrew, C., Calder, A. J., et al. (1997, October 2). A specific neural substrate for perceiving facial expressions of disgust. *Nature, 389,* 495–498.

Plutchik, R. (1980). A general psychoevolutionary theory of emotion. In R. Plutchik & H. Kellerman (Eds.), *Emotion: Theory, research, and experience: Vol. 1. Theories of emotion* (pp. 3–33). New York: Academic.

Rauch, S. L., Jenike, M. A., Alpert, N. M., Baer, L., Breiter, H. C., Savage, C. R., et al. (1994). Regional cerebral blood flow measured during symptom provocation in obsessive–compulsive disorder using oxygen 15-labeled carbon dioxide and positron emission tomography. *Archives of General Psychiatry, 51*, 62–70.

Rauch, S. L., Savage, C. R., Alpert, N. M., Miguel, E. C., Baer, L., & Breiter, H. C. (1995). A positron emission tomography study of simple phobic symptom provocation. *Archives of General Psychiatry, 52*, 20–28.

Rolls, E. T. (1999). *The brain and emotion.* New York: Oxford University Press.

Rozin, P., & Fallon, A. (1987). A perspective on disgust. *Psychological Review, 94*, 23–41.

Rozin, P., Haidt, J., & McCauley, C. R. (2000). Disgust. In M. Lewis & J. Haviland (Eds.), *Handbook of emotions* (2nd ed., pp. 637–653). New York: Guilford Press.

Schäfer, A., Schienle, A., & Vaitl, D. (2005). Stimulus type and design influence hemodynamic responses towards visual disgust and fear elicitors. *International Journal of Psychophysiology, 57*, 53–59.

Schienle, A., Schäfer, A., Hermann, A., Walter, B., Stark, R., & Vaitl, D. (2006). fMRI responses to pictures of mutilation and contamination. *Neuroscience Letters, 393*, 174–178.

Schienle, A., Schäfer, A., Stark, R., Walter, B., Kirsch, P., & Vaitl, D. (2003). Disgust processing in blood-injection-injury phobia: An fMRI study. *Journal of Psychophysiology, 17*, 87–93.

Schienle, A., Schäfer, A., Stark, R., Walter, B., & Vaitl, D. (2005a). Gender differences in the processing of disgusting and fear-inducing pictures: An fMRI study. *Neuroreport, 16*, 277–280.

Schienle, A., Schäfer, A., Stark, R., Walter, B., & Vaitl, D. (2005b). Relationship between disgust sensitivity, trait anxiety and brain activity during disgust induction. *Neuropsychobiology, 51*, 86–92.

Schienle, A., Schäfer, A., Walter, B., Stark, R., & Vaitl, D. (2005). Brain activation of spider phobics towards disorder-relevant, generally disgust- and fear-inducing pictures. *Neuroscience Letters, 388*, 1–6.

Schienle, A., Stark, R., Walter, B., Blecker, C., Ott, U., Sammer, G., & Vaitl, D. (2002). The insula is not specifically involved in disgust processing: An fMRI study. *NeuroReport, 13*, 2023–2026.

Schienle, A., Walter, B., Stark, R., & Vaitl, D. (2002). A questionnaire for the assessment of disgust sensitivity. *Zeitschrift für Klinische Psychologie und Psychotherapie, 31*, 110–120.

Schroeder, U., Hennenlotter, A., Erhard, P., Haslinger, B., Stahl, R., Lange, K. W., et al. (2004). Functional neuroanatomy of perceiving surprised faces. *Human Brain Mapping, 23*, 181–187.

Shapira, N., Yijun, L., He, A. G., Bradley, M. M., Lessig, M. C., James, G. A., et al. (2003). Brain activation by disgust-inducing pictures in obsessive–compulsive disorder. *Biological Psychiatry, 54*, 751–756.

Sprengelmeyer, R., Rausch, M., Eysel, U. T., & Przuntek, H. (1998). Neural structures associated with recognition of facial expressions of basic emotions. *Proceedings of the Royal Society of London, 265,* 1927–1931.

Stark, R., Schienle, A., Girod, C., Walter, B., Kirsch, P., Blecker, C., et al. (2005). Erotic and disgust-inducing pictures: Differences in the hemodynamic responses of the brain. *Biological Psychology, 70,* 19–29.

Stark, R., Schienle, A., Sarlo, M., Palomba, D., Walter, B., & Vaitl, D. (2005). Influences of disgust sensitivity on hemodynamic responses towards a disgust-inducing film clip. *International Journal of Psychophysiology, 57,* 61–67.

Stark, R., Schienle, A., Walter, B., Kirsch, P., Blecker, C., Ott, U., et al. (2004). Hemodynamic effects of negative emotional pictures: A test–retest analysis. *Neuropsychobiology, 50,* 108–118.

Stark, R., Schienle, A., Walter, B., Kirsch, P., Sammer, G., Ott, U., et al. (2003). Hemodynamic responses to fear- and disgust-inducing pictures. *International Journal of Psychophysiology, 50,* 225–234.

Surguladze, S. A., Brammer, M. J., Young, A. W., Andrew, C., Travis, M. J., Williams, S. C. R., et al. (2003). A preferential increase in the extrastriate response to signals of danger. *Neuroimage, 19,* 1317–1328.

Wicker, B., Keysers, C., Plailly, J., Royet, J.-P., Gallese, V., & Rizzolatti, G. (2003). Both of us are disgusted in my insula: The common neural basis of seeing and feeling disgust. *Neuron, 40,* 655–664.

Williams, L. M., Das, P., Liddell, B., Olivieri, G., Peduto, A., Brammer, M. J., et al. (2005). BOLD, sweat and fears: fMRI and skin conductance distinguish facial fear signals. *Neuroreport, 16,* 49–52.

Winston, J. S., O'Doherty, J., & Dolan, R. J. (2003). Common and distinct neural responses during direct and incidental processing of multiple facial expressions. *Neuroimage, 20,* 84–97.

Wright, P., He, G., Shapira, N. A., Goodman, W. K., & Liu, Y. (2004). Disgust and the insula: fMRI responses to pictures of mutilation and contamination. *Neuroreport 15,* 2347–2351.

III

DISORDERS OF DISGUST

8

DISGUST AND ANIMAL PHOBIAS

GRAHAM C. L. DAVEY AND SARAH MARZILLIER

Animal fears are arguably the most common set of fears and phobias experienced. Large epidemiological studies of phobias have indicated that the most common phobic category cited is "bugs, mice, snakes and bats," and individuals who report fears in this category represent 46% of the total group of individuals who report any phobia (Chapman, 1997). Factor analysis studies have identified animal phobias as a clearly defined, integrated cluster of fears (Arrindell, Pickersgill, Merckelbach, Ardon, & Cornet, 1991; Bernstein & Allen, 1969; Landy & Gaupp, 1971), and although animal fears represent one of the most commonly referred clinical phobias (Marks, 1987), they also occur regularly at a nonclinical level in the normal population (Costello, 1982; Davey, 1994c; Davey et al., 1998). Animals that are the common focus of everyday fears and phobias in Western cultures include spiders; snakes; rodents such as rats and mice; insects such as cockroaches, beetles, and moths; invertebrates such as maggots, slugs, snails, and worms; and reptiles such as lizards (Davey, 1994c). Arguably, the most common specific fear in Western societies

Some of the research reported in chapter 8 was supported by the Economic and Social Research Council Grants RES-000-23-0839 and R000237622 to Graham C. L. Davey. We acknowledge the contributions of Karen Barker, Kate Cavanagh, and Benie MacDonald to the research on disgust and psychopathology that has been carried out at the University of Sussex over the past 10 years.

169

is fear of spiders, and in a U.K. survey, 55% of women and 18% of men reported being fearful of spiders (Davey, 1994c).

There have been a number of theories addressing the etiology of animal fears. The most prominent of these is the classical conditioning model (Watson & Rayner, 1920) and the preparedness hypothesis (Seligman, 1971). Attempts to explain animal phobias in terms of classical conditioning date back to the famous "Little Albert" study reported by Watson and Rayner (1920). Albert was an 11-month-old infant, and Watson and Rayner attempted to condition in him a fear to his pet white rat. They did this by pairing the rat—the conditioned stimulus (CS)—with the frightening event of a loud noise produced by striking an iron bar—the unconditioned stimulus (UCS)—which distressed Albert (the unconditioned response). After several pairings of the rat with the noise, Albert began to cry (the conditioned response) whenever the rat was introduced into the room. This type of explanation has been popular over the past 50 years, and more sophisticated contemporary conditioning models of specific phobias have been developed (Davey, 1992b, 1997). However, it is difficult to generally explain the range of features possessed by animal phobias with conditioning theories. Criticisms of the conditioning model of animal phobias include the following: (a) Traumatic experiences are essential for conditioning accounts, yet many animal phobics appear unable to recall any trauma or aversive conditioning experience at the time of the onset of their phobia, and this appears to be particularly true of many animal phobias, including snake and spider phobia (Davey, 1992b; Murray & Foote, 1979); and (b) simple conditioning models treat all stimuli as equally likely to enter into association with aversive consequences, yet fears and phobias are not evenly distributed across stimuli and experiences. People appear to develop phobias of some animals (e.g., snakes, spiders) more readily than other animals (e.g., tigers, bears) even though encounters with the latter type of animals could well be associated with pain or trauma (Seligman, 1971).

That animal phobias tend to be focused on a limited set of animals, some of which are venomous, has led some researchers to suggest that we may be biologically prepared or prewired to acquire animal phobias. For example, Seligman (1971) argued that evolutionary selection pressures have developed a biological predisposition to learn to associate fear with stimuli that were hazardous for our pretechnological ancestors. That is, we tend to have a built-in predisposition to learn to fear things such as snakes and spiders because these have been life threatening to our ancestors, and those of our ancestors that evolved a biological predisposition to learn to fear these kinds of animals will have been more likely to survive and pass that fear predisposition on to future generations. This account is known as *biological preparedness*, and it has been supported by two lines of evidence. First, if participants in a classical conditioning experiment are shown pictures of "fear-relevant" stimuli such as snakes and spiders (CSs) paired with electric shock (UCSs), they develop fear of the CSs more quickly and show a greater resistance to extinction than if pictures of less fear-irrelevant stimuli are used as CSs (e.g., pictures of houses; Öhman, Eriksson, & Lofberg, 1975). Second, Cook and Mineka (1989, 1990) found that laboratory-reared rhesus monkeys that had never before seen a snake rapidly acquired fear reactions to snakes after being shown a demonstration of another monkey who was frightened in the presence of a snake. They did not acquire fear reactions after watching a demonstration of another monkey being frightened in the presence of a stimulus such as a rabbit or a flower. Both studies suggest that humans and primates such as rhesus monkeys have an unlearned predisposition to rapidly acquire fear responses to some types of stimuli (i.e., animals such as snakes) and not to others (see Öhman & Mineka, 2001).

Although evolutionary accounts such as the preparedness hypothesis are appealing and appear to have at least some face validity, one must be cautious about accepting them on the basis of existing evidence (Davey, 1995; Delprato, 1980). First, such accounts depend on the fact that animals that are currently the focus of fears and phobias have actually acted as important selection pressures over our evolutionary past. However, this is very difficult to verify empirically. For example, do we tend to have phobic reactions to spiders because they once constituted an important life-threatening pressure on our pretechnological ancestors? There is no convincing evidence to suggest this. Second, evolutionary accounts can be constructed in a post hoc manner and are at risk of being either "adaptive stories" (McNally, 1995) or "imaginative reconstructions" (Lewontin, 1979; cf. Merckelbach & de Jong, 1997). This view argues that it is possible to construct, post hoc, an adaptive scenario for the fear and avoidance of almost any stimulus or event (McNally, 1995). This does not mean that evolutionary accounts are wrong (see Öhman & Mineka, 2001, for a contemporary evolutionary account of phobias), merely that they are tantalizingly easy to propose but very difficult to substantiate.

Given these problems with individual theories of animal phobias, an expanding body of evidence suggests that different types of animal phobias may be acquired in quite different ways (Merckelbach, de Jong, Muris, & van den Hout, 1996). For example, there is good evidence that some animal phobias—such as dog phobia—are caused by traumatic conditioning experiences (e.g., being bitten or chased by a dog; Doogan & Thomas, 1992). In contrast, many other animal phobias do not appear to be characterized by a traumatic experience at their outset—in fact, sufferers often cannot recall the exact onset of their phobia, which suggests that the onset may be gradual and precipitated by factors that are not immediately obvious to the individual. Phobias that fit this description include most animal phobias (e.g., snake phobia, spider phobia; Merckelbach, Muris, & Schouten, 1996; Murray & Foote, 1979).

A radically alternative approach to understanding the etiology of animal fears and phobias argues that many such fears are closely associated with the emotion of disgust. High levels of disgust sensitivity have been found to be associated with small animal phobias in general (Davey, 1994c; Ware, Jain, Burgess, & Davey, 1994) and spider phobia specifically (Mulkens, de Jong, & Merckelbach, 1996). Disgust is a food-rejection emotion whose main function is to prevent the transmission of illness and disease through the oral incorporation of contaminated items (Davey, 1994a; Rozin & Fallon, 1987), and elevated disgust sensitivity implies increased avoidance of disgust-relevant objects. Both Angyal (1941) and Rozin and Fallon (1987) have pointed out that nearly all disgust objects are animals, animal products, parts of animals, animal body products, or objects that have had contact with animals or animal products. Therefore, it seems that avoidance of animals generally is a central feature of the disgust emotion, and this may explain the close association between disgust sensitivity and animal fears and phobias.

In the remainder of this chapter we describe evidence for the involvement of the disgust emotion in animal fears and phobias. If the disgust emotion is central to an understanding of the acquisition and experience of animal fears and phobias, then a number of important issues remain to be explored. We first describe in detail the evidence for an association between animal fears and elevated levels of experienced disgust and then continue by exploring some of the important theoretical issues surrounding the role of disgust in animal fears. These include (a) why some animals have become associated with disgust more than others, and (b) whether disgust is simply experienced in animal phobias or whether it has a genuine causal or precipitating role in the origin of animal phobias.

EVIDENCE FOR THE RELATIONSHIP BETWEEN ANIMAL FEARS AND THE DISGUST EMOTION

This section reviews the way in which researchers have attempted to study the links between disgust and animal fears, and to determine whether (a) animals associated with disgust fall into clearly defined categories and (b) disgust is associated with cognitive factors that may maintain phobic fear.

Small Animal Fears and Phobias

Animal fears and phobias tend to fall into two rather separate categories. Ware et al. (1994, Study 1) conducted a factor analytic study of self-rated animal fear. This yielded two factors, the first representing predatory animals (e.g., tiger, alligator) that would be extremely dangerous if confronted in the wild. These have high fear and high predatory status. The second factor represented fear-relevant animals (e.g., slug, spider), which have high-fear and low-predatory status (i.e., they would not present a serious physical risk if confronted; Exhibit 8.1A). Davey (1994c, Study 1) also examined self-reported fears to animals indigenous to the United Kingdom. A factor analysis identified two separate categories, one representing invertebrate animals (e.g., slug, spider), and a second representing mainly vertebrate fear-relevant animals (e.g., mouse, bat). As with the Ware et al. (1994) findings, the latter category consisted of predatory, high-fear status animals. In this chapter, we adopt the term *fear relevant* to apply generally to that group of animals that have high-fear and low-predatory status. This contrasts with groups that have high-fear and high-predatory status (to be called predatory animals) or low-fear and low-predatory status (e.g., rabbits, kittens). In addition, a number of studies have found that the fear-relevant group can be divided into two further groups

EXHIBIT 8.1
Factor Analysis Studies of Animal Fears

A

Fear-relevant animals	Predatory animals
Snake	Tiger
Bat	Alligator
Rat	Crocodile
Lizard	Lion
Slug	Bear
Leech	Shark
Mouse	Wolf
Eel	Hippopotamus
Octopus	Snake
Cockroach	
Spider	

B

Fear-relevant small mammals and reptiles	Fear-relevant invertebrates
Mouse	Slug
Rat	Snail
Snake	Worm
Bat	Maggot
Lizard	Beetle
Eel	Cockroach
Frog	Fly
	Spider

Note. The following gives the reader an indication of the types of animals found in the various animal fear categories used in chapter 8. A: Fear-relevant animals are normally high-fear, low-predatory status, and they are the group normally most associated with the disgust emotion. (Data from Ware, Jain, Burgess, & Davey [1994]: *Snake* loaded significantly on both factors.) B: Fear-relevant animals have also been divided into two separate groups, covering (a) small fear-relevant mammals and reptiles and (b) invertebrate animals. (Data from Davey [1994c] was based on fear ratings to common indigenous animals in the United Kingdom.)

consisting of (a) relatively small fear-relevant mammals and reptiles (e.g., rats, frogs, lizards, mice) and (b) invertebrate animals (e.g., beetles, maggots, creepy crawlies; see Exhibit 8.1B).

These studies suggest that there is a significant number of animals with high-fear status that do not pose a serious physically aggressive threat to humans. The labeling of these categories of animals has varied considerably between studies. Therefore, it is advisable to set out definitions of these animals that will be used throughout this review. In Ware et al.'s (1994) study, this group is defined as one factor (fear-relevant animals) with high-fear and low-predatory status. In Davey's (1994c, Study 1) article, this group is represented by two factors (invertebrates and mainly vertebrate fear-relevant animals) where both have high-fear and low-predatory status.

Disgust Sensitivity and Animal Fear in a Nonclinical Population

A possible link between disgust and fear to fear-relevant animals has been investigated in several ways. Matchett and Davey (1991) reported a relationship between measures of disgust sensitivity and fear of small animals. One hundred and four participants completed the Fear Survey Schedule (FSS; Wople & Lang, 1964), a measure of disgust and contamination sensitivity (The Food Contamination Questionnaire [FCQ]; Rozin, Fallon, & Mandell, 1984), a measure of trait anxiety (Spielberger, 1983), and a measure of self-reported fear to predatory (high-fear, high-predatory), fear-relevant (high-fear, low-predatory), and invertebrate (revulsion evoking) animals. Matchett and Davey (1991) found that disgust sensitivity was significantly associated with scores on the animal subscale and the tissue-damage, illness, and death subscale of the FSS. Disgust sensitivity (DS) was not associated with other FSS subscales, such as social phobia, noises, and other classical phobias. Furthermore, disgust sensitivity was significantly associated with self-reported fear to fear-relevant and invertebrate animals, but not predatory animals. This study also included a measure of trait anxiety that was not related to the animal subscale or the tissue damage/illness death subscale of the FSS but was related to the social phobia, other classical phobias, and the miscellaneous subscales of the FSS. This suggests that the relationship between disgust sensitivity and animal and tissue damage/illness death subscales cannot be explained simply by a correlation between DS and trait anxiety.

Davey (1994c, Study 2) conducted a similar study that investigated the relationship between disgust sensitivity and animal fears in a U.K. population. Participants completed the FCQ as a measure of disgust sensitivity (Rozin et al., 1984) and a questionnaire that measured self-reported fear to fear-relevant and invertebrate animals. The results suggested a significant correlation between measures of disgust sensitivity and fear of both fear-relevant small animals and invertebrate animals.

Arrindell, Mulkins, Kok, and Vollenbroek (1999) investigated the relationships between disgust sensitivity and four subscales of an Animal Fears Questionnaire (fear-relevant animals, nonslimy invertebrates, slimy invertebrates, and farm animals) in a community sample. They found that disgust sensitivity was significantly associated with fear of fear-relevant animals, nonslimy invertebrates, and slimy invertebrates, but not with farm animals.

The studies described so far have one major drawback, and that is that the measure of disgust sensitivity used (FCQ) may be confounded with any measure of animal fears. This is because the FCQ measures disgust sensitivity by asking questions that include reference to animals—especially fear-relevant animals and creepy crawlies (e.g., "Consider a bowl of soup with a washed, dead grasshopper in the bottom. How much would you like to eat this soup?"). Nevertheless, similar relationships between disgust sensitivity and animal fear have been found using Haidt, McCauley, and Rozin's (1994) General Disgust Questionnaire (GDQ). This scale measures disgust to seven core disgust domains (food, body products, animals, sexual acts, hygiene, death, and violations of the body envelope) rather than measuring only food contamination sensitivity as the FCQ does. Tucker and Bond (1997) investigated the relationship between both the FCQ and the GDQ and a self-report questionnaire that measured fear to repulsive (invertebrate), fear-relevant, and predatory animals. Although the FCQ did not correlate with fear to any of the animal types, the GDQ correlated with fear to the repulsive (invertebrate) and fear-relevant animals, but not to the predatory animals. Thus, these results that use the GDQ to measure disgust sensitivity report similar findings to those of Arrindell et al. (1999) and Matchett and Davey (1991), where fear of fear-relevant and invertebrate animals are associated with disgust but not fear of larger predatory animals.

Muris, Merckelbach, Schmidt, and Tierney (1999) took a slightly different approach and looked for a relationship between a simplified version of the FCQ (Rozin et al., 1984) and several anxiety disorder symptoms (generalized anxiety disorder, separation anxiety disorder, social phobia, panic disorder, obsessive–compulsive disorder, blood-injury-injection [BII] phobia, situational–environmental phobia, and animal phobia) in a normal population of children. Significant relationships were found between the FCQ and all anxiety disorder symptoms. However when the effects of trait anxiety were partialed out, only correlations between the FCQ and animal phobia, the FCQ and BII phobia, the FCQ and situational–environmental phobia, and the FCQ and separation anxiety disorder remained significant. This finding suggests that the relationship between disgust sensitivity and animal fears is not simply mediated by anxiety and cannot also be accounted for by an overlap between measures of disgust and measures of anxiety.

Disgust Sensitivity and Spider Fear

Studies that investigate a possible relationship between disgust sensitivity and spider fear (a spider is a fear-relevant animal) have been conducted in both nonclinical and clinical populations. The spider is the most commonly used example of a fear-relevant animal, and many of the studies supporting the disease-avoidance model have concentrated on spider fear.

First, de Jong and Merckelbach (1998) found a significant relationship between disgust sensitivity (measured by both the FCQ and the GDQ) and scores on the Spider Phobia Questionnaire (SPQ) in female students. Similarly, Tolin, Lohr, Sawchuk, and Lee (1997) classified 157 students into spider phobic individuals (scoring at least 1 standard deviation above their gender means on the SPQ; Klorman, Weerts, Hastings, Melamed, & Lang, 1974) and nonphobic individuals. These two groups then completed the GDQ and the Disgust Emotion Scale (Walls & Kleinknecht, 1996), which measures aversion to eight disgust-relevant stimuli (e.g., rotting foods, smells). The students classified as spider phobic individuals scored significantly higher on both disgust sensitivity measures.

Sawchuk, Lohr, Tolin, Lee, and Kleinknecht (2000) divided 138 students into groups of BII phobic, spider phobic, and nonphobic individuals. They compared group means on two disgust questionnaires: the GDQ and the Disgust Emotion Scale (Walls & Kleinknecht, 1996). They also looked for group differences on two contamination fears questionnaires: the contamination subscale of the Padua Inventory (Burns, Keortge, Formea, & Sternberger, 1996) and the contamination subscale of the Vancouver Obsessional Compulsive Inventory (Thordarson, Radomsky, Rachman, Shafran, & Sawchuk, 1997). Sawchuk et al. (2000) found significant correlations between spider fear and both measures of disgust sensitivity. Moreover, BII and spider phobic individuals reported significantly higher disgust sensitivity than nonphobic individuals. However, spider fear was not significantly correlated with either contamination scale.

Studies that investigated the relationship between disgust sensitivity and spider fear have also been conducted on clinical populations. Two studies have investigated the relationship between disgust sensitivity and spider fear in female spider phobic individuals. Merckelbach, de Jong, Arntz, and Schouten (1993) compared female spider phobic individuals with female nonphobic individuals on measures of disgust sensitivity (measured by the FCQ). As predicted, they found that spider phobic individuals had significantly higher scores on the FCQ than the nonphobic group. Mulkens et al. (1996) also compared women with spider phobia with women who were nonphobic on the FCQ and found the same relationship. Furthermore, Mulkens et al. (1996) partialed out the effect of neuroticism and introversion (measured with Eysenck's Personality Questionnaire; Eysenck & Eysenck, 1984) and found that the relationship between disgust sensitivity and spider fear was relatively unaffected. No relationship was found between disgust sensitivity and measures of social phobia, BII phobia, and agoraphobia. In a similar approach, Davey and Bond (2006) found a significant correlation between disgust sensitivity (as measured by the Disgust Propensity and Sensitivity Scale [DPSS]—a tool that measures disgust sensitivity without asking questions about disgust to specific objects) and spider fear as measured by the SPQ. After partialing out measures of trait anxiety, they found that disgust sensitivity still predicted statistically significant variance in SPQ scores, suggesting that the relationship between disgust sensitivity and spider fear was not being mediated by trait anxiety.

Finally, de Jong, Andrea, and Muris (1997) compared spider phobic girls with nonphobic girls (mean age = 11.6 years, range = 9–14). Once again, they found that the spider phobic girls had a higher disgust sensitivity score (measured on the FCQ).

These findings suggest a significant relationship between disgust sensitivity and spider fear and phobia, and one that is unaffected by partialing out constructs such as neuroticism, introversion, and trait anxiety.

Disgust Beliefs About Spiders and Spider Fear and Phobia

Further evidence of a role for disgust in animal fears and phobias has come from studies of spider phobic individuals who report beliefs about the disgustingness of spiders. In a study by de Jong et al. (1997), spider phobic children saw spiders as more disgusting than did nonphobic children (measured by two questions that relate to the contaminating properties of spiders). Also, in a nonclinical sample, de Jong and Merckelbach (1998) found that views about the ability of spiders to contaminate were related to spider fear (but see conflicting results from Sawchuk et al., 2000). Armfield and Mattiske (1996) also found significant correlations between a scale measuring the disgustingness of spiders and spider fear in a nonclinical sample.

Mulkens et al. (1996) reported that spider phobic individuals were much more likely to refuse to eat a cookie after it had been in brief contact with a live spider than nonphobic individuals. They argued that this demonstrates that spider phobic individuals consider spiders to be disgusting (as contaminating properties are a central property of a disgust stimulus). Furthermore, no difference was found between spider phobic individuals and nonphobic individuals on a separate behavioral measure of disgust sensitivity (drinking tea from a cup covered in scale), suggesting that the disgust to spiders is not simply a consequence of heightened levels of disgust sensitivity. A number of studies have also shown that disgust beliefs about spiders are reduced by appropriate treatment for the spider phobia (de Jong et al., 1997; Mulkens et al., 1996; Thorpe & Salkovskis, 1997), which is consistent with disgust beliefs that play an important role in mediating spider fear.

However, Thorpe and Salkovskis (1995) also found that spider phobic individuals endorse disgust beliefs about spiders but that this does not appear to be related to the intensity of their fear. They argued that spiders are generally considered to be disgusting stimuli and that phobic fear may simply amplify disgust as a part of the universal negative evaluation of the spider. Thorpe and Salkovskis (1998, Study 2) found that when asked to generate words to describe a spider, spider phobic individuals did generate 15 disgust words from a total of 190 words (8%). This finding suggests that at least some phobic individuals do see spiders as disgusting. However the number of disgust words contrasts with the number of movement words (56/190, 29%) and physical appearance words (98/190, 52%), suggesting that disgust may not be the single most important descriptive element about spiders for spider phobic persons. Arntz, Lavy, van den Berg, and van Rijsoort (1993) also found that people with spider phobia endorsed beliefs about the disgustingness of spiders (e.g., that spiders are "dirty"); however, the majority of beliefs about spiders were related to harm, attack, and the predatory nature of spiders. Arntz et al. (1993) argued that their investigation into the beliefs of spider phobic individuals suggests that disgust beliefs are present in spider phobia but they do not play a particularly prominent role.

In summary, the results of these studies indicate that spider phobic individuals do endorse beliefs about the disgustingness of spiders, but researchers differ in their views about how important these beliefs are in maintaining clinically phobic responding. A recent study by Edwards and Salkovskis (2006) suggested that spider fear may enhance disgust levels in people with spider phobia but that disgust alone does not enhance the fear response. During habituation to spider fear, they introduced either a neutral, disgusting, or phobia-relevant stimulus. Exposure to the phobic stimulus resulted in a return of self-reported fear and increased disgust levels. However, exposure to the disgust stimulus increased disgust levels but not self-reported fear. We discuss these findings in more detail later when we look more closely at the causal relationships between disgust and animal fears.

Cognitive Bias for Spider and Contamination Words in Individuals With Spider Fear

Barker and Robertson (1997) investigated a cognitive bias for spider words in people with high spider fear. Using the emotional Stroop task (developed from Stroop, 1935), Barker and Robertson (1997) found that a nonclinical spider-fearing group showed greater Stroop interference for words relating to the physical attributes and movement of spiders and also to words relating to disgust and contamination.[1] This finding suggests that the interference for disgust and contamination words may reflect the influence of a cognitive bias toward disgusting stimuli. However, Barker and Robertson (1997) acknowledged that some research (e.g., Martin, Williams, & Clark, 1991) has suggested that anxiety may be associated with selective processing of any emotive material, which would include disgust words.

Thorpe and Salkovskis (1998, Study 4) also used the emotional Stroop task to investigate whether spider phobic individuals showed a cognitive bias for disgust words. Unlike Barker and Robertson (1997), Thorpe and Salkovskis (1998) included positive words to allow for the influence of the general emotionality of the word. They found a greater Stroop interference for spider words only in spider-phobic compared with nonphobic individuals. Thorpe and Salkovskis found no difference between spider-phobic and nonphobic individuals for disgust, positive, or neutral words. Using the dot probe paradigm, Wenzel and Holt (1999) also looked at attentional deployment to phobia relevant stimuli in spider phobic persons. Contrary to the findings from Thorpe and Salkovskis (1998), they found no attentional bias toward phobia-relevant stimuli in spider phobic individuals.

In summary, the available evidence on cognitive biases toward fear-relevant cues in people with spider phobia is equivocal and inconclusive at present, and it requires further detailed investigation.

Differential Outcome Beliefs in Animal Phobics

Most individuals who are fearful of animals develop a set of outcome beliefs about what will happen to them if they encounter their phobic animal. At least two studies have suggested that those who fear fear-relevant or invertebrate animals expect disgust-related outcomes (e.g., being contaminated, made dirty, or becoming ill) rather than outcomes involving physical harm (e.g., being attacked and physically harmed). Davey, Cavanagh, and Lamb (2003) used a hypothetical conditioning experiment to get participants to rate what outcomes they expected after being shown pictures of a range of animals (fear relevant, predatory, and fear irrelevant). They found that predatory animals (e.g., wolf, tiger) were selectively associated with pain-relevant outcomes, whereas fear relevant (e.g., spider, cockroach) were selectively associated with disease and disgust-relevant outcomes. In a similar hypothetical conditioning experiment, van Overveld, de Jong, and Peters (2006) asked spider-fearful individuals to estimate the probability that slides of spiders, maggots, pit bull

---

[1]The Stroop task (Stroop, 1935) involves naming the color that words are written in while ignoring the meaning of the word itself. The emotional Stroop task has been used to show that people take longer to name the color of the word if the word has emotional significance for them (e.g., spider phobic individuals take longer to name spider words; Watts, McKenna, Sharrock, & Trezise, 1986).

terriers, or rabbits would be followed by a sip of nauseating juice (a disgusting outcome) or an electric shock (physically harmful outcome). They found that maggots were selectively associated with the disgusting outcome, pit bull terriers with the physically harmful outcome, and spiders with both. In addition, a bias toward disgust-relevant consequences was the best single predictor of spider fear. These studies suggest that there is a predisposition to associate fear-relevant animals and invertebrates with disgusting consequences, and it may be that through this association with disgusting consequences that fear-relevant animals acquire their disgusting properties.

The body of research discussed above clearly indicates a significant relationship between measures of disgust sensitivity and measures of fear of fear-relevant animals and invertebrates. This relationship is found by using a range of measures of disgust sensitivity (including the FCQ, GDQ, and the DPSS) and is still present when measures of neuroticism, introversion, and trait anxiety are partialed out. This latter finding suggests that the relationship between disgust sensitivity and animal fears is unlikely to be mediated by levels of anxiety, per se, and does not result from measures of disgust being confounded with measures of anxiety (Davey & Bond, 2006; Muris et al., 1999). The relationship between disgust and fear-relevant animals is selective in that disgust sensitivity is not usually related to fear of other groups of animals, such as predatory animals (e.g., tigers, sharks, wolves), farm animals (e.g., cows, pigs, chickens), or fear-irrelevant animals (e.g., rabbits, kittens; Arrindell et al., 1999; Matchett & Davey, 1991). Nevertheless, despite this relationship between disgust and subclinical animal fears, the role of disgust in clinically diagnosable animal phobias is unclear. Disgust is certainly experienced in many clinical animal phobias, and phobic persons do develop beliefs about their phobic animal being disgusting. However, these beliefs are usually less frequent than other types of phobic beliefs (e.g., "the animal will physically harm me"), and disgust does not appear to trigger phobic fear when it is experimentally induced in animal phobic persons (Arntz et al., 1993; Edwards & Salkovskis, 2006; Thorpe & Salkovskis, 1998).

THEORETICAL ISSUES

Evidence from more than 10 years of research now indicates fairly unambiguously that disgust is an emotion that is experienced in animal phobias and especially in fear to that group of animals with high-fear, low-predatory status (known as *fear-relevant animals*). Unfortunately, research on this topic has not progressed much beyond this basic and simple finding, and a number of critical theoretical issues remain to be resolved. Two of the most important issues are (a) Why is fear of some animals (e.g., fear-relevant animals) associated with disgust when fear of other types of animals is not (e.g., predatory animals)? and (b) Is disgust merely an experienced consequence of acquiring an animal fear or phobia, or does disgust have a causal role to play in the acquisition of animal fears? We now address the relevant evidence on these two issues.

What Makes Animals Disgust Relevant?

Disgust sensitivity levels are directly associated with fear of certain types of animals (fear-relevant animals) but not with others (e.g., predatory animals). In this respect fear-relevant animals act like primary disgust objects and directly elicit disgust as well as fear. This is supported by the fact that fear-relevant animals appear as primary disgust-eliciting stimuli in cluster analyses of disgust-relevant objects and score higher on measures of disgust than many other negative emotions (Marzillier & Davey, 2004). Many people with animal phobia also develop beliefs about their feared animal being disgusting or disgust related in some way (Arntz et al., 1993; de Jong et al., 1997; Thorpe & Salkovskis, 1995). Therefore, why have those animals listed in the fear-relevant categories in Exhibit 8.1 acquired disgust relevance?

First, it is known that disgusting objects are nearly always associated with animals, animal products, parts of animals, animal body products, and so forth, so it is perhaps not surprising that animals themselves will also elicit disgust (Angyal, 1941; Rozin & Fallon, 1987). However, not all animals have a close association with disgust. Fear of predatory animals and many farm animals, for example, is not related to levels of disgust sensitivity, which might be expected if such animals are primary disgust objects (Arrindell et al., 1999; Matchett & Davey, 1991). There is, therefore, something more substantial than just being an animal that relates animals in the fear-relevant category to disgust.

Davey (1992a) outlined a number of possible reasons why those animals in the fear-relevant category have a close association with the disgust emotion. First, one function of the disgust emotion is as a food-rejection response that helps to prevent the transmission of disease. The main features of the disgust emotion include a physiological manifestation (nausea), a distancing of the self from the disgusting object (avoidance), and sensitivity to contamination from, or oral incorporation of, the offensive object (Rozin & Fallon, 1987). Thus, the adaptive benefit of the disgust emotion appears to be the prevention of oral incorporation of disgusting objects, and as a consequence the prevention of the transmission of disease (Davey, 1994a). This link between disgust and the prevention of the spread of disease, infection, and illness may be an important factor in defining why fear-relevant animals have such a strong association with disgust. Davey (1992b) outlined three possible ways in which fear-relevant animals might have acquired their disgust relevance: (a) by historically being directly associated with the spread of disease (e.g., rats, cockroaches) or the contamination of food (e.g., maggots, mice); (b) by possessing physical characteristics that resemble primary disgust-evoking stimuli such as mucus and feces (e.g., animals that are perceived as slimy such as snakes, lizards, slugs, worms, frogs); and (c) by being opportunistically or superstitiously associated with disease, or acting as signals for infection. Although the rationale for the first two groups is reasonably self-evident, the latter is included because, historically, many animals have become associated with illness and the spread of disease but in fact are entirely innocent of any involvement. One such example is the spider—arguably the most common animal fear in Western cultures. For instance, in most of Europe during the Middle Ages spiders were considered a source of contamination that absorbed poisons in their environment, and any food that had come into contact with a spider was considered to be infected (Renner, 1990). The spider's bite was also one way of explaining the causes of many of the terrible epidemics of plague and disease that swept across Europe in the Middle Ages onward (Gloyne, 1950). Although not fatally venomous, many European spiders do possess bites that cause painful systemic reactions, and these bites became opportunistically associated with causally unrelated diseases and illness (Gloyne, 1950; Hecker, 1846; Renner, 1990). During the Middle Ages, spiders were also perceived as harbingers of the Great Plagues that swept across Europe from the 10th century onward (Davey, 1994b), and it is interesting that cross-cultural studies of animal fears tend to suggest that spider fear features more prominently in lists of animal fears from cultures that consist mainly of European persons and their descendants (Davey et al., 1998). Therefore, although explicit knowledge of the spider's association with disease and illness may have been lost over time, it may still be manifest today in its ability to elicit disgust.

Nevertheless, there is still little in the way of definitive evidence on which to evaluate these views about the origins of animal disgust relevance. However, the hypotheses outlined by Davey (1992a) are empirically testable. For example, (a) Is sliminess (or other physical characteristics possessed by primary disgust objects) an important feature that contributes to the elicitation of disgust to fear-relevant animals such as snakes, lizards, slugs, worms, and so forth? (b) Does an individual's knowledge of an animal's involvement in the spread of disease affect its ability to elicit disgust? (c) Does pairing a disgust-irrelevant animal (e.g., predatory animal, farm animal, fear-irrelevant animal) with a disgust or disease-relevant outcome increase that animal's ability to elicit disgust? At the time of this writing, studies such as these are still waiting to be implemented.

Does Disgust Have a Causal Role to Play in the Acquisition of Animal Fears?

As we emphasized earlier, it is clear that disgust is an emotion that is experienced in many animal fears, but does disgust have a causal role to play in the acquisition of these fears? For example, if someone has high disgust-sensitivity levels (i.e., reacts strongly to disgusting objects) does this mean that an individual will be more likely to develop animal fears? Similarly, if an individual's disgust sensitivity is suddenly increased is that likely to increase experienced fear to fear-relevant animals? Measures of disgust sensitivity levels are known to be highly correlated with measures of fear to fear-relevant animals, but this could simply imply that possessing an animal fear increases disgust sensitivity and not vice versa.

The most obvious way to investigate any causal relationship between disgust sensitivity and animal fears is to experimentally manipulate disgust levels and then assess the effects of this manipulation on measures of animal fear. In an early study that manipulated disgust, Webb and Davey (1993) asked a nonclinical population to rate fear to four categories of animals (predatory, fear-relevant small mammals and reptiles, fear-relevant invertebrates, and neutral) before and after watching a violent, disgusting, or neutral video. They found that participants who watched the violent video showed increased fear ratings to predatory animals, whereas participants who watched the disgusting video showed increased fear to both groups of fear-relevant animals. At first sight, this appears to represent good evidence for a causal role for disgust in small animal fears as it suggests that disgust mood induction may directly act to increase fear to fear-relevant animals. However, this study has a number of limitations. First, the video used to manipulate disgust showed an open-heart surgery operation, and it may have been as likely to elicit anxiety as disgust. Second, Webb and Davey (1993) failed to make a mood manipulation check after the inductions, and therefore it cannot be verified whether the inductions facilitated the emotions they were supposed to target.

In a more controlled and thorough investigation, Marzillier and Davey (2005) looked at whether induced disgust facilitated experienced anxiety and vice versa. Using a range of mood-induction procedures and a variety of mood measures, Marzillier and Davey demonstrated that induced anxiety produced increases in reported disgust, but there was no evidence for an effect of induced disgust on reported anxiety. These findings were independent of the type of mood-induction procedure used (guided imagery vignette and music, video clips, and autobiographical recall and music), and the type of dependent mood measure used (visual analog scale, differential emotion scale, or a free-label questionnaire). These findings have important implications for the putative causal role for disgust in animal fears and phobias, and they suggest that if disgust does have a causal influence on animal fears, then this influence is not mediated simply by experienced disgust facilitating experienced anxiety. These findings are consistent with results reported by Edwards and Salkovskis (2006), who investigated the effect of disgust inductions on spider fear. They found that inducing disgust during the habituation of a spider phobia failed to enhance self-reported fear to spiders—

further evidence that increases in experienced disgust do not directly affect experienced fear or anxiety, even when that fear is directly related to a specific animal fear.

Is there any evidence that disgust directly influences animal fears? The evidence so far available suggests that if there is a causal effect of disgust on animal fears, then it is not as simple as experienced disgust facilitating experienced fear or anxiety. However, disgust may play an indirect role in influencing anxiety generally and animal fears specifically. Disgust is just one of a number of negative emotions that people experience, and negative emotions can often have important effects on how people process and store information. For example, Davey, Bickerstaffe, and MacDonald (2006) reported the results of an experiment that investigated the effect of induced disgust on interpretational bias using the homophone spelling task. Four groups of participants experienced disgust, anxiety, happy, or neutral mood inductions and then completed the homophone spelling task, which requires the participant to interpret ambiguous words presented through headphones. Both the disgust and anxiety groups interpreted significantly more threat/neutral homophones as threat than both the happy and neutral groups; the disgust group also interpreted significantly fewer positive/neutral homophones as positive than the happy group. If experienced disgust causes a shift away from positive toward threatening interpretations of ambiguous material, then this may provide the basis for a causal role for disgust in anxious psychopathology. Because the effect appears to be a nonspecific emotion-congruent one (i.e., a negative emotion causing negative interpretations of any ambiguous material), elevated disgust levels will result in a predisposition to interpret information in a threatening way across a broad range of anxiety- and threat-relevant domains. Applying these findings directly to animal fears implies that if an individual is processing information about an animal while experiencing disgust, then he or she is likely to interpret ambiguous information as threatening rather than positive, and this could provide the basis for establishing a fear of that animal. Nevertheless, the information-processing bias associated with disgust is almost certainly a general one that applies to the interpretation of ambiguous information generally. If this is so, then one would expect disgust to be associated with the development of fear to all animals and not just fear-relevant animals, but this is patently not the case (see Arrindell et al., 1999; Matchett & Davey, 1991; Ware et al., 1994).

One final route by which disgust may causally influence animal fears is by directly affecting the experience of disgust itself. It is known that disgust inductions significantly increase the experience of disgust (Edwards & Salkovskis, 2006; Marzillier & Davey, 2005), and there is some evidence that disgust inductions will increase disgust experienced to specific disgust-relevant animal stimuli such as spiders and crane flies (Marzillier, 2003). At least some of the response components of the disgust emotion are shared with anxiety and fear, and these include negatively valenced feelings and a tendency to avoid stimuli that evoke either disgust or anxiety. This being the case, then the shared response components may mean that evoked disgust may be confused with anxiety or fear by the individual and they may label evoked disgust as fear (see also Nabi, 2002). Studies that have attempted to measure whether induced disgust facilitates fear and anxiety have generally used only self-report methods to measure changes in fear, and this is likely to minimize any confusion between disgust and fear because it does not permit the experience of behavioral responses. However, if a behavioral avoidance task is also used, then this allows the participant to experience the avoidance component of the disgust emotion, and this may facilitate confusion between experiences of disgust and fear that result in reporting of increased fear to disgust-relevant stimuli in the wake of a disgust induction.

In summary, there are a number of possible routes by which disgust might have a causal influence on animal fears. However, there is relatively little convincing evidence to support any of these putative routes as yet, and no convincing evidence exists for a causal role of disgust in animal fears and phobias.

CONCLUSION

The ever-growing body of research on disgust and animal fears and phobias has undoubtedly demonstrated that disgust is an emotion experienced in animal fears—and especially in the fear of what we have called fear-relevant animals (e.g., snakes, spiders, rats, mice, slugs, snails, maggots, cockroaches, beetles). This may simply be because fear-relevant animals have developed a disgust relevance that means they evoke disgust as well as fear, and the more they are feared, the more they elicit disgust. So far there is no convincing evidence that disgust has a causal role to play in the acquisition of animal fears and phobias, and a number of possible routes by which disgust may influence animal fear are currently being actively researched. This research needs to examine whether it is the disgust-relevant status of an animal that is critical to disgust generating fear of the animal, or whether more general processes are responsible. For example, the link between disgust and animal fears may be mediated by the effect of disgust on information processing generally. If so, disgust may not possess a special significance for animal fears but may be merely one of many negatively valenced emotions that influence anxiety through emotion-congruent informational and interpretation biases. If disgust does turn out to have a causal role to play, then it is clear that ameliorative treatments for animal phobias will need to take this into account.

REFERENCES

Angyal, A. (1941). Disgust and related aversions. *Journal of Abnormal and Social Psychology, 36*, 393–412.

Armfield, J. M., & Mattiske, J. K. (1996). Vulnerability representation: The role of perceived dangerousness, uncontrollability, unpredictability, and disgustingness in spider fear. *Behaviour Research and Therapy, 34*, 899–909.

Arntz, A., Lavy, E., van den Berg, G., & van Rijsoort, S. (1993). Negative beliefs of spider phobics: A psychometric evaluation of the spider phobics belief questionnaire. *Advances in Behaviour, Research and Therapy, 15*, 257–277.

Arrindell, W. A., Mulkens, S., Kok, J., & Vollenbroek, J. (1999). Disgust sensitivity and the sex difference in fears to common indigenous animals. *Behaviour Research and Therapy, 37*, 273–280.

Arrindell, W. A., Pickersgill, M. J., Merckelbach, H., Ardon, A. M., & Cornet, F. C. (1991). Phobic dimensions. 3. Factor analytic approaches to the study of common phobic fears—an updated review of findings obtained with adult subjects. *Advances in Behaviour Research and Therapy, 13*, 73–130.

Barker, K., & Robertson, N. (1997). Selective processing and fear of spiders: Use of the Stroop task to assess interference for spider-related, movement, and disgust information. *Cognition & Emotion, 11*, 331–336.

Bernstein, D. A., & Allen, G. J. (1969). Fear Survey Schedule. II: Normative data and factor analyses based upon a large college sample. *Behaviour Research and Therapy, 7*, 403.

Burns, G. L., Keortge, S. G., Formea, G. M., & Sternberger, L. G. (1996). Revision of the Padua Inventory of obsessive compulsive disorder symptoms: Distinctions between worry, obsessions and compulsions. *Behaviour Research and Therapy, 34*, 163–173.

Chapman, T. F. (1997). The epidemiology of fears and phobias. In G. C. L. Davey (Ed.), *Phobias: A handbook of theory, research and treatment* (pp. 415–434). Chichester, England: Wiley.

Cook, M., & Mineka, S. (1989). Observational conditioning of fear to fear-relevant versus fear-irrelevant stimuli in rhesus monkeys. *Journal of Abnormal Psychology, 98*, 448–459.

Cook, M., & Mineka, S. (1990). Selective associations in the observational learning of fear in rhesus monkeys. *Journal of Experimental Psychology: Animal Behavior Processes, 16*, 372–389.

Costello, C. G. (1982). Fears and phobias in women: A community study. *Journal of Abnormal Psychology, 91*, 280–286.

Davey, G. C. L. (1992a). Characteristics of individuals with fear of spiders. *Anxiety Research, 4*, 299–314.

Davey, G. C. L. (1992b). Classical conditioning and the acquisition of human fears and phobias: A review and synthesis of the literature. *Advances in Behaviour Research and Therapy, 14*, 29–66.

Davey, G. C. L. (1994a). Disgust. In V. S. Ramachandran (Ed.), *Encyclopedia of human behavior* (Vol. 2, pp. 135–141). San Diego, CA: Academic Press.

Davey, G. C. L. (1994b). The 'disgusting' spider: The role of disease and illness in the perpetuation of fear of spiders. *Society & Animals, 2,* 17–25.

Davey, G. C. L. (1994c). Self-reported fears to common indigenous animals in an adult UK population: The role of disgust sensitivity. *British Journal of Psychology, 85,* 541–554.

Davey, G. C. L. (1995). Preparedness and phobias: Specific evolved associations or a generalized expectancy bias? *Behavioral and Brain Sciences, 18,* 289–297.

Davey, G. C. L. (1997). A conditioning model of phobias. In G. C. L. Davey (Ed.), *Phobias: A handbook of theory, research and treatment* (pp. 301–322). Chichester, England: Wiley.

Davey, G. C. L., Bickerstaffe, S., & MacDonald, B. A. (2006) Experienced disgust causes a negative interpretation bias: A causal role for disgust in anxious psychopathology. *Behaviour Research and Therapy, 44,* 1375–1384.

Davey, G. C. L., & Bond, N. (2006). Using controlled comparisons in disgust psychopathology research: The case of disgust, hypochondriasis and health anxiety. *Journal of Behavior Therapy and Experimental Psychiatry, 37,* 4–15.

Davey, G. C. L., Cavanagh, K., & Lamb, A. (2003). Differential aversive outcome expectancies for high- and low-predation animals. *Journal of Behavior Therapy and Experimental Psychiatry, 34,* 117–128.

Davey, G. C. L., McDonald, A. S., Hirisave, U., Prabhu, G. G., Iwawaki, S., Jim, C. I., et al. (1998). A cross-cultural study of animal fears. *Behaviour Research and Therapy, 36,* 735–750.

de Jong, P. J., Andrea, H., & Muris, P. (1997). Spider phobia in children: Disgust and fear before and after treatment. *Behaviour Research and Therapy, 35,* 559–562.

de Jong, P. J., & Merkelbach, H. (1998). Blood-injection-injury phobia and fear of spiders: Domain specific individual differences in disgust sensitivity. *Personality and Individual Differences, 24,* 153–158.

Delprato, D. J. (1980). Hereditary determinants of fears and phobias: A critical review. *Behavior Therapy, 11,* 79–103.

Doogan, S., & Thomas, G. V. (1992). Origins of fear of dogs in adults and children: The role of conditioning processes and prior familiarity with dogs. *Behaviour Research and Therapy, 30,* 387–394.

Edwards, S., & Salkovskis, P. M. (2006). An experimental demonstration that fear, but not disgust, is associated with the return of fear in phobias. *Journal of Anxiety Disorders, 20,* 58–71.

Eysenck, H., & Eysenck, S. B. G. (1984). *Manual of the Eysenck Personality Questionnaire (junior and adult)*. London: Hedder & Stoughton.

Gloyne, H. F. (1950). Tarantism: Mass hysterical reaction to spider bite in the Middle Ages. *American Image, 7,* 29–42.

Haidt, J., McCauley, C., & Rozin, P. (1994). Individual differences in sensitivity to disgust: A scale sampling seven domains of disgust elicitors. *Personality and Individual Differences, 16,* 701–713.

Hecker, J. F. C. (1846). *The epidemics of the Middle Ages*. (B. G. Babington, Trans.). London: Woodfall.

Klorman, R., Weerts, T. C., Hastings, J. E., Melamed, B. G., & Lang, P. J. (1974). Psychometric descriptions of some specific fear questionnaires. *Behavior Therapy, 5*, 401–409.

Landy, F. J., & Gaupp, L. A. (1971). A factor analysis of the fear survey schedule—III. *Behaviour Research and Therapy, 9*, 89–93.

Lewontin, R. C. (1979). Sociobiology as an adaptationist program. *Behavioral Science, 24*, 5–14.

Marks, I. M. (1987). *Fears, phobias and rituals*. New York: Academic Press.

Martin, M., Williams, R. M., & Clark, D. M. (1991). Does anxiety lead to selective processing of threat-related information? *Behaviour Research and Therapy, 29*, 147–160.

Marzillier, S. (2003). *The role of disgust in anxiety disorders*. Unpublished master's thesis, University of Sussex, Sussex, England.

Marzillier, S., & Davey, G. C. L. (2004). The emotional profiling of disgust-eliciting stimuli: Evidence for primary and complex disgusts. *Cognition & Emotion, 18*, 313–336.

Marzillier, S., & Davey, G. C. L. (2005). Anxiety and disgust: Evidence for a unidirectional relationship. *Cognition & Emotion, 19*, 729–750.

Matchett, G., & Davey, G. C. L. (1991). A test of a disease-avoidance model of animal phobias. *Behaviour Research and Therapy, 29*, 91–94.

McNally, R. J. (1995). Preparedness, phobias, and the Panglossian paradigm. *Behavioral and Brain Sciences, 18*, 303–304.

Merckelbach, H., & de Jong, P. J. (1997). Evolutionary models of phobias. In G. C. L. Davey (Ed.), *Phobias: A handbook of theory, research and treatment* (pp. 323–348). Chichester, England: Wiley.

Merckelbach, H., de Jong, P. J., Arntz, A., & Schouten, E. (1993). The role of evaluative learning and disgust sensitivity in the etiology and treatment of spider phobia. *Advances in Behaviour Research and Therapy, 15*, 243–255.

Merckelbach, H., de Jong, P. J., Muris, P., & van den Hout, M. (1996). The etiology of specific phobias: A review. *Clinical Psychology Review, 16*, 337–361.

Merckelbach, H., Muris, P., & Schouten, E. (1996). Pathways to fear in spider phobic children. *Behaviour Research and Therapy, 34*, 935–938.

Mulkens, S. A. N., de Jong, P. J., & Merckelbach, H. (1996). Disgust and spider phobia. *Journal of Abnormal Psychology, 105*, 464–468.

Muris, P., Merckelbach, H., Schmidt, H., & Tierney, S. (1999). Disgust sensitivity, trait anxiety and anxiety disorders symptoms in normal children. *Behaviour Research and Therapy, 37*, 953–961.

Murray, E., & Foote, F. (1979). The origins of fear of snakes. *Behaviour Research and Therapy, 17*, 489–493.

Nabi, R. L. (2002). The theoretical versus the lay meaning of disgust: Implications for emotion research. *Cognition & Emotion, 16*, 695–703.

Öhman, A., Eriksson, A., & Lofberg, I. (1975). Phobias and preparedness: Phobic versus neutral pictures as conditioned stimuli for human autonomic responses. *Journal of Abnormal Psychology, 84,* 41–45.

Öhman, A., & Mineka, S. (2001). Fears, phobias and preparedness: Towards an evolved module of fear and fear learning. *Psychological Review, 108,* 483–522.

Renner, F. (1990). *Spinnen: Ungeheuer—sympathisch.* Kaiserslautern, Germany: Rainar Nitzche Verlag.

Rozin, P., & Fallon A. E. (1987). A perspective on disgust. *Psychological Review, 94,* 23–41.

Rozin, P., Fallon, A. E., & Mandell, R. (1984). Family resemblances in attitudes to food. *Developmental Psychology, 20,* 309–314.

Sawchuk, C. N., Lohr, J. M., Tolin, D. F, Lee, T. C., & Kleinknecht, R. A. (2000). Disgust sensitivity and contamination fears in spider and blood-injection-injury phobias. *Behaviour Research and Therapy, 38,* 753–762.

Seligman, M. E. P. (1971). Phobias and preparedness. *Behavior Therapy, 2,* 307–320.

Spielberger, C. D. (1983). *State-Trait Anxiety Inventory.* Palo Alto, CA: Consulting Psychologists Press.

Stroop, J. R. (1935). Studies of interference in serial verbal reactions. *Journal of Experimental Psychology, 18,* 643–662.

Thordarson, D. S., Radomsky, A. S., Rachman, S., Shafran, R., & Sawchuk, C. (1997, November). *The Vancouver Obsessional Compulsive Inventory (VOCI).* Paper presented at the 31st annual meeting of the Association for the Advancement of Behavior Therapy, Miami Beach, FL.

Thorpe, S. J., & Salkovskis, P. M. (1995). Phobic beliefs: Do cognitive factors play a role in specific phobias. *Behaviour Research and Therapy, 33,* 805–816.

Thorpe, S. J., & Salkovskis, P. M. (1997). Information processing in spider phobics: The Stroop colour-naming task may indicate strategic but not automatic attentional bias. *Behaviour Research and Therapy, 35,* 131–144.

Thorpe, S. J., & Salkovskis, P. M. (1998). Studies on the role of disgust in the acquisition and maintenance of specific phobias. *Behaviour Research and Therapy, 36,* 877–893.

Tolin, D. F., Lohr, J. M., Sawchuk, C. N., & Lee, T. C. (1997). Disgust and disgust sensitivity in blood-injection-injury and spider phobia. *Behaviour Research and Therapy, 35,* 949–943.

Tucker, M., & Bond, N. W. (1997). The roles of gender, sex role, and disgust in fear of animals. *Personality and Individual Differences, 22,* 135–128.

van Overveld, M., de Jong, P. J., & Peters, M. L. (2006). Differential UCS expectancy bias in spider fearful individuals: Evidence toward an association between spiders and disgust relevant outcomes. *Journal of Behavior Therapy and Experimental Psychiatry, 37,* 60–72.

Walls, M. M., & Kleinknecht, R. A. (1996, April). *Disgust factors as predictors of blood-injury fear and fainting.* Paper presented to the annual meeting of the Western Psychological Association, San Jose, CA.

Ware, J., Jain, K., Burgess, I., & Davey, G. C. L. (1994). Disease-avoidance model: Factor analysis of common animal fears. *Behaviour Research and Therapy, 32,* 57–63.

Watson, J. B., & Rayner, R. (1920). Conditioned emotional reactions. *Journal of Experimental Psychology, 3,* 1–14.

Watts, F. N., McKenna, F. P., Sharrock, R., & Trezise, I. (1986). Color naming of phobia related words. *British Journal of Psychology, 77,* 97–108.

Webb, K., & Davey, G. C. L. (1993). Disgust sensitivity and fear of animals: Effect of exposure to violent or revulsive material. *Anxiety, Stress, & Coping, 5,* 329–335.

Wenzel, A., & Holt, C. S. (1999). Dot probe performance in two specific phobias. *British Journal of Clinical Psychology, 38,* 407–410.

Wolpe, L., & Lang, P. J. (1964). A fear survey schedule for use in behaviour therapy. *Behaviour Research and Therapy, 2,* 27–30.

9

DISGUST AND BLOOD-INJURY-INJECTION PHOBIA

ANDREW C. PAGE AND BENJAMIN J. TAN

Blood-injury-injection (BII) *phobia* is defined as persistent fear and avoidance that is both excessive and unreasonable, triggered by the anticipation or presence of blood, injury, injections, and conceptually similar stimuli (American Psychiatric Association, 2000). The phobic disorder, experienced by about 3% of the population (Fredrikson, Annas, Fischer, & Wik, 1996), is not only disabling but it may also bring an attendant risk of morbidity and mortality as sufferers avoid timely medical care (Marks, 1988; Page, 1996). However, if such a characterization were sufficient, BII phobia would have little place in this book. The phobia is complicated by two factors, namely fainting (Marks, 1988) and disgust (Page, 1994). This chapter begins by describing the nature of this phobia and after reviewing the relevant literature, it outlines a hypothetical model that can accommodate existing data and make predictions to guide future research.

Fainting in phobic situations is common among people with BII phobia (Öst, 1992; Öst, Sterner, & Lindahl, 1984; Page, 1996, 1998; Thyer, Himle, & Curtis, 1985). The emotional fainting observed has been described as *vasovagal syncope* (Lewis, 1932), in acknowledgement of the presumed vasovagal origin. Vasovagal syncope can be triggered by events of an emotional (e.g., blood) and nonemotional nature (e.g., body tilt; Gerlach et al., 2006; Thyer et al., 1985). The physiological mechanisms responsible for vasovagal syncope produce a diphasic response (Graham, 1961; Graham, Kabler, & Lunsford, 1961). In the first phase, there is dominance of sympathetic nervous system activity, consistent with elicitation of the fight-or-flight response (Thyer & Curtis, 1985; Thyer et al., 1985). Of particular relevance to fainting is the initial rise in blood pressure. In the second phase, there is a relative increase in parasympathetic nervous system activity, consistent with a conservation-withdrawal response (Marks, 1988; Vingerhoets, 1984). The occurrence of fainting appears related to the drop in blood pressure in the latter part of the diphasic response. If the drop is of sufficient magnitude to affect cerebral blood flow, syncope will occur as a consequence of cerebral anoxia. The second phase may occur while the blood-injury stimulus is present, but it can occur after some time. For instance, Ruetz, Johnson, Callahan, Meade, and Smith (1967) noted that among blood donors, fainting can occur after the cessation of venipuncture.

Although vasovagal syncope appears unique to BII phobia (Connolly, Hallam, & Marks, 1976), and present in about three quarters of these phobic persons (Kleinknecht & Lenz, 1989), it is not universal. Kleinknecht and Lenz (1989) found that BII fainting may occur among some individuals with minimal fear of BII stimuli. This led them to propose a three-fold distinction among fainters (Kleinknecht, Lenz, Ford, & DeBerard, 1990). First, there are *essential fainters*, who report minimal anxiety or fear in the presence of blood and injury stimuli. Avoidance among these nonfearful fainters is minimal. The remaining two groups of individuals can be considered to be variants of fearful fainters. The second group of fainters is *escape fainters*. These people faint in the presence of blood and injury stimuli when avoidance is impossible, but they would endeavor to escape before fainting occurs. The final group comprises the *relief fainters*. These people experience phobic fear, but they do not experience faintness until the perceived threat has terminated. Thus, it is clear is that there are two ways people react to blood, injury, and injection stimuli, one involving fear and the other involving fainting. Fear and fainting can occur together in the same individual, but each can also be present in the absence of the other (Page, 1994). Fear and fainting also appear to be triggered to greater extents by different stimuli. Both Öst (1992) and Page, Bennett, Carter, and Woodmore (1997) found that faintness was more common among people who were more concerned about blood than injections, whereas fear was the stronger response among those who were more concerned about injections than blood. Thus, situational and person-related factors appear to be associated with fainting.

The occurrence of fainting among a subset of individuals in response to a subset of phobic stimuli complicates the presentation of BII phobia, but the picture is still incomplete. The response to blood and injury can also involve disgust and associated avoidance (Rachman, 1990). For example, Sawchuk, Lohr, Westendorf, Meunier, and Tolin (2002) exposed individuals with either blood or spider phobia to stimuli relevant to their fears. They found that fear ratings could not discriminate groups, but elevated disgust scores were present among the participants with BII phobia (see also de Jong & Merckelbach, 1998; Koch, O'Neill, Sawchuk, & Connolly, 2002; Sawchuk, Lohr, Tolin, Lee, & Kleinknecht, 2000; Tolin, Lohr, Sawchuk, & Lee, 1997). BII phobic individuals exposed to BII stimuli exhibited greater disgust responses than nonfearful and anxious control individuals (Tolin, Sawchuk, & Lee, 1999). Likewise, in a series of studies that used an evaluative conditioning methodology, similar results were found (Olatunji, Lohr, Sawchuk, & Westendorf, 2005). Neutral facial expressions were paired with fearsome, disgusting, and neutral pictures in one experiment and BII-relevant stimuli in a second experiment. Evaluative conditioning would be demonstrated if the previously neutral stimuli acquired characteristics of the emotional response with which they had been paired. The authors showed that conditioned evaluative shifts toward disgust occurred with repeated pairings of facial and BII stimuli. In addition, they reported that the phobic stimuli elicited two correlated emotional reactions of fear and disgust, but it is important to note that the dominant emotional response among BII fearful participants was disgust. What is not yet apparent is whether some individuals respond to the phobic stimuli with fear, others with disgust, and a final group with a blended emotional experience typified by both fear and disgust (Woody & Teachman, 2000).

Although the relationship that disgust has to other emotions remains to be clarified, the construct of disgust itself does not appear to be unitary (Olatunji & Sawchuk, 2005). Disgust was initially described as a food-related emotion of oral revulsion (Rozin & Fallon, 1987). However, disgust is not only elicited by food stimuli (e.g., rotting foods, odors) but also by certain animals, body products, death, sex, and body envelope violations (Haidt, McCauley, & Rozin, 1994). *Body envelope violations* refer to the situation in which the exterior envelope of the human body (e.g., the skin) is breached or altered in some way (e.g., "You see a man with his intestines exposed after an accident"; Haidt et al., 1994). Accordingly, subsequent work has distinguished the core food-related disgust from other domains of disgust. *Animal-reminder disgust* is described as the emotion elicited by aspects of life that remind individuals of their animal origins (Rozin, Haidt, & McCauley, 1999). *Interpersonal disgust* describes disgust triggered by contact with attributes of undesirable people, and *moral disgust* is used to describe a disgust reaction to certain moral offenses (Rozin, Haidt, & McCauley, 2000).

Disgust is more commonly associated with contamination threat and serves to prevent contact with contaminants (Olatunji, Sawchuk, de Jong, & Lohr, 2006). Withdrawal from phobic objects may be related to disgust (associated with the threat of contamination) as well as to fear (associated with the threat of injury). Thus, de Jong and Muris (2002) found that the disgust-evoking properties in spiders were better predictors of spider phobia than were the actual threatening or harmful properties. In addition, some investigations have suggested that disgust is not a unitary construct, but rather, different domains of disgust are related to different disorders (de Jong & Merckelbach, 1998; Olatunji, Sawchuk, Lohr, & de Jong, 2004; Sawchuk, Lohr, Tolin, Lee, & Kleinknecht, 2000).

Notwithstanding issues about the co-occurrence of fear and disgust and the variety of stimuli that may elicit the emotion and facets thereof, it is clear that the phenomenon of BII phobia is more diverse than the fear-centered characterization presented in diagnostic schemes. By way of summary, the experience of fear appears strongly correlated with disgust, but the greater intensity of disgust (Olatunji & Sawchuk, 2005) may suggest that it is the primary emotion involved. In addition to fear and disgust, faintness and fainting can occur in phobic situations. It appears that the individual differences affect the extent to which these responses typify a reaction to BII stimuli, and these three responses of fear, fainting, and disgust are triggered to varying extents by different stimuli. Fear responses tend to occur more strongly among stimuli that signal future pain (e.g., injections; Öst, 1992; Page et al., 1997), and faintness tends to occur more strongly with stimuli associated with body envelope violations (e.g., blood; Öst, 1992; Page et al., 1997). BII phobic persons, in contrast to spider phobic persons, also are more likely to exhibit disgust in response to body envelope violations (de Jong & Merckelbach, 1998).

Thus, it is clear that disgust plays a key role in BII concerns, perhaps even being a more significant response than the fear implied by the disorder's designation as a phobia. Some have also argued that not only is disgust a response but it is also involved in a causal manner producing or exacerbating some of the observed responses or making treatment more difficult (see Woody & Teachman, 2000). However, before describing these accounts, we consider a conceptual structure to assist with the organization of the relevant theories and data. Having reviewed the literature, it is possible to return to this heuristic model to clarify some of the causal pathways in BII phobia.

A simplified heuristic for considering possible relationships among hypothetical variables in BII phobia can be outlined. Three correlated response (dependent) variables representing fear, fainting, and disgust can be postulated. These responses could be caused by three hypothetical latent (independent) variables. Each latent variable could be broken down into various components, and this is done in the remainder of the chapter. For example, the latent variable causally responsible for BII fears could include a variety of associative (e.g., conditioning, vicarious transmission, verbal acquisition; Mineka & Zinbarg, 1996; Rachman 1990) and nonassociative (e.g., innate tendency to fear particular stimuli; Menzies & Clarke, 1995) pathways. However, despite the model's simplicity, it provides a conceptual structure for considering the role of disgust in BII phobia. Because the focus of this chapter is on the role of disgust in BII phobia, the questions of interest are (a) What causes the emotional response of disgust around BII stimuli? (b) How is disgust related to BII fear? and (c) How is disgust related to BII fainting? We now consider each issue in turn.

WHAT CAUSES THE EMOTIONAL RESPONSE
OF DISGUST AROUND BII STIMULI?

Disgust is an emotional response that has state and trait components (Woody & Teachman, 2000). The trait of disgust sensitivity is an individual difference dimension. The reasons for the individual differences appear to include familial factors (Rozin et al., 2000; Rozin, Fallon, & Mandell, 1984), female gender (Haidt et al., 1994; Opplinger & Zillmann, 1997), and environmental experiences, including sociocultural factors (Rozin et al., 2000). These individual differences are predisposing variables that set the stage for disgust to be triggered in the presence of certain stimuli. These stimuli include food-related contaminants but also cues that remind humans of their relatedness to animals (Rozin et al., 2000).

Because blood and injury are objects that remind humans of their relatedness to other animals, they have potential to elicit disgust and presumably will be more likely to elicit these reactions among people with elevated disgust sensitivity. Disgust sensitivity itself seems to be related to personality dimensions, with one of the strongest relationships being with neuroticism (Druschel & Sherman, 1999; Haidt et al., 1994). The nature of the relationship between disgust and neuroticism is the focus of some debate, with some researchers who argue that the relationship is spurious and an artifact of neuroticism (Woody & Teachman, 2000; Woody & Tolin, 2002). However, Mulkens, de Jong, and Merckelbach (1996) found that the relationship between disgust sensitivity and spider fear did not change appreciably after controlling for neuroticism, suggesting that they are independent predictors of different constructs.

This implies that people with elevated disgust sensitivity are characterized by elevated emotional reactivity, particularly anxiety. Druschel and Sherman (1999) also found that *conscientiousness* played an important role, indicating that people with elevated disgust have traits of competence, order, dutifulness, achievement striving, self-discipline, and deliberation. Elevated *agreeableness* (indicating traits of sympathy, sensitivity to others' interpersonal needs, altruism) and low *openness* (indicating minimal experience seeking) also characterized individuals high in disgust sensitivity. Similar to the negative relationship with openness, Haidt et al. (1994) found that disgust sensitivity was negatively correlated with sensation seeking. Therefore, the individual high in disgust sensitivity "might be a highly sociable individual, one who is very sensitive to social and emotional stimuli, but also one who may suffer personally as a result of this sensitivity" (Druschel & Sherman, 1999, p. 746). This is not to say that disgust sensitivity is wholly explained by these five personality dimensions (because together they only account for a third of the variance), but the strong relationship with neuroticism would predict disgust to have other correlates. Because elevated neuroticism is associated with anxiety and its disorders (Andrews et al., 2003), individuals high in disgust sensitivity would be more likely to exhibit higher anxiety and anxiety disorders. Therefore, the trait of disgust sensitivity as well as the emotional state of disgust would be associated with BII phobia.

Consistent with these suggestions, the elevated disgust reaction found among BII phobic individuals does not appear specific to emotional reactions to BII stimuli. As discussed in detail in chapter 6, BII phobic individuals described greater disgust reactions and showed stronger facial expressions of disgust to disgusting (but fear-irrelevant) stimuli when compared with control individuals (Schienle, Stark, & Vaitl, 2001). Replicating these results, Schienle, Schäfer, Stark, Walter, and Vaitl (2005a) found that BII phobic persons reported greater general disgust sensitivity and experienced greater disgust while viewing disgust-related images as well as greater activation of the visual association cortex when observing disgust-relevant slides (which could imply greater selection attention for disgust-evoking stimuli; Schienle et al., 2003).

These self-report questionnaire data linking disgust and neuroticism, or trait anxiety, have found parallels in studies of brain function. Although fear and disgust can be distinguished (implying some neural specificity; Williams et al., 2005), it may be that fear and disgust both recruit an integrative control system responsible for emotional processing (Vaitl, Schienle, & Stark, 2005; see also Schienle, Schäfer, Stark, Walter, & Vaitl, 2005b; and see chap. 6, this volume). In fact, during the disgust induction, individuals with higher trait-anxiety scores also show greater activation of the right amygdala, suggesting that these two emotions share a common neural basis (see also Stark et al., 2004). However, these studies examined the reactions to general disgust stimuli rather than BII stimuli.

When normal participants were exposed to images of contamination and mutilation, there was activation of the occipito-temporal cortex and the right superior parietal cortex (Wright, He, Shapira, Goodman, & Liu, 2004). There were also positive associations between self-reported disgust and activation in the insula and correlations between self-reported arousal and responses in the occipito-temporal cortex. These divergent correlations suggest that the insula may be involved in the processing of disgust-related stimuli that involve body envelope violations and the occipito-temporal cortex may be involved in processing general affective arousal.

In summary, it appears that trait disgust sensitivity is elevated among individuals with BII fears. This relationship is identifiable when studying the neural bases as well as the associated personality dimensions. In addition, BII stimuli can signal body envelope violations and remind people of their animal origins, thereby having the extra capacity to elicit one facet of disgust. How disgust itself is related to BII fears is considered in the next section.

HOW IS DISGUST RELATED TO BII FEARS?

State disgust appears to be elevated among BII phobic individuals when confronting stimuli that distress them (de Jong & Merckelbach, 1998; Koch et al., 2002; Olatunji et al., 2005; Sawchuk et al., 2002; Tolin et al., 1997, 1999). Furthermore, the trait of disgust sensitivity also appears to be strongly correlated with BII fears, with scores on a measure of the construct correlating highly with scores on the Mutilation Questionnaire (Schienle et al., 2001). However, different facets of disgust appear to be more strongly elicited by BII stimuli. For instance, using structural equation modeling to examine the relationships between disgust and BII stimuli, it was apparent that animal reminder disgust was related to BII fears, but there was no significant relationship between BII fears and core disgust (Olatunji et al., 2006). Thus, the relationship between disgust and BII fears appears more strongly related to the domain of animal-reminder disgust rather than being generalized to a broad range of disgust elicitors as have been previously speculated (e.g., Page, 1994). Therefore, future conceptualizations of BII phobia need to be more precise about the particular facet of disgust to which they are referring.

Woody and Teachman (2000) noted that one reason for a close relationship between fear and disgust in the presence of BII stimuli is the shared appraisal of the stimuli. To the extent that disgust appraisals focus on a contamination threat, they will have the capacity to elicit both fear and disgust (e.g., Davey, 1993). Specifically, they suggest appraisal of a stimulus as a signal of possible (a) bodily harm, (b) social rejection (i.e., disgust-related shame and fear of abandonment elicited by behavior interpreted as warranting social rejection), or (c) loss of bodily control (i.e., fear or shame disgust caused by the anticipation of lack of control over a bodily function). It is important to note that the presence of an objective danger is not necessary, but the appraisal that one of these types of threatening outcomes is possible is sufficient to elicit these emotional "false alarm" (Barlow, 2002) reactions. Problems with fear and disgust occur when individuals are not able to avoid, cognitively reframe, or minimize the perceived threats or when these threats have a personal significance because they are central to a person's self-concept.

In summary, disgust is related to BII fears. Woody and Teachman (2000) highlighted a variety of possible explanations for the existence of this relationship. First, fear and disgust may share a common vulnerability, such as the individual difference dimension of neuroticism. Second, people may label the emotional states of fear and disgust with imprecision. This may arise because of problems with the measures, a lack of sophistication on the part of participants, research tending to concentrate on low levels of emotional intensity, or even that fear and disgust are manifestations of disliking emotions (see Ortony, Clore, & Collins, 1988). Third, the relationship may arise from a bidirectional synergistic association shared by fear and disgust. Disgust may exacerbate fear because disgust is associated with vivid imagery and disgust-related imagery occurring in the presence of fear-related stimuli increases reported fear (Hepburn & Page, 1999). Likewise, threatening imagery can lead to sensitization of distress (Dorfan & Woody, 2006; Page, 1999) rather than the expected reduction when people are confronted with fear-relevant stimuli. Future research needs to clarify which of these explanations are more credible, and one place that may inform these theories is the occurrence of fainting, because some have argued that disgust plays a particular role in eliciting faintness.

HOW IS DISGUST RELATED TO BII FAINTING?

BII fainting appears to have some unique causes. Page and Martin (1998), in a multivariate genetic analysis, found that BII fainting was explained by additive genetic variance predictive of fainting in nonblood situations and unique environmental experiences unique to blood fainting. Similarly, Accurso et al. (2001) found that participants who fainted around blood and injury showed a predisposition toward vasovagal syncope when faintness was induced (using the head-up tilt procedure) in the absence of BII stimuli. These two sets of data converge on a view that BII phobic individuals who faint possess an autonomic substrate, not specific to BII stimuli, that predisposes them to respond with vasovagal syncope. Triggering this autonomic process produces the circulatory dysfunction responsible for fainting. Accurso et al. (2001) speculated that the fainting may produce fear secondarily, as sufferers avoid situations liable to elicit syncopal responses. Although this is consistent with Kleinknecht's (1994) suggestion, Page and Martin's genetic analysis found that the co-occurrence of blood fainting and fear arose from an additive genetic factor shared between nonblood fainting and blood fears. Thus, it seems reasonable to postulate that BII may involve a process in which aversive experiences of fainting condition fear to BII situations. It appears that people require this general autonomic dysregulation, but the question remains, how does this mechanism become activated by blood and injury stimuli?

One plausible explanation of the relationship between blood and injury stimuli and fainting has been offered by Page (1994, 2003). It begins with the observation that phobic reactions do not only involve the emotion of fear but also include disgust (e.g., Davey, 1994; Davey et al., 1998; Mattchett & Davey, 1991; Webb & Davey, 1992). Fearful phobic reactions tend to be associated with animals that are classifiable as predatory (i.e., capable of inflicting pain and injury). "Phobic" reactions that involve disgust tend to be associated with animals that are classifiable as potential contaminants (i.e., capable of causing illness if consumed or touched). Assuming that the processes responsible for fear and disgust are partially independent places stimuli involving blood and injury in a curious position. BII stimuli are arguably the point of intersection of the two emotions. That is, observing (Kleinknecht & Thorndike, 1990; Lumley & Melamed, 1992) or imagining (Page, 1999) an injury could elicit both fear and animal reminder of body envelope violation disgust. Thus, presenting an individual with a picture of an injury could first activate the normal sympathetically mediated rise in blood pressure (Page, 1994, 2003) and over time, this activation could be opposed by increases in homeostatic parasympathetic processes that would reduce blood pressure to a baseline level. However, state disgust involves vagal and parasympathetic activation (Levenson, 1992) and hence reductions in blood pressure. How could these effects interact with the homeostatic parasympathetic processes that return blood pressure to normal levels?

Before answering this question an aside is necessary. Disgust sometimes appears associated with increases in heart rate (Prkachin, Williams-Avery, Zwaal, & Mills, 1999; Vrana, 1993). Although this appears to contradict the preceding claim, McKay and Tsao (2005) noted that sympathetic activation occurs more often when the design involves the anticipation of a disgusting stimulus rather than its actual presence, at which time parasympathetic activation appears more usual. Thus, the stimulus presence appears important for the elicitation of disgust, a precondition that is consistent with one of the key criteria of disgust, namely that physical contact with the object is required (Rozin et al., 2000). It is also not clear whether disgust triggered by different domains (e.g., food-related vs. body envelope violation) is more likely to bring about greater parasympathetic activation.

Returning to the argument, some disgust-related stimuli appear to recruit parasympathetic processes, but to explain fainting it is necessary to make an additional assumption, namely that priority is typically accorded to the sympathetic activation of the fight-or-flight response over any other emotion (see Robinson, 1998). Therefore, the pattern of activation would involve a sympathetically mediated increase in blood pressure, followed by a decrease in blood pressure. This decrease would occur as the parasympathetic activation associated with disgust summed with the parasympathetic processes normally responsible for the homeostatic decline in blood pressure.

Examining the relationship between individual differences in disgust sensitivity, fear, and faintness, Kleinknecht, Kleinknecht, and Thorndike (1997) found positive relationships between measures of fear and faintness. However, in contrast to Page's (1994) prediction, they obtained a negative relationship between one of their measures of disgust and their index of faintness. They argued that "disgust-faint relationships are illusory and are mediated by disgust's shared covariance with fear" (p. 1083). Kleinknecht et al. (1997) further speculated that the fear–faint relationship is mediated by the differential interpretations of threat and differential baroreceptor sensitivity. People prone to vasovagal syncope are those who react to painful stimulation with an increase in baroreceptor sensitivity and a decrease in heart rate, which may set the stage for fainting (see Adler, France, & Ditto, 1991; France, 1995). More recently, Olatunji, Williams, Sawchuk, and Lohr (2006) used a similar analytic strategy to examine the relationships among disgust, fainting, and BII fears and replicated the key finding of Kleinkecht et al. (1997). They did find a relationship between the individual-difference variable of (animal-reminder) disgust sensitivity and BII faintness (predicted by Page, 1994), but when the path from BII fear to fainting was included, then the relationship between disgust sensitivity and faintness was no longer significant. Together, these articles present a strong case that self-reports of past BII fainting are related to trait disgust sensitivity by virtue of the correlation between disgust and BII fears.

One possible explanation for the apparently contradictory data is the absence of behavioral and physiological recording and the examination of state disgust. It is plausible that self-reports of faintness and the underlying physiological responses are desynchronous. Therefore, self-reports may vary depending on factors other than the changes in blood pressure that are ultimately responsible for fainting. Although both may be valid indexes of different constructs, in the case of fainting, the decreases in peripheral blood pressure are related to declines in cerebral blood flow and ultimately to the proximal cause of faintness, cerebral anoxia. Therefore, when explaining faintness, changes in blood pressure are potentially more informative than changes in self-reports of faintness.

Gerlach et al. (2006) examined responses around venipuncture and found that BII phobic individuals reported elevated anxiety and disgust during the procedure. Participants also evidenced greater heart rate, respiration, and minute ventilation, indicating increased arousal. However, the authors found no evidence of parasympathetic activation in either BII phobic subgroup or of an association between disgust and parasympathetic activation. Gerlach et al. concluded that these data disconfirm Page's (1994) prediction and suggest that the associations between disgust, parasympathetic activation, and fainting were absent because they do not exist. However, none of their participants viewed the venipuncture. Because participants were not exposed to a disgust-related stimulus, it is not apparent that the hypothesis was tested. In contrast, participants would have experienced the anticipation (and perhaps the occurrence) of pain associated with the injection, rather than contact with the disgust-relevant stimulus. Therefore, the conditions were ripe to generate sympathetic fearful arousal, which is what the authors observed.

In contrast to this scenario, when participants could view blood-injury stimuli, the effects on faintness were more likely to be found. Hepburn and Page (1999) exposed participants to a picture of mutilation and reported that images of pain increased symptoms of both fear and faintness relative to control participants, but images of disgust increased symptoms of faintness but not fear. Furthermore, the effects on self-reported faintness were strongest among individuals with stronger BII-related fears. A similar interaction between fear and disgust has been found in other research. Examining the effects on BII fear and fainting, Exeter-Kent and Page (2006) read scripts concerning pain and nausea to individuals (who varied in terms of trait anxiety and disgust sensitivity) while they viewed blood-injury slides. The pain scripts produced greater self-reported fear than the nausea script, and these symptoms of fear were unaffected by individual differences in trait anxiety and disgust sensitivity. One possible interpretation of this pattern of data involves the effects of different appraisals of particular stimuli. Appraisals concerning pain may recruit the sympathetic nervous system (and the associated fight-and-flight response). Disgust-related appraisals may elicit less sympathetic nervous system activation. However, the fear data contrasted with the symptoms of faintness. A blood stimulus produced the greatest increase in faintness when participants who were high in both trait anxiety and disgust sensitivity were exposed to the pain script. Thus, it may be that studies such as that reported by Kleinknecht et al. (1997) may fail to identify a positive relationship between disgust sensitivity and faintness if they do not consider the particular stimuli in addition to the interaction of individual difference variables.

These studies point to an interaction between disgust and fear, but other research has highlighted that different stimuli may be associated with different responses. Page (2003) exposed individuals high and low in disgust sensitivity who were more distressed either by blood or injections to both a blood picture and a needle picture. High-disgust individuals reported more faintness in response to both slides, but those who were more distressed by blood reported more faintness from the blood slide and those who were more distressed by needles reported more fear from the needle picture. Both systolic and diastolic blood pressure assessments manifested a diphasic-response characteristic of vasovagal syncope. The diphasic-response pattern was most evident among the high-disgust participants who were more distressed by blood than injections. Thus, it appears that when stimuli involving body envelope violations are likely to elicit the changes in blood pressure associated with fainting, but these relationships are not evident when the stimuli are not observed or when participants reflect on past experiences.

In summary, it appears that there are two possible pathways to fainting around blood, injury, and injections. The first pathway is a nonspecific tendency to faint in non-BII settings. The nature of the causes of this vulnerability is unclear, but they could well increase the likelihood of fainting around blood. The second pathway could involve disgust, and there is some evidence that disgust and fear when elicited by the same stimuli may increase the likelihood of fainting. However, the co-occurrence of fear and disgust cannot be a complete explanation for fainting in the presence of BII stimuli because fainting is not found among other phobic individuals who find their fear-provoking stimuli disgusting (see Woody & Teachman, 2000). It is possible that the explanation may lie in the nature of the disgust stimuli (e.g., body envelope violation, animal-reminder disgust), the disgust response involved (e.g., trait, state), the way the stimuli are appraised, or the predispositions of the participants (e.g., perhaps they need to have the nonspecific tendency to faint), or the dependent variables chosen (e.g., physiological, behavioral, self-report). At present the reasons for these differences are not clear, and further research is needed. To assist research, a speculative model will be outlined that draws together the themes outlined in the preceding review about the role of disgust in BII phobia.

AN INTEGRATIVE MODEL OF BII PHOBIA

Considering first the causes of BII fear, two sets of pathways have been identified. The associative pathways of conditioning, vicarious acquisition, and verbal transmission (Mineka & Zinbarg, 1996; Rachman, 1990) and non-associative pathways (Menzies & Clarke, 1995) serve to increase the probability that fear will be triggered by BII stimuli. When BII stimuli are present, fear is increased when they are appraised as signals of likely pain and injury. In addition to the emotional reaction of fear, individuals can react to BII stimuli with disgust. The predisposing variables appear to include gender (with female individuals being more likely to react with disgust than male individuals), particular personality profiles (involving neuroticism, agreeableness, conscientiousness, low openness), and environmental factors (e.g., learning history, sociocultural influences) that will reduce the threshold to elicit a disgust reaction and also identify the stimuli that will elicit this emotion. Broadly, this propensity to experience disgust can be thought of as trait disgust, and individuals high on this trait will be more likely to experience state disgust when confronted by disgusting stimuli. Two classes of relevant stimuli include those that involve body envelope violations and those that serve as reminders of our animal origins. These cues seem particularly effective in eliciting the emotion of disgust. However, as evident in Figure 9.1 by the upward arrow from BII disgust to the casual pathway leading to BII fears, the experience of BII disgust also affects BII fear. As described by Woody and Teachman (2000), disgust appears to play a role in amplifying fears. It may do this in a variety of ways, perhaps because fear and disgust share predisposing variables (e.g., neuroticism), tend to blend as emotions, or because the emotions are hard to distin-

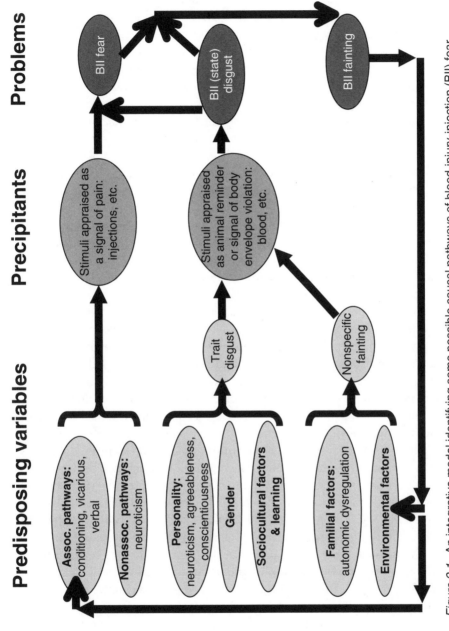

Figure 9.1. An integrative model identifying some possible causal pathways of blood-injury-injection (BII) fear, disgust, and faintness. Assoc. = associative. Nonassoc. = nonassociative.

guish. Although future research will likely clarify these various processes, the key point is that disgust and fear combine to generate a fear response that is greater than would otherwise be the case.

Page (1994, 2003) proposed that the simultaneous presence of fear and facets of disgust increases the probability of faintness. The details of this pathway were outlined earlier, but what is apparent from Figure 9.1 is that Woody and Teachman's view that disgust may amplify fear is not necessarily incompatible with the view that fear and certain types of disgust may interact to generate faintness. However, the model does include some additional factors that appear to predispose individuals to faint in the presence of blood and injury. These factors include an autonomic dysregulation that results in people being more likely to faint in nonblood and injury situations. An important question that needs to be addressed is the degree to which the presence of this general autonomic dysregulation that predisposes a person to faint is a necessary precondition for BII faintness. The model assumes that this is necessary, but future research will need to answer this question. Notwithstanding this issue, the model identifies some of the effects of having fainted. Fainting in BII situations appears to serve as an environmental factor associated both with subsequent fainting in BII situations as well as increasing the amount of fear. That is, people who have fainted in medical situations may well fear and avoid the contexts that they associate with faintness.

The two main purposes in articulating the speculative integrative model are to organize the existing research in a way that the different conclusions can be considered in a complementary manner and to stimulate research. Some variables and pathways may have been omitted; future research can identify these. That is, when directional arrows are not included in the model, this should be taken to signal that a strong or meaningful relationship does not exist. However, some variables and pathways may turn out to be more important than others, and future research will allow the model to be modified accordingly. Some variables and pathways may be unnecessary; future research can identify which ones need to be removed. Some possible future research questions include the following: (a) To what extent are disgust domains specific to particular disorders and are particular domains of disgust differentially related to BII phobia? (b) What particular variables (or interactions among variables) predispose an individual toward a fainting response? and (c) What is the nature of the relationship between disgust, anxiety, and neuroticism? Identify whether the relationship is an artifact of neuroticism. However, the model outlined in this chapter does emphasize a couple of important points with which the chapter opened. BII involves more than phobic fear, and any conceptualization needs to address the various manifestations of problems. Second, disgust plays an important role in BII phobia, certainly as a part of the response to phobic stimuli but also as a cause of some of the responses. Therefore, there stand to be reciprocal benefits as our understanding of BII phobia and disgust continues to develop.

REFERENCES

Accurso, V., Winnicki, M., Shamsuzzaman, A. S. M., Wenzel, A., Johnson, A. K., & Somers, V. K. (2001). Predisposition to vasovagal syncope in subjects with blood/injury phobia. *Circulation, 104,* 903–907.

Adler, P. S. J., France, C., & Ditto, B. (1991). Baroreflex sensitivity at rest and during stress in individuals with a history of vasovagal syncope. *Journal of Psychosomatic Research, 35,* 591–597.

American Psychiatric Association. (2000). *Diagnostic and statistical manual of mental disorders* (4th ed., text rev.). Washington, DC: Author.

Andrews, G., Creamer, M., Crino, R. D., Hunt, C., Lampe, L. A., & Page, A. C. (2003). *The treatment of anxiety disorders: Clinician guides and patient manuals* (2nd ed.). New York: Cambridge University Press.

Barlow, D. H. (2002). *Anxiety and its disorders: The nature and treatment of anxiety and panic* (2nd ed.). New York: Guilford Press.

Connolly, J., Hallam, R. S., & Marks, I. M. (1976). Selective association of fainting with blood-injury-illness fear. *Behavior Therapy, 7,* 8–13.

Davey, G. C. L. (1993). Factors influencing self-rated fear to a novel animal. *Cognition & Emotion, 7,* 461–471.

Davey, G. C. L. (1994). Self-reported fears to common indigenous animals in an adult UK population: The role of disgust sensitivity. *British Journal of Psychology, 85,* 541–554.

Davey, G. C. L., McDonald, A. S., Hirisave, U., Prabhu, G. G., Iwawaki, S., Jim, C. I., et al. (1998). A cross-cultural study of animal fears. *Behaviour Research and Therapy, 36,* 735–750.

de Jong, P. J., & Merckelbach, H. (1998). Blood-injection-injury phobia and fear of spiders: Domain specific individual differences in disgust sensitivity. *Personality and Individual Differences, 24,* 153–158.

de Jong, P. J., & Muris, P. (2002). Spider phobia interaction of disgust and perceived likelihood of involuntary physical contact. *Journal of Anxiety Disorders, 16,* 51–65.

Dorfan, N. M., & Woody, S. R. (2006). Does threatening imagery sensitize distress during contaminant exposure? *Behaviour Research and Therapy, 44,* 395–413.

Druschel, B. A., & Sherman, M. F. (1999). Disgust sensitivity as a function of the Big Five and gender. *Personality and Individual Differences, 26,* 739–748.

Exeter-Kent, H. A., & Page, A. C. (2006). The role of cognitions, trait anxiety and disgust sensitivity in generating faintness around blood-injury phobic stimuli. *Journal of Behavior Therapy and Experimental Psychiatry, 37,* 41–52.

France, C. (1995). Baroreflex sensitivity during noxious stimulation in vasovagal reactors to blood donation. *Journal of Psychophysiology, 19,* 13–22.

Fredrikson, M., Annas, P., Fischer, H., & Wik, G. (1996). Gender and age differences in the prevalence of specific fears and phobias. *Behaviour Research and Therapy, 34,* 33–39.

Gerlach, A. L., Nat, R., Spellmeyer, G., Vogele, C., Huster, C., Stevens, S., et al. (2006). Blood-injury phobia with and without a history of fainting: Disgust sensitivity does not explain the fainting response. *Psychosomatic Medicine, 68,* 331–339.

Graham, D. T. (1961). Prediction of fainting in blood donors. *Circulation, 23,* 901–906.

Graham, D. T., Kabler, J. D., & Lunsford, L. (1961). Vasovagal fainting: A diphasic response. *Psychosomatic Medicine, 23,* 493–507.

Haidt, J., McCauley, C., & Rozin, P. (1994). Individual differences in sensitivity to disgust: A scale sampling seven domains of disgust elicitors. *Personality and Individual Differences, 16,* 701–713.

Hepburn, T., & Page, A. C. (1999). Effects of images about fear and disgust upon habituation of responses to blood-injury phobic stimuli. *Behavior Therapy, 30,* 63–77.

Kleinknecht, R. A. (1994). Acquisition of blood, injury, and needle fears and phobias. *Behaviour Research and Therapy, 32,* 817–823.

Kleinknecht, R. A., Kleinknecht, E. A., & Thorndike, R. M. (1997). The role of disgust and fear in blood and injection-related fainting symptoms: A structural equation model. *Behaviour Research and Therapy, 35,* 1075–1087.

Kleinknecht, R. A., & Lenz, J. (1989). Blood/injury fear, fainting and avoidance of medically-related situations: A family correspondence study. *Behaviour Research and Therapy, 27,* 537–547.

Kleinknecht, R. A., Lenz, J., Ford, G., & DeBerard, S. (1990). Types and correlates of blood/injury-related vasovagal syncope. *Behaviour Research and Therapy, 28,* 289–295.

Kleinknecht, R. A., & Thorndike, R. M. (1990). The Mutilation Questionnaire as a predictor of blood/injury fear and fainting. *Behaviour Research and Therapy, 28,* 429–437.

Koch, M. D., O'Neill, H. K., Sawchuk, C. N., & Connolly, K. (2002). Domain-specific and generalized disgust sensitivity in blood-injection-injury phobia: The application of behavioral approach/avoidance tasks. *Journal of Anxiety Disorders, 16,* 511–527.

Levenson, R. W. (1992). Autonomic nervous system differences among emotions. *Psychological Science, 3,* 23–27.

Lewis, T. (1932). Vasovagal syncope and the carotid sinus mechanism. *British Medical Journal, 1,* 873–876.

Lumley, M. A., & Melamed, B. (1992). Blood phobics and nonphobics: Psychological differences and affect during exposure. *Behaviour Research and Therapy, 30,* 425–434.

Marks, I. M. (1988). Blood-injury phobia: A review. *American Journal of Psychiatry, 145,* 1207–1213.

Mattchett, G., & Davey, G. C. L. (1991). A test of a disease-avoidance model of animal phobias. *Behaviour Research and Therapy, 29,* 91–94.

McKay, D., & Tsao, S. D. (2005). A treatment most foul: Handling disgust in cognitive-behavior therapy. *Journal of Cognitive Psychotherapy: An International Quarterly, 19,* 355–367.

Menzies, R. G., & Clarke, J. C. (1995). The etiology of phobias: A non-associative account. *Clinical Psychology Review, 15*, 23–48.

Mineka, S., & Zinbarg, R. (1996). Conditioning and ethological models of anxiety disorders: Stress-in-dynamic-context anxiety models. In D. A. Hope et al. (Eds.), *Nebraska Symposium on Motivation: Vol. 43. Perspectives on anxiety, panic, and fear. Current theory and research in motivation* (pp. 135–210). Lincoln: University of Nebraska Press.

Mulkens, S. A. N., de Jong, P. J., & Merckelbach, H. (1996). Disgust and spider phobia. *Journal of Abnormal Psychology, 105*, 464–468.

Olatunji, B. O., Lohr, J. M., Sawchuk, C. N., & Westendorf, D. (2005). Using facial expressions as CSs and fearsome and disgusting pictures as UCSs: Affective responding and evaluative learning of fear and disgust in BII phobia. *Journal of Anxiety Disorders, 19*, 539–555.

Olatunji, B. O., & Sawchuk, C. N. (2005). Disgust: Characteristic features, social manifestations, and clinical implications. *Journal of Social and Clinical Psychology, 24*, 932–962.

Olatunji, B. O., Sawchuk, C. N., de Jong, P. J., & Lohr, J. M. (2006). The structural relation between disgust sensitivity and blood-injection-injury fears: A cross-cultural comparison of US and Dutch data. *Journal of Behavior Therapy and Experimental Psychiatry, 37*, 16–29.

Olatunji, B. O., Sawchuk, C. N., Lohr, J. M., & de Jong, P. J. (2004). Disgust domains in the prediction of contamination fear. *Behaviour Research and Therapy, 42*, 93–104.

Olatunji, B. O., Williams, N. L., Sawchuk, C. N., & Lohr, J. M. (2006). Disgust, anxiety and fainting symptoms associated with blood-injection-injury fears: A structural model. *Journal of Anxiety Disorders, 20*, 23–41.

Opplinger, P. A., & Zillmann, D. (1997). Disgust in humour: Its appeal to adolescents. *Humour: International Journal of Humour Research, 10*, 421–437.

Ortony, A., Clore, G. L., & Collins, A. (1988). *The cognitive structure of emotions*. New York: Cambridge University Press.

Öst, L.-G. (1992). Blood and injection phobia: Background and cognitive, physiological, and behavioral variables. *Journal of Abnormal Psychology, 101*, 68–74.

Öst, L.-G., Sterner, U., & Lindahl, I. L. (1984). Physiological responses in blood phobics. *Behaviour Research and Therapy, 22*, 109–117.

Page, A. C. (1994). Blood-injury phobia. *Clinical Psychology Review, 14*, 443–461.

Page, A. C. (1996). Blood-injury-injection fears in medical practice. *Medical Journal of Australia, 164*, 189.

Page, A. C. (1998). Blood-injury-injection fears: Nature, assessment, and management. *Behaviour Change, 15*, 160–164.

Page, A. C. (1999). Effects of images on the renewal of blood-injury fears. *Behaviour Change, 16*, 105–110.

Page, A. C. (2003). The role of disgust in faintness elicited by blood and injection stimuli. *Journal of Anxiety Disorders, 17*, 45–58.

Page, A. C., Bennett, K. S., Carter, O., & Woodmore, K. (1997). The Blood-Injection Symptom Scale (BISS): Assessing a structure of phobic symptoms elicited by blood and injections. *Behaviour Research and Therapy, 35,* 457–464.

Page, A. C., & Martin, N. G. (1998). Testing a genetic structure of blood-injury-injection fears. *American Journal of Medical Genetics (Neuropsychiatric Genetics), 81,* 377–384.

Prkachin, K. M., Williams-Avery, R. M., Zwaal, C., & Mills, D. E. (1999). Cardio-vascular changes during induced emotion: An application of Lang's theory of emotional imagery. *Journal of Psychosomatic Research, 47,* 255–267.

Rachman, S. (1990). *Fear and courage* (2nd ed.). New York: Freeman.

Robinson, M. D. (1998). Running from William James' bear: A review of preatten-tive mechanisms and their contributions to emotional experience. *Cognition & Emotion, 12,* 667–696.

Rozin, P., & Fallon, A. E. (1987). A perspective on disgust. *Psychological Review, 94,* 32–41.

Rozin, P., Fallon, A. E., & Mandell, R. (1984). Family resemblances in attitudes to food. *Developmental Psychology, 20,* 309–314.

Rozin, P., Haidt, J., & McCauley, C. R. (1999). Disgust: The body and soul emotion. In T. Dalgleish & M. J. Power (Eds.), *Handbook of cognition and emotion* (pp. 429–446). New York: Wiley.

Rozin, P., Haidt, J., & McCauley, C. R. (2000). Disgust. In M. Lewis & J. M. Haviland (Eds.), *Handbook of emotions* (2nd ed., pp. 637–653). New York: Guilford Press.

Ruetz, P. P., Johnson, S. A., Callahan, R., Meade, R. C., & Smith, J. J. (1967). Fainting: A review of its mechanisms and a study in blood donors. *Medicine, 46,* 363–384.

Sawchuk, C. N., Lohr, J. M., Tolin, D. F., Lee, T. C., & Kleinknecht, R. A. (2000). Disgust sensitivity and contamination fears in spider and blood-injection-injury phobias. *Behaviour Research and Therapy, 38,* 753–762.

Sawchuk, C. N., Lohr, J. M., Westendorf, D. A., Meunier, S. A., & Tolin, D. F. (2002). Emotional responding to fearful and disgusting stimuli in specific pho-bia. *Behaviour Research and Therapy, 40,* 1031–1046.

Schienle, A., Schäfer, A., Stark, R., Walter, B., Kirsch, P., & Vaitl, D. (2003). Disgust processing in blood-injection-injury phobia: An fMRI study. *Journal of Psychophysiology, 17,* 87–93.

Schienle, A., Schäfer, A., Stark, R., Walter, B., & Vaitl, D. (2005a). Elevated dis-gust sensitivity in blood phobia. *Cognition & Emotion, 19,* 1329–1241.

Schienle, A., Schäfer, A., Stark, R., Walter, B., & Vaitl, D. (2005b). Relationship between disgust sensitivity, trait anxiety, and brain activity during disgust induc-tion. *Neuropsychobiology, 51,* 86–92.

Schienle, A., Stark, R., & Vaitl, D. (2001). Evaluative conditioning: A possible explanation for the acquisition of disgust responses? *Learning and Motivation, 32,* 65–83.

Stark, R., Schienle, A., Walter, B., Kirsch, P., Blecker, C., Ott, U., et al. (2004). Hemodynamic effects of negative emotional pictures: A test–retest analysis. *Neuropsychobiology, 50,* 108–118.

Thyer, B. A., & Curtis, G. C. (1985). On the diphasic nature of vasovagal fainting associated with blood-injury-illness phobia. *Pavlovian Journal of Biological Science, 20,* 84–87.

Thyer, B. A., Himle, J., & Curtis, G. C. (1985). Blood-injury-illness: A review. *Journal of Clinical Psychology, 41,* 451–459.

Tolin, D. F., Lohr, J. M., Sawchuk, C. N., & Lee, T. C. (1997). Disgust and disgust sensitivity in blood-injection-injury and spider phobia. *Behaviour Research and Therapy, 35,* 949–953.

Tolin, D. F., Sawchuk, C. N., & Lee, T. C. (1999). The role of disgust in blood-injury-injection phobia. *The Behavior Therapist, 22,* 96–99.

Vaitl, D., Schienle, A., & Stark, R. (2005). Neurobiology of fear and disgust. *International Journal of Psychophysiology, 57,* 1–4.

Vingerhoets, A. J. (1984). Biochemical changes in two subjects succumbing to syncope. *Psychosomatic Medicine, 46,* 95–103.

Vrana, S. R. (1993). The psychophysiology of disgust: Differentiating negative emotional contexts with facial EMG. *Psychophysiology, 30,* 279–286.

Webb, K., & Davey, G. C. L. (1992). Disgust sensitivity and fear of animals: Effect of exposure to violent or repulsive material. *Anxiety, Stress, & Coping, 5,* 329–335.

Williams, L. M., Das, P., Liddell, B., Olivieri, G., Peduto, A., Brammer, M. J., et al. (2005). BOLD, sweat and fears: fMRI and skin conductance distinguish facial fear signals. *Neuroreport, 16,* 49–52.

Woody, S. R., & Teachman, B. A. (2000). Intersection of disgust and fear: Normative and pathological views. *Clinical Psychology: Science and Practice, 7,* 291–311.

Woody, S. R., & Tolin, D. F. (2002). The relationship between disgust sensitivity and avoidant behavior: Studies of clinical and nonclinical samples. *Journal of Anxiety Disorders, 16,* 543–559.

Wright, P., He, G., Shapira, N. A., Goodman, W. K., & Liu, Y. (2004). Disgust and the insula: fMRI responses to pictures of mutilation and contamination. *Neuroreport, 15,* 2347–2351.

10

THE INTERSECTION OF DISGUST AND CONTAMINATION FEAR

DEAN McKAY AND MELANIE W. MORETZ

Over the past 8 years, the emerging literature on the role of disgust in psychopathology has increasingly included *contamination fear*. Contamination fear is most frequently associated with obsessive–compulsive disorder (OCD). In fact, concerns over contamination represent one of the primary symptom dimensions of OCD (McKay et al., 2004), consistently identified in factor analyses of symptom checklists for OCD. A common conceptualization of contamination fear involves anxious appraisals of environmental toxins that would lead to disease or illness (see e.g., Riggs & Foa, 2007). However, many individuals with contamination fear are motivated by disgust as much or in some cases more than by fear (McKay, 2006). Contamination fear, however, is also a central feature of the avoidance patterns associated with disgust, irrespective of the presence of OCD. This chapter focuses on the role of disgust in contamination fear in psychopathology, with special attention to contamination fear associated with OCD. Basic features of psychopathology as well as patterns of habituation for disgust in contamination are covered. Given that this is an emergent area of research, suggestions for future research are provided throughout the chapter.

THE NATURE OF CONTAMINATION FEAR

Concerns over contamination are not restricted to people with OCD. Many individuals avoid stimuli out of a concern over contamination, and the early investigations into the role of disgust in psychopathology largely centered on fears of contamination. The following section describes the range of areas in which avoidance out of concern with contamination.

Animal Phobias and Blood-Injection-Injury Phobia

Disgust has been described as a basic emotion that serves the adaptive function of protecting humans from contact with contaminated stimuli (Woody & Teachman, 2000). Disgust is no longer defined in the psychological literature as solely food related, as originally proposed by Rozin and Fallon (1987), but the concept has been expanded to encompass seven different domains of disgust elicitors, including food, animals, body products, sex, body envelope violations, death, and hygiene. Although these elicitors represent classes of stimuli that provoke disgust reactions, cognitive components of disgust have been categorized as well. Rozin, Haidt, and McCauley (2000) conceptualized two subtypes of disgust: *core disgust* and *animal-reminder disgust*. Core disgust comprises stimuli that suggest offensiveness and the threat of contamination, such as rotting foods, waste products, and small animals. Animal reminder disgust is elicited by stimuli that remind individuals of their animal origins, such as culturally inappropriate sexual acts, poor hygiene, death, and body envelope violations or mutilation.

Disgust, specifically disgust sensitivity, has been hypothesized to play a key role in the etiology and maintenance of some anxiety disorders. Disgust sensitivity has been conceptualized as a dispositional trait that increases the likelihood of an individual developing avoidance reactions (McNally, 2002), and the bulk of the research conducted on disgust sensitivity has involved phobias of small animals, such as spiders and snakes (Matchett & Davey, 1991), or blood-injury-injection (BII) phobias (Sawchuk, Lohr, Tolin, Lee, & Kleinknecht, 2000; Tolin, Lohr, Sawchuk, & Lee, 1997). Assessment of disgust sensitivity has been based on the aforementioned disgust elicitors, as well as resulting from the two different subtypes of disgust (core and animal reminder).

Concerns over contamination are related to the construct *sympathetic magic* (Rozin & Fallon, 1987). This important concept posits that items can become disgusting on the basis of different events. First, it is possible for an item to become a disgust elicitor by coming into momentary contact with a core disgust item (e.g., a pen cap comes in momentary contact with dog feces) or a secondary disgust domain (e.g., going into a hotel room and learning that a dead body had been found there a week earlier). Second, an item can be deemed disgusting by taking on the physical shape of a core disgust item (e.g., a candy bar shaped like feces). The ability of disgust stimuli to effectively transfer properties to otherwise neutral objects creates serious disruptions in functioning for individuals with pronounced contamination fear, as will be discussed in the next section.

Obsessive–Compulsive Disorder-Related Contamination Fear

A growing body of research has indicated that there is also a relationship between disgust sensitivity and *obsessive–compulsive disorder* (OCD). OCD is an anxiety disorder characterized by the presence of disturbing intrusive thoughts and/or repetitive behaviors (*Diagnostic and Statistical Manual of Mental Disorders, Fourth Edition, Text Revision*; American Psychiatric Association, 2000). The condition is a serious and disabling disorder. There are effective treatments for OCD, namely cognitive–behavior therapy (CBT; Antony, Purdon, & Summerfeldt, 2007), with large effect sizes associated (Abramowitz, 1996). However, there are substantial proportions of people with OCD who either fail to respond to treatment or only do so to a limited extent (Eddy, Dutra, Bradley, & Westen, 2004). In part, the partial or nonresponse to treatment could result from an inadequate focus on disgust components of the condition. The component of CBT associated with the greatest behavioral and cognitive change in OCD is exposure and response prevention (ERP; Abramowitz, Taylor, & McKay, 2005). In this approach to treatment, individuals with OCD are exposed to stimuli that provoke anxiety, and compulsions are prevented until habituation is achieved (a detailed description of the methods of ERP are provided in Abramowitz & Larsen, 2007). Indeed, most of the theoretical perspectives on ERP focus on the role of exposure in reducing anxiety (e.g., Foa & Kozak, 1986) with little attention to other emotional states associated with avoidance reactions.

Individuals with OCD can present with a wide range of different primary symptoms, making it a highly heterogeneous condition (McKay et al., 2004). Fear of contamination, with associated cleaning rituals, has been identified as one of the most common obsessive–compulsive concerns among people with OCD (Foa & Kozak, 1995; Foa et al., 1995). Other common symptom subtypes include concerns with symmetry or ordering, pure obsessions (i.e., sexual and aggressive obsessions), checking, and hoarding (Abramowitz, McKay, & Taylor, 2005). Among individuals with contamination fear, this preoccupation with avoiding contamination points to a plausible relationship between disgust sensitivity and OCD, given that disgust sensitivity serves as a means of avoiding potential sources of contamination or infection. Tolin, Woods, and Abramowitz (2006) suggested that disgust may uniquely contribute to contamination-based OCD because feelings of disgust lead to phobic avoidance of certain stimuli that are relieved through compulsive behavior and the behavior is sustained through negative reinforcement. This is consistent with the diagnostic criteria for OCD, whereby compulsions are described as behaviors maintained as a result of alleviating upsetting and unwanted thoughts and emotions. Although the prior literature has emphasized anxiety to the exclusion of other emotional states, disgust is likewise experienced as aversive and would be a potent source of negative reinforcement.

Empirical Research

Some investigations have linked disgust sensitivity to OCD. Muris et al. (2000) investigated the relationship between disgust sensitivity and several types of psychopathology among a sample of college undergraduates. They found that phobias, specifically agoraphobia-related fears, and obsessive–compulsive symptoms, especially cleaning concerns, were significantly related to disgust.[1] Cleaning behaviors serve the function of alleviating disgust reactions and are therefore negatively reinforced. This study was somewhat limited because the researchers used the Disgust Sensitivity Questionnaire (DSQ; Rozin, Fallon, & Mandell, 1984), a measure of disgust that addresses only one specific aspect of disgust sensitivity—food contamination—but it provided some early empirical support for the connection between OCD and disgust sensitivity.

Mancini, Gragnani, and D'Olimpio (2001) also found a significant positive relationship between disgust and obsessive symptoms in a nonclinical sample, using a more comprehensive measure of disgust sensitivity, the Disgust Scale (DS; Haidt, McCauley, & Rozin, 1994). These researchers found that washing and checking behaviors were significantly and uniquely predicted by disgust sensitivity in male and female individuals in a multiple regression analysis, after controlling for age, state and trait anxiety, and depression. Mancini et al. (2001) did not find a strong link between disgust sensitivity and other OCD subscales, for example, impulses and rumination among female participants. For male participants, however, disgust was a weak but significant predictor of the rumination subscale along with trait anxiety. Disgust did not solely predict washing and checking behavior among female participants in the sample. Depression was also a significant predictor of washing and checking behavior among female participants.

Considered together, these results suggest that, in OCD, disgust may be most strongly associated with washing and checking problems. However, this specificity has not been firmly established, in part because of the various measures available for OCD. For example, in contrast to Mancini et al.'s (2001) findings, Scheinle, Stark, Walter, and Vaitl (2003) found a positive significant association between disgust sensitivity and all four subscales of the Maudsley Obsessional Compulsive Inventory (Hodgson & Rachman, 1977): washing,

---

[1]Agoraphobia-related fears include concerns over the inability to escape different places or situations out of a concern that a panic attack might occur.

checking, slowness-repetition, and doubting-conscientiousness. Thorpe, Patel, and Simonds (2003) found that disgust sensitivity was significantly correlated with all Obsessive Compulsive Inventory (OCI; Foa, Kozak, Salkovskis, Coles, & Amir, 1998) subscales, except for hoarding, as well as with a measure of health anxiety. The OCI measures both the frequency and distress associated with obsessive–compulsive symptoms along the following dimensions: washing, checking, doubting, ordering, obsessing, hoarding, and neutralizing. Disgust sensitivity was found to best predict washing frequency. Washing distress, however, was best predicted by health anxiety, with disgust sensitivity entering into the subsequent model. These results indicate that disgust is related to the frequency of compulsive behavior, but "subsequent processing, such as worry" may lead to experiencing distress (Thorpe et al., 2003, p. 1407).

The problem that must still be examined is which aspects of OCD are most clearly associated with disgust. The aforementioned studies do not adequately shed light on this issue. Part of this problem is due to measurement. There are numerous assessment tools available for OCD, and no single measure has become a dominant "gold standard" measure of its diverse symptoms. Furthermore, many of the popular measures are sensitive to treatment effects (Taylor, 1998). The effects of scaling, item wording, and anchors for items are important issues (Schwarz, 1999) that have not been examined carefully in relation to assessments of OCD. Nonetheless, the research findings consistently find an association between contamination fear and disgust. These findings do not necessarily rule out mediating or moderating variables. In light of the historical view of OCD as almost exclusively a result of anxiety, with acknowledgement that depression often occurs secondary to the disorder (Barlow, 2002; Clark, 2004), the contributory role of disgust must also be examined.

Gender Differences

Mancini et al.'s (2001) results suggest that gender differences might be important in the relationship between disgust sensitivity and OCD. As noted earlier, depression mediated the association between contamination and disgust but only among female participants in the sample. As far as disgust sensitivity is concerned, there are well-documented gender differences. Female individuals typically report higher levels of disgust sensitivity than male individuals (Arrindell, Mulkens, Kok, & Vollenbroek, 1999; Haidt et al., 1994), and the pattern of gender differences in disgust sensitivity is similar to the pattern of gender differences for OCD. Female individuals have been found to be at higher risk for developing OCD (Weissman et al., 1994), as with all anxiety disorders (Craske, 2003). Olatunji, Sawchuk, Arrindell, and Lohr (2005) found that disgust sensitivity was a predictor of high levels of contamination fear as measured by the contamination obsessions and washing compulsions subscales of the Padua Inventory (Sanovio, 1988) and the Vancouver Obsessional

Compulsive Inventory (Thordarson et al., 2004) in an undergraduate sample. Furthermore, these authors found that women reported higher levels of disgust sensitivity and more contamination fears. Finally, the effect size of the association between disgust sensitivity and contamination fear was greater for female than male individuals. This is in keeping with the finding that female individuals have higher sensitivity to negative affectivity that may play a critical role in their increased risk for anxiety disorders (Craske, 2003).

Specific Disgust Domains

There is some evidence that particular domains of disgust may be more closely related to OCD symptoms than others. Using a clinical sample, Woody and Tolin (2002) found that OCD patients with washing compulsions reported significantly higher disgust sensitivity on the DS than nonanxious control participants and somewhat higher disgust sensitivity than OCD patients with nonwashing related symptoms. These researchers found that the OCD sample with washing compulsions had significantly higher scores on the DS animals and body products subscales. In this study, the correlation between the DS and compulsions was notably stronger than the correlation between the DS and obsessions, which suggests that washing compulsions may be strongly related to disgust sensitivity whereas other OCD symptoms are related to disgust to a lesser extent.

Tsao and McKay (2004) provided additional support for the hypothesis that multiple disgust domains are associated with contamination fear. As opposed to using a self-report measure of disgust sensitivity, Tsao and McKay found that participants who scored high on self-report washing compulsions, categorized as "contamination fearful," could be differentiated from participants with high trait anxiety, using behavioral avoidance tasks (BATs) designed to assess six domains of disgust. They found that on two of the BATs—animal-related disgust and sympathetic magic—the contamination fearful group had significantly higher disgust sensitivity than did the high trait-anxiety group. However, four of the tasks revealed no significant differences between disgust and trait-anxiety groups.

Olatunji, Sawchuk, Lohr, and de Jong (2004) also conducted a study that examined the relationship between specific domains of disgust elicitors and contamination fear. The researchers predicted that all disgust domains would contribute to the prediction of contamination fear but that sympathetic magic and hygiene would be the best predictors given their relationship with contamination fear. Disgust sensitivity was measured using both the DS and the Disgust Emotion Scale (DES; Walls & Kleinknecht, 1996). The DES is a 30-item measure on which respondents rate how disgusted they would feel if they were exposed to items across five domains of disgust elicitors: animals, injections and blood draws, mutilation and death, rotting foods, and smells.

Contamination fear was assessed by using the Padua Inventory–Washington State University Revision, contamination obsessions and washing compulsions subscale (Burns, Keortge, Formea, & Sternberger, 1996). The authors found that participants high on contamination fear scored higher on disgust sensitivity on all DES and DS disgust domains than those scoring low on contamination fear. Using stepwise multiple regression analyses, they found that seven disgust domains together best predicted contamination fear (DS hygiene, food, and death; DES smells, injections, mutilation, and animals). These results suggest that contamination fear is best predicted by taking a generalized, rather than domain-specific, approach to disgust assessment. The hygiene subscale was found to contribute the most to the regression equation. Notably, sympathetic magic did not enter into the regression equation, but, as was predicted, it was found to be significantly correlated with contamination fear.

Although it appears from the evidence accumulated to date that disgust is best conceptualized as a global construct in relation to contamination fear, the aforementioned studies have limits that merit noting. First, it is possible that these findings are limited by the nature of assessment (i.e., self-report). Disgust is an emotion with limited, or as yet unclear, cognitive involvement (McKay & Tsao, 2005), but it has clear psychophysiological (see chap. 6, this volume) and neurobiological correlates (see chap. 7, this volume). This level of specificity suggests that reactions to different domains would likely also show similar specificity. Additional measurement development focusing on developing valid behavioral assessments of disgust is clearly warranted. (see chap. 2, this volume).

Disgust and Obsessions

Although ample evidence exists to support a connection between disgust, obsessions, and compulsions, there is less research on the relation between disgust sensitivity and pure obsessions. Olatunji et al. (2004) found a significant relationship between religious obsessions and disgust sensitivity when controlling for general fearfulness and cleanliness fears among college undergraduates. Fear and disgust were both found to significantly contribute to religious obsessions, but the interaction was not significant. Although these authors investigated a rather specific type of obsessional thinking, they found evidence for a relationship between disgust sensitivity and obsessional thinking in a nonpatient sample.

As discussed, there has frequently been an association between diverse symptoms of OCD and disgust. In this instance, obsessions only (while controlling for cleanliness) were associated with disgust. As noted earlier, disgust has two subtypes. Core disgust, which encompasses disgust in the broadest sense, would be operating for religious obsessions, particularly given the importance of cleanliness in many religious traditions. Some evidence suggests that morally reprehensible acts (defined as moral disgust) lead to increased washing (Zhong & Liljenquist, 2006).

Sympathetic Magic

Two types of distorted thinking are prevalent among individuals with OCD contamination concerns that are hypothesized to increase their sensitivity to disgust. Patients with contamination fears might be more disgust sensitive because of the effects of "magical thinking" (Woody & Teachman, 2000). Magical thinking can be described as the belief that thoughts about an action are equivalent to performing the action or the belief that thoughts alone can increase the likelihood of a particular action. This has been referred to as *thought–action fusion* (Shafran, Thordarson, & Rachman, 1996). In other words, people who believe that a particular disgusting stimulus has the ability to contaminate might perceive that they have actually been contaminated when in the presence of that stimuli. No real contact is necessary when engaged in magical thinking. *Sympathetic magic* is a similar cognitive process. Sympathetic magic is characterized by distorted beliefs about how contamination spreads. Rozin, Millman, and Nemeroff (1986) described the two laws of sympathetic magic, which shape the circumstances under which people may perceive a threat of contamination, even when there is no actual danger of becoming contaminated. The first is the law of contagion, which states that objects pass on some of their properties when they touch other things in such a way that the effect of contact is sustained even after the connection has been broken (i.e., "once in contact, always in contact," p. 703). The second is the law of similarity. This law states that objects that are similar to one another share important properties (i.e., "the image equals the object," p. 703). It is not known whether individuals with contamination fear show greater levels of the specific components of sympathetic magic as described by Rozin et al. (1986).

Rozin et al. (1986) found experimentally that most people tend to make appraisals about possible contamination according to the laws of sympathetic magic, but not everyone is prone to magical thinking to the same extent as people with OCD. Woody and Teachman (2000) suggested that the difference between normal and pathological responding, according to sympathetic magic, may be due to the finding that people with obsessive contamination fears often have a low tolerance for uncertainty (Sookman & Pinard, 2002), which makes it difficult to ignore or reevaluate potential threats. Sympathetic magic is also more prevalent and powerful in individuals with OCD because they are likely to attribute more significance to their thoughts than other people, especially the intrusive thoughts that comprise their obsessions (Thordarson & Shafran, 2002).

Tolin, Worhunsky, and Maltby (2004) experimentally illustrated the "implausible chain of contagion" (p. 195) that operates through sympathetic magic. These authors found that people with OCD symptoms perceived that when a pencil was briefly touched to an idiosyncratic "contaminated" object, it also became contaminated. Furthermore, when this newly contaminated pencil touched another new, clean pencil, the second pencil also became fully contaminated. People with OCD rated the second pencil to be just as contaminated as the first pencil, and the level of contamination did not decrease significantly across a number of new pencils successively tapped to the previous contaminated pencil. It follows that because disgust sensitivity leads to more frequent appraisals of contamination threat and sympathetic magic dictates that disgusting objects can pass along their properties easily and fully, disgust sensitivity among people with OCD can magnify the distress they experience as a result of increasing the amount of intrusive thoughts of being contaminated.

Despite strong theoretical ties with OCD, the sympathetic magic subscale of the DS has not been consistently associated with contamination-related OCD. Using BATs, however, Tsao and McKay (2004) provided some evidence to support this connection beyond simply self-report assessment. As discussed earlier, this study showed that individuals with elevated levels of contamination fear showed greater avoidance on a sympathetic magic BAT (drinking spring water from a cup with a label "saliva sample") and animals (holding a live earthworm). There were four other BATs used in this study that were not significant in discriminating between contamination fearful participants and either high trait anxious or nonanxious control participants.

It appears that, on the basis of the research reviewed, self-report approaches to assessing disgust have the greatest promise in evaluating global disgust sensitivity, or core disgust, but they represent a less promising approach to specific disgust elicitor domains. By comparison there has been much less research that examines the role of disgust in contamination by using behavioral assessment procedures, in which specific disgust elicitors have been found to be related to contamination concerns. Furthermore, no studies have as yet examined this relationship using psychophysiological assessments. These latter assessment approaches are important in light of the etiology of disgust reactions and contamination, which is detailed subsequently.

Evaluative Conditioning, Disgust, and Contamination

Evaluative conditioning (EC) moves past classical conditioning by including appraisals of the target conditioned stimuli. Essentially, EC involves labeling of stimuli as positive or negative. This labeling process occurs rapidly, and the speed of acquisition is partially dependent on the intensity of positive or negative experiences associated with the stimuli. For example, if one consumes bitter food in conjunction with otherwise enjoyable food (e.g., bitter taste on a candy bar), the enjoyable food will be labeled negative. Once this labeling process begins, the object labeled takes on the characteristics of the unconditioned stimuli (for a detailed review of EC, see De Houwer, Thomas, & Baeyens, 2001). Gustatory stimuli are among the most potent ones for establishing disgust reactions given that disgust itself has strong gastrointestinal ties.

The appeal of EC as a model for disgust acquisition rests with the fact that there are no universal disgust elicitors, in contrast to anxiety (startle reflex). In fact, according to the model described by Rozin and Fallon (1987), disgust is learned from caregivers, giving the emotional response cultural and contextual specificity. This would account for the relative lack of universal disgust elicitors.

EC is an appealing model for sympathetic magic. Sympathetic magic is a reaction that has specificity. The following case illustration is instructive in this regard. A woman with a 10-year history of severe contamination fear seeks treatment for her condition. She cannot touch any items with her bare hands out of a concern she will come in contact with either HIV/AIDS or hepatitis. She wears gloves at all times but still cannot escape the obsessional idea that she has possibly contracted an illness or has put herself at risk. When treatment began, and ERP exercises were developed, one type of place that was a source of avoidance was the drugstore. An early exercise involved touching a tissue to a pill jar with a prescription label on it. After contact with the pill jar, the tissue had acquired the contamination of the drugstore. At this point, she was still unable to handle the tissue. Only after the tissue came in contact with another tissue was there a low enough risk in her view to handle it; however, she still felt that the second tissue was contaminated. Figure 10.1 illustrates the sequence of contamination for this client. EC is a valuable way of conceptualizing this case because each succession of contact involves naming a specific object *contaminated* or *disgusting*, which was exactly how this client described it.

Habituation to Disgust

Habituation to stimuli that provoke obsessions is a fundamental basis for treatment of OCD. This is true whether one is relying on pure behavioral approaches, such as exposure and response prevention, or modifications of exposure in cognitive therapy, such as behavioral experiments (Abramowitz, Taylor, & McKay, 2005). The following section reviews findings on habituation for disgust.

Self-Report Findings

Early in the development of exposure-based interventions, clinical researchers documented changes in self-report disgust (along with more general distress) among individuals with problems associated with phobias and avoid-

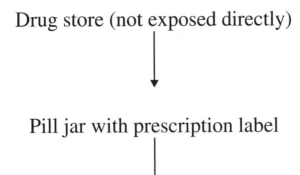

Drug store (not exposed directly)

↓

Pill jar with prescription label

↓

Clean tissue in contact with pill jar

↓

Second clean tissue in contact with first tissue
(Client holds for exposure exercise)

Figure 10.1. Sequence of sympathetic magic in exposure exercise.

ance. For example, D'Zurilla, Wilson, and Nelson (1973) described a study in which 48 female participants with fears of "dead and bloody rats" were treated with prolonged exposure with a cognitive intervention. Their results showed significant decreases in both fear and disgust among the women following the combination of exposure and cognitive interventions.

Some research that examines the patterns of self-report habituation to disgust has been limited. Smits, Telch, and Randall (2002) found with a sample of spider-phobic participants that in vivo exposure produced improvement in both fear and disgust, partially independent of each other. The results indicated that spider-related disgust was reduced through this intervention; however, overall disgust sensitivity remained unchanged after the treatment. These findings suggest that both fear and disgust may be reduced with exposure therapy and, furthermore, that disgust does not interfere with treatment of fear.

Other Treatment Data

Self-report approaches to determining improved functioning follow-ing exposure treatment are common and widely accepted. However, there is ample reason to suggest that other response modalities would show smaller effect sizes for the same treatment period in relation to exposure for disgust. Disgust activates the parasympathetic nervous system (see chap. 6, this volume). As noted earlier, most of the theoretical conceptualizations of avoidance problems, particularly for OCD, have focused on anxiety, an emotional state associated with sympathetic nervous system arousal (Phelps, 2006). Far less is known about how the parasympathetic system responds to prolonged exposure. For example, Gianaros and Quigley (2001) found different rates of heart-rate habituation for exposure associated with sympathetic activation compared with heart-rate habituation associated with parasympathetic activation.

Tsao and McKay (2006) examined physiological assessments of disgust in response to prolonged exposure to disgust-eliciting cues. Psychophysiological assessments included respiration, heart rate, peripheral skin temperature, and muscle tension at the levator labii, all of which are involved in disgust reactions. Participants were not selected on the basis of preexisting conditions or avoidance problems. All participants were exposed to stage blood and fake vomit. Only heart rate and muscle tension significantly changed during the prolonged exposure, whereas the self-report disgust significantly declined for all participants. These findings suggest that whereas participants can report global changes in disgust reduction, psychophysiological assessments show a varied pattern of change following prolonged exposure to disgust.

McKay (2006) found that when directly targeted with exposure methods, disgust was significantly reduced among patients with OCD. However, McKay also found that OCD patients with contamination concerns did not respond to treatment for disgust as quickly as did other OCD patients, although there were no differences between groups found in the reduction of anxiety. These findings indicate that treatment specifically targeted to disgust may be a necessary additional component of treatment for individuals with contamination-related OCD; the findings also highlight the importance of disgust-related research in the context of OCD treatment.

SUMMARY AND FUTURE DIRECTIONS

It appears that disgust is critically involved in contamination fear. In fact, from the available evidence, there are reasons to suggest that disgust and contamination fear are tied when examined by use of self-report methods or psychophysiological approaches, or in treatment. However, from a review of the empirical data, the association is not a straightforward one. Prior research on contamination fear has focused primarily on anxiety. This is appropriate if for no other reason than that it is labeled *fear* rather than contamination *concerns* or *avoidance*. This approach has provided the necessary focus on a primary and important emotional motivator for avoidance caused by contamination fear. However, the emotional concomitants of contamination fear are more complicated than merely anxiety. The patterns of avoidance support the role of sympathetic magic and, by extension, disgust.

Future research is still warranted. First, although self-report findings support the hypothesis that contamination and disgust are linked, the problems associated with measurement have not conclusively pointed to contamination fear specifically, and they have not allowed for more precise hypotheses relative to other symptoms of OCD. This may be because OCD is a highly heterogeneous condition, even within primary presenting symptoms (e.g., McKay et al., 2004). That is, individuals with contamination fear differ considerably among one another, as well as from individuals with other major presenting symptoms of OCD. For example, many individuals with contamination fear avoid stimuli associated with blasphemy or ideas deemed reprehensible (see examples in Taylor, Abramowitz, & McKay, 2007). Although these forms of contamination fears fit well with the experimental data on washing and exposure to morally reprehensible ideas (Zhong & Liljenquist, 2006), they do not completely account for the role of disgust and problems associated with OCD in general.

One way this may be resolved is with better models to account for OCD. There has been a call to reevaluate the adequacy of models of OCD. To date, there has not been a model of OCD that adequately explains the diverse and complex presenting symptoms associated with this disorder (Taylor, McKay, & Abramowitz, 2005a, 2005b). In part, this problem may be resolved with an agreed-on taxonomy for OCD. At this point, presenting symptoms do not completely address the myriad presentations of the condition (McKay et al., 2004) even though contamination fear is the most common presenting problem of the condition.

In a more general way, the problem of contamination fear and disgust is consistent with a movement to put psychopathology on dimensions (e.g., Watson, 2005). Dimensional models would allow for better testing of the role of different emotional states because the accompanying criteria of artificially created diagnostic categories would not be necessary. Some of the research described here adheres to that approach. For example, Tsao and McKay (2004) relied on elevated scores for measures of contamination in lieu of diagnostic criteria to examine the relation between disgust elicitors and disgust reactions. Because contamination is a central aspect of disgust, irrespective of OCD, it is necessary to fully examine these links.

REFERENCES

Abramowitz, J. S. (1996). Variants of exposure and response prevention in the treatment of obsessive–compulsive disorder: A meta-analysis. *Behavior Therapy*, *27*, 583–600.

Abramowitz, J. S., & Larsen, K. E. (2007). Exposure therapy for obsessive–compulsive disorder. In D. C. S. Richard & D. L. Lauterbach (Eds.), *Handbook of exposure therapies* (pp. 185–208). Amsterdam: Academic Press.

Abramowitz, J. S., McKay, D., & Taylor, S. (2005). Special series: Subtypes of obsessive–compulsive disorder. *Behavior Therapy, 36,* 367–369.

Abramowitz, J. S., Taylor, S., & McKay, D. (2005). Potentials and limitations of cognitive treatments for obsessive–compulsive disorder. *Cognitive Behaviour Therapy, 34,* 140–147.

American Psychiatric Association. (2000). *Diagnostic and statistical manual of mental disorders* (4th ed., text rev.). Washington, DC: Author.

Antony, M. M., Purdon, C., & Summerfeldt, L. J. (2007). *Psychological treatment of obsessive–compulsive disorder: Fundamentals and beyond.* Washington, DC: American Psychological Association.

Arrindell, W. A., Mulkens, S., Kok, J., & Vollenbroek, J. (1999). Disgust sensitivity and the sex difference in fears to common indigenous animals. *Behaviour Research and Therapy, 37,* 273–280.

Barlow, D. H. (2002). *Anxiety and its disorders* (2nd ed.). New York: Guilford Press.

Burns, G. L., Keortge, S. G., Formea, G. M., & Sternberger, L. G. (1996). Revision of the Padua Inventory of obsessive–compulsive disorder symptoms: Distinctions between worry, obsessions, and compulsions. *Behaviour Research and Therapy, 34,* 163–173.

Clark, D. A. (2004). *Cognitive–behavioral therapy for OCD.* New York: Guilford Press.

Craske, M. G. (2003). *Origins of phobias and anxiety disorders: Why more women than men?* Amsterdam: Elsevier.

De Houwer, J., Thomas, S., & Baeyens, F. (2001). Associative learning of likes and dislikes: A review of 25 years of research on human evaluative conditioning. *Psychological Bulletin, 127,* 853–869.

D'Zurilla, T. J., Wilson, G. T., & Nelson, R. O. (1973). A preliminary study of the effectiveness of graduated prolonged exposure in the treatment of irrational fear. *Behavior Therapy, 4,* 672–685.

Eddy, K. T., Dutra, L., Bradley, R., & Westen, D. (2004). A multidimensional meta-analysis of psychotherapy and pharmacotherapy for obsessive–compulsive disorder. *Clinical Psychology Review, 24,* 1011–1030.

Foa, E. B., & Kozak, M. J. (1986). Emotional processing of fear: Exposure to corrective information. *Psychological Bulletin, 99,* 20–35.

Foa, E. B., & Kozak, M. J. (1995). DSM–IV field trial: Obsessive–compulsive disorder. *American Journal of Psychiatry, 152,* 90–96.

Foa, E. B., Kozak, M. J., Goodman, W. K., Hollander, E., Jenike, M. A., & Rasmussen, S. A. (1995). 'DSM–IV field trial: Obsessive–compulsive disorder': Correction. *American Journal of Psychiatry, 152,* 654.

Foa, E. B., Kozak, M. J., Salkovskis, P., Coles, M. E., & Amir, N. (1998). The validation of a new Obsessive–Compulsive Disorder Scale: The Obsessive–Compulsive Inventory. *Psychological Assessment, 10,* 206–214.

Gianaros, P. J., & Quigley, K. S. (2001). Autonomic origins of a nonsignal stimulus-elicited bradycardia and its habituation in humans. *Psychophysiology, 38*, 540–547.

Haidt, J., McCauley, C., & Rozin, P. (1994). Individual differences in sensitivity to disgust: A scale sampling seven domains of disgust elicitors. *Personality and Individual Differences, 16*, 701–713.

Hodgson, R. J., & Rachman, S. J. (1977). Obsessional-compulsive complaints. *Behaviour Research and Therapy, 15*, 389–395.

Mancini, F., Gragnani, A., & D'Olimpio, F. (2001). The connection between disgust and obsessions and compulsions in a non-clinical sample. *Personality and Individual Differences, 31*, 1173–1180.

Matchett, G., & Davey, G. C. L. (1991). A test of a disease-avoidance model of animal phobias. *Behaviour Research and Therapy, 29*, 91–94.

McKay, D. (2006). Treating disgust reactions in contamination-based obsessive–compulsive disorder. *Journal of Behavior Therapy and Experimental Psychiatry, 37*, 53–59.

McKay, D., Abramowitz, J., Calamari, J., Kyrios, M., Radomsky, A., Sookman, D., et al. (2004). A critical evaluation of obsessive–compulsive disorder subtypes: Symptoms versus mechanisms. *Clinical Psychology Review, 24*, 283–313.

McKay, D., & Tsao, S. (2005). A treatment most foul: Handling disgust in cognitive-behavior therapy. *Journal of Cognitive Psychotherapy: An International Quarterly, 19*, 355–367.

McKay, D., & Tsao, S. (2006). *The effects of exposure on the generalization of habituation on multiple indices of disgust.* Unpublished manuscript.

McNally, R. J. (2002). Disgust has arrived. *Journal of Anxiety Disorders, 16*, 561–566.

Muris, P., Merckelbach, H., Nederkoorn, S., Rassin, E., Chandel, I., & Horselenberg, R. (2000). Disgust and psychopathological symptoms in a nonclinical sample. *Personality and Individual Differences, 29*, 1163–1167.

Olatunji, B. O., Sawchuk, C. N., Arrindell, W. A., & Lohr, J. M. (2005). Disgust sensitivity as a mediator of the sex differences in contamination fears. *Personality and Individual Differences, 38*, 713–722.

Olatunji, B. O., Sawchuk, C. N., Lohr, J. M., & de Jong, P. J. (2004). Disgust domains in the prediction of contamination fear. *Behaviour Research and Therapy, 42*, 93–104.

Phelps, E. A. (2006). Emotion and cognition: Insight from studies of the human amygdale. *Annual Review of Clinical Psychology, 2*, 27–53.

Riggs, D. S., & Foa, E. B. (2007). Treating contamination concerns and compulsive washing. In M. M. Antony, C. Purdon, & L. J. Summerfeldt (Eds.), *Psychological treatment of obsessive–compulsive disorder: Fundamentals and beyond* (pp. 149–168). Washington, DC: American Psychological Association.

Rozin, P., & Fallon, A. E. (1987). A perspective on disgust. *Psychological Review, 94*, 23–41.

Rozin, P., Fallon, A. E., & Mandell, R. (1984). Family resemblance in attitudes to foods. *Developmental Psychology, 20*, 309–314.

Rozin, P., Haidt, J., & McCauley, C. R. (2000). Disgust. In M. Lewis & J. M. Haviland (Eds.), *Handbook of emotions* (2nd ed., pp. 637–653). New York: Guilford Press.

Rozin, P., Millman, L., & Nemeroff, C. (1986). Operation of the laws of sympathetic magic in disgust and other domains. *Journal of Personality and Social Psychology, 50*, 703–712.

Sanovio, E. (1988). Obsessions and compulsions: The Padua Inventory. *Behaviour Research and Therapy, 26*, 169–177.

Sawchuk, C. N., Lohr, J. M., Tolin, D. F., Lee, T. C., & Kleinknecht, R. A. (2000). Disgust sensitivity and contamination fears in spider and blood-injection-injury phobias. *Behaviour Research and Therapy, 38*, 753–762.

Scheinle, A., Stark, R., Walter, B., & Vaitl, D. (2003). The connection between disgust sensitivity and blood-related fears, faintness symptoms, and obsessive–compulsiveness in a non-clinical sample. *Anxiety, Stress, & Coping, 16*, 185–193.

Schwarz, N. (1999). Self-reports: How the questions shape the answers. *American Psychologist, 54*, 93–105.

Shafran, R., Thordarson, D., & Rachman, S. (1996). Thought-action fusion in obsessive–compulsive disorder. *Journal of Anxiety Disorders, 10*, 379–391.

Smits, J. A. J., Telch, M. J., & Randall, P. K. (2002). An examination of the decline in fear and disgust during exposure-based treatment. *Behaviour Research and Therapy, 40*, 1243–1253.

Sookman, D., & Pinard, G. (2002). Overestimation of threat and intolerance of uncertainty in obsessive–compulsive disorder. In R. O. Frost & G. Steketee (Eds.), *Cognitive approaches to obsessions and compulsions: Theory, assessment, and treatment* (pp. 63–90). Oxford, England: Elsevier.

Taylor, S. (1998). Assessment of obsessions and compulsions. In R. Swinson, M. Antony, S. Rachman, & M. Richter (Eds.), *Obsessions and compulsions: Theory, assessment, and treatment* (pp. 229–257). New York: Guilford Press.

Taylor, S., Abramowitz, J. S., & McKay, D. (2007). Cognitive–behavioral models of obsessive–compulsive disorder. In M. M. Antony, C. Purdon, & L. J. Summerfeldt (Eds.), *Psychological treatment of obsessive–compulsive disorder: Fundamentals and beyond* (pp. 9–29). Washington, DC: American Psychological Association.

Taylor, S., McKay, D., & Abramowitz, J. (2005a). Is obsessive–compulsive disorder a disturbance of security motivation? Comment on Szechtman and Woody (2004). *Psychological Review, 112*, 650–657.

Taylor, S., McKay, D., & Abramowitz, J. (2005b). Problems with the security motivation model remain largely unresolved: Response to Woody & Szechtman (2005). *Psychological Review, 112*, 656–657.

Thordarson, D. S., Radomsky, A. S., Rachman, S., Shafran, R., Sawchuk, C. N., & Hakstian, A. R. (2004). The Vancouver Obsessional Compulsive Inventory. *Behaviour Research and Therapy, 42*, 1289–1314.

Thordarson, D. S., & Shafran, R. (2002). Importance of thoughts. In R. O. Frost & G. Steketee (Eds.), *Cognitive approaches to obsessions and compulsions: Theory, assessment, and treatment* (pp. 15–28). Amsterdam: Pergamon.

Thorpe, S. J., Patel, S. P., & Simonds, L. M. (2003). The relationship between disgust sensitivity, anxiety, and obsessions. *Behaviour Research and Therapy, 41,* 1397–1409.

Tolin, D. F., Lohr, J. M., Sawchuk, C. N., & Lee, T. C. (1997). Disgust and disgust sensitivity in blood-injection-injury and spider phobia. *Behaviour Research and Therapy, 35,* 949–953.

Tolin, D. F., Woods, C. M., & Abramowitz, J. S. (2006). Disgust sensitivity and obsessive–compulsive symptoms in a non-clinical sample. *Journal of Behavior Therapy and Experimental Psychiatry, 37,* 30–40.

Tolin, D. F., Worhunsky, P., & Maltby, N. (2004). Sympathetic magic in contamination-related OCD. *Journal of Behavior Therapy and Experimental Psychiatry, 35,* 193–205.

Tsao, S. D., & McKay, D. (2004). Behavioral avoidance tests and disgust in contamination fears: Distinctions from trait anxiety. *Behaviour Research and Therapy, 42,* 207–216.

Walls, M. M., & Kleinknecht, R. A. (1996, April). *Disgust factors as predictors of blood–injury fear and fainting.* Paper presented at the annual meeting of the Western Psychological Association, San Jose, CA.

Watson, D. (2005). Rethinking the mood and anxiety disorders: A quantitative hierarchical model for *DSM–V. Journal of Abnormal Psychology, 114,* 522–536.

Weissman, M. M., Bland, R. C., Canino, G. J., Greenwald, S., Hwu, H. G., Lee, C. K., et al. (1994). The cross national epidemiology of obsessive–compulsive disorder: The cross national collaborative group. *Journal of Clinical Psychiatry, 55,* 5–10.

Woody, S. R., & Teachman, B. A. (2000). Intersection of disgust and fear: Normative and pathological views. *Clinical Psychology: Science and Practice, 7,* 291–311.

Woody, S. R., & Tolin, D. F. (2002). The relationship between disgust sensitivity and avoidant behavior: Studies of clinical and nonclinical samples. *Journal of Anxiety Disorders, 16,* 543–559.

Zhong, C. B., & Liljenquist, K. (2006, October 13). Washing away your sins: Threatened morality and physical cleansing. *Science, 313,* 1451–1452.

11

FOOD, BODY, AND SOUL: THE ROLE OF DISGUST IN EATING DISORDERS

NICHOLAS TROOP AND ANNA BAKER

FOOD-BASED ORIGINS OF DISGUST

Definitions of core disgust emphasize its role in the avoidance of oral incorporation of offensive substances (Angyal, 1941; Rozin & Fallon, 1987). These substances are not necessarily considered noxious but, rather, contaminating in that they render otherwise acceptable food unacceptable (Rozin & Fallon, 1987). There is also a fear of becoming soiled because the contaminating properties of the offensive substance have the same effect on the self (Angyal, 1941). For example, Angyal (1941) stated that "the [disgust] reaction is mainly against ingestion, even in cases where there is no apparent danger of the disgusting materials reaching the mouth . . . in particular, faeces is the first object to which we become disgusted" (p. 394). Davey (1994) provided a more comprehensive definition but similarly emphasized ingestion: *Disgust* is defined as "a type of rejection response characterised by a specific facial expres-

Much of the discussion in this chapter is the result of collaborations on a series of studies carried out with colleagues and students whose contributions we acknowledge: Alyson Bond, Elvira Bramon, Jeff Dalton, Jayne Griffiths, Toni Harvey, Fay Murphy, Tara Murphy, Lucy Serpell, and Janet Treasure.

229

sion, a desire to distance oneself from the object of disgust, a physiological manifestation of mild nausea, a fear of oral incorporation of the object of disgust and a feeling of 'revulsion' " (p. 54).

It is no surprise, therefore, that the role of disgust has been explored in relation to food choice and food avoidance in general (see Rozin & Fallon, 1987). However, although Phillips, Senior, Fahy, and David (1998) suggested that the role of disgust has been neglected in psychiatry in general, this is particularly true in eating disorders. This is all the more surprising because accounts of their experience by individuals with an eating disorder are replete with references to feelings of disgust (we discuss this further in the "Disgust and Eating Disorder Symptoms" section below).

Nonfood objects can also be the object of disgust. For example, Rozin and colleagues (Rozin & Fallon 1987; Rozin, Haidt, & McCauley, 1999) described the importance of disgust in communicating cultural and moral values. Thus, disgust is associated with rejection, either of undesirable foods (at its most basic level) or undesirable characteristics (e.g., moral corruption or deviant behavior; Miller, 1997; Rozin, Haidt, et al., 1999). In spite of what may seem like such an obvious association in eating disorders (disgust and food avoidance or rejection), in this chapter we argue that it is not so much a role for *core* disgust but rather for *ideational* (Rozin, Haidt, et al., 1999) or even *complex* (Power & Dalgleish, 1997) disgust. In other words, even though eating disorders involve abnormal relationships with food, the role of disgust in eating disorders is not primarily one of "animal disgust origins centered on food selection and protecting the body from harmful ingestants" (Rozin, Haidt, et al., 1999) but one of "ideational disgust serving to protect the soul from harmful influences" (p. 431).

ANOREXIA NERVOSA AND BULIMIA NERVOSA

Anorexia nervosa refers to a refusal or inability to maintain a body weight above 85% of that expected (this approximates to a body mass index of 17.5 kilograms/meter^2), concomitant amenorrhoea, and a fear of weight gain (*Diagnostic and Statistical Manual of Mental Disorders, Fourth Edition* [*DSM–IV*]; American Psychiatric Association [APA], 1994). Although some individuals maintain their low weight purely through dietary restriction (restricting anorexia nervosa), others experience episodes of binge eating (even while at low weight) and/or maintain their low weight by using purging methods such as vomiting, laxative, or diuretic abuse (anorexia nervosa of the binge–purge subtype). *Bulimia nervosa* generally occurs in women of normal weight and refers to episodes of binge eating and compensatory behaviors that occur on average at least twice a week for a period of at least 3 months. Binge eating is defined as an amount of food that is eaten in a discreet period of time (operationalized at about 2 hours) in which there is a sense of loss of control over eating. Compensation for binge eating in bulimia nervosa, similar to anorexia nervosa, can take the form of purging (e.g., vomiting, laxative, diuretic abuse) or nonpurging behaviors (e.g., fasting, excessive exercise).

Common to both types of eating disorder is an overidentification of self-esteem with weight and shape (i.e., a belief that self-esteem can be measured by weight or body shape; Fairburn, Shafran, & Cooper, 1999; Garner & Bemis, 1982). The result of this is that weight gain and food (consumption of which leads to weight gain) are perceived as threats to self-esteem. Implicit in this perception of threat is the assumption that the underlying emotion in eating disorders is one of fear: Phrases used in clinical descriptions such as "morbid dread of fatness" (Russell, 1970), "weight phobia" (Crisp, 1967), and "fear of weight gain" (APA, 1994) make this explicit. Indeed, one of the reasons we began our research on disgust in eating disorders is that we were particularly struck by Graham Davey's disease-avoidance model of animal phobias (e.g., Davey, 1994; Davey, Forster, & Mayhew, 1993; Matchett & Davey, 1991; Ware, Jain, Burgess, & Davey, 1994). Here is a disorder that is, by definition, a disorder of "fear." Nevertheless, in a series of studies, Davey and colleagues have shown that the phobia associated with some animals is related to the degree to which they are perceived as disgusting. Specifically, the category of animal for which phobia is thought to be based on disgust is restricted to *revulsive animals* (e.g., slugs and snails) and *fear-relevant animals* (e.g., rats and spiders), whereas other animal fears, such as those of dogs, seem much more likely to be due to the classical conditioning account of phobias or else due to a genuine and realistic perception of danger, as is the case with predatory animals (Davey, 1994; Matchett & Davey, 1991; Ware et al., 1994).

Davey (1992) suggested that the link between disgust and (some) animal phobias may have evolved in three ways: (a) animals that may be associated with the spread of disease and infection (e.g., rats, mice, flies); (b) animals that may resemble (or possess features that resemble) disgust-evoking stimuli such as mucus or feces (e.g., slugs, snails, frogs, and others such as snakes and lizards that are at least perceived as slimy); (c) animals that may act as signals for dirt, disease, and infection (e.g., spiders). It is probably unlikely that the disease-avoidance model translates directly from animal phobias to eating disorders. However, although negative affect in general plays a role in the development of eating disorder symptoms (Serpell & Troop, 2003), for example, through its effect on inducing overeating in women with high levels of dietary restraint (Greeno & Wing, 1994; Ruderman, 1986), it is an intriguing possibility that disgust may play a specific role in disorders such as anorexia nervosa and bulimia nervosa that are so consistently referred to in terms of the importance of fear.

DISGUST AND EATING DISORDER SYMPTOMS

Although core disgust is a response to foodstuff, examples from online resources such as the beat: beating eating disorders Web site (http://www.b-eat.co.uk/Home; formerly the Eating Disorders Association [EDA]) suggest that even when disgust is expressed toward food, disgust of the body is also a prominent feature. The following extract from the Royal College of Psychiatrists (RCP) Web site refers to an individual with anorexia nervosa. In this example disgust is directed toward the self in relation to the body as well as the eating of food. There is reference to nausea as well as to avoidance. However, the avoidance described seems to be in terms of hiding the self rather than avoiding the food and is in keeping with the notion of self-concealment described by Rozin, Haidt, et al. (1999):

> When she looks in the mirror this girl sees a fatty. She is blind to the hip bones and the ribs. She sees the slightly swollen belly. The bud of a breast. The curve of a thigh. And they disgust her. As she disgusts herself when she eats a cream cake. As they make her want to be sick. Or hide. Under huge jumpers, massive coats. Invisible and shrinking under layers of cloth. (RCP, 2008, ¶1–2)

The EDA Web site similarly describes people with bulimia as being

> obsessed with calories and dieting . . . Whenever they feel angry, sad, unsuccessful, depressed, patronised, rejected etc they resort to bingeing. This is followed by feelings of self-disgust at the amount they have eaten [and] they go to extreme lengths to rid their bodies of food. (EDA, 2008a, ¶1)

Again, even when the consumption of food is mentioned, the disgust refers to the self as a consequence of having overeaten rather than because of the inherently disgusting properties of the food per se. The following quotes from individuals who have had an eating disorder further emphasize this point:

> I didn't think of food as fuel, as the energy I needed to be able to do all of that exercising in the first place, I thought food was fat. If I ate like everybody around me, it would destroy my exercise rituals, it would kill the new 'me' I was inventing for myself. If I ate a normal meal without puking afterwards, my body would disappear into a disgusting pile of pure fat. (EDA, 2008b, n.p.)

> When I was bulimic, I often met average sized women who wore size 16 clothes. Women who had self respect, who enjoyed living in their bodies, these women disgusted me. Surely, they didn't really like being so fat? Yes they did. My disgust was jealousy. (EDA, 2008b, n.p.)

A qualitative study with eating disorder patients explored emotional responses to the sight of different types of food. McNamara, Chur-Hansen, and Hay (2008) identified a core theme of control with participants who spontaneously expressed fear as well as disgust toward themselves (and others) in relation to loss of control over eating.

As well as contemporary accounts such as those mentioned earlier, Stunkard (1990) discussed a series of cases of bulimia originally described by the psychoanalyst Moshe Wulff in 1932 in which references to disgust are highly salient for 3 of the 4 patients. For example, Patient A referred to ". . . a tormenting feeling of inferiority and a strong disgust with myself, of my own body; I appear to myself as dirty, loathsome, repulsive" (p. 265). In discussing Patient B, Wulff said,

> At such times she had a particularly strong feeling of disgust toward her own body. If she let her hand fall even very lightly on her body she twitched full of disgust and pulled it back quickly with a look on her face as if she disturbed something terrible, dirty, and disgusting; at such times she would also say, "disgusting." (Stunkard, 1990, p. 265)

Wulff continued on to say of Patient B that

> This feeling of disgust toward her own body also began in this patient in puberty . . . and the first signs of a female body form and her breasts, in particular, became noticeable. . . . This feeling of disgust was closely connected with strong feelings of shame. These feelings of shame and of disgust were concentrated on her face and particularly strongly on her abdomen, in addition to her breasts. (Stunkard, 1990, p. 265)

A slightly different perspective on expressions of discuss are apparent in Patient D:

> "As if now everything is lost, my whole life has now lost its value, impossible, completely impossible, to live any longer now; I will always be loathsome like this, dirty, spoiled, turned into an animal, and I can never again be a human being. I feel disgust for myself, feel soiled and in order to be clean I would have to take a lot of castor oil . . . I feel so fat, so fat, and that is frightening . . ." Even when it was very hot she had to go out on the street in a large dark coat "so that people cannot see my disgusting fat body . . . The circumstances of her addictive eating were released primarily through some insult, particularly in her erotic affairs, when, for example, a young man from her host of admirers let her notice his indifference. Then she felt that she was ugly, repulsive, disgusting because she was fat and big and then began to eat out of spite, as she said, "out of feelings of revenge": "If I am not loved because I am like this, good;

now more than ever, I will be completely bestial, completely disgusting, completely dirty, and I will do what is harmful, what is forbidden, that is, eat a great deal." (Stunkard, 1990, p. 266)

The kinds of comments relating to feeling that the self is disgusting because of perceived fatness or overeating are reminiscent of those from the EDA Web site. However, references to being bestial and animal-like more closely relate to Rozin, Haidt, et al.'s (1999) description of animal-nature disgust. Although such descriptions are not new, they seem to have remained within clinical experience and have gone largely unresearched. Nevertheless, even before discussing what empirical literature there is, it can already be seen that references to disgust by individuals with an eating disorder focus on the link between the body being disgusting and, by implication, that the self is therefore disgusting: disgust of the physical transfers to disgust of the spiritual. However, it is still possible that the experience of disgust in bulimia nervosa (characterized by overeating) is different from that in anorexia nervosa (characterized by food avoidance).

THE INTERSECTION OF DISGUST AND MORALITY IN EATING DISORDERS

A number of other features commonly reported in people with eating disorders may share an association with disgust. Here we briefly consider that disgust may also contribute to eating pathology through moral, religious, and sexual attitudes. Although it is possible that these associations are secondary, perhaps even incidental, their consideration may still enable us to understand the putative role of disgust in eating disorders more fully.[1]

Moral and Religious Values

It has been proposed that disgust processes underlie the transmission of social and moral values (Rozin, Haidt, et al., 1999). Indeed, women with anorexia nervosa have been found to report greater adherence to social norms, both while symptomatic and when recovered (Casper, 1990; Casper, Hedeker, & McClough, 1992), suggesting this is a stable feature of anorexia. Another aspect of avoidance of food or weight loss that is connected with disgust is that of "purification." Rozin, Lowery, Imada, and Haidt (1999) provided evidence

---

[1]Perfectionism, obsessionality, obsessive–compulsive disorder, and obsessive–compulsive personality disorders are also relatively common features of eating disorders, particularly anorexia nervosa, features that also have a strong association with disgust processes, and therefore a complete understanding of the role of disgust in eating disorders might also usefully consider these disorders. However, because this is dealt with in chapter 10 of this volume, we do not discuss these issues here.

that disgust is the moral emotion associated with the violation of purity, divinity, and spirituality, and purification is an idea that has been expressed in anorexia nervosa throughout its history (Schmidt & Treasure, 1993), for example, through denial of food (e.g., "holy anorexia"). Abstinence of all kinds reflects discipline among the more austere religious groups, but even apart from these higher aims, the notion of denying oneself food comes strikingly close to Rozin's suggestion that disgust is generally a reaction to anything that reminds us that we are animals. If eating and defecating are bestial, then not eating (and, as a result, not defecating) are not animal-like behaviors.

Attitudes Toward Sex and Sexuality

Among others, Crisp (1965) suggested that the repudiation of sexual maturity is of key importance in anorexia nervosa. Although there is evidence that women report more disgust in response to erotic material than do men (Koukounas & McCabe, 1997), it has also been reported that women with primary anorexia (when weight loss is valued) tend to be more disgusted by sexual activity than are women with secondary anorexia (when weight loss is not valued; King, 1963).

RESEARCH ON DISGUST IN EATING DISORDERS

In the previous section, we presented clinical descriptions of disgust. In this section, we discuss studies that have been addressed empirically and present them under headings relating to individual differences, eating disorder-relevant stimuli, and recognition of expressions of disgust.

Individual Differences in Disgust and Disgust Sensitivity

A number of studies are beginning to consider the relationship between eating pathology and individual differences on disgust and disgust sensitivity more directly. These studies have generally operationalized disgust and disgust sensitivity, using the Disgust Sensitivity Questionnaire (DSQ; Rozin, Fallon, & Mandell, 1984), the Disgust Scale (DS; Haidt, McCauley, & Rozin, 1994), or the Disgust Questionnaire (DQ; Barker & Davey, 1994). Table 11.1 summarizes correlations between eating pathology and various measures of disgust from several studies. On the basis of the weight of evidence, it appears that eating pathology does generally correlate with disgust. However, findings from this body of literature are not unequivocal. For example, Muris et al. (2000) found no association between disgust and eating disorder symptoms in a nonclinical sample, whereas Troop, Murphy, Bramon, and Treasure (2000) found no

TABLE 11.1
Correlations Between Disgust and Eating Pathology

Questionnaire and sample	r
Davey et al. (1998)	
Rozin's DSQ (female students)[a]	−.51**
Rozin's DSQ (male students)[a]	−.09
Barker & Davey's DQ (female students)[a]	.41**
Barker & Davey's DQ (male students)[a]	.11
Muris et al. (2000)	
Rozin's DSQ (students, "corrected" for sex)[b]	.07
Troop et al. (2000)	
Haidt's DQ (patients, mostly female)[c]	.12
Troop et al. (2002)[g]	
Barker & Davey's DQ (eating disorder volunteer sample)[d]	
• Anorexia nervosa symptoms	.28**
• Bulimia nervosa symptoms	.23**
Harvey et al. (2002)	
Barker & Davey's DQ (female students)[a]	.46**
Griffiths & Troop (2006)	
Barker & Davey's DQ (female students)[e]	.37**
Muris et al. (2008)	
Haidt's DQ (girls age 9–13 years)[f]	.12
Haidt's DQ (boys age 9–13 years)[f]	.08
Rozin's DSQ (girls age 9–13 years)[f]	.19*
Rozin's DSQ (boys age 9–13 years)[f]	.24*

Note. DSQ = Disgust Sensitivity Questionnaire; DQ = Disgust Questionnaire.
[a]Eating Attitudes Test (Garner, Olmsted, Bohr, & Garfinkel, 1982). [b]Restraint Questionnaire (Herman & Polivy, 1975). [c]Eating Disorders Inventory (Garner, Olmsted, & Polivy, 1983). [d]Short Evaluation for Eating Disorders (Bauer, Winn, Schmidt, & Kordy, 2005). [e]Dutch Eating Behavior Questionnaire (Van Strien, Frijters, Bergers, & Defares, 1986). [f]Children's Eating Attitude Test (Maloney, McGuire, & Daniels, 1988). [g]This is an unpublished reanalysis.
*p < .05. **p < .001.

significant correlation between eating pathology and disgust sensitivity in an eating disorder sample. Schienle et al. (2002) also found no significant difference between outpatients with bulimia nervosa and healthy comparison women on disgust sensitivity. Also, even when an association is found (e.g., Troop, Treasure, & Serpell, 2002, Study 1), this may be due to unusually low levels of disgust sensitivity in comparison women rather than elevated levels of disgust sensitivity in eating-disordered women (see Figure 11.1, comparing Troop et al. [2002] with Haidt et al.'s [1994] data on female students).

It is important to note, however, that when significant correlations are found between disgust and eating disorder symptoms, these generally remain even after partialing out the effects of depression, anxiety, fear, and neuroticism (Davey, Buckland, Tantow, & Dallos, 1998; Griffiths & Troop, 2006; Harvey, Troop, Treasure, & Murphy, 2002; Muris, van der Heiden, & Rassin, 2008; Troop et al., 2000). Although such studies typically use nonclinical samples and the associations are generally found only in female (and not male) participants, Table 11.1 also presents a reanalysis of data from Troop et al.

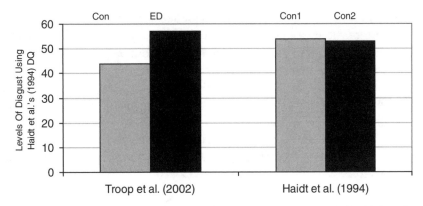

Figure 11.1. Comparison of ED women (Study 1: Troop et al., 2002) with female non-ED samples from Haidt et al. (1994). Con = female control/comparison samples; ED = eating disorder group (mixed AN and BN); AN = anorexia nervosa; BN = bulimia nervosa; DQ = disgust questionnaire.

(2002, Study 2) showing that anorexic and bulimic symptoms correlate with disgust in women with a current or past eating disorder, although only the correlation with anorexic symptoms remains significant after controlling for depression.

However, although results that indicate an association between disgust and eating pathology are not unequivocal, disgust is a multidimensional construct and therefore the use of global measures of disgust limits the conclusions that may be drawn. Across two studies, Davey et al. (1998) found that associations between eating disorder symptoms and disgust were restricted to domains related to foodstuff of animal origin (e.g., tripe, kidneys) and body products (e.g., feces, dandruff, obesity). In another study, although eating disorder patients were found to be significantly more sensitive to disgust stimuli overall than were comparison women (see Troop et al., 2002, Study 1), further analyses showed that these patients were more sensitive to disgust on items relating to food, animals, body products, and sex but not more sensitive to disgust on items relating to body envelope violations, death, hygiene, and magical contagion.

The specificity of disgust domains in eating disorders has also been found in studies that have examined course of diagnosis. For example, Troop et al. (2002, Study 2) found that currently ill and remitted eating disorder groups reported higher levels of disgust than noneating disordered women but only in the domains of foodstuff of animal original and the human body or body products. In addition, remitted women were less disgusted by the human body or body products than were currently ill women but did not differ on disgust of foodstuff of animal origin.

Therefore, although there is some evidence for increased levels of disgust sensitivity in eating disorder patients and/or a correlation between disgust sensitivity and eating pathology, the evidence is not unequivocal. This may be because of the measurement of global rather than of specific domains of disgust in some studies or even because of the differences in the measures themselves. For example, positive associations are more often found in studies that use the DQ (Barker & Davey, 1994) than those that use the DS (Haidt et al., 1994). Why this should be the case is not immediately clear. Nevertheless, the weight of evidence is that there is an association between disgust and eating pathology, and it seems to be restricted to the categories of foodstuff of animal origin and the human body or body products rather than a global disgust response or sensitivity.

Fear and Disgust in Response to Eating Disorder-Relevant Stimuli

From the previous section, it appears that the role of disgust in eating disorders is restricted to those domains that are most obviously relevant to eating disorders, namely food and the body. However, because most studies do not take account of emotions other than disgust we cannot be sure that the associations with eating pathology are not simply due to a greater negative affectivity in eating-disordered women in general or, more specifically, that fear is not still the primary emotion in eating disorders. However, Harvey et al. (2002) found that female students who scored high on abnormal eating attitudes rated images of high calorie foods as both more disgusting and more fearful than did those scoring low on abnormal eating attitudes. Female students who scored high on abnormal eating attitudes also rated images of overweight body shapes as both more disgusting and more fearful than did those who scored low on abnormal eating attitudes. However, groups did not differ in their fear and disgust ratings of images of slim body shapes. That levels of fear and disgust to eating disorder-relevant stimuli (high calorie foods and overweight body shapes) did not differ from each other but were higher in participants with abnormal eating attitudes confirms that disgust and fear are equally salient emotional responses.

More recently, Griffiths and Troop (2006) also found that higher levels of dietary restraint were associated with higher ratings of fear and disgust in response to images of high calorie foods and overweight body shapes but there was no significant association between dietary restraint and ratings of fear and disgust in response to images of low calorie food and slim body shapes. It is interesting to note that there was no correlation between amount of daily calories consumed in fat and ratings of fear or disgust to any of the images (even images of high calorie foods and overweight body shapes). It was therefore concluded from this study that disgust ratings of eating disorder-relevant stimuli do not reflect core disgust, because core disgust is associated with avoidance of those foods. Rather, it is suspected that disgust in this context is related to personal rules about what should or should not be eaten rather than what is or is not actually eaten. As such, it may simply form part of the dietary restraint construct. Dietary restraint refers specifically to cognitive efforts to restrict intake therefore it may be that the disgust and fear responses to high calorie and overweight stimuli are an affective component of this general construct of restraint.

Factor analyses of ratings from Harvey et al. (2002) and Griffiths and Troop (2006) seem to confirm this (see Table 11.2 and Table 11.3). In both analyses, eating concerns (abnormal eating attitudes or dietary restraint, respectively) load with fear and disgust ratings to threatening eating disorder-relevant stimuli (i.e., high calorie foods, overweight body shapes) to form a single factor. Fear and disgust ratings to nonthreatening eating disorder-relevant stimuli (i.e., slim body shapes and low calorie foods) and to eating disorder-irrelevant emotional stimuli (frightening and disgusting images such as attack dogs and severed hands) form separate factors. The results are taken to confirm the suggestion that disgust and fear responses to high calorie and overweight stimuli may represent a negative affective component of dietary restraint and are not simply a measure of general affectivity. This account may explain the results of Schienle et al.'s (2004) functional magnetic resonance imaging (fMRI) study in which bulimic patients and control participants did not differ significantly on subjective ratings or brain activation in response to disgust-inducing pictures. As these authors themselves pointed out, the stimuli they used combined disorder-relevant and disorder-irrelevant stimuli, and they suggested that future studies should consider these separately.

TABLE 11.2
Factor Analysis of Visual Analog Scale Ratings
and Abnormal Eating Attitudes

Stimulus	Emotion	1	2	3
Eating Attitudes Test		.81		
High calorie foods	Fear	.97		
High calorie foods	Disgust	.96		
High calorie drinks	Fear	.81		
High calorie drinks	Disgust	.86		
Overweight body shapes	Fear	.95		
Overweight body shapes	Disgust	.88		
Slim body shapes	Fear			.76
Slim body shapes	Disgust			.84
Frightening images	Fear		.89	
Frightening images	Disgust		.86	
Disgusting images	Fear		.81	
Disgusting images	Disgust			.73
Eigenvalue		6.84	2.45	1.64
% variance accounted for		52.6	18.9	12.6

Note. Analysis using data from Harvey et al. (2002). Factor analysis used oblique rotation and number of factors identified by examination of the scree plot. Only factor loadings that are greater than .5 are shown as indicating inclusion on the relevant factor. $n = 40$.

TABLE 11.3
Factor Analysis of Visual Analog Scale Ratings, Dietary Restraint, and Fat Intake

Stimulus	Emotion	1	2	3	4
Dietary restraint		.71			
High calorie foods	Fear	.98			
High calorie foods	Disgust	.87			
Overweight body shapes	Fear	.98			
Overweight body shapes	Disgust	.97			
Low calorie foods	Fear		.68		
Low calorie foods	Disgust		.76		
Slim body shapes	Fear		.71		
Slim body shapes	Disgust		.93		
Frightening images	Fear			.93	
Frightening images	Disgust			.89	
Disgusting images	Fear				
Disgusting images	Disgust			.66	
% fat intake					.96
Eigenvalues		4.27	2.51	1.76	1.44
% variance accounted for		30.5	17.9	12.6	10.3

Note. Analysis using data from Griffiths and Troop (2006). Factor analysis used oblique rotation and number of factors identified by examination of the scree plot. Only factor loadings that are greater than .5 are shown as indicating inclusion on the relevant factor. $n = 69$.

More recently, McNamara, Hay, Katsikitis, and Chur-Hansen (2008) found no significant association between eating pathology and visual analog scale (VAS) ratings of disgust and fear to images of foods. However, one explanation as to why these results differ from those of Harvey et al. (2002) and Griffiths and Troop (2006) is that the stimuli used in this study were chosen on the basis of likely emotional responses rather than their relevance to eating pathology per se (P. Hay, personal communication, 2008). Specifically, these authors used images of four groups of foods: those that might arouse disgust, those that might arouse a "happy response," unfamiliar foods, and threatening or binge foods.

Murphy et al. (2008) further examined differences in ratings of eating disorder-relevant images in women with an eating disorder. Women with anorexia nervosa reported higher levels of subjective fear and disgust to food versus nonfood stimuli, whereas no differences in emotional responses between food and nonfood stimuli were found between the bulimia nervosa and noneating-disordered groups. However, both the anorexia nervosa and bulimia nervosa groups were equally fearful and disgusted by overweight body shapes (relative to underweight and normal weight body shapes), and both groups were higher on these emotions than were the noneating-disordered women. Although generally higher on fear and disgust overall, women with anorexia nervosa and bulimia nervosa responded in a similar way to noneating-disordered women in their ratings of standard emotional stimuli. In fact, this was also true for women with high and low levels of abnormal eating concerns in the studies reported by Harvey et al. (2002) and Griffiths and Troop (2006) and collectively is taken to mean that general emotional responses in women with eating pathology are "normal" and appropriate and that, therefore, high ratings of fear and disgust to eating disorder-relevant stimuli cannot be dismissed on the basis that women with eating pathology simply show greater affective response or that they cannot differentiate between fear and disgust.

One further study is of note. Uher et al. (2005) conducted an fMRI study in a mixed group of patients with eating disorders and explored subjective ratings and brain activation in response to images of underweight, normal weight, and overweight body shapes. Although there were no significant differences in brain activation between patients and control participants, patients gave higher subjective ratings of fear and disgust overall but especially in response to overweight body shapes (in contrast, control participants gave higher subjective ratings of fear and disgust to underweight than to overweight body shapes). Comparison of the results of this study with those discussed previously is not entirely straightforward, however. Although previous research has tended to keep ratings of fear and disgust separate (in spite of admittedly high correlations) to determine whether patients can still differentiate between these two emotions or if they simply report high levels of negative emotions generally, Uher et al. (2005) combined scores on fear and disgust into a single variable that they termed *aversion*. Nevertheless, the results are broadly consistent with those of Murphy et al. (2008), who used patient samples, and Harvey et al. (2002) and Griffiths and Troop (2006), who used nonclinical samples.

In summary, in patients and nonclinical samples high in dietary restraint,

1. fear and disgust are equally salient emotions in relation to eating pathology;
2. high ratings of both of these emotions are not due to an inability to differentiate the two emotions;
3. fear and disgust are elevated specifically in relation to threatening eating disorder-relevant stimuli (i.e., overweight body shapes, high calorie foods) but not nonthreatening (e.g., slim body shapes, low calorie foods) or irrelevant or neutral stimuli; and
4. fear and disgust ratings of threatening eating disorder-relevant stimuli load on a single factor with dietary restraint.

To expand on this final point, it may be that fear and disgust represent an emotional component of (cognitive) restraint. However, precisely how these affective and cognitive components might relate cannot be determined from the results discussed earlier, for example, whether disgust of overweight body shapes or high calorie foods are a cause or consequence of dietary restraint is open to speculation. It may be that the fear and disgust expressed toward threatening foods causes this restraint; as if to say, "being overweight is disgusting so high calorie foods are disgusting and therefore I will attempt to avoid them." However, ratings of disgust may be a post hoc rationalization that provides the justification to the individual (and others) for their dietary restraint; for example, it may not be the case that the disgust causes the restraint but that a restrained individual can account for their restraint by proposing that these high calorie foods and overweight body shapes are in some way disgusting. A third alternative is that cognitive restraint may lead more successfully to the avoidance of high calorie foods (perhaps even overriding the desire to eat when hungry or even starving) if individuals can tap into this evolved capacity to experience disgust. Although this latter point is consistent with evidence from anorexia nervosa patients (Murphy et al., 2008) it is not consistent with the results of Griffiths and Troop (2006), who found that disgust of high calorie foods did not relate to actual consumption. It is clear that further research is required to explore these possibilities.

Recognition of Expressions of Emotion

There is evidence that patients with eating disorders have difficulty recognizing emotions in facial and vocal stimuli, in particular to negative emotions (Kucharska-Pietura, Nikolaou, Masiak, & Treasure, 2004), and it is suggested that this difficulty may contribute to problems in interpersonal communication. Although difficulties in the recognition and naming of emotions in general (so-called alexithymia) have long been recognized in eating disorders (e.g., Bourke, Taylor, Parker, & Bagby, 1992; Cochrane, Brewerton, Wilson, & Hodges, 1993; Schmidt, Jiwany, & Treasure, 1993; Troop, Schmidt, & Treasure, 1995), we argued in the previous section that this does not seem to be true for disgust (or fear) responses to eating disorder-relevant stimuli. It is reasonable to wonder, therefore, whether recognition of facial displays of disgust may show a different pattern in women with eating disorders than in those without. L. K. Murray, Murphy, Perrett, and Treasure (2008) measured accuracy and sensitivity in the recognition of facial displays of the six basic emotions (anger, disgust, fear, sadness, happiness, and surprise). The results showed that patients with eating disorders were equally accurate in the recognition of facial displays as noneating-disordered women. However, eating-disordered women were significantly more sensitive to the recognition of disgust in facial displays than were noneating-disordered women. This evidence of a specific sensitivity to the recognition of facial displays of disgust as a social signal brings us to one final strand in the discussion of the role of disgust in eating disorders and that relates to the experience of self-disgust or shame.

DISGUST AND SHAME IN EATING DISORDERS

There are several ways of conceptualizing shame (Gilbert, 1998). *Internalized shame* refers to how one sees or judges the self (e.g., worthless, flawed, morally defective, or unattractive), whereas external shame refers to how a perception of others see the self (e.g., the self is an object of scorn, ridicule, and contempt). Shame involves issues concerning rank, power, and status and is experienced when one perceives oneself to be judged as flawed and inadequate by some real or imagined observer who is more powerful. Gilbert (1992, 1997) proposed that the function of the feeling of shame is to signal to an individual that an involuntary loss of social status has occurred. Although Gilbert approached shame primarily from an evolutionary perspective, similar ideas of rank, power, and status have been expressed from a sociological perspective (Strongman, 1996) as well as in the literature that is more explicitly related to disgust, for example, the communication of moral norms, rejection, and the experience of the self as unattractive, base, or low rank (e.g., Miller, 1997; Rozin, Haidt, et al., 1999). An even more explicit connection between disgust and shame has been made by Power and Dalgleish (1997), who described shame as the complex variant of the basic emotion of disgust.

Beyond simply identifying elevated levels of shame in eating-disordered women (e.g., Sanftner, Barlow, Marschall, & Tangney, 1995), research on shame in eating disorders has taken three main directions: (a) the role of shame as a mediator of adverse life experiences, (b) the differential contribution of general shame and bodily shame to eating disorder symptoms, and (c) specificity in the particular type of shame experience that relates to eating disorder symptoms. Unfortunately these have often overlapped and all are complicated by the fact that shame is also intimately associated with depression (e.g., Gilbert & Andrews, 1998).

For example, proneness to experiencing shame moderated and feelings of shame mediated the effects of parental care in childhood on adult eating pathology in a student sample (C. Murray, Waller, & Legg, 2000). Bodily shame also mediated the relationship between childhood abuse and *DSM–III* bulimia (APA, 1980) in a community sample of women (Andrews, 1997). Bodily shame was found to be a stronger predictor of eating pathology than was general shame (Burney & Irwin, 2000), although bodily shame has been further delineated into shame that is experienced in relation to one's current body size and shame that is anticipated if one were to gain weight, so-called current and anticipated bodily shame, and these have different associations with different eating disorder symptoms (Troop, Sotrilli, Serpell, & Treasure, 2006). Specifically, current bodily shame was the strongest predictor of binge eating in a sample of women with a history of eating disorders, whereas anticipated bodily shame (were the individual to gain weight) was the strongest predictor of behaviors associated with the avoidance of weight gain (use of diet foods, fasting, and excessive exercise).

In terms of specific associations between different approaches to shame and eating disorder symptoms, Gee and Troop (2003) found in a student sample that depression was uniquely associated with external shame (using the Other As Shamer Scale; Goss, Gilbert, & Allan, 1994), whereas eating pathology was uniquely associated with internalized shame (using the Test of Self-Conscious Affect; Tangney, Wagner, & Gramzow, 1992). However, in a sample of women with a history of eating disorders, Troop, Allan, Serpell, and Treasure (in press) found that external shame (using the Other As Shamer Scale; Goss et al., 1994) was uniquely predictive of anorexia nervosa symptoms, whereas internalized shame (using the Personal Feelings Questionnaire; Harder & Zalma, 1990) was uniquely predictive of bulimia nervosa symptoms. The difference between external and internal shame is the difference between being shamed and feeling ashamed. Precisely why this specificity might exist is unclear. The specific link with external shame may mean that anorexia nervosa is more closely linked to issues of social rank than is bulimia nervosa. Although we do have some unpublished longitudinal data that suggest this may be the case, it would be premature to present this here. However, Goss and Gilbert (2002) suggested the development of a shame–pride cycle in relation to anorexic symptoms, whereby shame negatively reinforces and pride positively reinforces the primary symptoms of restriction and weight loss, that is, internal and external shame lead to restriction and the subsequent weight loss leads to feelings of pride. However they suggested that bulimic or binge symptoms may be involved in a shame–shame cycle, whereby feelings of shame lead individuals to use food or eating to regulate negative affect but that both the binge eating and subsequent compensatory behavior (e.g., vomiting) perpetuate feelings of shame and, therefore, reinforce attempts at affect regulation.

More evidence on the specificity of disgust and shame in anorexia nervosa comes from research on life events. Although a number of studies have revealed that severe life events (in particular, interpersonal ones) trigger onset of both anorexia nervosa and bulimia nervosa (see Serpell & Troop, 2003, for a review), to our knowledge only one study has explored the meaning (as opposed to the type) of triggering events. Schmidt, Tiller, Andrews, Blanchard, and Treasure (1997) found that rates of severe life events and difficulties (as identified using the Life Events and Difficulties Schedule; Brown & Harris, 1978) in the year before onset of eating disorders were similar to those found in depression. However, Schmidt et al.(1997) also explored the hypothesis that onset of anorexia nervosa was provoked specifically by *pudicity* events, that is, events of a sexual nature which are perceived as disgusting, shameful, or embarrassing. Pudicity events were indeed found more commonly to provoke the onset of anorexia nervosa than bulimia nervosa or depression. Such events were also rarely reported by women with no psychiatric disorder. Although consistent with this discussion of the role of disgust processes in eating disorders, it was still only a minority of anorexic women (24%) who experienced such a provoking agent. However, the specificity of this disgust-based meaning of events may be important in the development of anorexia nervosa in a considerable number of women.

CONCLUSION

In this chapter we argued that disgust processes (including basic disgust responses and the complex variant of shame) may play an underrecognized role in eating disorders. Studies on individual differences in disgust and disgust sensitivity, although not conclusive, do suggest that it is only disgust in relation to categories of food and body products that relates to eating disorder symptoms rather than disgust in general. Further studies on specific emotional responses to threatening eating disorder-relevant stimuli are generally more consistent, finding that disgust, together with fear, is high in relation to overweight body shapes and high calorie foods.

We further argued that not only are such processes related to eating disorder symptoms directly but that other personality features considered typical of individuals with an eating disorder (e.g., religiosity) are also related to disgust emotions as well as other key aspects, such as stress, dietary restraint, and shame. Thus, although there has been a great deal of research on apparently disparate features of eating disorders, a theme common to many of them is that of disgust.

It is not clear whether disgust plays a causal role in eating disorders or is simply an emotional component of the cognitive constructs already shown to be of importance (e.g., dietary restraint). Mayer, Bos, Muris, Huijding, and Vlielander (2008) showed that using foul-smelling odors to induce disgust did not decrease body esteem or preference for high calorie foods. They argued, therefore, that disgust does not cause eating pathology. However, because the disgusting odor did not emanate from these high calorie foods or relate to participants' (or others') bodies and was in no way bound up with other known causal factors, it is not entirely clear why a bad odor should have been causal. That dietary restraint itself plays a causal role (e.g., Stice, Akutagawa, Gaggar, & Agras, 2000) and that shame may be involved in mediating between risk factors and (some) triggering events and the onset of eating disorders, the causal role of disgust and disgust-based emotions remains a possibility. However, further research is required to test this more directly. In particular, evidence for some disgust processes is stronger for anorexia nervosa whereas for others evidence also exists for bulimia nervosa. It is possible that disgust plays different roles in the different eating disorders.

Another question that has arisen from this review concerns the overlap between the emotions of fear and disgust. Some authors have combined disgust and fear ratings because of their high intercorrelations (e.g., Uher et al., 2005). However, others (e.g., Griffiths & Troop, 2006; Harvey et al., 2002; Murphy et al., 2008) have shown that, in spite of their high intercorrelations, participants can still distinguish between them in relation to different stimuli. Nevertheless, whether these two emotions have different or complementary roles in relation to eating pathology is for future research to address.

Finally, although self-evaluation in terms of body weight and shape is not a new idea in eating disorders (e.g., Fairburn et al., 1999; Garner & Bemis, 1982; Wolff & Serpell, 1998), the specificity of disgust and its complex derivative shame in relation to this may prove to be important components in future models of eating disorders. Self-evaluations are generally viewed in cognitive terms, whereas Bornholt et al. (2005) found that affective components (including guilt or shame and disgust, as well as feeling okay, worrying, and feeling anger about the body) were related to, but distinct from, cognitive self-evaluations of the body and that a consideration of both provided a better fit of the data than did either one on its own. Findings presented in this chapter that disgust and fear ratings loaded on the same factors as dietary restraint and eating attitudes are consistent with this notion.

According to Miller (1997),

> Disgust figures centrally in our everyday moral discourse . . . It is bound up intimately with our responses to the ordinary vices of hypocrisy, betrayal, cruelty and stupidity. But disgust ranges more widely than we may wish, for it judges ugliness and deformity to be moral offences. It knows no distinction between the moral and the aesthetic, collapsing failures in both into an undifferentiated revulsion. Is this a necessary cost of a sentiment which does so much of the work of keeping us sociable and preventing us from being sources of offence and alarm? (p. 17)

The conflation of physical attractiveness and shame is certainly a prominent feature in eating disorders, regardless of whether shame is conceived as a failure to live up to an internalized set of standards, that the self is morally defective, or that the individual is perceived as having lost social rank. Disgust (core and interpersonal) evolved as an adaptive process that facilitated appropriate selection of foods, partners, and social contacts, and the rejection of inappropriate ones (Rozin, Haidt, et al., 1999). However, Gilbert (1995) argued that even evolved systems that are adaptive can have costs: For example, cell replication evolved as a process for repairing tissue, but one cost is that it is a source for cancer. Similarly, it can be argued that although disgust may have evolved as an adaptive process for the rejection of inappropriate foods, partners, and ways of behaving, this has a cost when the object of disgust becomes the self. When attractiveness becomes bound up with issues of body size (and, as a consequence, the consumption of foods that threaten the maintenance of an "attractive" body size) eating disorders (possibly) and bodily shame (probably) are costs of that evolved system.

REFERENCES

American Psychiatric Association. (1980). *Diagnostic and statistical manual of mental disorders* (3rd ed.). Washington, DC: Author.

American Psychiatric Association. (1994). *Diagnostic and statistical manual of mental disorders* (4th ed.). Washington, DC: Author.

Andrews, B. (1997). Bodily shame in relation to abuse in childhood and bulimia: A preliminary investigation. *British Journal of Clinical Psychology, 36*, 41–49.

Angyal, A. (1941). Disgust and related aversions. *Journal of Abnormal and Social Psychology, 36*, 393–412.

Barker, K., & Davey, G. C. L. (1994). *Categories of disgust: A factor analysis study.* Unpublished manuscript.

Bauer, S., Winn, S., Schmidt, U. H., & Kordy, H. (2005). Construction, scoring and validation of the Short Evaluation for Eating Disorders (SEED). *European Eating Disorders Review, 13*, 191–200.

Bornholt, L., Brake, N., Thomas, S., Russell, L., Madden, S., Anderson, G., et al. (2005). Understanding affective and cognitive self-evaluations about the body for adolescent girls. *British Journal of Health Psychology, 10*, 485–503.

Bourke, M. P., Taylor, G. J., Parker, J. D., & Bagby, J. M. (1992). Alexithymia in women with anorexia nervosa: A preliminary investigation. *British Journal of Psychiatry, 161*, 240–243.

Brown, G. W., & Harris, T. O. (1978). *Social origins of depression: A study of psychiatric disorder in women.* London: Tavistock.

Burney, J., & Irwin, H. J. (2000). Shame and guilt in women with eating disorder symptomatology. *Journal of Clinical Psychology, 56*, 51–61.

Casper, R. C. (1990). Personality features of women with good outcome from restricting anorexia nervosa. *Psychosomatic Medicine, 52*, 156–170.

Casper, R. C., Hedeker, D., & McClough, J. F. (1992). Personality dimensions in eating disorders and their relevance for subtyping. *Journal of the American Academy of Child and Adolescent Psychiatry, 31*, 830–840.

Cochrane, C. E., Brewerton, T. D., Wilson, D. B., & Hodges, E. J. (1993). Alexithymia in the eating disorders. *International Journal of Eating Disorders, 14*, 219–222.

Crisp, A. H. (1965). Clinical and therapeutic aspects of anorexia nervosa: A study of 30 cases. *Journal of Psychosomatic Research, 9*, 67–78.

Crisp, A. H. (1967). The possible significance of some behavioural correlates of weight and carbohydrate intake. *Journal of Psychosomatic Research, 11*, 117–131.

Davey, G. C. L. (1992). Characteristics of individuals with fear of spiders. *Anxiety Research, 4*, 299–314.

Davey, G. C. L. (1994). Self-reported fears to common indigenous animals in an adult UK population: The role of disgust sensitivity. *British Journal of Psychology, 85*, 541–554.

Davey, G. C. L., Buckland, G., Tantow, B., & Dallos, R. (1998) Disgust and eating disorders. *European Eating Disorders Review, 6*, 201–211.

Davey, G. C. L., Forster, L., & Mayhew, G. (1993). Familial resemblances in disgust sensitivity and animal phobias. *Behaviour Research and Therapy, 31*, 41–50.

Eating Disorders Association. (2008a). *Eating disorders: Bulimia nervosa and binge eating.* Retrieved January 24, 2008, from http://www.stardrift.net/survivor/eating.html

Eating Disorders Association. (2008b). *What are eating disorders? Survivors stories.* Retrieved January 24, 2008, from http://www.edauk.com/_baks/skinnyfragile .htm.0002.c7da.bak

Fairburn, C. G., Shafran, R., & Cooper, Z. (1999). A cognitive behavioural theory of anorexia nervosa. *Behaviour Research and Therapy, 37*, 1–13.

Garner, D. M., & Bemis, K. (1982). A cognitive-behavioral approach to anorexia nervosa. *Cognitive Therapy and Research, 6*, 123–150.

Garner, D. M., Olmsted, M. P., Bohr, Y., & Garfinkel, P. E. (1982). The Eating Attitudes Test: Psychometric features and clinical correlates. *Psychological Medicine, 12*, 871–878.

Garner, D. M., Olmsted, M. P., & Polivy, J. (1983). Development and validation of a multidimensional eating disorder inventory for anorexia nervosa and bulimia. *International Journal of Eating Disorders, 2*, 15–34.

Gee, A., & Troop, N. A. (2003). Shame, depressive symptoms and eating, weight and shape concerns in a non-clinical sample. *Eating and Weight Disorders, 8*, 72–75.

Gilbert, P. (1992) *Depression: The evolution of powerlessness.* Hove, England: Erlbaum.

Gilbert, P. (1995). Biopsychosocial approaches and evolutionary theory as aids to integration in clinical psychology and psychotherapy. *Clinical Psychology and Psychotherapy, 2*, 135–156.

Gilbert, P. (1997). The evolution of social attractiveness and its role in shame, humiliation, guilt and therapy. *British Journal of Clinical Psychology, 70*, 113–147.

Gilbert, P. (1998). What is shame? In P. Gilbert & B. Andrews (Eds.), *Shame: Interpersonal behaviour, psychopathology and culture* (pp. 3–38). New York: Oxford University Press.

Gilbert, P., & Andrews, B. (1998). *Shame: Interpersonal behaviour, psychopathology and culture.* New York: Oxford University Press.

Goss, K., & Gilbert, P. (2002). Eating disorders, shame and pride: A cognitive-behavioural functional analysis. In P. Gilbert & J. Miles (Eds.), *Body shame: Conceptualisation, research and treatment* (pp. 219–255). Hove, England: Brunner-Routledge.

Goss, K., Gilbert, P., & Allan, S. (1994). An exploration of shame measures. I: The Other As Shamer Scale. *Personality and Individual Differences, 17*, 713–717.

Greeno, C. G., & Wing, R. R. (1994). Stress-induced eating. *Psychological Bulletin, 115*, 444–464.

Griffiths, J., & Troop, N. A. (2006). Disgust and fear ratings of eating disorder-relevant stimuli: Associations with dieting concerns and fat intake. *Anxiety, Stress, & Coping, 19*, 421–433.

Haidt, J., McCauley, C., & Rozin, P. (1994). Individual differences in sensitivity to disgust: A scale sampling seven domains of disgust elicitors. *Personality and Individual Differences, 16*, 701–713.

Harder, D. W., & Zalma, A. (1990). Two promising shame and guilt scales: A construct validity comparison. *Journal of Personality Assessment, 55*, 729–745.

Harvey, T., Troop, N. A., Treasure, J. L., & Murphy, T. (2002). Fear, disgust and abnormal eating attitudes: A preliminary study. *International Journal of Eating Disorders, 32*, 213–218.

Herman, C. P., & Polivy, J. (1975). Anxiety, restraint and eating behavior. *Journal of Abnormal Psychology, 84*, 666–672.

King, A. (1963) Primary and secondary anorexia nervosa syndromes. *British Journal of Psychiatry, 109*, 470–479.

Koukounas, E., & McCabe, M. (1997). Sexual and emotional variables influencing sexual response to erotica. *Behaviour Research and Therapy, 35*, 221–230.

Kucharska-Pietura, K., Nikolaou, V., Masiak, M., & Treasure, J. L. (2004). The recognition of emotion in the faces and voice of anorexia nervosa. *International Journal of Eating Disorders, 35*, 42–47.

Maloney, M. J., McGuire, J. B., & Daniels, S. R. (1988). Reliability testing of a children's version of the Eating Attitude Test. *Journal of the American Academy of Child and Adolescent Psychiatry, 27*, 541–543.

Matchett, G., & Davey, G. C. L. (1991). A test of a disease-avoidance model of animal phobias. *Behaviour Research and Therapy, 29*, 95–97.

Mayer, B., Bos, A. E. R., Muris, P., Huijding, J., & Vlielander, M. (2008). Does disgust enhance eating disorder symptoms? *Eating Behaviors, 9*, 124–127.

McNamara, C., Chur-Hansen, A., & Hay, P. (2008). Emotional responses to food in adults with an eating disorder: A qualitative exploration. *European Eating Disorders Review, 16*, 115–123.

McNamara, C., Hay, P., Katsikitis, M., & Chur-Hansen, A. (2008). Emotional responses to food, body satisfaction and other eating disorder features in children, adolescents and young adults. *Appetite, 50*, 102–109.

Miller, W. (1997). *The anatomy of disgust*. Cambridge, MA: Harvard University Press.

Muris, P., Merckelbach, H., Nederkoorn, S., Rassin, E., Candel, I., & Horselenberg, R. (2000). Disgust and psychopathological symptoms in a nonclinical sample. *Personality and Individual Differences, 29*, 1163–1167.

Muris, P., van der Heiden, S., & Rassin, E. (2008). Disgust sensitivity and psycho-pathological symptoms in non-clinical children. *Journal of Behavior Therapy and Experimental Psychiatry, 39*, 133–146.

Murphy, T., Troop, N. A., Bond, A., Dalgleish, T., Dalton, J., Sanchez, P., et al. (2008). *Subjective and psychophysiological responses to food, body shape and emotional stimuli in anorexia nervosa and bulimia nervosa.* Manuscript in preparation.

Murray, C., Waller, G., & Legg, C. (2000). Family dysfunction and bulimic psychopathology: The mediating role of shame. *International Journal of Eating Disorders*, *28*, 84–89.

Murray, L. K., Murphy, F., Perrett, D. I., & Treasure, J. L. (2008). *Altered facial expression sensitivity in eating disorders*. Manuscript in preparation.

Phillips, M. L., Senior, C., Fahy, T., & David, A. S. (1998). Disgust—The forgotten emotion of psychiatry. *British Journal of Psychiatry*, *172*, 373–375.

Power, M., & Dalgleish, T. (1997). *Cognition and emotion: From order to disorder*. Hove, England: Erlbaum.

Royal College of Psychiatrists. (2007). *Changing minds: Anorexia and bulimia (section 5)*. Retrieved February 6, 2007, from http://www.rcpsych.ac.uk/default.aspx?page=1428

Rozin, P., & Fallon, A. E. (1987). A perspective on disgust. *Psychological Review*, *94*, 23–41.

Rozin, P., Fallon, A. E., & Mandell, R. (1984). Family resemblance in attitudes to disgust. *Developmental Psychology*, *20*, 309–314.

Rozin, P., Haidt, J., & McCauley, C. R. (1999). Disgust: The body and soul emotion. In T. Dalgleish & M. Power (Eds.), *Handbook of cognition and emotion* (pp. 429–446). Chichester, England: Wiley.

Rozin, P., Lowery, L., Imada, S., & Haidt, J. (1999). The CAD triad hypothesis: A mapping between the other-directed moral emotions, disgust, contempt and anger and Shweder's three universal moral codes. *Journal of Personality and Social Psychology*, *76*, 574–586.

Ruderman, A. J. (1986). Dietary restraint: A theoretical and empirical review. *Psychological Bulletin*, *99*, 247–262.

Russell, G. F. M. (1970). Anorexia nervosa: Its identity as an illness and its treatment. In J. H. Price (Ed.), *Modern trends in psychological medicine* (pp. 131–164). London: Butterworth.

Sanftner, J. L., Barlow, D. H., Marschall, D. E., & Tangney, J. P. (1995). The relation of shame and guilt to eating disorder symptomatology. *Journal of Social and Clinical Psychology*, *14*, 315–324.

Schienle, A., Schäfer, A., Stark, R., Walter, B., Franz, M., & Vaitl, D. (2002). Disgust sensitivity in psychiatric disorders: A questionnaire study. *The Journal of Nervous and Mental Disease*, *191*, 831–834.

Schienle, A., Stark, R., Schäfer, A., Walter, B., Kirsch, P., & Vaitl, D. (2004). Disgust and disgust sensitivity in bulimia nervosa: An fMRI study. *European Eating Disorders Review*, *12*, 42–50.

Schmidt, U. H., Jiwany, A., & Treasure, J. L. (1993). A controlled study of alexithymia in eating disorders. *Comprehensive Psychiatry*, *34*, 54–58.

Schmidt, U. H., Tiller, J. M., Andrews, B., Blanchard, M., & Treasure, J. L. (1997). Is there a specific trauma precipitating onset of anorexia nervosa? *Psychological Medicine*, *9*, 523–530.

Schmidt, U. H., & Treasure, J. L. (1993). From medieval mortification to Charcot's rose-red ribbon and beyond: Modern explanatory models of eating disorders. *International Review of Psychiatry, 5,* 3–7.

Serpell, L., & Troop, N. A. (2003). Psychological factors. In J. L. Treasure, U. H. Schmidt, & E. van Furth (Eds.), *Handbook of eating disorders* (2nd ed., pp. 151–167). London: Wiley.

Stice, E., Akutagawa, D., Gaggar, A., & Agras, S. (2000). Negative affect moderates the relation between dieting and binge eating. *International Journal of Eating Disorders, 27,* 218–229.

Strongman, K. T. (1996). *The psychology of emotion: Theories of emotion in perspective* (4th ed.). Chichester, England: Wiley.

Stunkard, A. (1990). A description of eating disorders in 1932. *American Journal of Psychiatry, 147,* 263–268.

Tangney, J. P., Wagner, P., & Gramzow, R. (1992). Proneness to shame, proneness to guilt and psychopathology. *Journal of Abnormal Psychology, 101,* 469–478.

Troop, N. A., Allan, S., Serpell, L., & Treasure, J. L. (in press). Shame in women with a history of eating disorders. *European Eating Disorders Review.*

Troop, N. A., Murphy, F., Bramon, E., & Treasure, J. L. (2000). Disgust sensitivity in eating disorders: A preliminary investigation. *International Journal of Eating Disorders, 27,* 446–451.

Troop, N. A., Schmidt, U. H., & Treasure, J. L. (1995). Feelings and fantasy in eating disorders: Factor analysis of the Toronto Alexithymia Scale. *International Journal of Eating Disorders, 18,* 151–157.

Troop, N. A., Sotrilli, S., Serpell, L., & Treasure, J. L. (2006). Establishing a useful distinction between current and anticipated bodily shame in eating disorders. *Eating and Weight Disorders, 11,* 83–90.

Troop, N. A., Treasure, J. L., & Serpell, L. (2002). A further exploration of disgust in eating disorders. *European Eating Disorders Review, 10,* 218–226.

Uher, R., Murphy, T., Friederich, H.-C., Dalgleish, T., Brammer, M. J., Giampietro, V., et al. (2005). Functional neuroanatomy of body shape perception in healthy and eating-disordered women. *Biological Psychiatry, 58,* 990–997.

Van Strien, T., Frijters, J. E. R., Bergers, G. P. A., & Defares, P. B. (1986). Dutch Eating Behavior Questionnaire for assessment of restrained, emotional and external eating behavior. *International Journal of Eating Disorders, 5,* 295–315.

Ware, J., Jain, K., Burgess, I., & Davey, G. C. L. (1994). Disease avoidance model: Factor analysis of common animal fears. *Behaviour Research and Therapy, 32,* 57–63.

Wolff, G., & Serpell, L. (1998). A cognitive model and treatment strategies for anorexia nervosa. In H. Hoek, J. L. Treasure, & M. Katzman (Eds.), *The neurobiology of eating disorders* (pp. 407–430). Chichester, England: Wiley.

12

SEX AND THE SEXUAL DYSFUNCTIONS: THE ROLE OF DISGUST AND CONTAMINATION SENSITIVITY

PETER J. de JONG AND MADELON L. PETERS

Current psychological views of sexual behavior roughly consider sexual dysfunction to be a consequence of a negative emotional reaction to erotic stimulation, which then becomes the focus of attention (e.g., Barlow, 1986; Janssen & Everaerd, 1993). Although disgust seems an obvious candidate for being one of these negative emotional reactions that interferes with healthy sexual behavior and/or sexual pleasure, current theories and empirical research focus predominantly on emotional and cognitive processes related to fear and pain (e.g., Payne, Binik, Amsel, & Khalifé, 2005), whereas the reference to disgust is mainly anecdotal (e.g., Carnes, 1998; Kaneko, 2001). In a similar vein, current cognitive–behavioral interventions often include some form of fear reduction exercises (exposure or cognitive restructuring) and pain management techniques (e.g., van Lankveld et al., 2006), whereas interventions targeted at reducing or neutralizing disgust-related feelings, appraisals, and/or action tendencies are virtually absent in the literature (for a short overview of current psychological interventions, see Heiman, 2002).

Therefore, it appears that disgust is largely overlooked as a potentially relevant factor in the etiology of sexual dysfunction. In this chapter we defend the notion that disgust nevertheless has a great promise for improving our understanding of common sexual behavior and sexual complaints and may

253

provide potentially interesting clues for treatment as well. We first succinctly outline how disgust and contamination sensitivity may play roles in common sexual behaviors and may contribute to the generation of sexual complaints. We then briefly discuss how disgust and contamination sensitivity may be involved in the major sexual dysfunctions described in the *Diagnostic and Statistical Manual of Mental Disorders, Fourth Edition, Text Revision* (DSM–IV–TR; American Psychiatric Association [APA], 2000). A major part of this chapter then focuses on vaginismus and illustrates on the basis of research how a disgust conceptualization of vaginismus may help explain this "most perplexing problem" (Leiblum, 2000, p. 181). In the final part of this chapter we discuss the clinical implications of such a disgust conceptualization for the treatment of vaginismus and related concerns.

DISGUST AND SEX

Rozin, Haidt, and McCauley (1999) argued that disgusting stimuli can be classified into several broad categories of disgust elicitors (see also chap. 1, this volume). In this section, we discuss the categories of disgust that seem most relevant for the present context of sexual behaviors: core disgust, animal-reminder disgust, and sociomoral disgust.

Core Disgust

From an evolutionary perspective, disgust is seen as a defensive mechanism that has evolved to protect the organism from contamination by pathogens and toxins present in the environment (Curtis, Aunger, & Rabie, 2004). Accordingly, disgust is focused on the intersection between the body and the environment and concentrates on the skin and body apertures (Fessler & Haley, 2006; Rozin, Nemeroff, Horowitz, Gordon, & Voet, 1995). The various body parts differ with respect to their sensitivity to contamination. It has been found that the mouth, vagina, and penis are the body parts with the highest subjective contamination sensitivity. Given the central role of these organs in the context of sexual behavior, together with the fact that bodily products (e.g., saliva, sweat, semen) and smells are among the strongest disgust elicitors (Rozin & Fallon, 1987), it is not very difficult to envisage that feelings of disgust and disgust-related appraisals may arise during sex, which in turn may influence sexual behaviors as well.

Feelings of Disgust

The notion that feelings of disgust may be elicited by sexual stimuli or sexual behaviors is not only theoretically and intuitively plausible but is also supported by empirical evidence (e.g., Carnes, 1998; Koukounas & McCabe, 1997). Consistent with the idea that disgust may interfere with sexual pleasure, it was found that the level of experienced disgust correlated negatively with positive feelings, sexual arousal, and absorption, whereas there was a positive relationship with experienced anxiety (Koukounas & McCabe, 1997). Future studies in which state disgust is experimentally manipulated are necessary to test more rigorously the alleged causal influence of disgust in reducing sexual arousal.

Avoidant Behavior

Disgust is a defensive emotion associated with avoidance tendencies motivated to create distance from the disgusting situation or object. This may be accomplished by removal of the self from the situation but also by withdrawal of attention (closing eyes or nose, engaging in some distraction). Research in the context of spider phobia, blood-injection distress, and washing compulsions provided clear evidence that feelings of disgust (state disgust) may indeed motivate avoidant behaviors. Experimentally evoked disgust was the strongest predictor of avoidance and less compliance in a series of behavioral-approach tasks involving disgusting food, nondangerous disgusting animals, a surgery video, and simulated vomit (e.g., Olatunji, Lohr, Sawchuk, & Tolin, 2007; see also Woody, McLean, & Klassen, 2005). In a similar vein, state disgust may motivate withdrawal or avoidance of particular sexual behaviors or sex-related stimuli. In support of this, a vignette study showed that anticipated feelings of disgust were closely related to participants' willingness to carry out an action that implied physical contact with certain sexual stimuli (e.g., touching the face with a towel that has been previously used for wiping off sperm or vaginal fluids of the partner; Genten, 2005). In addition, some clinical cases have been described in the literature, in which sexual stimuli seem to elicit such profound feelings of disgust that people even attempt to avoid anything sexual in themselves and others, a condition known as *sexual anorexia* (Carnes, 1998).

Defensive Reflexes

It is conceivable that disgust and fear of contamination elicit defensive reflexes that may interfere with functional sexual behaviors. From its function to protect the organism from contamination, disgust may give rise to reflexes that are associated with the expulsion of potentially hazardous pathogens from our body. Accordingly, disgust may elicit retching during oral sex or French kissing. In addition, disgust and fear of contamination may give rise to defensive muscular contractions that are associated with the prevention of contaminants crossing the intersection of the environment and the body. There is evidence that involuntary contraction of the pelvic floor muscles is part of a general defense mechanism (van der Velde, Laan, & Everaerd, 2000) that may be elicited by (the anticipation of) fearful and/or painful occurrences (e.g., van der Velde & Everaerd, 2001). It seems reasonable to assume that similar defensive contractions of the pelvic floor muscles can be elicited or potentiated by disgust-related appraisals (e.g., Yartz & Hawk, 2002). Following this, the prospect of mere physical contact with the vagina or anus (highly contamination-sensitive body parts) and/or the anticipation of penetration by the partner's penis (a body part with very high contamination potency; Rozin et al., 1995) may well elicit involuntary pelvic floor muscle activity (cf. van der Velde & Everaerd, 2001). In its turn, increased activity of these muscles will result in enhanced friction between penis and vulvar or anal skin, eventually giving rise to genital pain during intercourse or adding to the impossibility of having intercourse (or anal sex) altogether. This type of experience may be the start of a cascade of negative sexual experiences that not only seriously detract from sexual pleasure or satisfaction but may also result in all kinds of relational conflicts (e.g., Rathus, Nevid, & Fichner-Rathus, 2005). It would be important for future research to test whether indeed feelings of intense disgust and/or fear of contamination are accompanied by increased pelvic floor muscle activity.

Cognition

Disgust may influence pertinent cognitive processes as well. In the context of anxiety and fear, it has been consistently found that people direct their attention toward stimuli in the environment that are central to their concerns (i.e., threat cues; Harvey, Watkins, Mansell, & Shafran, 2004). The initial orientation toward threatening stimuli has been argued to be adaptive in the sense that it helps the individual to readily escape from potentially dangerous situations (Mogg, Bradley, Miles, & Dixon, 2004). Meanwhile, in sexual situations, vigilance for threat is likely to be antithetical to an efficient attentional focus on erotic cues, a requirement for functional sexual performance (e.g., Barlow, 1986; Janssen & Everaerd, 1993).

It is interesting to note that some research showed that disgust-related stimuli might have involuntary attention-attracting properties (Charash & McKay, 2002). Similar to the attention bias for threat, attention bias for disgust-related stimuli is likely to interfere with becoming absorbed in current sexual activities. Hence increased vigilance for disgusting stimuli will logically undermine the generation of sexual arousal (e.g., erection or lubrication) and will interfere with functional sexual performance. Consistent with this, it has been found that individuals who experienced relatively strong feelings of disgust indicated that they had problems in becoming absorbed in the activities portrayed in an erotic film and reported lower levels of sexual arousal (Koukounas & McCabe, 1997).

Some experimental work showed that disgust not only affects attentional processes but also may influence interpretational processes. More specifically, it has been found that experienced disgust facilitated negative interpretations of potentially negative ambiguous cues, whereas it reduced the chance of interpreting potentially positive ambiguous cues as positive (Davey, Bickerstaffe, & MacDonald, 2006). Such disgust-induced negative interpretation bias may add further to the activation of negative emotional reactions and withdrawal responses in the context of sexual behaviors (e.g., Dorfan & Woody, 2006).

Animal-Reminder Disgust

It has been argued that the defensive mechanism of disgust originally evolved to prevent the body from contamination by pathogens and toxins from the outside environment is extended to stimuli and/or behaviors that remind us of our animal nature (Rozin et al., 1999). This disgust-mediated rejection of our animal nature is argued to serve a defensive function by maintaining the hierarchical division between humans and animals through distancing the self from animals and animal properties (Haidt, McCauley, & Rozin, 1994). Because sexual behavior is highly suggestive of our underlying animal nature, sexual behaviors and/or sexual advances may well elicit disgust to guard the human–animal border and may thus give rise to avoidance behaviors that interfere with functional sexual behaviors.

This type of disgust-relevant appraisal may also be problematic for experiencing orgasm because orgasm involves a sudden loss of voluntary control. Disgust-induced reluctance of "letting go" may thus block sexual arousal. The impossibility of experiencing orgasms may also give rise to all kinds of dysfunctional thoughts or appraisals (e.g., "I am not a normal person"; "I am a failure"; "My partner will think that I find him/her not attractive"), which in turn may result in various secondary problems, whereas the negative preoccupations with the failure of experiencing orgasms may further strengthen the original problem (e.g., through detracting the attentional focus from the arousing features of sex).

Sociomoral Disgust

A third category of disgust that may be relevant for a proper understanding of people's sexual behavior is sociomoral disgust (Rozin et al., 1999). This type of disgust is argued to be linked to the protection and internalization of (sub)culture-based rules, and it is elicited by behaviors that apparently violate such rules (Rozin et al., 1999). For example, parents who grew up in a strict heterosexual peer group may react with disgust when seeing their daughter having sex with another woman (or their son with another man) because their child's behavior violates the heterosexual standard of the parent's reference group. Rozin et al. (1999) further stressed the importance of disgust in learning to adhere to dominant sociomoral rules by arguing that disgust is a major force for negative socialization in children: "a very effective way to internalize culturally prescribed rejections (perhaps starting with feces) is to make them disgusting" (p. 439). Accordingly, learning strict moral rules concerning sexual behaviors, or even more explicitly learning that sex is dirty altogether, may strongly influence individuals' subsequent emotional responding toward particular sexual behaviors in later life, which may contribute to the generation of sexual complaints.

What is morally correct and what is not is a very subjective and sensitive issue that may differ widely even within one culture. It is therefore possible that a specific sexual activity will elicit highly positive feelings in one person (e.g., sexual masochism, transvestism), whereas another person may consider exactly the same activity as highly disgusting because he or she feels it is not "right," it is something you should not be doing, or it is even immoral just because it is not compliant with the person's internalized sociomoral values. In a similar vein it has been shown that women with relatively liberal moral values were more inclined to be sexually active during menses and were also more unconventional in their attitudes toward sex in general (e.g., Rempel & Baumgartner, 2003). Supporting the idea that *moral disgust* may be involved in sexual behaviors, it has been shown that women with relatively restrictive attitudes toward sexual behaviors experienced more disgust when they viewed erotic slides and/or videos and had more difficulty in becoming immersed in a situation without getting distracted (Koukounas & McCabe, 1997).

On the basis of research in the context of anxiety showing that people tend to infer danger from experienced anxiety ("If I feel anxious, there must be danger"; Arntz, Rauner, & van den Hout, 1995), one could speculate that elicited feelings of disgust may also further confirm the importance of adhering to certain sociomoral rules through a similar form of emotional reasoning of the type, "if I feel disgusted it must be an inappropriate behaviour" (cf. Rachman, 2004, p. 1252). Making these kinds of emotion-based inferences will logically act in a way to further inhibit individuals' motivation to get involved in these particular disgust-eliciting sexual behaviors or in addition motivate people to refrain from sex altogether. In support of the notion that the experience of disgust may indeed bolster already internalized sociomoral rules, there is evidence that experimentally augmenting feelings of disgust can increase the severity of moral judgments (Wheatley & Haidt, 2005).

DISGUST AND SEXUAL DYSFUNCTIONS

In this section, we discuss how disgust may be involved in the generation of sexual problems and how considering the potential role of disgust may help to improve therapeutic interventions.

Desire, Arousal, and Orgasm

Sexual dysfunctions are defined as persistent or recurrent sexual problems that interfere with normal performance and cause distress for the individual and his or her partner (e.g., McAnulty & Burnette, 2004). The categories of sexual dysfunctions as described in the *DSM–IV–TR* (APA, 2000) closely follow Kaplan's three-stage model of the sexual response cycle, which consists of desire, excitement, and orgasm. Accordingly, dysfunctions are defined on the basis of problems involving desire (hypoactive sexual desire disorder, sexual aversive disorder), excitement (female sexual arousal disorder, male erectile disorder), and orgasm (female orgasmic disorder, male orgasmic disorder, premature ejaculation). As an additional category the *DSM–IV–TR* refers to sexual pain disorders, including dyspareunia and vaginismus.

As we argued in the previous section, anticipated feelings of disgust will logically motivate sexual avoidance and withdrawal, whereas cognitive biases may further confirm the negative appreciation of sex. Accordingly, enhanced feelings of disgust may well contribute to hypoactive sexual desire disorder and sexual aversive disorder. In support of this, there is clinical evidence that disgust-related appraisals are prominent in these conditions (e.g., Carnes, 1998), which led Kaneko (2001) to argue that it would be important to more fully appreciate the potential role of disgust in the diagnostic process. However, thus far the particular role of disgust in these disorders has not been the focus of empirical research. Therefore, it remains for future research to determine what type of disgust is most prominently involved (core, animal reminder, and/or sociomoral), whether the particular disgust-related preoccupations vary across patients, and whether disgust should be considered as a cause, a consequence of the complaints, or both. Yet, on theoretical grounds it seems reasonable to argue that any factor that may enhance individuals' disgust and contamination sensitivity, and/or the particular sensitivity of the body parts that are involved in sexual behavior, and/or enhance the anticipated contamination potency of relevant body parts or body products of sexual partners may set people at risk for developing sexual disorders linked to reduced sexual desire (e.g., Rempel & Baumgartner, 2003).

A very similar line of reasoning can be followed for the other disorders that are based on the stages of the sexual response cycle, with the addition that feelings of disgust and disgust-related appraisals will logically oppose the generation of sexual arousal and may thus also contribute to problems associated with reduced sexual arousal (e.g., erection problems) as well as to male or female orgasmic disorder. It may be the interaction of disgust with other factors that eventually determines the exact phenomenology of an individual's complaints. Feelings of disgust and disgust-related appraisals may perhaps be best considered as transdiagnostic phenomena (see Harvey et al., 2004). Following from this, it may well be that a more thorough appreciation of the role of disgust in the various complaints may help to improve the current diagnostic categories (see, e.g., Basson, 2002) and provide more specific clues for more tailored interventions.

Disgust may not only help improving our understanding of the dysfunctions associated with the sexual response cycle (for both men and women), but it may also provide some fresh and promising clues that may help to explain the most perplexing and ill-understood sexual dysfunction: vaginismus. In the final section of this chapter, "The Case of Vaginismus," we therefore focus more extensively on the potential role of disgust in the generation of vaginistic complaints in a way that illustrates how considering the potential role of disgust in sexual behaviors may help to improve the conceptualization of the sexual disorders and may point to fresh starting points for therapeutical interventions.

The Case of Vaginismus

Vaginismus is defined as recurrent or persistent involuntary spasm of the musculature of the outer third of the vagina that interferes with intercourse (APA, 2000). The vaginistic complaints are characterized by persistent difficulties to allow vaginal entry of a penis, a finger, or an object, despite the woman's expressed wish to do so (Basson et al., 2003). Vaginismus may result in considerable emotional distress and often takes a chronic course (Weijmar Schultz & van der Wiel, 2005). Unfortunately, the etiology of this "perplexing condition" is largely unknown (Leiblum, 2000) and currently available treatment strategies are not very effective in reducing these complaints (e.g., van Lankveld et al., 2006).

Although the first published case reports of vaginistic complaints stem from the 19th century, still little is known about the factors that are responsible for this condition (Beck, 1993). This state of affairs led Beck to conclude that vaginismus is "an interesting illustration of scientific neglect" (p. 381). For a long time the dominant view implied that vaginismus essentially reflected a medical problem, and much effort has been invested in designing and testing various surgical solutions for the impossibility of having sexual intercourse (Abromov, Wolman, & David, 1994). More recently, injection with botuline (perhaps better known as Botox) has been used to paralyze the pelvic floor muscles to allow penetration (Ghazizadeh & Nikzad, 2004; Münchau & Bhatia, 2000).

Dominant psychological explanations imply highly aversive sexual experiences and/or sexual harassment as an important factor in the etiology of vaginismus (Rathus et al., 2005). Accordingly, the *DSM–IV–TR* (APA, 2000) refers to sexual trauma as an etiological feature of vaginismus. However, some empirical studies showed that sexual trauma is neither a necessary nor a sufficient condition for the generation of vaginistic complaints. Although a considerable proportion of women with vaginismus report a history of sexual abuse (in terms of attempts of sexual abuse and/or forced sexual touching or being touched with hands, mouth, or objects; e.g., Reissing, Binik, Khalifé, Cohen, & Amsel, 2003), a considerable number of women with these complaints indicate that they have not experienced such abuse (e.g., ter Kuile et al., 2007). The specificity of a history of sexual abuse in the etiology of vaginismus is further questioned by the finding that sexual abuse is also quite frequent in women with complaints that certainly do not involve difficulties in allowing vaginal entry, such as sexual addiction (Carnes, 1998). Hence it appears that this type of specific aversive-conditioning experience is not relatively frequent in women with vaginistic complaints (see also Weimar Schultz & van der Wiel, 2005).

More recently, it has been argued that pain-related fears may be critically involved in vaginismus (e.g., Reissing, Yitzchak, Khalifé, Cohen, & Amsel, 2004). Although the report of pain is not a requirement for the diagnosis of vaginismus, women with vaginismus indeed often have comorbid pain complaints (e.g., Reissing et al., 2004). Accordingly, it has been shown that a considerable percentage of women with lifelong vaginismus report vestibular pain on touch with a cotton swab (e.g., ter Kuile, van Lankveld, Vlieland, Willekes, & Weijenborg, 2005). Following on from this, one could argue that vaginistic reactions may reflect a defensive response that is elicited by fear of pain associated with penetration. However, although such a fear-of-pain conceptualization of vaginismus may help in explaining the maintenance of vaginistic complaints, it is not immediately evident how such a view could explain the etiology of vaginismus, especially for those women who report a lifelong course of the condition.

The validity of a fear-of-pain explanation is further questioned by a randomized waiting-list controlled treatment trial that tested the efficacy of cognitive–behavioral therapy, aiming at reducing fearful preoccupations with vaginal entry in women with lifelong vaginismus (van Lankveld et al., 2006). Although this intervention was found to be successful in reducing vaginistic complaints (van Lankveld et al., 2006), the effect size of this cognitive–behavioral intervention was modest at best, and only a very small minority (12%) of treated individuals eventually reported successful intercourse at 1-year follow up. The disappointing effect size of the treatment of vaginismus on this target outcome measure not only points to the importance of future efforts to improve the available interventions but also casts further doubt on the validity of the current fear of pain conceptualization of vaginistic complaints. Therefore, it seems that other factors are critically involved in vaginismus apart from fear of pain.

Disgust and fear of contamination are probable candidates in this respect. Accordingly, it was proposed that the involuntary contraction of the pelvic floor muscles in women with vaginismus may be elicited by the prospect of penetration by a potential contaminant (e.g., penis) rather than by the prospect of pain per se (de Jong, van Overveld, Weijmar Schultz, Peters, & Buwalda, in press). Such a disgust conceptualization of vaginismus would give rise to at least three testable hypotheses. First, it might be that these women are extremely sensitive to disgust and contamination. Such enhanced disgust sensitivity could reflect a general tendency to respond with the emotion of disgust to any given stimulus and/or a more focused tendency to respond with extreme disgust that is restricted to sexual stimuli. Second, women with vaginismus may be characterized by restricted moral values in general or with respect to sexual behaviors in particular, which may result in moral-disgust-induced defensive responses in the prospect of sexual intercourse (cf. Rozin et al., 1999). Third, women with vaginismus may be characterized by a particular individual physiological response stereotype to react with extreme contraction of the pelvic floor muscles in response to acute feelings of threat and/or disgust (for a test of a conceptually similar hypothesis in the context of chronic low back pain, see Vlaeyen et al., 1999).

Vaginismus: Enhanced Contamination Potency of Sexual Stimuli

As a first exploration of the possible role of disgust in vaginistic complaints, we examined whether sexual stimuli have indeed relatively strong contaminating potency in women with lifelong vaginistic complaints compared with patients with *dyspareunia* (defined as recurrent genital pain associated with sexual intercourse) and women without sexual complaints (de Jong et al., in press). In support of the idea that disgust may indeed be involved in vaginismus, results showed that women with vaginistic complaints displayed a relatively strong avoidance of stimuli that were potentially contaminated by sexual stimuli compared with women with dyspareunia or without sexual complaints.

It is interesting to note that the enhanced sensitivity for disgust and contamination in women with vaginistic complaints was not restricted to sexual stimuli but was evident in other domains of possible disgust elicitors as well. The difference between the vaginistic group on the one hand and the dyspareunia and control groups on the other hand was mainly carried by their differential scores on the Hygiene and Death subscales of the Disgust Scale (DS; developed by Haidt et al., 1994). The items of these scales represent disgust elicitors capable of producing contaminating agents (cf. Olatunji, Sawchuk, Lohr, & de Jong, 2004). High scores on these items seem therefore to imply some aversion toward, and avoidance of coming into contact with, objects that may transmit contaminating agents (e.g., DS Hygiene: "I never let any part of my body touch the toilet seat in a public washroom"; DS Death: "It would bother me tremendously to touch a dead body"). In other words, the high levels of disgust propensity in the vaginistic group seem to reflect a fearful preoccupation with contamination.

The preliminary finding that vaginistic women show a generally enhanced aversion toward coming into contact with stimuli that are capable of producing or transmitting contaminating agents, points to the possibility that high levels of disgust and contamination sensitivity are a premorbid characteristic that makes people liable to develop vaginistic complaints. That is, intercourse-related stimuli (e.g., penis) are more likely to acquire inflated contamination potency in women with high, than in women with low, levels of disgust and contamination sensitivity. In a similar vein, the vagina is more likely to acquire strong contamination sensitivity in women with high disgust propensity (cf. Davey, Forster, & Mayhew, 1993). Both characteristics will logically facilitate the generation of disgust-motivated avoidance tendencies, such as the contraction of the pelvic musculature in the prospect of penetration.

One way to further explore the potential role of enhanced disgust and contamination sensitivity in the development of vaginismus would be to test whether the generally enhanced disgust and contamination sensitivity (e.g., as indexed by the DS) is affected by treatment. If indeed strong contamination sensitivity sets people at risk for developing vaginismus rather than being a consequence of these complaints, one would expect an individual's general contamination sensitivity to remain largely unaffected by successful treatment (cf. de Jong, Andrea, & Muris, 1997).

Vaginismus: Enhanced Disgust-Eliciting Properties of Sexual Stimuli

As a more direct test of the role of disgust in vaginismus, we subsequently investigated whether individuals with vaginistic complaints reacted with (enhanced) feelings of disgust in response to erotic slides and video materials displaying sexual intercourse (de Jong, 2007). In support of the idea that disgust and fear of contamination is somehow involved in vaginismus, women with vaginistic complaints reported considerably higher levels of experienced disgust on a visual analog scale ranging from 0 to 100 than did women without these complaints (55 vs. 31). In addition, the women with vaginistic complaints reported higher levels of experienced threat (35 vs. 5), higher levels of annoyance (53 vs. 30), and lower levels of pleasant feelings (22 vs. 43). These between-groups differences were specific for the erotic slides or videos and were absent for generally disgusting pictures selected from the domain of core-disgust elicitors (e.g., unflushed feces, maggots, vomit).

Unexpectedly, this pattern of subjective feelings was not accompanied by participants' facial electromyographic (EMG) responding. In line with previous research, the generally disgusting pictures evoked stronger EMG responses of the m. levator labii superioris alaeque nasi (the muscle that is responsible for wrinkling the nose) than did the neutral pictures (e.g., de Jong, Peters, & Vanderhallen, 2002; Vrana, 1993; see chap. 5, this volume). However, similar responses were absent for the erotic slides. Although there was a trend in the predicted direction, indicating that specifically the vaginistic group responded with an increase of levator activity in response to the erotic slides, the effect size was small (eta² = .12) and did not reach significance. One explanation might be that the elicited disgust was not so much motivated by core-disgust related appraisals but by moral disgust. The nose wrinkle (that is indexed by levator activity) has been most closely associated with disgust situations related to oral incorporation, whereas raising the upper lip has been most associated with more elaborated disgust elicitors such as dead bodies and certain moral violations (Rozin, Lowery, & Ebert, 1994). Following on from this, it would be important to replicate this procedure, measuring both nose wrinkle and upper lip raise to see whether indeed the induced feelings of disgust reflect moral rather than core disgust.

Vaginismus and Moral Disgust

A parallel vignette study provided some tentative evidence for the idea that enhanced moral disgust may be involved in vaginismus (de Jong, Peters, Weijmar Schultz, & van Overveld, 2008). Women with relatively high scores on the vaginismus subscale of the Golombok Rust Inventory of Sexual Satisfaction (Rust & Golombok, 1986) indicated expecting relatively strong feelings of disgust when they imagined getting involved in particular uncommon sex-related behaviors that may violate the sociomoral rules of particular subgroups, such as watching a video showing your partner while he or she is masturbating (de Jong et al., 2008). In a similar vein there was a strong negative correlation between the willingness to get involved in this type of situations and participants' level of vaginistic complaints. These findings seem consistent with the hypothesis that women with vaginismus are characterized by relatively restricted sexual standards. Restricted sexual values set people at risk for experiencing disgust during sexual behaviors (i.e., as a result of some violation), which in turn may facilitate the generation of vaginistic complaints.

To see whether vaginismus would be more generally connected with strict moral values irrespective of the sexual domain, we also asked participants to complete the Schwartz Value Survey (Schwartz & Bilsky, 1987). Most important for the present context, the vaginistic women rated "conformity," which was defined as restraint of actions and impulses that may harm others or violate social expectations, as much more important than women without sexual complaints (Trautman, 2006). Hence it appears that vaginistic women are characterized by relatively strict sociomoral values irrespective of the domain of concern. To get some insight into whether relatively restrictive (sexual) standards have a causal influence on the generation of vaginistic complaints, it would be interesting to see whether challenging the rigidity of individuals' sexual moral and/or learning a more flexible attitude toward the full range of socially acceptable sexual behaviors has a favorable influence on the intensity of vaginistic complaints. If so, this would not only be of theoretical interest but it may also provide a relatively unexplored starting point for the treatment of vaginismus.

Some Speculations in Regard to Clinical Implications

Although there is some tentative empirical evidence that disgust and contamination sensitivity may contribute to the various sexual dysfunctions, much research remains to be done to get a clearer picture of the actual role of disgust in this domain of psychopathology and of how, for example, disgust interacts with other relevant emotions such as shame, fear, and pain in generating particular complaints. Meanwhile, a disgust conceptualization of sexual dysfunctions provides some fresh clues that may help to improve the available interventions. For example, it suggests that it might be worthwhile in cognitive–behavioral therapy to add a focus on contamination-related preoccupations and to include exposure exercises aimed at reducing the contamination potency of sexual products and/or the sensitivity to contamination of the individual's body parts (cf. de Jong, Vorage, & van den Hout, 2000). In addition, it suggests that it might be helpful to include exposure exercises to more generally reduce individuals' disgust propensity irrespective of the particular domain of sex-related stimuli.

In their review, Rozin and Fallon (1987) reported three different mechanisms that may act to unmake disgust responses, and all of these mechanisms may be integrated in regular treatment. The first mechanism concerns the initiation of accepting expressions by others toward the relevant object or action. Following this, the framing of homework assignments as well as the therapist's expressed attitudes toward the ingredients of the assignments both during the instruction and the evaluation stage may well contribute to a positive change in the evaluation of particular behaviors as well as of particular stimuli. It is important to note, however, that Rozin and Fallon expressed doubt concerning the efficacy of this type of process for well-established disgust elicitors (as might be the case in sexual dysfunctions).

As the second mechanism, Rozin and Fallon (1987) mentioned *conceptual reorientation*. This notion refers to the phenomenon that the disgust response can disappear when, for example, a person discovers that what he or she thought was rotting milk is actually yogurt. Such a cognitive switch may also be of relevance in the context of sexual complaints. For example, a meaningful proportion of people with sexual complaints might never have had a close and detailed look at their own sex organs or at their sex partner's. Homework assignments to get a more elaborated and accurate view of the sex organs and their responding to the various stages of the sexual response cycle may, for example, contribute to a reorientation of a penis from being an atrocious, uncontrollable, attacking, dirty monster toward the conception of the penis as a cute, caring body part that can share love and sexual pleasure with a loved sex partner. To the extent that moral disgust is involved it might be helpful to use cognitive–behavioral therapy-like techniques to facilitate change of a dysfunctional conception of sex as being dirty, sinful, and immoral acts into a more functional (and arousing) conception of sex.

Finally, Rozin and Fallon (1987) argued that the strength of the disgust response can weaken through extinction or habituation, for example, when someone is consistently forced into close contact with the disgusting item (e.g., when cleaning toilets is part of your job, the aversion to dirty toilets gradually declines). In a similar vein, there is preliminary evidence to suggest that exposure may be helpful in the modification of food aversions (de Silva, 1988). Yet, as for disgusting items in general, individuals experiencing disgust-relevant sexual dysfunctions will ordinarily avoid opportunities that would provide for the extinction or habituation of the disgust response. They are likely to use all kinds of strategies, such as distracting attention, withdrawing particular behaviors, or avoiding sustained contact with particular sexual products, and so forth. Therefore, it might be useful to arrange homework assignments that help the clients to force themselves to tolerate close and sustained direct physical contact with disgusting stimuli. It may be most efficient to arrange these assignments in a gradual manner (disgust hierarchy) from stimuli or situations that are only mildly disgusting or aversive to stimuli or situations that are maximally disgusting. Given the lack of effective, theory derived psychological interventions for sexual dysfunctions (Heiman, 2002), future efforts to further develop and test interventions targeted at reducing disgust-related feelings and appraisals may lead to welcome contributions to the available intervention techniques.

REFERENCES

Abromov, L., Wolman, I., & David, M. P. (1994). Vaginismus: An important factor in the evaluation and management of vulvar vestibulitis syndrome. *Gynecologic and Obstetric Investigation, 38,* 194–197.

American Psychiatric Association. (2000). *Diagnostic and statistical manual of mental disorders* (4th ed., text rev.). Washington, DC: Author.

Arntz, A., Rauner, M., & van den Hout, M. A. (1995). "If I feel anxious, there must be danger": Ex-consequential reasoning in inferring danger in anxiety disorders. *Behaviour Research and Therapy, 33,* 917–925.

Barlow, D. H. (1986). Causes of sexual dysfunction: The role of anxiety and cognitive interference. *Journal of Consulting and Clinical Psychology, 54,* 140–148.

Basson, R. (2002). Are our definitions of women's desire, arousal and sexual pain disorders too broad and our definition of orgasmic disorder too narrow? *Journal of Sex & Marital Therapy, 28,* 289–300.

Basson, R., Leiblum, S., Brotto, L., Derogatis, L., Foucroy, J., Fugl-Meyer, K., et al. (2003). Definitions of women's sexual dysfunction reconsidered: Advocating expansion and revision. *Journal of Psychosomatic Obstetrics and Gynecology, 34,* 221–229.

Beck, J. G. (1993). Vaginismus. In W. O'Donohue & J. G. Geer (Eds.), *Handbook of sexual dysfunctions: Assessment and treatment* (pp. 381–397). Needham Heights, MA: Allyn & Bacon.

Carnes, P. J. (1998). The case for sexual anorexia: An interim report on 144 patients with sexual disorders. *Sexual Addiction & Compulsivity, 5,* 293–309.

Charash, M., & McKay, D. (2002). Attention bias for disgust. *Journal of Anxiety Disorders, 16,* 529–541.

Curtis, V., Aunger, R., & Rabie, T. (2004). Evidence that disgust evolved to protect from risk of disease. *Proceedings of the Royal Society B: Biological Sciences, 271* (Suppl. 4), S131–S133.

Davey, G. C. L., Bickerstaffe, S., & MacDonald, B. A. (2006). Experienced disgust causes a negative interpretation bias: A causal role for disgust in anxious psycho-pathology. *Behaviour Research and Therapy, 44,* 1375–1384.

Davey, G. C. L., Forster, L., & Mayhew, G. (1993). Familial resemblances in disgust sensitivity and animal phobias. *Behaviour Research and Therapy, 31,* 41–50.

de Jong, P. J. (2007, July). *Vaginismus: Automatic vs. deliberate associations with threat and disgust.* Paper presented at the World Congress of Behavioral and Cognitive Therapies, Barcelona, Spain.

de Jong, P. J., Andrea, H., & Muris, P. (1997). Spider phobia in children: Disgust and fear before and after treatment. *Behaviour Research and Therapy, 35,* 559–562

de Jong, P. J., Peters, M., & Vanderhallen, I. (2002). Disgust and disgust sensitivity in spider phobia: Facial EMG in response to spider and oral disgust imagery. *Journal of Anxiety Disorders, 16,* 477–493.

de Jong, P. J., Peters, M. L., Weijmar Schultz, W., & van Overveld, M. (2008). *Enhanced socio-moral disgust sensitivity and vaginismus.* Manuscript in preparation.

de Jong, P. J., van Overveld, M., Weijmar Schultz, W., Peters, M. L., & Buwalda, F. (in press). Disgust and contamination sensitivity in vaginismus and dyspareunia. *Archives of Sexual Behavior.*

de Jong, P. J., Vorage, I., & van den Hout, M. A. (2000). Counterconditioning in the treatment of spider phobia: Effects on disgust, fear, and valence. *Behaviour Research and Therapy, 38,* 1055–1069.

de Silva, P. (1988). The modification of human food aversions: A preliminary study. *Journal of Behavior Therapy and Experimental Psychiatry, 19,* 217–220.

Dorfan, N. M., & Woody, S. R. (2006). Does threatening imagery sensitize distress during contaminant exposure? *Behaviour Research and Therapy, 44,* 395–413.

Fessler, D. M. T., & Haley, K. J. (2006). Guarding the perimeter: The outside-inside dichotomy in disgust and bodily experience. *Cognition & Emotion, 20,* 3–19.

Genten, M. H. (2005). *Psychometric quality of the Sexual Disgust Questionnaire (SDQ)*. Unpublished doctoral dissertation, University of Maastricht, Maastricht, the Netherlands.

Ghazizadeh, S., & Nikzad, M. (2004). Botulinum toxin in the treatment of refractory vaginismus. *Obstetrics and Gynecology, 104*, 922–925.

Haidt, J., McCauley, C., & Rozin, P. (1994). Individual differences in sensitivity to disgust: A scale sampling seven domains of disgust elicitors. *Personality and Individual Differences, 16*, 701–713.

Harvey, A., Watkins, E., Mansell, W., & Shafran, R. (2004). *Cognitive behavioral processes across psychological disorders: A transdiagnostic approach to research and treatment*. Oxford, England: Oxford University Press.

Heiman, J. R. (2002). Psychological treatments for female sexual dysfunction: Are they effective and do we need them? *Archives of Sexual Behavior, 31*, 445–450.

Janssen, E., & Everaerd, W. (1993). Determinants of male sexual arousal. *Annual Review of Sex Research, 4*, 211–245.

Kaneko, K. (2001). Penetration disorder: Dyspareunia exists on the extension of vaginismus. *Journal of Sex & Marital Therapy, 27*, 153–155.

Koukounas, E., & McCabe, M. (1997). Sexual and emotional variables influencing sexual response to erotica. *Behaviour Research and Therapy, 35*, 221–231.

Leiblum, S. R. (2000). Vaginismus: A most perplexing problem. In S. R. Leiblum & R. C. Rosen (Eds.), *Principles and practice of sex therapy* (3rd ed., pp. 181–202). New York: Guilford Press.

McAnulty, R. D., & Burnette, M. M. (2004). *Exploring human sexuality, making healthy decisions*. Boston: Pearson.

Mogg, K., Bradley, B. P., Miles, F., & Dixon, R. (2004). Time course of attentional bias for threat scenes: Testing the vigilance-avoidance hypothesis. *Cognition & Emotion, 18*, 689–700.

Münchau, A., & Bhatia, K. P. (2000). Uses of botulinum toxin injection in medicine today. *British Medical Journal, 320*, 161–165.

Olatunji, B. O., Lohr, J. M., Sawchuk, C. N., & Tolin, D. F. (2007). Multimodal assessment of disgust in contamination-related obsessive-compulsive disorder. *Behaviour Research and Therapy, 45*, 263–276.

Olatunji, B. O., Sawchuk, C. N., Lohr, J. M., & de Jong, P. J. (2004). Disgust domains in the prediction of contamination fear. *Behaviour Research and Therapy, 42*, 93–104.

Payne, K. A., Binik, Y. M., Amsel, R., & Khalifé, S. (2005). When sex hurts, anxiety and fear orient attention towards pain. *European Journal of Pain, 9*, 427–436.

Rachman, S. (2004). Fear of contamination. *Behaviour Research and Therapy, 42*, 1227–1255.

Rathus, S. A., Nevid, J. S., & Fichner-Rathus, L. (2005). *Human sexuality in a world of diversity*. Boston: Pearson Education.

Reissing, E. D., Binik, Y. M., Khalifé, S. M. D, Cohen, D. M. D, & Amsel, R. M. A. (2003). Etiological correlates of vaginismus: Sexual and physical abuse, sexual knowledge, sexual self-schemata, and relationship adjustment. *Journal of Sex & Marital Therapy, 29*, 47–59.

Reissing, E. D., Yitzchak, B. M., Khalifé, S. M. D., Cohen, D. M. D., & Amsel, R. M. A. (2004). Vaginal spasm, pain and behavior: An empirical investigation of the diagnosis of vaginismus. *Archives of Sexual Behavior, 33*, 5–17.

Rempel, J. K., & Baumgartner, M. S. W. (2003). The relationship between attitudes towards menstruation and sexual attitudes, desires, and behavior in women. *Archives of Sexual Behavior, 32*, 155–163.

Rozin, P., & Fallon, A. E. (1987). A perspective on disgust. *Psychological Review, 94*, 23–41.

Rozin, P., Haidt, J., & McCauley, C. R. (1999). Disgust: The body and soul emotion. In T. Dalgleish & M. Power (Eds.), *Handbook of cognition and emotion* (pp. 429–446). Chichester, England: Wiley.

Rozin, P., Lowery, L., & Ebert, R. (1994). Varieties of disgust faces and the structure of disgust. *Journal of Personality and Social Psychology, 66*, 870–881.

Rozin, P., Nemeroff, C., Horowitz, M., Gordon, B., & Voet, W. (1995). The borders of the self: Contamination sensitivity and potency of the body apertures and other body parts. *Journal of Research in Personality, 29*, 318–340.

Rust, J., & Golombok, S. (1986). *The Golombok Rust Inventory of Sexual Satisfaction* [Manual]. Windsor, England: NFER.

Schwartz, S. H., & Bilsky, W. (1987). Toward a universal psychological structure of human values. *Journal of Personality and Social Psychology, 53*, 550–562.

ter Kuile, M. M., van Lankveld, J. J. D. M., de Groot, E., Melles, R., Nefs, J., & Zandbergen, M. (2007). Cognitive-behavioral therapy for women with lifelong vaginismus: Process and prognostic factors. *Behaviour Research and Therapy, 45*, 359–373.

ter Kuile, M. M., van Lankveld, J. J. D. M., Vlieland, C. V., Willekes, C., & Weijenborg, P. T. M. (2005). Vulvar vestibulitis syndrome: An important factor in the evaluation of lifelong vaginismus? *Journal of Psychosomatic Obstetrics & Gynecology, 26*, 245–249.

Trautman, J. (2006). *Vaginismus and dyspareunia: The role of disgust and disgust sensitivity*. Unpublished bachelor's thesis, University of Groningen, Groningen, the Netherlands.

van der Velde, J., & Everaerd, W. (2001). The relationship between involuntary pelvic floor muscle activity, muscle awareness and experienced threat in women with and without vaginismus. *Behaviour Research and Therapy, 39*, 395–408.

van der Velde, J., Laan, E., & Everaerd, W. (2001). Vaginismus, a component of a general defensive reaction. An investigation of pelvic floor muscle activity during exposure to emotion-inducing film excerpts in women with and without vaginismus. *International Urogynecology Journal and Pelvic Floor Dysfunction, 12,* 328–331.

van Lankveld, J. J. D. M., ter Kuile, M. M., de Groot, H. E., Melles, R., Nefs, J., & Zandbergen, M. (2006). Cognitive–behavioral therapy for women with lifelong vaginismus: A randomized waiting-list controlled trial of efficacy. *Journal of Consulting and Clinical Psychology, 74,* 168–178.

Vlaeyen, J. W., Seelen, H. A., Peters, M., de Jong, P. J., Aretz, E., Beisiegel, E., et al. (1999). Fear of movement/(re)injury and muscular reactivity in chronic low back pain patients: An experimental investigation. *Pain, 82,* 297–304

Vrana, S. R. (1993). The psychophysiology of disgust: Differentiating negative emotional contexts with facial EMG. *Psychophysiology, 30,* 279–286.

Weijmar Schultz, W. C., & van de Wiel, H. B. (2005). Vaginismus. In R. Balon & R. T. Segraves (Eds.), *Handbook of sexual dysfunction* (pp. 273–292). New York: Marcel Dekker.

Wheatley, T., & Haidt, J. (2005). Hypnotic disgust makes moral judgments more severe. *Psychological Science, 16,* 780–784.

Woody, S. R., McLean, C., & Klassen, T. (2005). Disgust as a motivator of avoidance of spiders. *Journal of Anxiety Disorders, 19,* 461–475.

Yartz, A. R., & Hawk, L. W., Jr. (2002). Addressing the specificity of affective startle modulation: Fear versus disgust. *Biological Psychology, 59,* 55–68.

13

THE TREATMENT OF DISGUST

SUZANNE A. MEUNIER AND DAVID F. TOLIN

Research on the topic of disgust and its contribution to psychopathology has increased in recent years. Despite this increased interest, there has been little discussion about the relationship between disgust and psychosocial treatment. Research has revealed that several disorders involve significant disgust-based components. Treatment models of these disorders can be improved by incorporating the influence of disgust into the functional analysis of these problems.

PSYCHOLOGICAL TREATMENT OF EMOTIONAL DISORDERS

Numerous variations of cognitive–behavioral therapy (CBT) have been developed that have proved helpful for such diverse conditions as major depressive disorder (Hollon et al., 1992), panic disorder (Barlow, Gorman, Shear, & Woods, 2000), specific phobia (Öst, Fellenius, & Sterner, 1991), social phobia (Heimberg et al., 1998), and obsessive–compulsive disorder (OCD; Foa et al., 2005). Common to most CBT models is the tripartite conceptualization of emotion advanced by Lang (1979). According to this model, emotions can be divided into (a) psychophysiological activity, (b) subjective/

cognitive experience, and (c) behavioral action tendencies. In a case of specific phobia of snakes, for example, the individual's emotion of fear can be conceptualized as including (a) sympathetic activation such as increased heart rate, (b) a subjective sense of fear and a belief that snakes are harmful, and (c) a tendency to avoid snake-related stimuli. An individual with anger-control problems, however, might be conceptualized as experiencing (a) sympathetic activation, (b) a subjective sense of anger and thoughts that someone has violated a "rule" or norm, and (c) a tendency to engage in aggressive action.

In light of emerging evidence of overlap among the emotional disorders (Brown, Chorpita, & Barlow, 1998), there is increasing interest in identifying common mechanisms across cognitive–behavioral interventions that apply to multiple emotional difficulties. Barlow, Allen, and Choate (2004) suggested that three fundamental aspects of CBT for emotional disorders are (a) altering the maladaptive cognitions that precede emotional arousal, (b) preventing emotional avoidance, and (c) facilitating mood-incongruent action tendencies. Therefore, for example, treatment of contamination-related OCD would include (a) altering, through rational discussion or behavioral experiments, the patient's beliefs that everyday objects are contaminated and will cause illness; (b) encouraging abstinence from compulsive behaviors such as hand-washing; and (c) encouraging exposure to commonly avoided situations, such as using public restrooms. Treatment of major depressive disorder might include (a) challenging the person's hopelessness-related beliefs, such as, "Why bother? I'm just going to fail"; (b) reducing the interpersonal withdrawal and rumination that serve to attenuate the experience of acute discomfort; and (c) encouraging greater frequency of potentially rewarding activities.

We suggest that these core principles may be useful in the treatment of pathological disgust. We begin by discussing the relationships between disgust and other emotions, followed by the potential role of disgust in several common emotional disorders. We conclude our chapter by describing efforts to alter disgust-related psychopathology and suggesting future directions for treatment development.

STATE VERSUS TRAIT DISGUST

In describing the clinical aspects of disgust, it is potentially useful to distinguish between *trait* and *state* disgust. Trait disgust, typically referred to as *disgust sensitivity* (DS), is considered a general predisposition to experiencing disgust. DS has been typically assessed through self-report ratings of how much an individual expects that he or she would experience disgust or repugnance to a variety of stimuli. State disgust, is the elicited emotion experienced in reaction to an external stimulus of some kind. Presumably, individuals with high levels of trait disgust (DS) would be more likely to experience state disgust, rather than some other emotion, when confronted with certain situations.

Trait and state disgust can affect the development of an emotional disorder. Trait disgust may contribute to the development of an emotional disorder through its pervasiveness by affecting the likelihood that an individual will develop negative cognitions about their disgust reactions (e.g., the feeling is out of their control or may overwhelm them) and experiential avoidance. In a similar way, state disgust may contribute to the development of an emotional disorder when it is experienced intensely. Therefore, treatment of disgust might focus on altering cognitions and reducing behavioral avoidance regardless of an individual's level of trait or state disgust.

Because the disorders of disgust are discussed in the chapters included in Part III of this volume, please consult the following chapters for related topics. Disgust and animal phobia are discussed in chapter 8. Chapter 9 includes the study on disgust and its relation with blood-injury-injection (BII) phobia, and chapter 10 includes the discussion on contamination fear and how is it associated with OCD. In chapter 11, the authors discuss how disgust relates to eating disorders.

IMPLICATIONS OF DISGUST
FOR COGNITIVE–BEHAVIORAL THERAPY

In this section, we discuss the relevance of disgust to CBT for emotional disorders. First, we consider whether disgust and disgust sensitivity predict treatment outcome. If disgust were associated with poorer outcome of CBT, this would suggest a need to modify procedures according to the emotional status of the patient. Second, we consider whether disgust can be alleviated by using CBT procedures. Although CBT is well established as a treatment for exaggerated emotional states such as fear (in anxiety disorders) and sadness (in depressive disorders), it is not clear whether disgust responds similarly to treatment. Finally, we discuss whether CBT procedures can be modified in a manner that more effectively addresses the disgust elements of psychiatric disorders.

Does Disgust Predict Treatment Outcome?

Several studies have investigated the role of disgust reactions in response to exposure treatment for spider phobia. One study investigated the effect of DS on the decline in spider fear after a 2-hour exposure session during which participants watched the therapist model interactions with spiders and then engaged in a hierarchy of exposures to the spider (Merckelbach, de Jong, Arntz, & Schouten, 1993). The results revealed that individuals high in DS (on the basis of median split) demonstrated less of a decline in the spider phobia symptoms than did those low in DS (Merckelbach et al., 1993). A study of the relationship between DS and reduction of BII-phobia symptoms revealed that global DS was not predictive of fear reduction, whereas a marginally significant relationship between BII-specific DS and reductions in fear was found (Olatunji, Smits, Connolly, Willems, & Lohr, 2007).

To date, we are unaware of any studies that examine the predictive value of disgust in disorders other than specific phobia. However, the role of disgust might be inferred from subtypes of OCD. As described earlier, patients with contamination-related OCD appear more likely than do patients with other forms of OCD (e.g., checking) to rate avoided stimuli as disgusting, and at least some evidence suggests that these patients may present with greater DS. Most studies have found that patients with contamination-related OCD fared about as well as did patients with other symptom subtypes (Abramowitz, Franklin, Schwartz, & Furr, 2003; Mataix-Cols, Marks, Greist, Kobak, & Baer, 2002). Mataix-Cols et al. (2002) reported a 64% responder rate (defined as a 40% or greater reduction in scores on the Yale–Brown Obsessive–Compulsive Scale) among patients with contamination-related OCD; these figures did not differ significantly from those of other subtypes. Abramowitz et al. (2003) reported a 70% rate of clinically significant change (Jacobson & Truax, 1991), which again did not differ from other subtypes. However, in a study of group CBT and exposure and response prevention (ERP), McLean et al. (2001) found that only 9% of patients classified as "washers," compared with 20% of primarily "obsessional" patients, 33% of "checkers," and 58% of patients with "miscellaneous" OCD symptoms, were classified as having recovered. Further examination of the response rates among washers revealed that 0% of those who received CBT (focused on altering faulty appraisals) and 20% of those who received ERP (focused on habituation) were considered recovered (McLean et al., 2001). Attempts to alter faulty cognitions in the absence of habituation may be insufficient for change, as evidenced by the lack of treatment response among those who received group CBT. Some studies have found that disgust reactions may habituate more slowly than fear reactions (Olatunji, Smits, et al., 2007; Smits, Telch, & Randall, 2002). Therefore, the low response rate among those who received ERP may be the result of insufficient time for significant habituation of their disgust reactions. Group formats may not allow for the flexibility of continuing an exposure long enough to ensure sufficient habituation of disgust reactions.

Does Disgust Decrease During Treatment?

Within the anxiety disorders, generalized DS appears to be affected little by treatment. In two studies of spider-phobic patients (de Jong, Andrea, & Muris, 1997; Smits et al., 2002) and one study of analogue BII phobics (Olatunji,

Smits, et al., 2007), overall DS did not decrease following successful exposure-based therapy to phobia-related stimuli. However, in all three studies, measures of phobia-specific DS did decrease following treatment. The declines in spider-specific fear and DS were correlated in one study (de Jong et al., 1997). The decline in BII-specific fear was independent of the decline in BII-specific disgust; however, disgust declines were partially dependent on the decline of fear (Olatunji, Smits, et al., 2007). These findings suggest that fear and disgust reactions may become interconnected. The elicited emotion of disgust, unlike general DS, is alleviated with exposure-based treatment. Two studies have examined the rates of decline of fear and disgust reactions during exposure. Both emotions declined over the course of treatment; however, disgust reactions were noted to decrease more slowly than fear reactions (Olatunji, Smits, et al., 2007; Smits et al., 2002). The decline in fear and disgust ratings was correlated; however, neither emotion entirely accounted for reductions in the other.

Habituation of disgust reactions to contamination-related stimuli was examined among a group of individuals with contamination-related OCD and a group with different types of primary OCD symptoms (McKay, 2006). Participants were exposed to OCD-related stimuli and disgust stimuli that were not related to their OCD symptoms. Both groups exhibited a reduction in their disgust reactions; however, those with contamination-related OCD exhibited a smaller reduction in disgust that habituated more slowly.

A slower rate of decline for disgust reactions may negatively affect treatment. If treatment sessions do not allow for sufficient time and repetitions of exposure, then patients may not attain sufficient habituation of their disgust reactions to benefit from treatment. One study compared the decline of disgust reactions in analogue spider-phobic individuals who received exposure to spiders in one context or multiple contexts (Vansteenwegen et al., 2007). Results revealed a significant decline in disgust ratings only for those who received many trials of exposure to spiders in one context. Those who received exposure to spiders in multiple contexts experienced the same number of exposure trials but experienced fewer trials for each context. Furthermore, when tested in a new context, individuals who received exposure in only one context exhibited a return of fear. These findings indicate that disgust reactions may require additional time or repetitions for habituation to occur and also suggest that exposure in multiple contexts cannot be sacrificed to allow for the additional time.

Although disgust reactions appear to respond to exposure treatment, its rate of decline may be slower than that of fear and may be influenced by individual difference variables. These findings may be because of a difference in the acquisition process. It has been proposed that disgust reactions are acquired through sympathetic magic beliefs or evaluative conditioning, which may be influenced by individual difference variables such as DS. Responses that have been acquired through evaluative-conditioning processes have been found to be highly resistant to extinction (Baeyens, Crombez, van den Bergh, & Eelen, 1988). For example, food aversions that are mediated by negatively valenced information (e.g., disgust-related mental images) are found to be stronger and longer lasting than traditional food aversions (Batsell & Brown, 1998). If disgust reactions develop through evaluative shifts, then treatments may be improved by specifically addressing the valence of the disgust-eliciting stimulus.

CAN TREATMENT BE MODIFIED TO ADDRESS DISGUST?

As previously discussed, treatment for emotional disorders should address the maladaptive cognitions, emotional avoidance, and action tendencies associated with that particular emotion (Barlow et al., 2004). Treatment of disgust, therefore, should include direct attention to altering the perceived valence of the disgust-elicitors and the likelihood that contact with a stimulus will result in illness. Treatment should also address tolerance of parasympathetic nervous system reactions and the avoidance and withdrawal behavior associated with disgust reactions.

Maladaptive Cognitions

Treatments have been developed to address the negative appraisals of disgust-eliciting stimuli in specific anxiety disorders. A treatment that included in vivo exposure and counterconditioning was developed to address the negative valence of spiders (de Jong, Vorage, & van den Hout, 2000). The counterconditioning component involved reference to the disgusting properties of spiders and an explanation that a spider's disgust-eliciting status can be reduced through prolonged and close contact of spiders with tasty food items and by listening to one's favorite music after in vivo exposure is completed (de Jong et al., 2000). Both exposure and the combined exposure and counterconditioning treatments resulted in significant reductions in avoidance behavior, fear reactions, and disgust reactions, as well as a more favorable perception of spiders (de Jong et al., 2000).

One novel and intense variant of cognitive therapy for patients with contamination-related OCD (danger ideation reduction therapy [DIRT]) involves traditional cognitive restructuring with experiences designed to alter negative appraisals of threat by providing evidence that refutes the likelihood of becoming ill from contact with possible contaminants and discussion aimed at generating realistic probability estimates (Jones & Menzies, 1997). The DIRT intervention appeared effective in reducing symptoms of contamination-related OCD in a small controlled trial (Jones & Menzies, 1998) as well as in an open pilot study of 5 adult patients who had previously failed to respond to pharmacotherapy and exposure and response prevention (Krochmalik, Jones, & Menzies, 2001).

Although treatments have been developed to address negative appraisals specifically, they may not be necessary for a shift in valence to occur. Treatment of food aversions, including graded in vivo exposure, verbal reinforcement, and modeling of target behavior, has resulted in the majority of participants (71%) completing their exposure hierarchy and experiencing a shift in the valence of target foods from dislike to neutral (de Silva, 1989). Traditional exposure-based interventions may be sufficient to produce alterations in valence for the majority of individuals. However, as with the DIRT intervention, it may be useful to test whether these modified treatments may benefit those who fail traditional approaches.

Treatment might also include behavioral experiments to address the perceived likelihood of contagion- or illness-related consequences as well as the individual's beliefs about his or her ability to cope with consequences. Potential consequences may be general to negative emotions (e.g., feeling overwhelmed, losing control), or specific to disgust (e.g., fear that one may faint or vomit in the presence of a disgust-eliciting stimulus, belief that certain foods will be likely to cause weight gain).

Emotional Avoidance and Mood-Incongruent Action Tendencies

The majority of individuals do not faint or vomit as a result of parasympathetic activation following exposure to a disgust-eliciting stimulus. However, as previously discussed, some individuals with BII phobia experience fainting when confronted with phobia-relevant stimuli; fainting in turn inhibits the individual's ability to confront disgust-eliciting stimuli. Page (1994) suggested that treatment should be matched to the presence of fearful avoidance and fainting symptoms. Specifically, individuals who reported fainting symptoms would receive treatments designed to focus on parasympathetic activation, whereas those who reported fearful avoidance symptoms would receive treatments designed to focus on sympathetic activation. Applied tension was developed specifically to address the diphasic response pattern consisting of a rapid drop in blood pressure and cerebral blood flow. This treatment involves learning to tense gross body muscles and identify the first signs of a drop in blood pressure to use as a cue for applying the technique (Öst & Sterner, 1987). Studies have demonstrated that applied tension is an effective treatment for blood phobia with benefits superior to in vivo exposure alone (Hellström, Fellenius, & Öst, 1996; Öst, Fellenius, & Sterner, 1991; Öst, Sterner, & Fellenius, 1989). Applied tension may be necessary for those who experience fainting so that they are able to engage in mood-incongruent behaviors such as exposure.

The primary action tendency associated with disgust is avoidance. Treatment for disgust-based problems must include a focus on reducing avoidance behaviors. For individuals with anxiety disorders, exposures will be similar to those that are conducted for anxiety-related avoidance but with a focus on the disgust-producing properties of the situation. For example, an individual who is phobic of snakes may report disgust by the snake's movement or by the idea of touching the snake's skin. Exposure that is limited to viewing pictures of snakes would be unlikely to address these concerns. Exposure that allows for direct contact with a snake and the ability to watch its movement would be preferable.

Individuals with eating disorders may report feeling disgusted when they break a dietary rule or binge. These individuals would be encouraged to eat foods that may cause feelings of nausea or bloating and refrain from compensatory behaviors. In addition, they would be encouraged to look at body parts that they may view as disgusting because of their shape or size in a mirror.

DIRECTIONS FOR FUTURE RESEARCH

Because very little research has been conducted on the treatment of disgust reactions, many important questions remain unanswered. First, the roles of DS and disgust reactions are unclear. Second, although self-reports of disgust have been found consistently in several disorders, there has been little study of whether individuals with those disorders also experience physiological activity that corresponds with their verbal reports. Third, findings suggest that disgust may habituate more slowly than do other emotional reactions; however, there has not been any study of whether slower habituation is related to increased rates of relapse, and so forth. Fourth, we do not yet know whether it will be important to modify current treatments for anxiety disorders to incorporate strategies that focus more directly on disgust reactions. Fifth, the relationship between disgust variables and eating behaviors is not understood. Sixth and last, the constructs of interpersonal and sociomoral disgust are not well understood and may also have implications for treatment.

Disgust Sensitivity Versus Disgust Reactivity

Generalized DS has been found to correlate with some psychological symptoms. Studies have also demonstrated that an individual's report that he or she is likely to experience disgust when confronted with a particular stimulus (DS) is discordant with the actual experience of disgust when exposed to the stimulus (state disgust). Through exposure, it appears that state disgust and stimulus-relevant DS are decreased, whereas generalized DS is unaffected. The evidence from one study suggests that generalized DS may negatively predict treatment outcome. However, additional studies are needed to investigate the extent to which predictions of disgust reactions and actual disgust reactions affect the likelihood that an individual will benefit from treatment.

Does Self-Reported Disgust Correspond With Physiological Measures?

Investigations of disgust variables have largely relied on self-report measures of disgust reactions. Although some studies have found that the relationships between disgust variables and psychological symptoms remain when controlling for other traits (e.g., negative affectivity, neuroticism), it is unclear whether these self-reports translate into physiological differences. There is some evidence to suggest that disgust may influence the physiological reactions such as fainting symptoms experienced in some individuals with BII phobia. It is not yet known whether individuals experience significant parasympathetic nervous system reactions in other disorders linked to disgust. Anecdotally, we have observed some individuals with contamination fears gagging or even vomiting when confronting contaminants during exposures. Clarification of the degree to which the parasympathetic nervous system becomes activated in these individuals may provide insight into the importance of designing exposures to elicit that activation. Examination of the relationship between subjective, behavioral, and physiological measures of disgust may also clarify the degree to which each should be attended to during treatment.

Does It Matter That Disgust Habituates More Slowly Than Fear?

Although studies suggest that disgust reactions may be slower to habituate, it is unclear whether the same level of habituation can be achieved with additional sessions. It is possible that disgust habituates more slowly to traditional exposure-based approaches because they are designed to elicit anxiety and sympathetic nervous system reactions. Future studies may investigate whether habituation occurs more rapidly when the focus of exposure is to elicit disgust and parasympathetic nervous system reactions. The length of time required to achieve sufficient habituation of disgust and the potential risk of relapse associated with a slower habituation process also need to be examined. Treatment provided in group settings may limit a therapist's ability to provide longer exposure sessions. Studies that compare individual versus group treatments may clarify whether disgust reactions can be significantly reduced by using each treatment approach.

Are Modifications to Current Treatments Necessary?

Treatments that were designed to address the unique physiological responses observed in BII-phobic individuals appear to have added benefit over in vivo exposure alone. If strong parasympathetic activation is found in other disorders, then a focus on inducing that activation may provide additional benefit. Findings demonstrating that many individuals appear to achieve symptom reduction without treatments that directly target disgust-related appraisals indicate that these interventions may not be necessary. However, there may be a group of individuals who do not respond to first-line treatments but who receive benefit from such approaches (e.g., DIRT). Studies that compare the efficacy of these modified approaches with traditional exposure treatments are needed.

Disgust and Disordered Eating Behaviors

Evidence demonstrates a relationship between DS and self-reported eating disorder symptoms. We are unaware of any studies that have investigated the role of disgust in disordered eating. Individuals who binge often report feelings of disgust, but the degree to which their disgust reactions result in compensatory strategies is not known. Future studies can investigate how strong disgust reactions to food may affect the likelihood that an individual will purge, and so forth. Disgust toward overweight body shapes has also been found in those with disordered eating. It is unclear whether those reactions translate into other common eating disorder behaviors, such as frequent checking of weight and aspects of appearance, including body shape and size. Once the relationship between disgust reactions and eating disorder behaviors is better understood, suggestions for possible treatment modifications can be made.

Complex Disgust Reactions

As suggested previously, the basic emotion of disgust appears consistent with reactions to core disgust elicitors and other disgust elicitors related to the prevention of illness and disease. However, it is unclear whether being disgusted by the violation of a social norm is the same experience as being disgusted by rotten food. It is possible that the former evokes a more complex emotional response. The constructs of interpersonal and sociomoral disgust are not as well understood. Theoretically, they are described as an expansion of the disgust reaction to include social functions. One study demonstrated that interpersonal and sociomoral disgust elicitors loaded on a separate factor from core and hygiene-related disgust (Meunier, Lohr, & Olatunji, 2004). Future research is needed to define the constructs of interpersonal and sociomoral disgust and to examine similarities and differences in reactions to these and other disgust elicitors. Once these constructs are validated, their possible involvement in psychological disorders can also be examined.

CONCLUSION

Because there has been limited research on the treatment of disgust to date, guidelines for conceptualization and treatment planning can be derived from basic cognitive–behavioral principles. The research literature has provided information to understand the psychophysiological activity, cognitions, and behavioral action tendencies associated with disgust, which may lead to improved identification of disgust reactions that may be contributing to an emotional disorder. Future research may provide additional guidance about whether specific disgust-targeted interventions are necessary and when they are likely to add to treatment efficacy.

REFERENCES

Abramowitz, J. S., Franklin, M. E., Schwartz, S. A., & Furr, J. M. (2003). Symptom presentation and outcome of cognitive-behavioral therapy for obsessive–compulsive disorder. *Journal of Consulting and Clinical Psychology, 71*, 1049–1057.

Baeyens, F., Crombez, G., van den Bergh, O., & Eelen, P. (1988). Once in contact always in contact: Evaluative conditioning is resistant to extinction. *Behaviour Research and Therapy, 10*, 179–199.

Barlow, D. H., Allen, L. B., & Choate, M. L. (2004). Toward a unified treatment for emotional disorders. *Behavior Therapy, 35*, 205–230.

Barlow, D. H., Gorman, J. M., Shear, M. K., & Woods, S. W. (2000, May 17). Cognitive-behavioral therapy, imipramine, or their combination for panic disorder: A randomized controlled trial. *JAMA, 283*, 2529–2536.

Batsell, W. R., & Brown, A. S. (1998). Human flavor-aversion learning: A comparison of traditional aversions and cognitive aversions. *Learning and Motivation, 29*, 383–396.

Brown, T. A., Chorpita, B. F., & Barlow, D. H. (1998). Structural relationships among dimensions of the *DSM–IV* anxiety and mood disorders and dimensions of negative affect, positive affect, and autonomic arousal. *Journal of Abnormal Psychology, 107*, 179–192.

de Jong, P. J., Andrea, H., & Muris, P. (1997). Spider phobia in children: Disgust and fear before and after treatment. *Behaviour Research and Therapy, 35*, 559–562.

de Jong, P. J., Vorage, I., & van den Hout, M. A. (2000). Counterconditioning in the treatment of spider phobia: Effects on disgust, fear and valence. *Behaviour Research and Therapy, 38*, 1055–1069.

de Silva, P. (1989). The modification of human food aversions: New application of behaviour therapy. In H. G. Zapotoczky & T. Wenzel (Eds.), *Scientific dialogue: From basic research to clinical interventions* (pp. 177–180). Vienna, Austria: European Association of Behaviour Therapy.

Foa, E. B., Liebowitz, M. R., Kozak, M. J., Davies, S., Campeas, R., Franklin, M. E., et al. (2005). Randomized, placebo-controlled trial of exposure and ritual prevention, clomipramine, and their combination in the treatment of obsessive-compulsive disorder. *The American Journal of Psychiatry, 162*, 151–161.

Heimberg, R. G., Liebowitz, M. R., Hope, D. A., Schneier, F. R., Holt, C. S., Welkowitz, L. A., et al. (1998). Cognitive behavioral group therapy versus phenelzine therapy for social phobia: 12-week outcome. *Archives of General Psychiatry, 55*, 1133–1141.

Hellström, K., Fellenius, J., & Öst, L. G. (1996). One versus five sessions of applied tension in the treatment of blood phobia. *Behaviour Research and Therapy, 34*, 101–112.

Hollon, S. D., DeRubeis, R. J., Evans, M. D., Wiemer, M. J., Garvey, M. J., Grove, W. M., et al. (1992). Cognitive therapy and pharmacotherapy for depression: Singly and in combination. *Archives of General Psychiatry, 49*, 774–781.

Jacobson, N. S., & Truax, P. (1991). Clinical significance: A statistical approach to defining meaningful change in psychotherapy research. *Journal of Consulting and Clinical Psychology, 59*, 12–19.

Jones, M. K., & Menzies, R. G. (1997). Danger ideation reduction therapy (DIRT): Preliminary findings with three obsessive-compulsive washers. *Behaviour Research and Therapy, 35*, 955–960.

Jones, M. K., & Menzies, R. G. (1998). Danger ideation reduction therapy (DIRT) for obsessive-compulsive washers. A controlled trial. *Behaviour Research and Therapy, 36*, 959–970.

Krochmalik, A., Jones, M. K., & Menzies, R. G. (2001). Danger ideation reduction therapy (DIRT) for treatment-resistant compulsive washing. *Behaviour Research and Therapy, 39*, 897–912.

Lang, P. J. (1979). Presidential address, 1978. A bio-informational theory of emotional imagery. *Psychophysiology, 16*, 495–512.

Mataix-Cols, D., Marks, I. M., Greist, J. H., Kobak, K. A., & Baer, L. (2002). Obsessive-compulsive symptom dimensions as predictors of compliance with and response to behaviour therapy: Results from a controlled trial. *Psychotherapy and Psychosomatics, 71*, 255–262.

McKay, D. (2006). Treating disgust reactions in contamination-based obsessive-compulsive disorder. *Journal of Behavior Therapy and Experimental Psychiatry, 37*, 53–59.

McLean, P. D., Whittal, M. L., Thordarson, D. S., Taylor, S., Sochting, I., Koch, W. J., et al. (2001). Cognitive versus behavior therapy in the group treatment of obsessive-compulsive disorder. *Journal of Consulting and Clinical Psychology, 69*, 205–214.

Merckelbach, H., de Jong, P. J., Arntz, A., & Schouten, E. (1993). The role of evaluative learning and disgust sensitivity in the etiology and treatment of spider phobia. *Advances in Behavior Research and Therapy, 15*, 243–255.

Meunier, S. A., Lohr, J. M., & Olatunji, B. O. (2004, November). *The psychometric properties of a new measure of disgust sensitivity: The search for a valid measure*. Paper presented at the annual meeting of the Association for the Advancement of Behavior Therapy, New Orleans, LA.

Olatunji, B. O., Smits, J. A., Connolly, K., Willems, J., & Lohr, J. M. (2007). Examination of the decline in fear and disgust during exposure to threat-relevant stimuli in blood-injection-injury phobia. *Journal of Anxiety Disorders, 21*, 445–455.

Öst, L. G., Fellenius, J., & Sterner, U. (1991). Applied tension, exposure in vivo, and tension-only in the treatment of blood phobia. *Behaviour Research and Therapy, 29*, 561–574.

Öst, L. G., & Sterner, U. (1987). Applied tension. A specific behavioral method for treatment of blood phobia. *Behaviour Research and Therapy, 25*, 25–29.

Öst, L. G., Sterner, U., & Fellenius, J. (1989). Applied tension, applied relaxation, and the combination in the treatment of blood phobia. *Behaviour Research and Therapy, 27*, 109–121.

Page, A. C. (1994). Blood-injury phobia. *Clinical Psychology Review, 14*, 443–461.

Smits, J. A., Telch, M. J., & Randall, P. K. (2002). An examination of the decline in fear and disgust during exposure-based treatment. *Behaviour Research and Therapy, 40*, 1243–1253.

Vansteenwegen, D., Vervliet, B., Iberico, C., Baeyens, F., Van den Bergh, O., & Hermans, D. (2007). The repeated confrontation with videotapes of spiders in multiple contexts attenuates renewal of fear in spider-anxious students. *Behaviour Research and Therapy, 45*, 1169–1179.

14

DISGUST AND PSYCHOPATHOLOGY: NEXT STEPS IN AN EMERGENT AREA OF TREATMENT AND RESEARCH

DEAN McKAY AND BUNMI O. OLATUNJI

As the chapters in this book illustrate, disgust is an important emotion in a wide range of psychopathology. Beginning with the initial recognition of the role of disgust in specific forms of phobic avoidance (Matchett & Davey, 1991), disgust is now implicated in conditions as varied as contamination fear associated with obsessive–compulsive disorder (OCD), sexual dysfunction, and eating disorders. Research on the role of disgust has been growing steadily through the years (Olatunji & McKay, 2007), but the literature is dwarfed when compared with that on other emotions traditionally associated with psychopathology. More programmatic research will be needed for researchers and clinicians to gain a better understanding of the implications of excessive disgust reactions for various forms of psychopathology.

DISGUST AND PSYCHIATRIC ILLNESS: SCOPE OF EMPIRICAL FINDINGS

Since the introduction of the disease-avoidance model (Matchett & Davey, 1991), research has shown that disgust significantly contributes to many different disorders. The following section outlines what has been found and what additional research is necessary regarding disgust and the disorders that it can affect.

Phobic Avoidance

As noted earlier, the development of empirical evaluations that involve disgust in psychopathology began with phobic avoidance, wherein many individuals with specific phobias for insects, animals, and some other objects report strong feelings of disgust rather than fear when faced with those stimuli (Matchett & Davey, 1991). Since that time, the accumulated research suggested strongly that this is in fact a robust relationship. Moreover, individuals with specific phobias for insects and small animals tend to have greater disgust reactions, in general, as well as for the specific phobic object (e.g., Mulkens, de Jong, & Merckelbach, 1996). As research has accumulated on specific phobias, special attention has been paid to blood-injury-injection phobia (BII). BII phobia has been associated with a number of additional individual and family psychiatric conditions that set it apart from the other phobias (for a review, see Öst & Hellstrom, 1994). That disgust is associated with BII phobia appears reasonable at this point given the role of parasympathetic activation in fainting. The extent to which parasympathetic activation is involved in other phobias with a disgust component requires additional investigation.

To expand on current knowledge on the role of disgust in phobic avoidance, more laboratory-based research in which findings can be translated into the real world will be needed. Such research must begin to identify the temporal relations between disgust and phobic fear. That is, does disgust actually enhance phobic fear or is the elevated disgust responsivity a mere artifact of phobic anxiety? An important observation is that there is a relative absence of disgust responding during the early years of life (Haidt, Rozin, McCauley, & Imada, 1997; Rozin & Fallon, 1987). This observation implies the role of social influence and cultural shaping in the learning of disgust, and prospective research is needed to examine how social and cultural factors also shape disgust to motivate phobic avoidance. More cross-cultural research may be particularly informative along these lines.

BII phobia is, in particular, a good condition to study to determine the relative contributions of anxiety and disgust to the condition. There is debate in the literature as to whether phobic avoidance has a component of disgust or whether participants incorrectly label the internal state as disgust when it is actually anxiety (i.e., Edwards & Salkovskis, 2006). However, anxiety and disgust are associated with different nervous system responses and different brain areas (Schienle, chap. 7, this volume). BII phobia is associated with activation in both of these systems, with sympathetic arousal during anticipation of exposure (Sarlo, Palomba, Angrilli, & Stegagno, 2002) and parasympathetic arousal during actual exposure (Friedman et al., 1993).

Other Psychiatric Conditions

As the chapters in this text amply illustrate, disgust has become associated with a number of other psychiatric conditions beyond the phobias. This is not a surprising development because disgust itself is a complex defense emotion beyond the evolutionary significance of preventing disease. Rozin and Fallon (1987) showed that disgust can be described along a number of dimensions, with classes of stimuli referred to as elicitors. Many of these elicitors do not necessarily correspond to disease avoidance, such as unusual or culturally unique food combinations.

Although the chapters in this volume illustrate the role of disgust in conditions as diverse as sexual dysfunction, eating disorders, and OCD, there are other psychiatric conditions in which disgust plays a prominent role. The emergent findings are as varied as the aforementioned chapters related to nonphobic conditions in this volume. For example, Schienle et al. (2003) found that individuals with schizophrenia had elevated global proneness to disgust. Carey and Harris (2005) found that BII phobia developed in cancer patients after initiating treatment, suggesting that exposure to medical procedures increases the salience of concerns over blood and injection, and enhances disgust reactions to the associated medical procedures. This effect has been observed in a more general way with patients who are undergoing a blood test—a small but significant minority reported disgust reactions as they were about to have blood drawn (Deacon & Abramowitz, 2006). In addition to these findings, social anxiety disorder has been associated with reduced sensitivity for detecting disgust (and anger) facial expressions (Montagne et al., 2006).

A CALL FOR A COMPREHENSIVE MODEL OF DISGUST IN PSYCHOPATHOLOGY

Research on disgust is an emergent area in psychopathology. Therefore, perhaps it is premature to make the case that a theoretical framework is necessary at this point. Indeed, although, for example, there is little debate that panic disorder is based on extreme anxiety, there is still debate about the role disgust might play in psychopathological states (i.e., Edwards & Salkovskis, 2006; Thorpe & Salkovskis, 1998). Instead, it has been suggested that disgust is merely an epiphenomena and that individuals with psychiatric disorders merely label all aversive states as elevated. It will be difficult to resolve this conflict without an organizing framework that generates testable hypotheses about the role of disgust in psychopathology. We may be approaching a point where some preliminary model development might be undertaken in the service of ultimately developing a comprehensive theory of disgust. Although a comprehensive theory of disgust has been described in chapter 1 of this volume (see also, Rozin & Fallon, 1987), it does not readily predict psycho-pathology or specific psychiatric disorders. Certainly the case can be forcefully made that disgust plays a role in phobic avoidance in light of the diversity of assessments showing the relationship.

At this time, models and hypotheses derived from the models are limited to specific conditions rather than driven by diagnostic considerations or psy-chiatric conditions in general. In many ways this is a consequence of the current diagnostic framework. The *Diagnostic and Statistical Manual of Mental Disorders*, *Fourth Edition* (*DSM–IV*; American Psychiatric Association, 1994) is structured to support discrete diagnostic entities. However, examination of emotional states and their contributions to different psychopathological states assumes a dimensional structure. Presently there are plans for increasing the dimen-sional features of the *DSM* as the fifth edition is prepared (i.e., Watson, 2005). Some analyses show that disgust is best considered dimensional (e.g., Olatunji & Broman-Fulks, 2008).

Relying on a dimensional perspective for disgust would be in keeping with the dimensional approach advocated for the planned revisions for the *DSM*. The publication of the "white papers" lays out a research agenda for the planned revisions to the *DSM* that specifically addresses the potential for including a dimensional component to diagnosis (Kupfer, First, & Regier, 2002). Currently, research on dimensional models does not allow for fine dis-tinctions among psychiatric conditions. For example, Watson (2005) found that all mood and anxiety disorders could be described in three different cat-egories (bipolar disorders, distress disorders, and fear disorders), with OCD not fitting into any category. Although this may simplify matters in diagnostic schemes, adopting a dimensional view that reduces psychopathology down to only three categories risks losing some of the fundamental characteristics of diagnosis, such as facilitating communication between health professionals, fostering theory development, predicting clinical course, or matching treat-ments to clients (Blashfield & Livesley, 1999). Inclusion of disgust as a dimensional component for specific disorders that have an established disgust component could sharpen the distinctions between and among disorders.

Disorders Associated With Low Disgust?

For a comprehensive theory of the role of disgust in psychopathology to be viable, it must also explain the phenomena of very low disgust reactions. Thus far, the majority of the research has emphasized the importance of sig-nificantly elevated disgust reactions. However, as emphasized previously, disgust is an important adaptive emotional reaction that protects from disease and poisoning (Rozin & Fallon, 1987). There are psychopathological states that lie at each extreme for major emotional states. For example, high levels of anxiety are associated with a wide range of emotional problems, and very low levels of anxiety are also associated with specific emotional problems, such as antisocial personality and some impulse-control disorders. Depression exists at one extreme, whereas the extreme absence of depression can also be construed as mania.

Because disgust is an emergent area of research, some of the findings thus far could be contradictory and could be cleared up with additional investigation. Although it was noted that Schienle et al. (2003) found that individuals with schizophrenia had elevated levels of disgust, other findings suggest that low levels of disgust reactivity are associated with schizoid personality and psychoticism (Quigley, Sherman, & Sherman, 1997; Wronska, 1990).

THE TREATMENT OF DISGUST

If disgust is associated with psychopathology, then treatments aimed at alleviating it will be necessary. In the coming years, as research progresses on this emotion and its role in different psychological disorders, presumably there will be a rise in the sophistication of approaches to treatment. At the current time, few studies have attempted to directly address disgust in the context of treatment. These approaches have assumed that disgust would respond in a manner similar to anxiety, whereby exposure leads to habituation. For example, McKay (2006) found that disgust required a longer period of time, using exposure for the treatment of contamination-based OCD. It is not known, however, whether disgust could be alleviated more readily by other methods that could even be contraindicated for other emotional problems. This has been demonstrated in other emotional states. For example, repeated exposure to anxiety-provoking information tends to reduce anxiety, but repeated exposure to depressing information does not alleviate depression (Williams et al., 1997).

Evidence is emerging that disgust is resistant to treatment that uses exposure-based interventions, which are commonly used for most problems associated with avoidance. For example, McKay (2006) showed that habituation to disgust was slower than for anxiety in a group of individuals with contamination OCD. In a study by de Jong, Vorage, and van den Hout (2000), a group of successfully treated spider-phobic women remained highly disgusted by spiders 1 year following treatment.

Investigators point to evaluative conditioning as an explanatory framework for the resistance to extinction observed in disgust (De Houwer, Thomas, & Baeyens, 2001; McKay & Tsao, 2005). Essentially, the problem involves identifying and naming the emotional reaction that co-occurs with the presentation of specific stimuli. Once this occurs, repeated exposure does not necessary change the labeling that has been generated for the stimuli, reducing the likelihood that habituation will occur. As a result of this finding, models of intervention that rely on pure exposure may be considered crude approximations to treating disgust as though it were analogous to anxiety. It is possible that treatments that might be ineffective for anxiety, such as direct cognitive challenge or relabeling, could be efficacious in the treatment of disgust. This is an important area that requires investigation as models of disgust become more sophisticated.

Cognitive–behavior therapy (CBT) has the most accumulated support for the various conditions described in this book (Hayes, Barlow, & Nelson-Gray, 1999, Chambless & Ollendick, 2001). It is therefore little surprise that the early efforts at intervention have been based on exposure methods. However, contemporary CBT relies heavily on specific cognitive interventions aimed at adjusting assumptions made about different environmental events and situations. The current state of the research does not allow for any assumptions to be made about the accessibility of cognitions related to disgust. Some have suggested that these cognitions are largely inaccessible although present in specific tests of attention, memory, and judgment (McKay & Tsao, 2005). This important area requires considerable attention if there are to be effective therapies developed to alleviate disgust in the diverse conditions affected by this emotion.

REFERENCES

American Psychiatric Association. (1994). *Diagnostic and statistical manual of mental disorders* (4th ed.). Washington, DC: Author.

Blashfield, R. K., & Livesley, W. J. (1999). Classification. In T. Millon, P. H. Blaney, & R. D. Davis (Eds.), *Oxford textbook of psychopathology* (pp. 3–28). New York: Oxford University Press.

Carey, C., & Harris, L. M. (2005). The origins of blood-injection fear/phobia in cancer patients undergoing intravenous chemotherapy. *Behaviour Change, 22,* 212–219.

Chambless, D. L., & Ollendick, T. O. (2001). Empirically supported psychological interventions: Controversies and evidence. *Annual Review of Psychology, 52,* 685–716.

Deacon, B., & Abramowitz, J. (2006). Fear of needles and vasovagal reactions among phlebotomy patients. *Journal of Anxiety Disorders, 20,* 946–960.

De Houwer, J., Thomas, S., & Baeyens, F. (2001). Association learning of likes and dislikes: A review of 25 years of research on human evaluative conditioning. *Psychological Bulletin, 127,* 853–869.

de Jong, P. J., Vorage, I., & van den Hout, M. A. (2000). Counterconditioning in the treatment of spider phobia: Effects on disgust, fear and valence. *Behaviour Research and Therapy, 38,* 1055–1069.

Edwards, S., & Salkovskis, P. M. (2006). An experimental demonstration that fear, but not disgust, is associated with return of fear in humans. *Journal of Anxiety Disorders, 20,* 58–71.

Friedman, B. H., Thayer, J. F., Borkovec, T. D., Tyrell, R. A., Johnson, B. H., & Columbo, R. (1993). Autonomic characteristics of nonclinical panic and blood phobia. *Biological Psychiatry, 34,* 298–310.

Haidt, J., Rozin, P., McCauley, C., & Imada, S. (1997). Body, psyche, and culture: The relationship between disgust and morality. *Psychology and Developing Societies, 9,* 107–131.

Hayes, S. C., Barlow, D. H., & Nelson-Gray, R. O. (1999). *The scientist-practitioner: Research and accountability in the age of managed care.* Boston: Allyn & Bacon.

Kupfer, D. J., First, M. B., & Regier, D. A. (2002). *A research agenda for* DSM–V. Washington, DC: American Psychiatric Association.

Matchett, G., & Davey, G. C. L. (1991). A test of a disease-avoidance model of animal phobias. *Behaviour Research and Therapy, 29,* 91–94.

McKay, D. (2006). Treating disgust reactions in contamination-based obsessive-compulsive disorder. *Journal of Behavior Therapy and Experimental Psychiatry, 37,* 53–59.

McKay, D., & Tsao, S. (2005). A treatment most foul: Handling disgust in cognitive-behavior therapy. *Journal of Cognitive Psychotherapy: An International Quarterly, 19,* 355–367.

Montagne, B., Schutters, S., Westenberg, H. G., van Honk, J., Kessels, R. P., & de Haan, E. H. (2006). Reduced sensitivity in the recognition of anger and disgust in social anxiety disorder. *Cognitive Neuropsychiatry, 11,* 389–401.

Mulkens, S. A., de Jong, P. J., & Merckelbach, H. (1996). Disgust and spider phobia. *Journal of Abnormal Psychology, 105,* 464–468.

Olatunji, B. O., & Broman-Fulks, J. (2007). A taxometric study of the latent structure of disgust sensitivity: Converging evidence for dimensionality. *Psychological Assessment, 19,* 437–448.

Olatunji, B. O., & McKay, D. (2007). Disgust and psychiatric illness: Have we remembered? *British Journal of Psychiatry, 190,* 457–459.

Öst, L. G., & Hellstrom, K. (1994). Blood-injury-injection phobia. In G. C. L. Davey (Ed.), *Phobias: A handbook of theory, research, and treatment* (pp. 63–78). Chichester, England: Wiley.

Quigley, J. F., Sherman, M. F., & Sherman, N. C. (1997). Personality disorder symptoms, gender, and age as predictors of adolescent disgust sensitivity. *Personality and Individual Differences, 22,* 661–667.

Rozin, P., & Fallon, A. E. (1987). A perspective on disgust. *Psychological Review, 94,* 23–41.

Sarlo, M., Palomba, D., Angrilli, A., & Stegagno, L. (2002). Blood phobia and spider phobia: Two specific phobias with different autonomic cardiac modulations. *Biological Psychology, 60,* 91–108.

Schienle, A., Schafer, A., Stark, R., Walter, B., Franz, M., & Vaitl, D. (2003). Disgust sensitivity in psychiatric disorders: A questionnaire study. *Journal of Nervous and Mental Disease, 191*, 831–834.

Thorpe, S. J., & Salkovskis, P. M. (1998). Studies on the role of disgust in the acquisition and maintenance of specific phobias. *Behaviour Research and Therapy, 36*, 877–893.

Watson, D. (2005). Rethinking the mood and anxiety disorders: A quantitative hierarchical model for DSM–V. *Journal of Abnormal Psychology, 114*, 522–536.

Williams, J. M. G., Watts, F. N., MacLeod, C. M., & Mathews, A. (1997). *Cognitive psychology and emotional disorders* (2nd ed.). Chichester, England: Wiley.

Wronska, J. (1990). Disgust in relation to emotionality, extraversion, psychoticism, and imagery abilities. In P. J. D. Drenth, J. A. Sergeant, & R. Takens (Eds.), *European perspectives in psychology* (Vol. I, pp. 125–138). Oxford, England: Wiley.

AUTHOR INDEX

Numbers in italics refer to listings in the references.

Abe, J. A., 99, *118*

Abramowitz, J. S., 27, 35, 36, *54*, *56*, 213, 220, 223, *224*, *225*, *226*, *227*, *274*, *281*, *287*, *290*

Abreu, K., 59, 89, *72*, *95*

Abromov, L., 260, *266*

Accurson, V., 198, *205*

Adler, C. M., 157, 158, *161*

Adler, P. S. J., 200, *205*

Adolphs, R., 149, 150, *161*

Agras, S., 245, *251*

Ahern, G. L., 154, *163*

Akutagawa, D., 245, *251*

al'Absi, M., 123, *139*

Alaoui-Ismaili, O., 130, 137, *139*

Allan, S., 244, 248, *251*

Allen, G. J., 169, *186*

Allen, L. B., 272, *281*

Alpert, N. M., *164*

Ameli, R., 129, *140*

American Psychiatric Association, 191, *205*, 213, *224*, 230, 243, *247*, 254, 260, *266*, 288, *290*

Amin, J. M., 68, 69

Amir, N., 65, *70*, 215, *224*

Amsel, R. M. A., 253, 261, 268, 269

Ancoli, S., 78, 93

Andersen, G. V., 84, 92

Anderson, A. K., 152, 153, 159, 161, *161*

Anderson, G., *247*

Andrea, H., *52*, 177, *187*, 263, *276*, *274*, *281*

Andreasen, N. C., 94, *163*

Andrew, C., 27, *94*, *163*, *165*

Andrews, B., 243, 244, *247*, *248*, *250*

Andrews, C., 27

Andrews, G., 195, *205*

Angrilli, A., 286, *291*

Angyal, A., 10, *24*, 172, 181, *186*, 229, *247*

Annas, P., 157, *162*

Antony, M. M., 213, *224*

Arcuri, L., 103, *119*

Ardon, A. M., 169, *186*

Aretz, E., *270*

Arguello, A. P., 84, 86, 93

Armfield, J. M., 177, *186*

Arndt, S., *161*

Arntz, A., 34, *53*, 90, 92, 171, 176, 178, 180, *186*, 188, 258, *266*, 273, *282*

Arrindel, W. A., 34, *52*, *54*, 82, 92, 94, 169, 175, 181, 184, *186*, 215, *224*, *225*

Ashmore, M., 14, 28, 36, 55

Augustine, J. R., 151, 160, *161*

Augustoni-Ziskind, M. L., 40, *55*, 79, 95

Aunger, R., 23, *24*, 254, *267*

Bacon, A. K., 61, *70*

Baer, L., *164*, 274, *282*

Baeyens, F., 87, 92, 220, *224*, 275, 276, *281*, *283*, *289*, *290*

Bagby, J. M., 242, *247*

Baker, A., xi

Baker, J. R., 156, *161*

Balaban, M. T., 130, *139*

Baraldi, P., *162*

Barker, K., 178, 179, *186*, 235, 238, *247*

Barker, W. A., 15, *25*

Barlow, D. H., 197, *205*, 215, *224*, 243, 250, 253, 256, *266*, 271, 272, *276*, *281*, *290*, *291*

Barnes, D. S., 19, *24*

Basson, R., 260, *266*, *267*

Batsell, W. R., 276, *281*
Bauer, S., *247*
Baumgartner, M. S. W., 258, 259, *269*
Beaudoin, G., *163*
Bechara, A., *162*
Beck, A. T., 61, *69*
Beck, J. G., 260, *267*
Becker, E., 13, 17, *24*, 61, 62, *69, 72*
Beckham, J. C., 127, *139*
Beisiegel, E., *270*
Bemis, K., 231, 246, *248*
Bench, C. J., *163*
Bennett, D., 79, *92*
Bennett, K. S., 192, *208*
Berenbaum, H., 50, *52*
Berenstein, I. L., 84, 87, *92, 96*
Bergers, G. P. A., *251*
Berle, D., 15, *24*
Bernstein, D. A., 169, *186*
Berntson, G. G., 136, *139*
Best, M. R., 84, *93*
Bhatia, K. P., 260, *268*
Bickerstaffe, S., 62, *70*, 184, *187*, 257, *267*
Biehl, M., 101, 102, 103, 109, 116, 117, *118*
Bilsky, W., 264, *269*
Binik, Y. M., 253, *268, 269*
Biran, A., 23, *24*, 111, *119*
Birch, L. L., 84, *92*
Bjork, R. A., 91, *93*
Bjorklund, F., 20, *26*, 35, 36, 37, *26, 52*
Blanchard, E. B., 61, *69*
Blanchard, M., 244, *250*
Bland, R. C., 215, *227*
Blashfield, R. K., 288, *290*
Blecker, C., 154, *164, 165, 209*
Bloom, P., 11, 21, *24, 26*
Bohr, Y., *248*
Boiton, F., 134, *139*
Bolls, P. D., 136, *141*
Bond, A., *249*
Bond, N. W., 82, 97, 175, *189*
Bond, N., 36, 41, 49, *52*, 177, 180, *187*
Bongard, S., 123, *139*
Borke, M. P., 242, *247*
Borkovec, T. D., *291*
Bornjholt, L., 246, *247*

Bos, A. E. R., 245, *249*
Boucher, J. D., 103, *118*
Boucsein, W., 134, *139*
Bourgouin, P., *163*
Bouton, M. E., 91, *92*
Bovbjerg, D. H., 84, *96*
Bradley, B. P., 61, *69, 71*, 256, *268*
Bradley, C. R., 61, *71*
Bradley, M. M., 124, 126, 127, 128, 129, 130, 131, 136, *139, 141*, 160, *161, 164*
Bradley, R., 213, *224*
Brake, N., *247*
Bramati, I. E., *27*
Brammer, M. J., *27, 163, 165, 209, 251*
Bramon, E., 36, 56, 235, *251*
Braun, C., 129, *142*
Bredart, S., 66, *70*
Breiter, H. C., 156, *161, 164*
Breitholtz, E., 62, *70*
Brewerton, T. D., 242, *247*
Bristow, W. S., 111, 114, *119*
Brody, S., 129, *142*
Broman-Fulks, J., 288, *291*
Brooner, R. K., 82, *96*
Brotto, L., *267*
Brown, A. S., 276, *281*
Brown, G. W., 244, *247*
Brown, S., 130, *140*
Brown, T. A., 272, *281*
Bryant, R. A., 61, *69*
Buchanan, J. B., 134, *141*
Büchel, C., 160, *162*
Buckland, G., 17, *25*, 236, *248*
Buckley, T. C., 61, *69*
Bundesen, C., 61, *70*
Burgess, I., 172, 173, *190*, 231, *251*
Burnette, M. M., 259, *268*
Burney, J., 243, *247*
Burns, G. L., 176, *186*, 217, *224*
Buwalda, F., 261, *267*
Byrnes, D., 86, *96*

Cacioppo, J. T., 150, *162*
Calamari, J., *225*
Calder, A. J., *27, 29*, 83, *92, 94, 96*, 156, *161, 163*

Callahan, R., 192, *208*
Camaras, L., 78, *92*
Cameron, M., 62, *72*
Campbell, L., 61, *71*
Campeas, R., *282*
Candel, I., *53, 249*
Canino, G. J., 215, *227*
Cannon, D. S., 84, *93*
Caparelli, D. E. M., *27*
Carey, C., 287, *290*
Carlson, G. E., 103, *118*
Carnes, P. J., 253, 255, 259, 261, *267*
Carrell, L. E., 84, *93*
Carstensen, L. L., 134, *141*
Carter, O., 192, *208*
Casper, R. C., 234, *247*
Cavanagh, K., 32, 41, *52, 56*, 126, *139*,
    179, *187*
Ceschi, C., 66, *70*
Chambless, D. L., 290, *290*
Chan, A., *93, 119*
Chan, R. M., *162*
Chandel, I., *225*
Chanel, J., *139*
Chapman, T. F., 169, *186*
Charash, M., *52*, 61, 62, 66, *70*, 256, *267*
Checkley, S. A., 130, *141*
Chentsova-Dutton, Y., 107, 109, 110,
    117, *122*
Chirot, D., 20, *24*
Choate, M. L., 272, *281*
Chorpita, B. F., 272, *281*
Christoff, K., *161*
Chrosniak, L. K., 59, *72*
Chur-Hansen, A., 233, 240, *249*
Cisler, J. M., xi, 36, 42, 49, *52, 54*, 61,
    64, 68, *70, 71*
Clark, D. A., 61, 69, 215, *224*
Clark, D. M., 62, *70*, 179, *188*
Clarke, J. C., 194, 202, *207*
Clore, G. L., 198, *207*
Coan, J. A., 136, *142*
Cochrane, C. E., 242, *247*
Codispoti, M., 126, *139*
Cohen, D. M. D., 261, *269*
Coles, M. E., 215, *224*
Collins, A., 198, *207*
Columbo, R., *291*

Comwell, R., *25*
Connolly, J., 192, 193, *205, 206*
Connolly, K. M., xi, 32, 35, 42, 44, *53,
    54, 56*, 60, 64, *71, 73*, 193, *206*,
    274, *283*
Cook, M., 63, *73*, 171, *186*
Cooper, Z., 231, *248*
Corgiat, M., 82, *96*
Cornet, F. C., 169, *186*
Cortina, J. M., 59, *72*
Cosmides, L., 133, *139*
Costello, C. G., 169, *186*
Costello, K., 20, *26*
Cox, B. J., 88, *96*
Cox, C. R., 13, *24*
Craske, M. G., 91, *93*, 215, 216, *224*
Creamer, M., 195, *205*
Crino, R. D., 195, *205*
Crisp, A. H., 231, 235, *247*
Crombez, G., 87, *92*, 276, *281*
Cuddy, A. J. C., 20, *25*
Curtis, A., 15, 83, *25, 93*
Curtis, G. C., 191, 192, *209*
Curtis, V., 23, 111, *24, 119*, 254, *267*
Cuthbert, B. N., 124, 125, 126, 127,
    139, 140, 141, 143

Daher, M., 79, *93*
Dalgleish, T., 15, 17, *27, 54*, 82, *94*,
    230, 243, *249, 250, 251*
Dallos, R., 17, *25, 236, 248*
Dalton, J., *249*
Damasio, A. R., 147, 149, *162*
Daniels, S. R., *249*
Darwin, C., 9, 11, 19, 23, *24, 25*, 99,
    100, *119*, 131, *139*
Das, P., *165, 209*
Davey, G. C. L., xi, xvi, 4, 15, 16, 17, 18,
    23, *25, 26*, 32, 36, 41, 49, *52, 56*,
    60, 62, 68, *70, 71*, 85, 90, *94*, 114,
    119, 126, *139*, 169, 171, 172, 173,
    174, 175, 177, 179, 180, 181, 182,
    183, 184, *186, 187, 188*, 190,
    197, 198, *205, 206, 209*, 212,
    225, 229, 231, 235, 236, 237, 238,
    247, 248, 249, 251, 257, 263,
    267, 285, 286, 289, *291*

David, A. S., 31, *54*, 230, *250*
David, M. P., 260, *266*
Davidson, R. J., *94*, 106, *120*, 147, 148, 154, *162*, *163*
Davies, S., *282*
Davis, M., 129, *140*
de Groot, E., *269*
de Groot, H. E., 253, *269*
de Haan, E. H., 287, *291*
De Houwer, J., 220, *224*, 289, *290*
de Jong, A., 34, *53*
de Jong, P. J., xi, xvi, 31, 32, 34, 36, 37, *52, 53, 54*, 62, 63, 64, *70, 73*, 114, 115, *121*, 171, 176, 177, 179, 181, *187*, 188, *189*, 193, 194, 195, 197, 200, *205*, 207, 216, *225*, 261, 262, 263, 264, 265, *267*, 268, *270*, 273, 274, 275, 276, *281*, 282, 286, 289, *290, 291*
de Rosa, E., *161*
de Silva, P., 84, *93*, 266, *267*, 277, *281*
Deacon, B., 42, *54*, 287, *290*
DeBerard, S., 192, *206*
Defares, P. B., *251*
Delhomme, G., *139*
Delprato, D. J., 171, *187*
Demellweek, C., 84, *93*
Demeree, H. A., 136, *139*
deOliveira-Souza, R., *27*
Derogatis, L, *267*
DeRubeis, R. J., *282*
Des Pres, T., 20, *25*
Desai, P., *161*
Diacoyanni-Tarlatzis, I., *93, 119*
Dias, M., 13, *26*
Diekmann, H., 129, *142*
Diessner, R., 83, *95*
Dilger, S., 157, *162*
Dimberg, U., 131, *139*
Dittmar, A., 130, 137, *139*
Ditto, B., 200, *205*
Dixon, R., 256, *268*
D'Mello, G. D., 84, *93*
Dolan, R. J., 152, *163, 165*
D'Olimpio, F., *53*, 82, *94*, 214, *225*
Doogan, S., 171, *187*
Dorfan, N. M., 198, *205*, 257, *267*

Downhill, J. E., *94, 163*
Drevets, W. C., 150, *163*
Druschel, B. A., 33, 36, *52*, 195, *205*
Ducci, L., 103, *119*
Duncan, L. A., 20, *25*
Dunlop, L., 14, 36, 28, *55*
Dutra, L., 213, *224*
D'Zurilla, T. J., 221, *224*

Eating Disorders Association, 232, *248*
Ebert, R., 43, *55*, 264, *269*
Ebsworthy, G., 61, *71*
Eddy, K. T., 213, *224*
Edwards, S., 178, 180, 183, 184, *187*, 286, 287, *291*
Eelen, P., 87, *92*, 276, *281*
Ehrlichman, H., 130, 137, *140*
Ekman, P., 10, *25*, 78, 88, *93*, 99, 101, 102, 103, 104, 105, 106, 107, 108, 109, 110, 116, 117, *118*, *119, 120*, 127, 128, 131, 134, 136, 137, *140, 141*, 145, *162*
Elias, N., 19, *25*
Ellwart, T., 61, 62, *72*
Elwood, L. S., xi, 32, *56*, 60, *73*
Erhard, P., *162, 164*
Ericson, K., 157, *162*
Eriksson, A., 171, *189*
Esteves, F., 61, *71*
Evans, M. D., *282*
Everaerd, W., 253, 255, 256, 268, *269*
Everhart, D. E., 136, *139*
Exeter-Kent, H. A., 33, *53*, 201, *205*
Eysel, U. T., 83, *96*, 150, *165*
Eysenck, H., 176, *187*
Eysenck, S. B. G., 176, *187*

Fahy, T., 31, *54*, 230, *250*
Fairburn, C. G., 231, 236, *248*
Fallon, A. E., 5, 12, 14, 18, *25*, 28, 31, 32, 40, *55*, 58, *72*, 77, 79, 80, 82, 83, 85, 86, 87, 88, 90, *93, 95*, 127, *142*, 145, 155, *164*, 172, 174, 181, *189*, 193, 195, *208*, 212, 214, 220, *225*, 229, 230, 235, *250*, 254, 265, 266, *269*, 286, 287, 288, *291*

Faulkner, J., 20, 23, *25*
Fellenius, J., 271, 277, *282, 283*
Fenichel, O., 3
Ferenczi, S., 18, *25*
Fessler, D. M. T., 20, 22, 23, *25, 27*, 84, 86, *93*, 254, 267
Fichner-Rathus, L., 256, *268*
Fine, G. A., 23, *25*
Finlay-Jones, R. A., *140*
First, M. B., 288, *291*
Fiske, S. T., 20, *25*
Fitek, C., *162*
Fitzsimmons, J. R., *161*
Flykt, A., 61, *71*
Foa, E. B., 60, 62, 65, 66, 67, *70*, 138, *140*, 211, 213, 215, *224, 225*, 271, *282*
Foote, F., 170, 171, *188*
Ford, G., 192, *206*
Formea, G. M., 176, *186*, 217, *224*
Forster, L., 18, *25*, 231, *248*, 263, *267*
Foucroy, J., *267*
Frackowiak, R. S. J., *163*
France, C., 200, *205*
Franklin, M. E., 274, *281, 282*
Franz, M., *29*, 250, *291*
Fredrickson, M., 157, *162*, 191, *205*
Freshman, M., 65, *70*
Fridlund, A. J., 106, *119*, 125, 131, 133, *140*
Friederich, H.-C., *251*
Friedman, A. G., 84, *94*
Friedman, B. H., 286, *291*
Friere-Bebeau, L., 107, 117, *122*
Friesen, W. V., 78, *93*, 99, 101, 103, 104, 105, 110, 116, 117, *119*, *120, 127, 128, 134*, 134, 136, *140, 141*
Frijters, J. E. R., *251*
Friston, K. J., 160, *162*
Frith, S. D., *163*
Fugl-Meyer, K., *267*
Furr, J. M., 62, *70*, 274, *281*

Gabrieli, J. D. E., *161*
Gaggar, A., 245, *251*
Galati, D., 112, *119*

Gallese, V., *165*
Ganchrow, J. R., 79, *93*
Garcia, J., 84, 87, *93*
Garcia-Gutierrez, A., 91, *92*
Garfinkel, P. E., *248*
Garner, D. M., 231, 246, *248*
Garvey, M. J., *282*
Gaupp, L. A., 169, *188*
Gee, A., 244, *248*
Genten, M. H., 255, *268*
Georgis, T. W., 103, *119*
Gerlach, A. L., 200, *206*
Gershuny, B., 65, *70*
Gessner, T. L., 59, *72*
Ghazizadeh, S., 260, *268*
Giampietro, V., *94, 251*
Gianaros, P. J., 222, *225*
Gibson, D., 15, *25*, 83, *93*
Gilbert, P., 243, 244, 246, *248*
Gilboa-Schechtman, E., 65, *70*
Girod, C., 154, *165*
Glick, P., 20, *25*
Globisch, J., 125, *140*
Gloyne, H. F., 182, *187*
Gobbini, M. I., 149, *162*
Goldenberg, J. L., 13, *24, 25*
Golombok, S., 264, *269*
Gomez, J., 50, *52*
Goodman, W. K., 15, *26*, 155, *165*, 196, 209, *224*
Gordon, B., 22, *28*, 254, *269*
Gorman, J. M., 271, *281*
Gorno-Tempini, M. L., 152, 153, *162*
Goss, K., 243, 244, *248*
Goudie, A. J., 84, *93*
Grabowski, T. J., *162*
Gragnani, A., 53, 82, *94*, 214, *225*
Graham, D. T., 191, 192, *206*
Graham, F. K., 129, *140*
Gramzow, R., 244, *251*
Gray, J. A., 130, *141*
Gray, J. M., 15, 16, *25*, 83, *93*
Greenberg, J., 13, *25, 29*
Greeno, C. G., 231, *248*
Greenwald, M. K., 129, *141*
Greenwald, S., 215, *227*
Greer, J., 49, *53*

Greist, J. H., 274, *282*
Griffiths, J., 236, 238, 239, 240, 241, 242, 246, *249*
Grill, H. J., 131, *140*
Grillon, C., 129, *140*
Gross, J., 136, *140*
Grove, W. M., *282*
Grunfeld, D. I., 22, *25*
Gur, R. C., 153, *162*
Gursky, D. M., 88, *95*
Gustafson, D. J., 127, *139*
Gustafson, L., *163*

Habekost, T., 61, *70*
Haidt, J., xi, xvi, 9, 12, 13, 14, 16, 20, 24, 25, 26, 28, 29, 31, 32, 33, 34, 35, 36, 37, 49, *53*, *55*, 69, *72*, 77, 82, 88, 93, *95*, 100, 102, 103, 104, 106, 107, 108, 111, 113, 115, 116, 117, 118, *120*, *121*, 128, 136, 137, *140*, *142*, 145, 155, *162*, *164*, 175, *187*, 193, 195, 206, 208, 212, 214, 215, 225, 226, 230, 234, 235, 236, 237, 238, *249*, *250*, 254, 257, 258, 262, 268, 269, 270, 286, *291*
Hakstian, A. R., *226*
Haley, K. J., 22, 23, *25*
Hallam, R. S., 192, *205*
Hamm, A. O., 125, 129, 131, 136, *140*, *141*
Hammer, L., 85, *95*
Harder, D. W., 244, *249*
Harris, L. M., 287, *290*
Harris, T. O., 244, *247*
Harvey, A. G., 61, *69*, 256, 259, *268*
Harvey, T., *53*, 236, 238, 239, 240, 241, 246, *249*
Haslam, N., 20, *26*
Haslinger, B., *162*, *164*
Hastings, J. E., 176, *188*
Hatfield, E., 150, *162*
Hawk, L. W., Jr., 129, 131, *143*, 256, *270*
Hawkins, A., 36, *56*
Haxby, J. V., 149, *162*
Hay, P., 233, 240, *249*
Hayes, S. C., 290, *291*

He, G., 155, *165*, 196, *209*, *164*
Hearn, V., 101, 102, 103, 109, 116, 117, *118*
Hecht, H., 61, *71*, *162*
Hecker, J. F. C., 182, *188*
Hedeker, D., 234, *247*
Heider, K., 93, 101, 102, 103, 109, 110, 116, 117, *118*, *119*, *120*
Heiman, J. R., 253, 266, *268*
Heimberg, R. G., 271, *282*
Heining, M., *163*
Hejmadi, A., 18, *26*, 104, 106, 108, 116, 117, *120*
Hellström, K., 277, *282*, 286, *291*
Helmeste, D., *120*
Hemenover, S. H., 24, *26*
Hennenlotter, A., 157, *162*, *164*
Hepburn, T., 198, 200, *206*
Herba, C. M., *163*
Herman, C. P., *249*
Hermann, A., *164*
Hermans, D., 275, *283*
Heuer, K., 61, 62, *72*
Hickling, E. J., 61, *69*
Hildebrand, M., 90, *92*
Himle, J., 191, *209*
Hirisave, U., *119*, *187*, *205*
Hodges, E. J., 242, *247*
Hodgson, R. J., 127, *142*, 214, *225*
Hodson, G., 20, *26*
Hoffmann, E. A., 149, *162*
Hogman, L., 61, *73*
Holker, L., 61, *71*
Holland, E. A., 78, *92*
Hollander, E., *224*
Hollon, S. D., 271, *282*
Holt, C. S., 179, *190*, *282*
Holt, R., 59, *72*, 89, *95*
Homberg, V., 29, *96*
Hood, J., 36, *56*
Hope, D. A., *282*
Horowitz, M., 22, 28, 254, *269*
Horowitz, T., 85, *95*
Horselenberg, R., *53*, 225, *249*
Hu, S., 134, *141*
Huang, Y., 103, *120*
Hugdal, K., 136, *141*

Huijding, J., 245, *249*
Hunsberger, B., 83, *95*
Hunt, C., 195, *205*
Huppert, J. D., 33, *54*, 62, *70*
Hursti, T. J., 35, 36, 37, *52*
Husted, D. S., 15, *26*
Huster, C., *206*
Huygens, K., 62, *73*
Hwu, H. G., 215, *227*

Iberico, C., 275, *283*
Ignacio, F. A., *27*
Ilai, D., 62, *70*
Imada, S., 12, 13, *28*, 82, *95*, 100, 107, *120*, *121*, 128, *140*, 234, *250*, 286, *291*
Inbar, Y., 21, *26*
Irwin, H. J., 243, *247*
Irwin, W., 148, *162*
Ishida, N., 106, *121*
Iwawaki, S., *119*, 187, *205*
Izard, C. E., 10, *26*, 57, *70*, *71*, 78, *93*, 99, 100, 101, *120*, 127, 131, *140*, *141*, 145, *162*

Jackson, D. C., *162*
Jacobsen, P. B., 84, *96*
Jacobson, N. S., 274, *282*
Jain, K., 172, 173, *190*, 231, *251*
James, G. A., *164*
James, W., 10, *26*
Janssen, E., 253, 256, *268*
Jenike, M. A., *164*, *224*
Jiang, T., 78, *96*
Jim, C. I., *119*, 187, *205*
Jiwany, A., 242, *250*
Johanson, A., 157, *163*
Johnsen, B. H., 136, *141*
Johnson, A. K., *205*
Johnson, B. H., *291*
Johnson, P. A., 84, *92*
Johnson, S. A., 192, *208*
Johr, J. M., 280, *283*
Jones, J. K., 11, *27*
Jones, M. K., 276, 277, *282*

Kabler, J. D., 192, *206*
Kalin, N. H., *162*

Kaneko, K., 253, 259, *268*
Karnat, A., 29, *96*
Kaspi, S. P., 61, *71*
Kasri, F., 108, *120*
Kass, L., 19, *26*
Katsikitis, M., 240, *249*
Kaviani, H., 130, *141*
Kellerman, H., *142*
Keltner, D., 102, 103, 104, 106, 111, 115, 116, 117, *120*
Kennedy, D. N., *161*
Keortge, S. G., 176, *186*, 217, *224*
Kessels, R. P., 287, *291*
Keysers, C., *165*
Khalifé, S. M. D., 261, *268*, 269
Khalifé, S., 253, *268*
King, A., 235, *249*
King, F. L., 82, *96*
King, W., *161*
Kirchner, P. T., *94*, *163*
Kirsch, P., 154, *164*, *165*, 208, 209, *250*
Kirschstein, R. L., xvi
Klassen, T., 255, *270*
Kleinknecht, E. E., 31, 38, *53*
Kleinknecht, R. A., 31, 32, 37, 38, *53*, *55*, *56*, 176, *189*, 192, 193, 194, 198, 199, 200, *206*, 208, 212, 216, *226*, *227*
Klorman, R., 176, *188*
Kluk, B., *25*
Knieps, L., 78, *97*
Knight, R. G., 130, 136, *142*
Kobak, K. A., 274, *282*
Koch, M. D., 44, 45, *53*, 193, 197, 201, *206*
Koch, W. J., *282*
Koelling, R. A., 84, 87, *93*
Kok, J., 34, *52*, 82, *92*, 175, *186*, 215, *224*
Koller, S., 13, *26*
Kooken, K., 108, *120*
Kordy, H., *247*
Koukounas, E., 235, *249*, 255, 256, 258, *268*
Kozak, M. J., 60, *70*, 130, *140*, 213, 215, *224*, *282*
Krieschel, S., 61, *71*
Kringlen, E., *96*

Krochmalik, A., 277, *282*
Kucharska-Pietura, K., 242, *249*
Kudoh, T., 101, 102, 103, 109, 116, 117, *118*
Kumari, V., 130, *141*
Kupfer, D. J., 288, *291*
Kwong, K. K., 156, *161*
Kyllingsbaek, S., 61, *70*
Kyrios, M., *225*

Laan, E., 255, *269*
Lacey, J. I., 125, *141*
Lamb, A., 126, *139*, 179, *187*
Lampe, L. A., 195, *205*
Landy, F. J., 169, *188*
Lane, R. D., 150, 154, *163*
Lang, A. J., 91, *93*
Lang, P. G., 60, *71*
Lang, P. J., 123, 124, 125, 126, 127, 129, *139*, *141*, *143*, *161*, 174, 176, *188*, *190*, 271, *282*
Lange, H., *29*, *96*
Lange, K. W., *164*
Lavy, E., 178, *186*
Lawrence, A. D., 156, *161*
Lazarus, R. S., 10, *26*
Le, H. N., 50, *52*
LeDoux, J. E., 147, 148, *163*
Lee, C. K., 215, *227*
Lee, T. C., 31, 38, *55*, *56*, 62, 72, 176, *189*, *193*, *194*, *208*, *209*, 212, *226*, *227*
Legg, C., 243, *250*
Leiblum, S. R., 254, 260, *267*, *268*
Leibowitz, J. A., 62, *72*
Lenz, J., 192, *206*
Leroux, J. M., *163*
Leshner, G., 136, *141*
Lessig, M. C., xi, *164*
Levenson, R. W., 23, *26*, 78, *93*, 99, 101, 110, 117, *119*, *120*, 134, 136, 137, *140*, *141*, 199, *206*
Lévesque, J., *163*
Levey, A. B., 86, *93*
Lewis, M., 77, 78, 79, 82, *96*
Lewis, T., 191, *206*
Lewontin, R. C., 171, *188*

Liberzon, I., 159, *163*
Liddell, B., *165*, *209*
Liebowitz, M. R., *282*
Lilienfeld, S. O., 41, *53*
Liljenquist, K., 21, *29*, 218, 223, *227*
Lindahl, I. L., 134, *142*, 191, *207*
Liu, Y., 155, *165*, *196*, *209*
Livesley, W. J., 288, *290*
Lofberg, I., 171, *189*
Lohr, J. M., xi, xvi, 17, *27*, 31, 32, 33, 35, 36, 37, 38, 42, 46, 47, 48, 49, *52*, *54*, *55*, 56, 58, 60, 62, 64, 65, 68, *70*, *71*, *72*, *73*, 82, 94, 114, *121*, 134, *142*, 176, *189*, 192, 193, 194, *207*, *208*, *209*, 212, 215, 216, *225*, *226*, *227*, 255, 262, 268, 274, *283*
Lovibond, P. F., 68, *69*
Lowery, L., 13, 19, *28*, 43, *55*, 82, *95*, 234, *250*, 264, *269*
Lumley, M. A., 199, *206*
Lundh, L., 61, *73*
Lunsford, L., 192, *206*
Lygren, S., *96*
Lythgoe, D., *163*

MacDonald, B. A., 62, *70*, 184, *187*, 257, *267*
Macias, R., 86, *93*
MacLeod, C. M., 57, 61, 65, *71*, *73*, 292
Madden, S., *247*
Mahapatra, M., 13, *29*, 107, *122*
Maloney, M. J., *249*
Maltby, N., 58, *73*, 218, *227*
Mancini, F., *53*, 82, 94, 214, 215, *225*
Mandell, R., 18, *28*, 31, 32, *55*, 174, *189*, 235, *250*
Mansell, W., 256, *268*
Manzano, M., *119*
Margraf, J., 61, *69*
Marks, I. M., *163*, 169, *188*, 191, 192, 193, *205*, *206*, 274, *282*
Marlier, L., 78, *96*
Marmora, V., 85, *95*
Marschall, D. E., 243, *250*
Martin, I., 86, *93*
Martin, M., 179, *188*

Marzillier, S., xii, 23, 26, 181, 183, 184, 188

Masiak, M., 242, 249

Mataix-Cols, D., 274, 282

Matchett, G., 4, 15, 26, 60, 71, 85, 90, 94, 174, 175, 180, 184, 188, 198, 206, 212, 225, 231, 249 285, 286, 289, 291

Mathews, A., 57, 61, 62, 65, 70, 73, 292

Matjak, M., 129, 142

Matsumoto, D., 101, 102, 103, 106, 108, 109, 116, 117, 118, 120, 122

Mattes, R. D., 84, 94

Mattiske, J. K., 177, 186

May, J. G., 127, 139

Mayer, B., 245, 249

Mayhew, G., 18, 25, 231, 248, 263, 267

McAndrew, F. T., 103, 121

McAnulty, R. D., 259, 268

McCabe, M., 235, 249, 255, 256, 258, 268

McCabe, R. E., 65, 71

McCarter, R., 99, 122

McCarthy, P. R., 62, 70

McCauley, C. R., xii, xvi, 9, 12, 14, 20, 23, 24, 26, 28, 31, 34, 36, 53, 55, 69, 72, 77, 82, 93, 95, 100, 113, 120, 121, 128, 140, 145, 155, 162, 164, 175, 187, 193, 206, 208, 212, 214, 225, 226, 230, 235, 249, 250, 254, 257, 268, 269, 286, 291

McChesney, K. A., 134, 141

McClough, J. F., 234, 247

McDonald, A. S., 119, 187, 205

McDonough-Ryan, P., 161

McGrath, C., 162

McGuire, J. B., 249

McGuire, P. K., 157, 163

McKay, D., xii, xvi, 4, 12, 26, 27, 45, 47, 52, 52, 53, 56, 61, 62, 66, 70, 199, 206, 211, 213, 216, 217, 219, 222, 223, 224, 225, 226, 227, 256, 267, 275, 282, 288, 289, 290, 291

McKenna, F. P., 179, 190

McLean, C., 255, 270

McLean, P. D., 274, 282

McNally, R. J., 4, 36, 53, 55, 61, 71, 82, 87, 88, 94, 95, 171, 188, 212, 225

McNamara, C., 233, 249, 249

McNeil, D. W., 125, 141

Meade, R. C., 192, 208

Meehan, O., 163

Mehrabian, A., 124, 141

Mekdara, J. M., 86, 93

Melamed, B. G., 125, 141, 176, 188, 199, 206

Melles, R., 253, 269, 270

Mensour, B., 163

Mentzel, H. J., 162

Menzies, R. G., 194, 202, 207, 276, 277, 282,

Merckelbach, H., 33, 34, 52, 53, 169, 171, 176, 186, 188, 192, 194, 195, 197, 205, 207, 225, 249, 273, 274, 282, 286, 291

Merikangas, K., 129, 140

Merkelbach, H., 176, 177, 187

Meunier, S. A., xii, 49, 55, 58, 64, 65, 71, 72, 192, 208, 280, 283

Miguel, E. C., 164

Miles, F., 256, 268

Miles, S., 136, 141

Miller, S. B., 11, 22, 26

Miller, W. I., 11, 19, 22, 23, 26, 230, 243, 246, 249

Millman, L., 14, 28, 88, 95, 218, 226

Mills, D. E., 199, 208

Miltner, W. H., 61, 71, 129, 130, 137, 142

Mineka, S., 63, 65, 71, 73, 171, 186, 189, 194, 202, 207

Mirenberg, M. C., 11, 27

Mogg, K., 61, 69, 71, 256, 268

Moll, F. T., 27

Moll, J., 16, 27

Montagne, B., 287, 291

Moody, E. W., 91, 92

Moretz, M. W., xii

Much, N. C., 13, 29, 107, 122

Mulkens, S. A. N., 34, 43, 49, 52, 53, 82, 92, 172, 175, 176, 177, 186, 188, 195, 207, 215, 224, 286, 291

Münchau, A., 260, 268

Mundy, P., 78, *94*
Murdock, T., 62, *70*
Muris, P., 33, 34, 36, *52, 53,* 171, 175,
    177, 180, *187, 188,* 193, *205,*
    225, 235, 236, 245, 249, 263,
    267, 274, *281*
Murphy, F., 36, *56,* 235, 242, *250, 251*
Murphy, T., 36, *53, 56,* 235, 236, 240,
    241, 242, 246, 249, *250, 251*
Murray, C., 243, *250*
Murray, E., 170, 171, *188*
Murray, L. K., 242, *250*

Nabi, R. L., 185, *188*
Nat, R., *206*
Navarette C. D., 20, *27*
Nederkoorn, S., *53, 225, 249*
Nefs, J., *270*
Nelson, R. O., 221, *224*
Nelson-Gray, R. O., 290, *291*
Nemeroff, C. J., 14, 17, 21, 22, *27, 28,*
    58, 59, *71, 72,* 81, 90, *94, 95,*
    121, 218, 226, 254, 269
Neuberg, S., 23, *28*
Nevid, J. S., 256, *268*
Nikolaou, V., 242, *249*
Nikzad, M., 260, *268*

O'Doherty, J., 152, *165*
O'Dwyer, A. M., *163*
Öhman, A., 61, 65, *71,* 171, *189*
Okifuji, A., 84, *94*
Olatunji, B. O., xii, xvi, 4, 10, 11, 12,
    14, 15, 17, 21, *27,* 31, 32, 33, 34,
    35, 36, 37, 38, 40, 42, 43, 46, 47,
    48, 49, *54, 56,* 57, 60, 64, 68, *70,*
    71, 73, 82, 86, 88, *94,* 114, 115,
    121, 134, *142,* 193, 194, 197,
    200, *207,* 215, 216, 217, *225,*
    255, 262, 268, 274, 275, 280,
    283, 285, 288, *291*
Olivieri, G., *165, 209*
Ollendick, T. O., 290, *290*
Olmsted, M. P., *248*
O'Neil, H. K., 44, *53,* 193, *206*
Onsrad, S., *96*
Opplinger, P. A., 195, *207*

Ortony, A., 198, *207*
Öst, L. G., 62, *70,* 85, *94,* 134, *142,*
    191, 192, 194, *207,* 271, 277,
    282, 283, 286, *291*
Oster, H., 78, 79, 85, *94,* 95
O'Sullivan, M., *93, 119*
Ott, U., *164, 165, 209*
Oxford American Dictionary, 128, *142*

Page, A. C., xii, xvi, 33, 49, *53, 54,* 85,
    94, 136, *142,* 191, 192, 194, 195,
    198, 199, 200, 201, 204, *205,*
    206, 207, 208, 277, *283*
Pagnoni, G., *162*
Palomba, D., *165,* 286, *291*
Panayiotou, G., 125, *142*
Pancer, S. M., 83, *95*
Panitz, D., *161*
Paquette, V., 157, *163*
Paradiso, S., 83, *94,* 153, *163*
Park, J. H., 20, *25*
Park, L., 13, *29,* 107, *122*
Parker, J. D., 242, *247*
Passant, U., *163*
Patel, S. P., 36, *55,* 215, *227*
Patterson, M. J., 78, *92*
Payne, K. A., 253, *268*
Peduto, A., *165, 209*
Pelham, B. W., 11, *27*
Perrett, D. I., 242, *250*
Perroud, A., 66, *70*
Peters, M. L., xii, 32, 36, *52, 56,* 63, 64,
    70, 179, *189,* 261, 263, 264, *267,*
    270
Peterson, R. A., 88, *95*
Phan, K. L., 159, 160, *163*
Phelps, E. A., 222, *225*
Phillips, E. S., 15, *24*
Phillips, M. L., 15, *27,* 31, *54,* 83, *94,*
    150, 151, 156, 158, 159, *163,*
    230, *250*
Philos, D. R., *96*
Picerno, M. R., 59, *72*
Pickering, A. D., 62, *72*
Pickersgill, M. J., 169, *186*
Pilner, P., 80, *93*
Pinard, G., 218, *226*

Pinker, S., 11, *27*
Pizarro, D. A., 21, *26*
Plailly, J., *165*
Player, A. B., 134, *141*
Pliner, P., 14, *25*
Plutchik, R., 10, *27*, 79, *94*, 127, *142*, 145, *163*
Polivy, J., *248, 249*
Porro, C., *162*
Power, M., 15, 17, *27*, 54, 82, *94*, 230, 243, *250*
Prabhu, G. G., *119, 187, 205*
Pradelli, S., *162*
Pratt, A., 83, *95*
Pratt, M., W., 83, *95*
Prkachin, K. M., 199, *208*
Prunty, M. J., 62, *72*
Przuntek, H., 83, *96*, 150, *165*
Przymus, D. E., 107, 117, *122*
Pu, J., 136, *139*
Purdon, C., 213, *224*
Pyszczynski, T., 13, *24, 25, 29*

Quigley, J. F., 289, *291*
Quigley, J., 33, 36, 49, *55*
Quigley, K. S., 222, *225*

Rabie, T., 23, *24*, 254, *267*
Rachman, S. J., 214, *225*
Rachman, S., 66, 67, *71*, 84, 85, 90, 93, *95*, 127, *142*, 176, *189*, 192, 194, 202, *208*, 218, *226*, 258, *268*
Rada, H., 130, 137, *139*
Radomsky, A. S., 66, *71*, 176, *189, 225, 226*
Raghavan, C., 50, *52*
Randall, P. K., 91, *96*, 221, *226*, 274, *283*
Rapson, R. L., 150, *162*
Rasmussen, S. A., *224*
Rassin, E., *53, 225*, 236, *249*
Rathus, S. A., 256, 260, *268*
Rauch, S. L., 150, 156, 157, *161, 163, 164*
Rauner, M., 258, *266*
Rausch, M., 83, *96*, 150, *165*
Reardon, J., 36, *52*

Regier, D. A., 288, *291*
Reichenbach, J., *162*
Reiman, E. M., 154, *163*
Reinecke, A., 61, 62, *72*
Reiss, S., 36, *55*, 88, *95*
Reissing, E. D., 261, *269*
Rempel, J. K., 258, 259, *269*
Remschmidt, H., 82, *95*
Renner, F., 182, *189*
Rescorla, R. A., 91, *95*
Riggs, D. S., 211, *225*
Rinck, M., 61, 62, 69, *72*
Risberg, J., *163*
Riskind, J. H., 39, *55*, 59, *72*, 89, *95*
Rizzolatti, G., *165*
Robertson, N., 178, 179, *186*
Robin, O., 130, 137, *139*
Robinson, J. L., 136, *139*
Robinson, M. D., 199, *208*
Robinson, R. G., *94, 163*
Roca, M., *119*
Rolls, E. T., 147, 148, 160, *164*
Rosen, A., 18, *27*
Rosenstein, D., 79, *95*
Roth, W. T., 61, 69
Royal College of Psychiatrists, 232, *250*
Royet, J.-P., *165*
Rozin, P., xii, xvi, 5, 9, 10, 11, 12, 13, 14, 15, 16, 17, 18, 20, 21, 22, 23, 24, 25, 26, *27*, 28, 31, 32, 34, 36, 40, 41, 43, 48, *53, 55*, 58, 59, 69, *71, 72*, 77, 79, 80, 81, 82, 83, 84, 85, 86, 87, 88, 90, 93, *94, 95*, 96, 100, 101, 106, 107, 113, 114, *120, 121*, 127, 128, *140, 142*, 145, 155, *162, 164*, 172, 174, 175, 181, *187, 189*, 193, 195, 199, *206, 208*, 212, 214, 218, *220, 225, 226*, 229, 230, 232, 234, 235, 243, 246, 249, *250*, 254, 256, 257, 262, 264, 265, 266, 268, 269, 286, 287, 288, *291*
Ruderman, A. J., 231, *250*
Ruetz, P. P., 192, *208*
Russell, G. F. M., 231, *250*
Russell, J. A., 100, 101, 103, 104, 106, 107, 115, 116, 117, *121, 122*, 124, *142*

Russell, L., *247*
Russell, T., *163*
Rust, J., 264, *269*
Rutherford, E., 61, *71*

Sabatinelli, D., *161*
Salkovskis, P. M., 34, 49, *56, 58, 62, 70,*
    73, 90, 96, 177, 178, 179, 180,
    181, 183, 184, *187, 189,* 215,
    224, 286, 287, *291, 292*
Sammer, G., *164, 165*
Sanchez, P., *249*
Sanftner, J. L., 243, *250*
Sanovio, E., 215, *226*
Sarlo, M., 155, *165,* 286, *291*
Sato, K., 116, 117, *121*
Savage, C. R., *164*
Sawchuk, C. N., xii, xvi, 6, 10, 11, 15,
    17, *27, 31,* 32, 33, 34, 35, 36, 37,
    38, 39, 40, 41, 43, 44, 46, 47, 49,
    53, 54, 55, 56, 57, 58, 62, 65, 66,
    71, 72, 82, 86, 88, *94,* 114, 115,
    121, 134, *142,* 176, 177, *189,*
    192, 193, 194, 197, 200, *206,*
    207, 208, 209, 212, 215, 216,
    225, 226, 227, 255, *262, 268*
Sax, K. W., *161*
Schaal, B., 78, *96*
Schafe, G. E., 84, *96*
Schafer, A., *29,* 82, *96,* 154, 155, 157,
    164, 196, 208, 291
Schaller, M., 20, 23, *25, 28*
Scheinle, A., 214, *226*
Scherer, K. R., 23, *29,* 112, 113, 117,
    121, 122
Schienle, A., xii, 2, 6, 17, 23, *29,* 35, 36,
    55, 96, 132, 136, *142,* 154, 155,
    156, 157, 158, 159, 160, 161, *164,*
    165, 196, 197, *208, 209,* 236,
    239, 250, 286, 287, *289, 291*
Schiller, D., 23, *28*
Schimmack, U., 24, *26*
Schmeichel, B. J., 136, *139*
Schmidt, H., 34, *53,* 175, *188*
Schmidt, S., *119*
Schmidt, U. H., 235, 242, 244, *247,*
    250, 251

Schneier, F. R., *282*
Schouten, E., 34, *53,* 171, 176, *188,*
    273, 282
Schroeder, U., 151, 158, 159, *162, 164*
Schutters, S., 287, *291*
Schwartz, G. E., 154, *163*
Schwartz, M. D., 84, *96*
Schwartz, S. A., 274, *281*
Schwartz, S. H., 264, *269*
Schwarz, N., 215, *226*
Scott, S. K., *94, 163*
Scozzafava, J. E., 134, *141*
Seelen, H. A., *270*
Seligman, M. E. P., 63, *72,* 87, *96,* 170,
    189
Senior, C., 27, 31, *54, 163,* 230, *250*
Serafini, M., *162*
Serpell, L., 231, 236, 243, 244, 246, *251*
Shäfer, A., *250*
Shafran, R., 176, *189, 218, 226,* 231,
    248, 256, 268
Shamsuzzamon, A. S. M., *205*
Shapira, N. A., 15, *26,* 155, 157, *164,*
    165, 196, 209
Shapiro, K. L., 60, *72*
Share, D. L., 80, *96*
Sharrock, R., 179, *190*
Shear, M. K., 271, *281*
Sherman, G. D., 136, *142*
Sherman, M. F., 33, 36, *52,* 195, *205,*
    195, 205, 289, *291*
Sherman, N. C., 36, *55,* 289, *291*
Shioiri, T., *120*
Shoyer, B., 62, *70*
Shweder, R. A., 13, *29,* 107, *122*
Siegal, M. S., 18, *26, 29,* 80, *96*
Simonds, L. M., 36, *55,* 215, *227*
Sineshaw, T., 103, *119*
Singh, L., 20, *28,* 86, *95*
Sini, B., *119*
Skinner, B. F., *3*
Skre, I., 87, *96*
Smith, G., *163*
Smith, G. R., 127, *139*
Smith, J. J., 192, *208*
Smits, J. A., 35, *54,* 91, *96,* 221, *226,*
    274, 275, *283*

Sochting, I., *282*
Solomon, S., 13, *25, 29*
Somers, V. K., 198, *205*
Someya, S., *120*
Sookman, D., 218, *225, 226*
Sorenson, E. R., 99, *119*
Sotrilli, S., 243, *251*
Soussignan, R., 78, *96*
Spellmeyer, G., *206*
Spence, E. L., 129, *143*
Spielberger, C. D., 174, *189*
Sprengelmeyer, R., 14, 16, *29*, 83, *96*,
    150, 151, 158, 159, *165*
Stahl, R., *164*
Stanley, J., 130, 136, *142*
Stark, R., 23, *29*, 35, 36, *55*, 82, *96*,
    132, 136, *142*, 154, 155, 157,
    164, 165, 196, *208, 209*, 214,
    226, 250, *291*
Starkowski, S. M., *161*
Stegagno, L., 286, *291*
Steiner, J. E., 78, 79, 93, *96*, 131, *142*
Sternberger, L. G., 176, *186*, 217, *224*
Sterner, U., 134, *142*, 191, *207*, 271,
    277, *283*
Stevens, S., *206*
Stice, E., 245, *251*
Stolerman, I. P., 84, *93*
Stone, M. J., 84, *93*
Stone-Elander, S., 157, *162*
Straube, T., *162*
Strauss, M., 59, *72*, 89, *95*
Strongman, K. T., 243, *251*
Stroop, J. R., 61, 66, 67, *72*, 178, *189*,
    189
Stunkard, A., 233, 234, *251*
Stzahl, R., *162*
Sullivan, M. W., 77, 78, 79, 82, *96*
Summerfeldt, L. J., 213, *224*
Surguladze, S. A., 152, *165*
Suzuki, N., 106, *121*

Tan, B. J., xii
Tang, S., *120*
Tangney, J. P., 243, 244, *250, 251*
Tantow, B., 17, *25*, 236, *248*
Tata, P. R., 62, *72*

Taussig, H. N., 130, *139*
Taylor, G. J., 242, *247*
Taylor, S. F., 159, *163*
Taylor, S., 41, *55*, 88, *96*, 213, 223,
    224, 226, 282
Teachman, B. A., 15, *29*, 39, 49, *55*,
    56, 57, 58, 60, 65, *73*, 83, 85, 87,
    97, 193, 194, 195, 197, 202, 204,
    209, 212, 218, *227*
Telch, M. J., 91, *96*, 221, *226*, 274, *283*
Templer, D. I., 82, *96*
Tenney, N., 62, *73*
ter Kuile, M. M., 261, *269, 270*
Thayer, J. F., 136, *141, 291*
Thomas, E., 136, *141*
Thomas, G. V., 171, *187*
Thomas, K., 19, *29*
Thomas, S., 220, *224, 247*, 289, 290
Thordarson, D. S., 176, *189*, 216, 218,
    226, 282
Thorndike, R. M., 31, 38, *53*, 199, *206*
Thorpe, S. J., 34, 36, 49, *55, 56, 58*, 62,
    73, 90, *96*, 177, 178, 179, 180,
    181, *189*, 215, *227*, 287, *292*
Thyer, B. A., 191, 192, *209*
Tierney, S., 34, *53*, 175, *188*
Tiller, J. M., 244, *250*
Tinti, C., *119*
Tolin, D. F., xii, xvi, 17, *27*, 31, 33, 35,
    36, 38, 44, 45, 46, 47, 48, 49, 50,
    54, 55, 56, 58, 59, 60, 62, *72, 73*,
    176, *189*, 192, 193, 194, 195,
    197, *208, 209*, 212, 213, 216,
    218, *227*, 255, *268*
Tomarken, A. J., 63, *73*
Tomkins, S. S., 10, 19, *29*, 99, *122*, 127,
    142
Ton, V., 101, 102, 103, 109, 116, 117, *118*
Tooby, J., 133, *139*
Torgersen, S., *96*
Toyama, N., 80, *97*
Tranel, D., 134, *142*
Trautman, J., 264, *269*
Travis, M. J., *165*
Treasure, J. L., 36, *53, 56*, 235, 236,
    242, 243, 244, 249, *250, 251*
Treneer, C. M., 84, *92*

Trezise, I., 179, *190*

Troop, N. A., xiii , 36, *53, 56,* 231, 235, 236, 237, 238, 239, 240, 241, 242, 243, 244, 246, *248, 249, 251*

Truax, P., 274, *282*

Tsai, J. L., 107, 109, 110, 117, *122*

Tsao, S. D., 45, 47, *56,* 199, *206,* 216, 217, 219, 222, 223, *225, 227,* 289, *291*

Tucker, M., 82, *97, 175, 189*

Turetsky, B. I., *162*

Turner, T., *162*

Tyrell, R. A., *291*

Uhr, R., 241, 246, *251*

Vaitl, D., 23, 29, 36, *55,* 82, 96 125, 132, 136, *140, 142,* 154, 155, 157, *164, 165,* 196, *208, 209,* 214, *226, 250, 291*

Valentiner, D., 36, 49, *56*

van de Wiel, H. B., 260, 261, *270*

van den Berg, G., 178, *186*

van den Bergh, O., 87, *92,* 275, 276, *281, 283*

van den Hout, M. A., 62, *73,* 90, *92, 188,* 258, 265, 266, *267,* 276, *281,* 289, *290*

van der Heiden, S., 236, *249*

Van der Linden, M., 66, *70*

van der Velde, J., 253, 255, 256, *269*

van Honk, J., 287, *291*

van Lankveld, J. J. D. M., 253, 260, 261, *269, 270*

van Oppen, P., 82, *97*

van Overveld, W. J. M., 32, 33, 35, 42, *56, 179, 189,* 261, 264, *267*

van Rijsoort, S., 178, *186*

Van Strien, T., *251*

Vanderhallen, I., 263, *267*

Vansteenwegen, D., 275, *283*

Veijenborg, P. T., *269*

Vernet-Maury, E., 130, 137, *139*

Vernon, L., 50, *52*

Vervliet, B., 275, *283*

Vianna, E. P. M., 134, *142*

Vingerhoets, A. J., *192, 209*

Vlaeyen, J. W., 262, *270*

Vlieland, C. V., 261, *269*

Vlielander, M., 245, *249*

Voet, W., 22, 28, 254, *269*

Vogele, C., *206*

Vollenbroek, J., 34, *52,* 82, *92,* 175, *186,* 215, *224*

Vorage, I., 265, 267, 276, *281,* 289, *290*

Vrana, S. R., xiii, 6, 124, 125, 127, 129, 131, 132, 136, 137, *139, 141, 142, 143,* 209, 263, *270*

Wager, T., 159, *163*

Wagner, P., 244, *251*

Walden, T., 78, *97*

Wallbott, H. G., 23, 29, 112, 117, *122*

Waller, G., 243, *250*

Walls, M. M., 32, 37, *56, 176, 189,* 216, *227*

Walter, B., 23, 29, 35, 36, *55,* 82, 96, 132, 136, *142,* 154, 155, 157, *164, 165,* 196, *208, 209,* 214, *226, 250, 291*

Ware, J., 172, 173, 174, 184, *190,* 231, *251*

Warkentin, S., *163*

Warrenburg, S., 130, *140*

Watkins, E., 256, *268*

Watson, D., 223, *227,* 288, *292*

Watson, J. B., 170, *190*

Watts, F. N., 57, *73, 179, 190, 292*

Webb, K., 183, *190, 198, 209*

Webster, M. M., 84, *92*

Weerts, T. C., 176, *188*

Weijenborg, P. T. M., 261, *269*

Weijmar Schultz, W. C., 260, 261, 264, *267, 270*

Weindl, A., *162*

Weise, D., *13*

Weiss, T., 61, *71*

Weisskoff, R. M., *161*

Weissman, M. M., 215, *227*

Welkowitz, L. A., *282*

Wenzel, A., 179, *190, 205*

Westen, D., 213, *224*

Westenberg, H. G., 287, *291*

Westendorf, D. A., 49, *55, 192, 208*

Westendorf, D. H., 58, 65, *72*

Westerlund, J., 61, *73*

Wheatley, T., 13, *29*, 258, *270*

Wheeler, D. J., 59, *72*

White, J., 61, 69

Whittal, M. L., *282*

Wicker, B., 151, 158, 159, *165*

Wiemer, M. J., *282*

Wik, G., 157, *162*

Wikstrom, J., 61, *73*

Willekes, C., 261, *269*

Willems, J. L., xiii, 35, 38, *54*, 274, *283*

Williams, J. M. G., 57, 60, 61, *73*, 289, *292*

Williams, L. M., 151, 152, 158, 159, *163*, *165*, 196, *209*

Williams, N. L., xiii, 17, 21, *27*, 32, 36, 39, 40, *52*, *54*, 56, 59, 61, *70*, *72*, 134, *142*, 200, *207*

Williams, R. M., 179, *188*

Williams, S. C. R., *165*

Williams-Avery, 199, *208*

Willoughby, J., 78, *94*

Wilson, D. B., 242, *247*

Wilson, G. D., 130, *141*

Wilson, G. T., 221, *224*

Wilson-Cohn, C., 106, *122*

Wing, R. R., 231, *248*

Winn, S., *247*

Winnicki, M., *205*

Winston, J. S., 152, *165*

Witvliet, C. V., 124, *143*

Wolff, G., 246, *251*

Wolman, I., 260, *266*

Wolpe, L., 174, *190*

Woodmore, K., 192, *208*

Woods, C. M., 35, 36, *56*, 213, *227*

Woods, S. W., 271, *281*

Woody, S. R., xiii, 15, *29*, 44, 45, 48, 49, 50, 56, 57, 58, 60, *73*, 83, 85, 87, 97, 193, 194, 195, 197, 198, 202, 204, 205, 209, 212, 216, 218, *227*, 255, 257, 267, *270*

Worhunsky, P., 58, *73*, 218, *227*

Wright, P., 155, *165*, 196, *209*

Wronska, J., 82, *97*, *292*

Wrzcsniewski, A., 86, *96*

Xu, J., 20, *25*

Yartz, A. R., 129, 131, *143*, 256, *270*

Yijun, L., *164*

Yik, M. S. M., 101, 103, 106, 107, 116, *122*

Yitzchak, B. M., *269*

Yoo, S. H., 118, *120*

Young, A. W., 15, *25*, *27*, *29*, 83, 93, 94, 96, 156, *161*, *163*, *165*

Yrizarry, N., 106, 107, *122*

Zalma, A., 244, *249*

Zandbergen, M., 253, *269*, *270*

Zeitlin, S. B., 61, *71*

Zellner, D. A., 84, 85, 86, *96*

Zhong, C. B., 21, *29*, 218, 223, *227*

Zhu, J., 130, *140*

Zillmann, D., 195, *207*

Zilski, J., 91, *92*

Zinbarg, R., 194, 202, *207*

Zwaal, C., 199, *208*

SUBJECT INDEX

Abstract representations of disgust, 82
Adaptation
    evolutionary theory, 23
    research needs, 21–22
    role of disgust, 87, 212
Agoraphobia, 177
Agreeableness, 195
Amygdala, 15, 147–148, 149, 150, 151,
        152, 153, 154, 155, 156, 157,
        159–160, 196
Anatomy of Disgust (Miller), 11
Anger
    disgust and, 138
    early research and theory, 10–11
    psychophysiology, 138
    research, 5
    See also CAD triad hypothesis
Animal-related disgust
    assessment of disgust sensitivity, 24,
        27, 44
    body-to-soul preadaptation theory
        of, 12–13
    centrality of, in emotion of disgust,
        172, 231
    characteristics of feared animals,
        181–182, 198–199
    conceptual basis, 12–13, 193
    conditioning experiences in develop-
        ment of, 85
    contamination fear in, 212, 216, 257
    cultural differences in, 111, 115
    disgust in BII phobia and, 197,
        198–199
    disgust in eating disorders and, 237
    disgust-related sexual dysfunction, 257
    disgust sensitivity and, 174–175,
        180, 181, 216, 217

etiological theories, 170–171
evolutionary theory and, 19
factor analysis studies, 172–174
future research directions, 17,
        180–181, 185
maintenance of, through stimulus
        generalization, 90
outcome beliefs, 179–180
predatory status of animal and,
        172–173, 174, 180–181
prevalence, 169
role of disgust in acquisition of,
        182–185, 185
See also Spider phobia
Anorexia nervosa, 230, 234, 245. *See
    also* Eating disorders
Anterior cingulate cortex, 149, 152,
        156, 157
Anterior insula, 15, 151, 152
Anxiety
    attentional biases in, 61
    in avoidance disorders, 6
    client description of disgust as, 4
    clinical significance of disgust in, 15, 58
    cognitive aspects of disgust and, 57–58
    cognitive processes research, 57
    cultural differences in disgust sensi-
        tivity and, 114
    decrease of disgust during treatment
        for disorders of, 274–275
    disgust sensitivity and, 34, 36,
        38–39, 44, 49, 175, 196, 212
    effects of induced disgust on, 183–185
    induced, disgust experience and,
        183–184
    spider fear and disgust sensitivity
        and, 177

Assessment
attentional bias assessment, 61
behavioral, 43–48
case data tradition in research, 3
dimensional aspects of diagnostic conceptualization of disgust, 288
disgust sensitivity as unique clinical
construct, 48–50
disgust sensitivity measurement, 31,
88
electromyography of facial response
to disgust, 131–132
emotional desynchrony, 127–128
facial expression in infants, 78–79
future research directions, 42–43, 48,
50, 51–52
historical and technical evolution,
31–32
instruments, 32, 40–41, 50–51. *See
also specific instrument*
memory biases, 65
obsessive–compulsive disorder, 215
obstacles to disgust recognition, 4
psychophysiology of emotional experience, 127
self-reported data, 43, 47, 49–50, 279
state–trait distinctions, 50–51
See also Disgust Scale
Attentional processes
biases in disgust, 60–62, 67–68
disgust-related sexual dysfunction, 256
facial expression recognition, 153
research needs, 62
Autonomic nervous system, 124–125,
134–137
Avoidance
appetitive and aversive motivation,
124, 128
assessment, 35
behavioral assessment of disgust sensitivity, 44
clinical significance of disgust in disorders of, 6
disgust and, 255
habituation therapy outcomes,
220–221
interpretive biases, 62–63

negative reinforcement of disgust, 89
in sexual behavior, 255
startle reflex response, 128–131
treatment for disgust-based problems,
278

Basal ganglia, 15, 83, 152, 156, 157, 158
Benign masochism, 23–24
BII. *See* Blood-injection-injury fear
Binge eating, 230–231. *See also* Eating
disorders
Biological functioning
acquisition of disgust, 87–88
assessment of emotional desynchrony, 127–128
behavioral dispositions in disgust,
131–134, 138
BII-fear response, 200
corrugator muscle activity in emotional processing, 131
cultural differences in physiological
response to disgust, 109–110
defensive reflexes in sexual dysfunction, 255–256
disgust sensitivity and, 36
facial expression in emotional
responding, 135
fainting, 134, 191–192, 198, 199, 200
fainting treatment, 277
gastric myoelectric response, 134
prolonged exposure to disgust-
eliciting cues, 222
psychophysiological assessment of
emotional experience,
126–127
psychophysiological research to date,
123
psychophysiological response to picture viewing, 136–137
psychophysiology of emotion,
124–126, 138
research needs, 138–139
response to odors, 137
self-reported disgust correlated with,
279
sexual arousal disorders, 259–260
startle reflex response, 128–131

See also Neurophysiology; Vaginismus

Blood-injection-injury (BII) fear
    animal-related disgust and, 12
    attentional bias for disgust, 62
    clinical features, 191
    clinical significance of disgust in,
        194–195, 274, 286
    conditioning experiences in onset of,
        85
    cultural differences in, 114–115
    decrease of disgust during treatment
        of, 274–275
    definition, 191
    disgust response in, 192–193,
        195–197
    disgust sensitivity and, 31, 34, 37,
        38, 44–47, 48, 196–197, 202
    fainting response, 134, 191–192,
        198–202
    fainting treatment, 277
    fear–disgust linkage in, 197–198,
        202–204
    future research directions, 204
    information processing biases in,
        63–64, 65, 66, 67
    integrative model, 202–204
    neurophysiology of disgust elicitation
        and, 158, 196
    prevalence, 191
    psychophysiological response to pic-
        ture viewing, 136–137
    spider fear and disgust sensitivity
        and, 177

Body-related disgust
    assessment instruments, 34
    body envelope violations, 12, 193,
        196–197
    body holes and, 22
    body-to-soul preadaptation theory of
        disgust, 12
    core disgust, 254
    cultural differences, 111
    in eating disorders, 237
    future research directions, 22
    sexual behavior and, 254
    See also Blood-injection-injury (BII)
        fear

Body-to-soul preadaptation theory, 12–13

Brain imaging
    advantages of disgust as research sub-
        ject, 14–15
    applications, 146
    during disgust elicitation, 153–156
    disgust in geriatric population, 83
    disgust perception studies, 150–153
    eating disorder, 241
    findings in disgust studies, 158–160
    future research directions, 16, 161
    implications for functional models of
        neural processing, 158–161
    technical basis, 146

Bulimia nervosa, 230, 234, 245. See also
    Eating disorders

Burkina Faso, 111

CAD triad hypothesis, 13, 19, 107

Canada, 104, 106–107

Cancer treatment-associated food aver-
    sion, 84

Cardiovascular function
    emotional responding, 134–135, 138
    emotional response to picture view-
        ing, 136–137, 199
    fainting, 134, 192
    response to odors, 137

Cerebellum, 154

Chemotherapy, 84–85

Childhood and adolescence
    development of disgust in, 79–82
    disgustingness beliefs about spiders,
        spider fear and, 177

China, 106–107, 116

Cigarette smoking, 20

Cingulate gyrus, 151

Cognitive–behavioral therapy
    common mechanisms for emotional
        disorder treatment, 272
    conceptualization of emotion in,
        271–272
    decrease of disgust during, 274–276
    disgust as outcome predictor,
        273–274
    disgust treatment, 276–278, 290
    implications of disgust, 273

Cognitive–behavioral therapy (*Continued*)
    maladaptive cognition interventions, 276–277
    for obsessive–compulsive disorder, 213, 272
    for sexual dysfunction, 265–266
Cognitive functioning
    anxiety–disgust linkage, 57–58
    in anxiety disorders, 57
    autonomic nervous system and, 135
    bias for disgusting stimuli in phobia, 178–179
    conceptual reorientation, 265–266
    conditioned aversion, 84–85
    contagion threat perception, 58
    dietary restraint, 241–242
    disgust development in adulthood, 82–83
    disgustingness beliefs about spiders, spider fear and, 177–178
    disgust research to date, 57
    effects of induced disgust on interpretational bias, 184
    expectancy evaluations, 90
    future research directions, 68–69
    learning processes in disgust acquisition, 85–87
    looming vulnerability to threat, 59–60
    outcome beliefs in animal phobics, 179–180
    perceived coping ability, 58
    sexual dysfunction, disgust-related, 256–257
    sympathetic magic, 58–59
    vulnerability to disgust, assessment of, 38–40
    See also Information processing
Conceptual reorientation, 265–266
Conditioned acquisition of disgust
    animal phobia etiology, 170
    associative processes, 84–85
    evaluative processes, 86–87, 219–220
    negative reinforcement, 89–90
    stimulus generalization, 90
Conscientiousness, 195
Contamination beliefs and fears
    adaptation to disgust, 21–22
    in animal phobias, 212

biased threat appraisal, 58
bias for contamination words in phobia, 178–179
childhood development and perception of, 79–81
clinical significance of disgust in psychopathology, 58, 211, 222–223
conceptual models, 21
defensive reflexes arising from, 255
disgust conceptualization of vaginismus, 261–263
disgust sensitivity and, 47
domains of disgust and, 216–217
emergence of germ theory and, 19
in food-based concepts of disgust, 229–230
future research directions, 16–17, 18, 21, 223
intergroup disgust, 20
looming vulnerability to threat, 59–60
maintenance of disgust-related responding, 89–90
material essence, 21
moral contagion, 21
in obsessive–compulsive disorder, 15, 211, 213–217, 223
perceived persistence, 80, 81
removal of object form source of contamination, 59
role of disgust, 87, 257
self-perceived coping ability, 58
sex differences, 82, 215–216
sexual behavior and, 254
sexual dysfunction treatment considerations, 265
spiritual essence, 21
sympathetic magic beliefs, 58–59, 212–213, 218
use of disgust in research on, 14
Contempt
    disgust and, 19
    See also CAD triad hypothesis
Coping ability, cognitive biases in self-evaluation, 58
Core disgust, 100, 212, 229
    sexuality and, 254–257

Corrugator supercilii muscle, 131, 132, 138
Covariation biases, 63, 64, 65, 68–69
Cuba, 112
Cultural differences
    CAD triad hypothesis, 107
    development of disgust, 18, 88
    elicitors of disgust, 110–114
    in emotional experience and expression, 99–100
    future directions in disgust research, 18, 20–21, 23, 117–118, 286
    historical development of eating behaviors, 18–19
    intensity of facial expression of emotion, 108–109, 117
    isolated cultures, 104–105, 117
    physiological response to disgust
    recognition of facial emotional expression, 101–107, 116–117
    relation between fear and disgust sensitivity, 114–115
    relived emotion task, 107–108
    sociomoral disgust in sexual dysfunction, 257–258
    translation issues, 115–116
    universal theories of emotion, 99, 101
Cuneus, 151

Danger ideation reduction therapy, 276–277
Darwinian algorithm, 133
Death
    body-to-soul preadaptation theory of disgust, 12, 13
    disgust assessment instruments, 34, 37
    future directions in disgust research, 17
Defensive reflexes in sexual dysfunction, 255–256
Definition of disgust, xv, 4, 193, 212, 229–230
    assessment of emotional desynchrony and, 127–128
    core disgust, 100
    diagnostic conceptualization, 288
    disgust as basic emotion, 100
    state–trait distinctions, 272–273

Dehumanization, 20
Depression
    cognitive–behavioral therapy, 272
    disgust sensitivity and, 36
    shame and, 243, 244
Desynchrony, emotional, 127–128, 132–133
Development of disgust
    in adulthood, 82–83, 91
    associative conditioning in, 84–85
    biological factors, 87, 88
    in childhood and adolescence, 79–82
    cultural differences, 18
    determinants of, 77–78, 83
    emergence of sympathetic magic, 81
    genetic factors, 87, 88
    in infancy, 78–79
    language development and, 81
    learning processes in, 85–86
    maintenance of disgust, 89–90
    research needs, 17–18, 91–92
    sociocultural factors, 88
    stimulus generalization and, 90
Diagnostic and Statistical Manual of Mental Disorders, 288
Disease-avoidance model, 4, 15
    disgust–fear relationship and, 58
    disgust in animal phobia and, 90, 181–182, 231
    eating disorders and, 231
Disgust and Contamination Sensitivity Questionnaire, 32–34, 50–51
Disgust Emotion Scale, 37–38, 50–51, 176
Disgust Propensity and Sensitivity Scale, 40–43, 50–51, 177
Disgust Questionnaire, 235
Disgust Scale, 14, 34–37, 49, 50–51, 155, 216, 219, 235
Disgust Sensitivity Questionnaire, 235
Domains of disgust
    childhood development, 81–82
    contamination fear and, 216–217
    current conceptualization, 21, 100, 212
    eating disorders and, 237
    sexual behavior and, 254–258
Dyspareunia, 262

Eating disorders
  clinical features, 230–231
  dietary restraint and, 238–239,
    241–242, 245, 246
  disease-avoidance model and, 231
  disgust linkage, 230, 245–247
  fear and disgust responses, 238–242,
    246
  fear as basis of, 231
  future research directions, 280
  individual differences in disgust and,
    36, 235–238
  moral values and, 234–235, 246
  recognition of emotional expressions
    and, 242
  severe life events in etiology of,
    244–245
  shame in, 243–245, 246–247
  symptoms of, disgust and, 232–234
  treatment, 278
Electrogastrography, 134
Electromyography, 131–132, 263–264
Emotional functioning
  affective neuroscience research,
    14–15
  appetitive and aversive motivation,
    124, 128
  associated context-specific behav-
    iors, 124, 125
  behavioral dispositions in disgust,
    131–134
  cognitive–behavioral therapy con-
    ceptualization, 271–272
  cognitive restraint and, 241–242
  common features of
    cognitive–behavioral therapy
    for problems of, 272
  corrugator supercilii muscle activity
    in, 131
  cultural differences in facial expres-
    sion recognition, 101–107
  cultural influences, 99–100
  definition of disgust, 4
  desynchrony, 127–128, 132–133
  difficulty in recognition of emotion
    expression, 14–15, 16, 83,
    157, 242

disgust as basic emotion, 100
evolution of disgust theory, 9–10
experimental evocation, 125
gastric myoelectrical response, 134
implications of disgust in treatment
    for disorders of, 273–278
motivational substrate, 124
neuropsychological models, 147–150
pattern of events in disgust experi-
    ence, 22–23
psychophysiological assessment,
    126–127
psychophysiological conceptualiza-
    tion, 124–126
reinforcement in, 148
relationship of disgust with other
    emotions, 19, 23
relived emotion task, 107–108, 137
role of brain imaging studies, 146, 147
in self-evaluation, 246
tripartite model, 271–272
universal theories, 99, 101, 117
valence and arousal in, 124
Estonia, 109
Evaluative learning
  acquisition of disgust, 86–87, 220
  concept, 219–220
  resistance to extinction, 275–276,
    289–290
Evolutionary theory
  animal-related disgust and, 19
  Darwin's disgust concepts, 9–10
  future directions in disgust research, 23
  neurophysiology of disgust and,
    145–146
  preparedness theory, 63, 87, 170–171
  role of disgust, 18, 87, 100, 145,
    246–247, 254, 257
Expectancy biases, 63–64, 65, 68–69, 90
  outcome beliefs in animal phobics,
    179–180
Experience of disgust, 22–23
Exposure therapy
  decrease of disgust during, 274–275
  for disgust, 289
  disgust reactions and, 273–274
  OCD treatment, 213

Extinction, 91
Extroversion, disgust sensitivity and, 36

Facial expression
    accuracy of disgust recognition,
        102–104, 108
    cultural differences, 88, 131
    cultural differences in emotion recog-
        nition, 101–107, 116–117
    of disgust, 100–101
    electromyography, 131–132
    free response studies, 105–106
    in infancy, 78–79
    intensity, 108–109, 117
    neuroanatomy of disgust perception,
        150–153
    neurophysiological development, 78
    neurophysiology of emotion recogni-
        tion, 149–150
    physiology of emotional responding,
        135
    recognition in eating disorders, 242
    recognition in Huntington's disease,
        14–15, 16, 83, 157
    social message in, 106–107, 125, 133
Fainting
    in blood-injection-injury phobia,
        134, 191–192, 198–202, 204
    fear–disgust relationship in,
        199–200, 202, 204
    physiology, 134, 191–192, 198, 199,
        200
    treatment, 277
    typology, 192
Fear
    classical conditioning, 170
    cognitive aspects of disgust and,
        57–58, 68
    conceptual relationship of disgust to,
        49–50, 194, 246
    cultural differences in disgust sensi-
        tivity and, 114–115
    decrease of, during cognitive–behav-
        ioral therapy, 274–275
    in dietary restraint, 241–242
    disgust in BII phobia and, 197–198,
        202–204

early research and theory, 10–11
    in eating disorders, 231, 246
    facial expressions, recognition of fear
        in, 151
    fainting and, 199–200, 202
    neurophysiology, 148, 151
    preparedness theory, 87, 170–171
    responses to eating disorder-relevant
        stimuli, 238–242
    See also Contamination beliefs and
        fears; Phobias
Fear Survey Schedule, 49, 174
Feces, 12, 17
Fight-or-flight response, 147–148
Food and eating
    body-to-soul preadaptation theory of
        disgust, 12
    in conceptual basis of disgust,
        229–230
    conditioned aversion, 84–85
    cultural differences in aversion, 111,
        113–114
    dietary restraint, 238–239, 241–242,
        245, 246
    disgust assessment instruments,
        32–34
    disgust in animal phobia and, 181
    historical development of disgust
        concepts, 18–19, 193
    neurophysiological aspects, 151
    obstacles to disgust research, 11
    oral expulsion of noxious substance,
        131, 133, 134, 145
    role of disgust, 100
    See also Eating disorders
Food Contamination Questionnaire,
    174, 175, 176–177
Frontal gyri, 158
Fusiform gyrus, 151, 153

General Disgust Questionnaire, 175, 176
Genetics, 87, 88, 198
Geriatric population, brain imaging
    studies, 83
Germany, 104, 109
Germ theory, 19
Greece, 106, 109, 111

Group behavior
    intergroup disgust, 20
    role of disgust, 23
    See also Interpersonal relations;
        Social psychology

Habituation
    decrease of disgust during OCD
        treatment, 275
    to disgust, 22, 220–222, 279,
        289–290
    fear–disgust relationship and, 178
    obsessive–compulsive disorder ther-
        apy, 213
    research needs, 278, 279
    sexual dysfunction treatment, 266
    strategies for unlearning disgust, 91
Happiness research, 5
Health behavior, gust and, 12
Hippocampus, 152, 155, 157
Hungary, 109
Huntington's disease, 14–15, 16, 83, 157
Hygiene
    behavioral assessment of disgust sen-
        sitivity, 43–44
    disgust assessment instruments, 34–35
    disgust in animal phobia and, 181
    disgust sensitivity and contamina-
        tion fear, 216, 217
    role of disgust, 87, 100
    washing compulsions, 156–157, 213

India, 105–106, 111, 112, 113–114
Individual differences
    future directions in disgust research, 21
    See also Sensitivity to disgust
Infancy, disgust in, 78–79
Inferior frontal gyrus, 151
Inferior occipital gyrus, 149
Information processing
    attentional biases, 60–62, 67–68
    biases in disgust, 57, 60
    findings in disgust studies, 67–68
    future research directions, 68–69
    interpretive biases, 62–65, 68–69, 184
    learning processes in disgust acquisi-
        tion, 85–86

memory biases, 65–67, 68
model of psychopathology, 60
Inhibition learning, 91
Injection fear. *See* Blood-injection-
    injury (BII) phobia
Inoculation, 92
Insula, 83, 149, 150, 151, 152, 153, 154,
    155, 156, 157, 158, 160, 196
International Affective Picture Set,
    126–127, 129–130, 131, 136
Interpersonal relations
    body-to-soul preadaptation theory of
        disgust, 12
    intergroup disgust, 20
    interpersonal disgust, 193, 280
    See also Group behavior; Social
        psychology
Interpretive biases, 62–65, 68–69
    disgust-related sexual dysfunction,
        256–257
Introversion, spider fear and disgust sen-
    sitivity and, 176–177
Intuitions, 20–21
Italy, 109, 112

Japan, 102, 106–107, 108, 109, 116

Language
    assessment of emotional experience,
        127
    bias for spider words in spider pho-
        bia, 178–179
    cultural differences in disgust vocab-
        ulary, 113
    development, 81
    effects of induced disgust on inter-
        pretational bias, 184
    translation issues in cross-cultural
        studies, 116
Lateral fusiform gyrus, 149
Learning
    associative conditioning in disgust
        acquisition, 84–85
    evaluative, 86–87
    information transfer, 86
    in maintenance of disgust, 90
    observational modeling, 85–86

preparedness theory of fear acquisition, 170–171
strategies for unlearning disgust, 91
Levator labii muscle, 36, 131–132,
263–264
Looming of Disgust Questionnaire,
38–40, 50–51
Looming vulnerability, 39, 59–60, 69

Magical thinking, 218
Maintenance of disgust, 89–90
Malaysia, 102
Memory
explicit, 65, 66–67
implicit, 65–66, 67
information processing biases,
65–67, 68
Moral disgust, 12, 19, 113, 128, 193,
217–218
contamination effects, 21
cultural differences, 111
eating disorders and, 234–235, 246
future research directions, 20–21, 280
in sexual dysfunction, 257–258,
264–265
Motivation
appetitive and aversive, 124, 128, 145
evolutionary basis of disgust,
145–146
neurophysiology, 160
startle reflex response, 128–131
substrate of disgust, 128–131

Nazis, 20
Netherlands, 111, 114–115
Neurophysiology
affective neuroscience research, 14–15
conceptual models of emotional processing, 147–150
of disgust feelings, 153–156
disgust perception, 150–153
of disgust-related disorders, 156–158
evolutionary basis, 145–146
fainting, 192, 199, 200
functional and effective connectivity
model, 160–161
future research directions, 16, 147, 161

gender differences, 154–155
gustatory system, 151
of Huntington's disease, 157
of infant facial expression, 78
integrative multisystem models of
emotional processing, 147,
159–160
neuroanatomy of disgust, 150–158
parasympathetic system disgust
response, 199, 200, 222
recognition of emotional expression,
149–150
research trends, 12
scope of emotional responses,
134–135
specific emotion processor model,
147, 158–159
threat perception, 147–148
trait linkages with disgust, 196
See also Brain imaging
Neuroticism
disgust sensitivity and, 36, 196
disgust sensitivity as component of,
48–49
spider fear and disgust sensitivity
and, 176–177
New Guinea, 102, 104–105

Observational modeling, 85–86
Obsessive–compulsive disorder
assessment, 215
attentional bias for disgust, 62
cleaning compulsions, 156–157, 213,
214–215, 216
clinical features, 156–157, 213
clinical significance of disgust in, 15,
58, 222–223, 274
conceptual model, 223
contamination fear in, 211,
213–217, 223
cultural differences in disgust sensitivity and, 115
decrease of disgust during treatment,
275
disgust linkage, 213–214
disgust sensitivity and, 38, 40, 49,
213, 214–215

Obsessive–compulsive disorder
  (*Continued*)
  domains of disgust related to, 216–217
  future research directions, 16–17, 223
  memory biases and, 66
  neurophysiology, 156
  sex differences, 214, 215–216
  sympathetic magic beliefs in, 59,
      218–219
  symptomology, 213
  treatment, 213, 272
  treatment for maladaptive cognition
      in, 276–277
Occipital gyrus, 151
Occipitotemporal cortex, 150, 152, 154,
    196
Odors
  contempt and, 19
  death and, 13
  effect of foul smells on eating disor-
      der behavior, 245
  infant facial response, 79
  psychophysiological response, 137
  startle reflex response and, 130–131
Openness to new experience, 195
Operculum, 158
Oral expulsion, 131, 133, 134, 145
Orbitofrontal cortex, 148, 150, 151,
    154, 156, 157, 159–160

Parietal lobe, 150, 157, 196
Personality
  BII-phobia risk, 202
  disgust sensitivity and, 34, 195–196
Phobias
  clinical significance of disgust in, 6,
      15, 58, 138, 286
  disease-avoidance model, 4
  disgust sensitivity and, 34, 36, 38,
      43–44, 49, 126, 172, 214
  etiological models, 170–172
  future research directions, 286
  habituation therapy outcomes,
      220–221
  information processing biases in,
      63–65

neurophysiology of disgust elicitation
    and, 157
  tripartite model of emotional func-
      tioning in, 272
  See also Animal nature and behav-
      iors, fear or disgust reactions
      to; *specific phobia*
Plagues, 182
Poland, 109
Political ideology, disgust sensitivity
    and, 20–21
Postcentral gyrus, 151
Prefrontal cortex, 148, 151, 152, 157
Prejudice, intergroup disgust, 20
Preparedness theory, 63, 87, 170–171
Propensity, disgust, 40–43, 88
Protective factors, 92
Psychoanalytic theory and therapy, 17
Psychopathology
  clinical significance of disgust in, 4,
      5, 6, 31, 138, 211, 285–287
  disorders with low disgust reactions,
      288–289
  evolutionary role of disgust and,
      246–247
  future research directions, 16–17
  information processing model, 60
  need for theoretical framework for
      disgust in, 287–289
  neurophysiology of disgust-related
      disorders, 156–158
  research trends, 12
  role of disgust in acquisition of ani-
      mal fears, 182–185
  state–trait disgust and emotional dis-
      orders, 273
  tripartite model of emotional func-
      tioning, 271–272
  See also specific diagnosis
Public perception and understanding
  frequency of disgust in conversation,
      11
  interest in disgust research, 15–16
  intergroup disgust, 20
Putamen, 151, 152

Questionnaire for the Assessment of
    Disgust, 155

Reactivity, disgust, 278–279
Religious obsession, 217
Relived emotion task, 107–108, 137
Research on disgust
  advantages of disgust as research sub-
    ject, 13–16
  case data tradition, 3
  cross-cultural studies, 118
  current shortcomings, xv–xvi, 138
  disgust treatment, 278
  experimental tradition, 3, 4
  experiment design, 13–14
  findings in anxiety studies, 126
  findings of brain imaging studies,
    158–161
  future directions, 5, 6, 16–24, 62,
    68–69, 91–92, 117–118, 134,
    138, 161, 180–181, 185, 204,
    223, 278–281, 286, 287–290
  historical development, 4–5, 10–11
  humor and, xvi–xvii, 23–24
  International Affective Picture Set
    studies, 126–127
  obstacles to, 10, 11
  public interest in, 15–16
  recent accomplishments, xvi, 4
  recent trends, 11–12
  translation issues in cross-cultural
    studies, 115–116

Schizophrenia and schizoid symptoms,
  36, 287
Scotland, 109
Sensitivity to disgust
  animal fear and, 174–175, 180, 181,
    182–183
  anxiety and, 34, 36, 38–39, 44, 49,
    175, 196, 212
  assessment instruments, 32, 40–41,
    50–51. See also specific instrument
  behavioral assessment, 43–48
  biological mechanisms, 87
  blood-injection-injury phobia and,
    31, 34, 37, 38, 44–47, 48,
    196–197, 201, 202
  clinical significance, 31, 51–52
  cognitive–behavioral therapy out-
    comes and, 273–274

decrease during cognitive–behavioral
    therapy, 274–276
  development, 18
  disgust propensity and, 40–41
  disgust reactivity versus, 278–279
  disorders with low disgust reactions,
    288–289
  eating disorders and, 235–238, 280
  fainting and, 201
  fear and, 114–115
  future directions in disgust research,
    21, 48, 50, 51–52
  measurement, 31, 88
  obsessional thinking or behavior
    and, 217–218
  obsessive–compulsive disorder and,
    38, 40, 49, 213, 214–216
  personality traits and, 195–196
  phobia and, 34, 172, 214
  political ideology and, 20–21
  psychopathology linkage, 31
  sex differences, 16–17, 82, 215–216
  spider fear and, 176–177
  as treatment outcome predictor,
    273–274, 278–279
  as unique clinical construct, 48–50
  vaginismus and, 262–263
  washing compulsions and, 216
Sex differences
  BII phobia, 202
  disgust sensitivity, 82
  disgust sensitivity in obsessive–
    compulsive disorder, 214,
    215–216
  neurophysiology of disgust, 154–155
  spider phobia, 170
Sexual anorexia, 255
Sexual dysfunction
  Animal-reminder disgust, 257
  avoidance behaviors, 255
  defensive reflexes in, 255–256
  definition, 259
  diagnostic classification, 259
  disgust linkage, 253–258
  disgust-related cognitions in, 256–257
  disorders of arousal, 259–260
  disorders of desire, 259

Sexual dysfunction (*Continued*)
    failure to experience orgasm, 257, 259
    research to date, 253
    sociomoral disgust in, 257–258
    therapeutic implications of disgust
        linkage in, 265–266
    trauma experience in, 260–261
    See also Vaginismus
Sexuality and sexual behavior
    body-to-soul preadaptation theory of
        disgust, 12
    disgust assessment instruments, 34
    domains of disgust and, 254–258
    eating disorders and attitudes
        toward, 235
    effects of disgust feelings on experi-
        ence of, 254–255
    pudicity events in eating disorder
        etiology, 244–245
    sexual obsession, 156
    See also Sexual dysfunction
Shame
    clinical conceptualization, 243
    depression and, 243, 244
    disgust and, 19, 243
    in eating disorders, 243–245, 246–247
Skin conductance response, 135, 136,
    137, 152
Social anxiety disorder, 287
Social phobia, 177
Social psychology
    CAD triad hypothesis, 13
    eating disorders and social values,
        234–235
    information transfer processes, 86
    intergroup disgust, 20
    moral disgust in sexual dysfunction,
        257–258
    observational modeling in disgust
        acquisition, 85–86
    social message in facial expression,
        106–107, 149
    terror management theory, 13
    See also Cultural differences; Group
        behavior; Interpersonal
        relations
Spain, 112

Spider fear and phobia, 157, 193–194
    assessment, 34, 36, 38, 43–44
    attentional bias for disgust, 62
    cognitive bias for disgusting stimuli
        in, 178–179
    decrease of disgust during treatment,
        274–275
    disgustingness beliefs about spiders
        and, 177–178
    disgust sensitivity and, 176–177
    epidemiology, 169–170
    habituation therapy outcomes, 221
    information processing biases in,
        64–65
    therapeutic significance of disgust
        reactions, 273–274
    treatment for maladaptive cognitions
        in, 276
    See also Animal-related disgust
Spider Phobia Questionnaire, 176
Startle response, 124, 128–131, 138
State–trait distinctions, 50–51,
    195–196, 272–273
Stroop task, 61, 66, 67, 178–179
Sumatra, 109, 110
Superior parietal cortex, 196
Superior temporal sulcus, 149
Sympathetic magic, 212–213, 216
    assessment, 34–35
    definition, 35, 58–59, 218
    development in childhood, 81
    evaluative conditioning and, 220
    obsessive–compulsive disorder and,
        59, 218–219

Tactile domain of disgust, 81–82
Taste
    distaste, disgust and, 19, 145
    infant facial response, 79
    oral expulsion of noxious substance,
        131, 133, 134
Taxonomy of disgust, 21
Terror management theory, 13
Thalamus, 83, 147–148, 152, 154
Theories of disgust
    animal phobia etiology, 170
    body-to-soul preadaptation theory,
        12–13

conceptual evolution, 9–11

dimensional aspects of diagnostic conceptualization, 288

disease-avoidance model, 4

disgust sensitivity as unique clinical construct, 48–50

experimental research tradition, 4

functional neurophysiological models, 158–161

need for psychopathology model, 287–289

neurophysiological models, 147–150

Thought–action fusion, 218

Threat evaluation

attentional biases, 61

childhood development, 81

disgust linkage with BII fear, 197–198

disgust sensitivity and, 58

etiology of eating disorders, 231

expectancy effects, 90

interpretive biases, 62–65

looming vulnerability model, 59–60

neurophysiology, 147–148

startle reflex response, 128–131

Toilet training, 12, 17

Treatment

of disgust, 276–281, 289–290

disgust as outcome predictor, 273–274, 278–279

disgust-based avoidance, 278

eating disorders, 278

expectancy biases in disgust and, 65

for fainting in BII phobia, 277

future research directions, 278–281, 289–290

habituation therapy, 220–222, 279

inhibition learning, 91

sexual dysfunction, 265–266

See also Cognitive–behavioral therapy

Turkey, 109

Twin studies, 88

United Kingdom, 111

Vaginismus

current clinical conceptualization, 260–261

definition, 260

disgust conceptualization of, 261–262

disgust response to sexual stimuli in, 263–264

disgust sensitivity and, 262–263

moral disgust and, 264–265

Valence asymmetry model of emotional processing, 148–149

Vasovagal syncope, 191–192, 198. See also Fainting

Vietnam, 109

Visual association cortex, 152–153, 154, 155, 157, 158, 159–160, 196

Visual domain of disgust

childhood development, 81–82

eating pathology and, 240

fainting in BII phobia and, 201

fear linkage, 198

levator labii EMG response to images, 132–133

neurophysiological response, 153–156

physiology of emotional responding, 136–137

startle reflex response and, 129–130

Vomiting, 134

Vulnerability to disgust. See Looming vulnerability

Washing compulsions, 156–157, 213, 214–215, 216, 217–218

Wounds, 12

disgust assessment instruments, 34, 37

See also Blood-injection-injury (BII) phobia

Wulff, M., 233

ABOUT THE EDITORS

Bunmi Olatunji, PhD, is an assistant professor in the Department of Psychology at Vanderbilt University in Nashville, Tennessee. He currently serves on the editorial boards of the journals *International Journal of Cognitive Therapy and Journal of Anxiety Disorders*. He has published more than 60 journal articles and book chapters and has participated in several conference presentations. As director of the Emotion and Anxiety Research Laboratory at Vanderbilt University, he is currently examining the role of basic emotions as they relate to the assessment, etiology, and maintenance of anxiety-related disorders. His research has been funded by the National Institutes of Health and the Anxiety Disorders Association of America. His research on the role of disgust in anxiety disorders has also been recognized by the American Psychological Association.

Dean McKay, PhD, ABPP, is an associate professor in the Department of Psychology at Fordham University in Bronx, New York. He is associate editor of *Journal of Cognitive Psychotherapy* and currently serves on the editorial boards of the journals *Behaviour Research and Therapy*, *Journal of Clinical Psychology*, and *Journal of Anxiety Disorders*. He has published more than 70 journal articles and book chapters and has participated in more than 100 conference presentations. He has been a member of the Obsessive Compulsive Cognitions

Workgroup since 1995 and a member of the Health Anxiety Workgroup since 2006. In addition to this volume, he is editor or coeditor of several published and forthcoming texts, including a volume on the treatment of refractory cases using cognitive behavior therapy to be published by the American Psychological Association with Jonathan Abramowitz and Steven Taylor. Other volumes he has edited or coedited include texts on obsessive–compulsive disorder (OCD), diagnosis in anxiety disorders, research methods, and treatment of refractory childhood and adolescent disorders. He is board certified in behavioral and clinical psychology by the American Board of Professional Psychology, is a fellow of the American Board of Behavioral Psychology and the Academy of Clinical Psychology, and a clinical fellow of the Behavior Research and Therapy Society. His research has focused primarily on OCD, body dysmorphic disorder and hypochondriasis and their link to OCD, and the role of disgust in psychopathology. Dr. McKay's research has also examined mechanisms of information-processing bias for anxiety states. He is codirector and founder of the Institute for Cognitive Behavior Therapy and Research, a private treatment and research center in White Plains, New York.